On Paper
A Course in College Writing

Johnston

Y0-AST-731

On Paper
A Course in College Writing

H. WENDELL SMITH
Santa Monica College

Wadsworth Publishing Company, Inc.
Belmont, California

© 1975 by Wadsworth Publishing Company, Inc., Belmont, California 94002. All rights reserved. No part of this book may be reproduced, stored in a retrieval system or transcribed, in any form or by any means, electronic, mechanical, photocopying, recording or otherwise, without the prior written permission of the publisher.

ISBN 0-534-00374-5
L. C. Cat. Card No. 74-84314
Printed in the United States of America

3 4 5 6 7 8 9 10---79 78 77

Acknowledgments

Encyclopaedia Britannica, Inc., for an excerpt from "Boxing," *Encyclopaedia Britannica,* 1972, IV, 43.

Robert Lescher Literary Agency, for an excerpt from "Little Boy Blues," copyright © 1972 by Judith Viorst.

McGraw-Hill Book Company, for an excerpt from *Soul on Ice,* copyright © 1968 by Eldridge Cleaver.

G. P. Putman's Sons, for an excerpt from Jackie Robinson, *I Never Had It Made,* 1972.

The Reader's Digest Association, Inc., for an excerpt from Lyndon Baines Johnson, "Toward a New Springtime," *Reader's Digest,* January 1973. Copyright 1972 by The Reader's Digest Association, Inc. Condensed from an address by Lyndon Baines Johnson, President of the United States, 1963–1969.

The Ronald Press Company, for excerpts from Lester Bromberg, *Boxing's Unforgettable Fights,* copyright © 1962 by The Ronald Press Company, New York.

Eric Sevareid, for an excerpt by Eric Sevareid.

Preface
To the Instructor

TWO ASSUMPTIONS underlie this book: (1) Effective writing is not the same as effective speaking, and (2) college students who are made aware of that difference and who are directed to specific studies in ways of effective writing can write better than they did before.

As the title suggests, students do not learn to write by being told about it; they learn by putting words *on paper*. That is why this book focuses upon a do-it-yourself method, more learning than teaching. The learning begins immediately. Within moments, no matter where the instructor chooses to have students begin, students are putting words on paper, learning to use principles of clear writing.

The book follows each bit of "study" material with quick reinforcement: review, do-it-yourself exercise, and check-up. Its full success will depend also upon feedback from the instructor to students, for the instructor's encouragement and help are, after all, more important to students than is any book.

The Tone of the Book

Students of college English often complain that their textbooks do not really make things clear. When the complaint is justified, the trouble may lie in a book's being written for teachers rather than for students: explanations perfectly clear to those who don't need them. Such a textbook becomes a burden to both instructor and students, and the teacher must continually be either defending or apologizing for the book. The tone and style of *On Paper* are designed to escape that paradox of *clear-only-if-known* and to disarm the student complaint.

Through its design and its tone *On Paper* pursues an elusive yet attainable goal: to impart both skill in writing and enthusiasm for it. Toward reaching that goal the book will be aided indispensably by the instructor's own enthusiasm for the students' success. Textbook and teacher are partners in the classroom; both fail unless each serves the other's aims.

Introducing the Book to Students

When assured that their speech habits are to be respected rather than changed, students can be brought to look upon written English as a special *dialect* with its own requirements necessarily more purposeful and controlled than those of everyday conversation. Where writing differs from the students' speech, it does so not simply because the speech habits are faulty but more importantly because the medium of words *on paper* is lacking in the gestures, intonations, smiles, challenges and revisions, and silent understandings that are the tools of conversation. To make up for what it lacks, writing uses other tools: firmer diction, more precise reference, more logical development, greater consistency, more direct movement toward point and effect. If the teacher is able to share this assumed difference between speech and writing and can bring students to understand it as well, then both instructor and students can find *On Paper* an enjoyable, productive guide for their work in the classroom.

Students will need coaching in how to use this book. They should be encouraged to study with pen in hand, always ready to write. The pen will help to slow their reading and study; reading with eyes alone, they should be told, is not enough for understanding. Until a principle has been taken in, it cannot be put to practice.

The "Time for Review" sections follow short "takes" of study material. The review should be carefully read before the student goes to work on the following "Do-It-Yourself Exercise" in which he is asked to apply what has just been learned. Following the exercise, a brief "Checking up" offers a self-evaluation of performance and often some variety of possible responses to the exercise. The instructor may decide to "grade" the do-it-yourself exercises only occasionally as a spot-check upon student progress. It should be made clear to students that the book and its exercises are aids to learning, not a collection of fill-in-the-blanks obstacles between student and grade.

Students should be guided toward conscious effort to use in their own writing the specific elements they have been studying and practicing in do-it-yourself exercises. The "Suggestions for Writing" have been geared to direct application of principles that have just been studied in the text. The suggestions are offered in groups of two or three so that students may have some choice of subject matter. Topics, of course, can be assigned instead by the instructor, who knows the local scene and student backgrounds. The book's suggestions for writing call for short passages so that students can do a larger number of them and get more opportunity for check-up and feedback. The instructor may, of course, change word-length designations to suit class purposes.

A key to instructor's marking symbols, provided in Supplement 3, makes possible quick communication with students about faults in their writing. The key directs students to study or review of relevant materials in the text.

Flexibility of Order

The sequence of chapters in *On Paper* has been designed to get students started immediately with easily understood fundamentals. It leads cumulatively to writing skills. But the instructor may find that a different order of things is better suited to class needs, and the book is easily adaptable. If the instructor's early diagnosis of class abilities indicates that students need work on diction, immediate assignment to Chapter 19 ("A Choice of Words") may help. If the instructor feels that students will benefit from early introduction to organization of ideas, assignment to Chapter 20 ("A Train of Thought") or Chapter 21 ("From Thought to Paragraph") may be made early in the course. What the instructor finds useful is what will determine the most suitable order of chapter assignments.

Assignments may also be adapted to personalized instruction if the teacher finds that method suitable to his students and their needs. Chapters, or even smaller sections of the book, may serve as individual assignments toward specific skills. Such personalized instruction may be facilitated by the book's thorough index.

Setting Up Assignments

Students can benefit greatly from being coached to know "the name of the game" before they play it: to know what to learn before they begin to study. The instructor may urge them to begin a chapter by scanning the divider page just ahead of it. On that page are listed the concepts that students are to learn about, including some faults they are to learn to avoid.

Short assignments are probably more effective than long ones, so the study-and-exercise units within each chapter have been spaced by groups of "Suggestions for Writing." These suggestion groups may make convenient end-of-assignment points, setting the students to work on their own compositions and guiding them to apply principles just learned.

Following each assignment, in addition to the instructor's comments upon student writing, reinforcement can be redoubled by in-class review of the materials covered in the assignment. The "Time for Review" sections may be of help in such reinforcement.

Using the Quizzes

Each chapter of *On Paper* concludes with a multiple-choice quiz. The five-choice format has been adapted to encourage thought and care rather than guesswork. Students are asked to write in full their selected completion of each item, then to mark the *letter* of that choice on an answer blank. But they are also asked to explain (on a "Because . . ." line) *why* the choice seems most appropriate. The multiple-choice format thus avoids thoughtless guesswork by the students, yet it provides flexibility and ease for the instructor's paper grading. Working with the master key provided in the accompanying Instructor's Manual, the teacher may mark and grade student quizzes by overlaying a dozen or more sheets and reading across the ganged sheets from left to right, one item at a time. The more extensive student responses on the "Because . . ." lines may, if the instructor elects, be spot-checked and used as a guide to what, if anything, has gone wrong in student work.

Still further time-saving is possible through the use of a Scan-tron (or other) electronic grading machine. If the college has such a machine available for the instructor's use, students may be asked to purchase printed answer blanks at their bookstore; they then mark their quiz responses in pencil on the printed blanks. When the instructor feeds the completed blanks through the machine, each is automatically scored and the class scores averaged. Some 50 quiz papers can be thus scored in less than two minures.

Classroom Follow Up

Useful follow up of quizzes may be accomplished by the instructor's taking note of which items have been most often missed by the group. If a significant number of students have chosen the wrong completion for a quiz item, the teacher may be sure that the class needs review and special explanation of the principle underlying that item. The Instructor's Manual includes with each quiz item a page-reference guide to pertinent material in the text.

The students should be continually reminded that scores on the quizzes are not the primary aim of their studies. What should count most is their writing, and the exercises and quizzes are best taken as learning devices, not as tests. If what they learn about writing does not result in better actual writing, the quizzes have led to nothing.

A Note on Teacher Effort

Since mere textbook quizzes may help students learn to write but cannot replace their writing, the tedious scoring of mere quizzes is not the best use of the instructor's time. That is why this book has been put together as a largely student-effort workbook: to encourage student writing and to free the instructor to read what they write. If *On Paper* provides adequate experience for students without excessive labor for the instructor, the book will have hit its intended mark.

Acknowledgments

My thanks to these reviewers for their helpful suggestions: Ray Kytle of Central Michigan University (whose comments on the early manuscript put the whole project on track), Jane Boisseau of Louisiana State University, Charles Bond of Ferris State College, E. Erickson of Weber State College, Frank Flack of Los Angeles Pierce College, Kathleen Holcomb of Angelo State University, C. Jeriel Howard of Bishop College, Sheila Juba of Lane Community College, Marian McClintock of Florissant Valley Community College, Mary McIver of Polk Community College, Marinus Swets of Grand Rapids Junior College, and Elera Zimmerman of Clayton Junior College. Loving thanks also to my wife, Nadine, who always believed, and to my son, Brad, who helped with the proofs and the index.

H. Wendell Smith

To the Student

AS YOU WORK WITH THIS BOOK, you will discover that getting your ideas down on paper is less important than getting them *off* the paper again and into the mind of your reader. But how you put the ideas down will largely determine how easily and clearly your reader picks them up. "Easy writing is curs'd hard reading," says one famous line; yet, you will discover that good writing, difficult as it is, becomes less difficult the more you know about how sentences work and how ideas develop into a clear-moving train of thought.

This book is designed to offer you both training and practice in writing. It is largely a do-it-yourself book, and you will learn from it only as much as you want to learn. If you follow the text with attention and then try your developing skill in the do-it-yourself exercises and other writings, the elements of good writing will become part of you.

Unless a classroom instructor directs otherwise, it will be best to follow the course as the book has set it forth, chapter by chapter. For the plan of *On Paper* is a step-by-step plan. The work of each chapter depends upon knowledge of what has gone before, and of course upon practice with that knowledge.

You will find your understanding of English and your skill in writing developing from the very first chapter and its exercises. But do not expect to learn everything at once. Necessarily you will be asked to write brief essays, or "passages," long before the book discusses how to write paragraphs and essays. If your early efforts in response to the "Suggestions for Writing" are not skilled essays, don't worry; the aim of each writing assignment is to help you practice the fine points introduced in the chapter. Smooth writing and finished essays are the final goal, but not necessarily the only goal along the way.

If you want to learn to write, you will not skimp the exercises and assignments. Use your pen and ink, not merely your eyes. What you read and study in this book will be of use to you only if you "do it yourself" and then thoughtfully consider what you have done—on paper.

When the course is done, you will find that it has been a course of discovery. Writing is a means of discovering your mind—of discovering yourself. And good writing will also help you discover a greater success in college work of all kinds, since so much depends upon how well you show what you are learning—especially how you show it on paper.

H. Wendell Smith

Contents

1   And   1

How to Work With: coordinators, parallelism, pairs and series, correlatives, verbs with paired subjects.

How to Avoid: faulty parallelism.

2   But   17

How to Work With: more coordinators, more correlatives, other uses of but *and* yet.

How to Avoid: faulty parallelism, faulty verb agreement.

3   A Touch of Grammar   35

How to Work With: the "rules" of grammar, subject and predicate, the "parts of speech," word groups as units.

4   Sentences   49

How to Work With: subject-predicate combinations, independent clauses, subordinate clauses, subordinators, four kinds of sentence.

How to Avoid: choppy sentences.

5   Therefore   67

How to Work With: conjunctive adverbs, the semicolon, other uses of therefore.

6   If, While, Until   77

How to Work With: subordinators, adverb clauses, incomplete clauses, restrictive clauses, nonrestrictive clauses.

How to Avoid: danglers, fragments

7   George, The Cherry Tree, and Truth   95

How to Work With: nouns, number (singular and plural), possessives (the apostrophe), appositives, noun clauses, verbal nouns, capitals.

How to Avoid: faulty possessives, faulty capitalization, faulty use of a and an.

8   Run, Fly, Sail   119

How to Work With: verbs, tenses (past and present), regular and irregular verbs, transitive and intransitive verbs, person, verb agreement, six troublesome verbs.

How to Avoid: faulty verb forms, faulty verb agreement.

9   Have Done, Will Do   143

How to Work With: auxiliary verbs, the future tense, the perfect tenses, sequence of tenses, consistency of tenses.

How to Avoid: faulty auxiliaries, faulty sequence of tenses, shifts of verb tense.

10   Be, Seem, Sound   161

How to Work With: linking verbs, noun complements, adjective complements, active voice, passive voice.

How to Avoid: faulty verb agreement, overuse of passive voice.

11   Which   181

>   ***How to Work With:*** *adjectives, determiners, comparatives and superlatives, compound adjectives, adjective phrases, adjective clauses.*
>
>   ***How to Avoid:*** *faulty parallelism, danglers, misplaced modifiers.*

12   When, Where, Why, and How   201

>   ***How to Work With:*** *adverbs, clipped forms of adverbs, adverb clauses.*
>
>   ***How to Avoid:*** *misplaced modifiers, faulty adverbs.*

13   Of, From, With, Between   215

>   ***How to Work With:*** *prepositions, prepositional phrases, the long possessive, indirect objects.*
>
>   ***How to Avoid:*** *misplaced modifiers, problems with prepositions.*

14   Me, Myself, and I   239

>   ***How to Work With:*** *pronouns, person, number, case, pronoun agreement, pronoun reference, eight kinds of pronoun.*
>
>   ***How to Avoid:*** *faulty pronoun case, faulty pronoun agreement, faulty use of* who *and* whom, *faulty use of* whose *and* who's.

15   Who and What   263

>   ***How to Work With:*** *interrogative pronouns, relative pronouns, adjective clauses,* who *and* whom, *noun clauses, appositive clauses, incomplete clauses, commas with nonrestrictive clauses.*

How to Avoid: misplaced adjective clauses, danglers, commas with restrictive clauses.

16   -Ing Words   285

How to Work With: gerunds (verbal nouns), gerund phrases, present participles (verbal adjectives), participial phrases, absolute phrases, commas with participial phrases, rephrasing danglers.

How to Avoid: danglers, faulty pronoun case with gerunds.

17   Borrowed, Stolen, Lost, or Sunk   303

How to Work With: past participles, past-participial phrases, restrictive and nonrestrictive modifiers, active voice and passive voice.

How to Avoid: misplaced modifiers, danglers, faulty use of commas.

18   To Live, to Love   321

How to Work With: infinitives, infinitive phrases, placement of infinitives.

How to Avoid: misplaced infinitives, danglers, commas with verbal nouns.

19   A Choice of Words   339

How to Work With: appropriate words, everyday words, exact words, concise words, fresh words.

How to Avoid: fancy words, slang words, jargon, out-of-date words, confused words, euphemisms, malapropisms, signposts, redundancies, fat phrasing, faulty comparisons, clichés.

20   A Train of Thought   373

How to Work With: expanding ideas, idea-linking devices, consistency of topic, consistency of reference, consistency of person, consistency of tense, parallelism, repetition.

How to Avoid: fragments, shift of topic, faulty pronoun reference, shift of person, shift of tense, awkward repetition.

21   From Thought to Paragraph   399

How to Work With: paragraphs, unity of idea, development of idea, coherence of idea, the topic sentence, controlling purpose, transition.

How to Avoid: underdevelopment of idea, incoherence, faulty transition.

22   From Idea to Essay   425

How to Work With: sources of ideas, attitudes, details, evaluating ideas, organizing, transitions, three kinds of essay.

How to Avoid: truisms, hedging, useless signposts, careless editing.

Supplement 1   A Guide to Punctuation   441

How to Work With: linking marks, separating marks, terminal marks, apostrophes, quotation marks.

How to Avoid: comma splices, comma faults, run-on sentences, other punctuation faults.

Supplement 2   Spelling: A Study List of Three Hundred
                  Useful Words   447

Supplement 3   A Guide to Revision   449

   How to Work With: the instructor's marking symbols.

Supplement 4   Review Quizzes   451

Index   481

And 1

How to work with . . . coordinators
parallelism
pairs and series
correlatives
verbs with paired subjects

How to avoid . . . faulty parallelism

WE START WITH *and*.

Few words in English are more useful than *and*. We use it to tie words together, to link ideas into sentences and sentences into longer trains of thought. And we use it often. To know something about that word and how it works can help a student write better almost immediately. So this book about putting ideas on paper begins with some study and practice with *and* as the first key to better writing.

Making Pairs With "And"

And connects two things: land *and* sea, up *and* down, rise *and* shine. In forming these pairs the word *and* suggests that we are to consider the two things equally, to give them equal rank in relation to something else. Perhaps *balance* is a good term: *And* allows us to balance things in pairs, like things on a seesaw or a set of scales:

All the rugs are *old* and *worn*.
Hank shouted at *the coach* and *the manager*.
He finished the job *quickly* and *quietly*.

When two things are joined by *and*, they are coordinated; that is, each of the items has the same job to do in the sentence. *The coach* and *the manager* are both *shouted at*, *old* and *worn* both describe *the rugs*; *quickly* and *quietly* both tell how he *finished the job*.

But we have to take care that the items we join by using *and* are really in balance. Suppose we write:

Hank shouted at *the coach* and *angry*.

Now the pairing doesn't work well; it appears to join a person *(the coach)* to a description of Hank *(angry)*. The description doesn't properly balance in the pair. The sentence perhaps means to say:

Hank *shouted* at the coach and *seemed* angry.

Then the items joined by *and* are both of the same sort—both things Hank did: he *shouted* and *seemed*.

Time for Review

And is a coordinator, a word used to link items in *pairs*.

The items linked in a pair should truly balance; that is, each should have the same relationship to some other element in the sentence:

Men and *women* enroll in the course. (Both *enroll*.)
She *dropped* the vase and *broke* it. (*She* did both.)
Dan is a *slow* and *careful* worker. (Dan, the *worker,* is both.)

Do-It-Yourself Exercise

Write in each blank a word that will form a *pair* in balance with the word shown in italics:

My *relatives* and _____ enjoy my jokes.

Apparently the boy *tossed* and _____ all night.

Do you ever *wash* your car and _____ it?

Take a *firm* and _____ grip on the drill handle.

That last pitch was *high* and _____ .

Now provide both items to form a pair in these sentences:

Very few drivers can _____ and _____ at the same time.

Riding a bicycle is _____ and _____ .

Hey, Jack, _____ and _____ the phone.

Barney built a model airplane of _____ and _____ .

You can trust your _____ and _____ to the Quickee Moving and Storage Company.

Finley has worked six years, _____ and _____ on his latest invention.

Checking up: Be sure you have written pairs whose items are *balanced*. You should not pair a *thing* with an *action* or a *description* with a *thing*. "Riding a bicycle is *exercise* and *cheap*" would be awkward, since *exercise* is a thing, *cheap* a description. If you had some trouble providing both items for a pair, try again—using some of these items: *run, wood, furniture, night, slow, long*.

"And" Forming a Series

So far we have used *and* to join items in *pairs*. Now we can try linking items in threes, fours—or as many as suit a purpose:

Some say that time *and* tide *and* taxes are inevitable.

We have added a third item to the list, forming a *series*. If the repetition of *and* seems too much, we may leave out the first *and*. Then we'll separate the items by using commas:

Perhaps time, tide, *and* taxes are inevitable.

The list may become even longer:

Perhaps *time, tide, taxes,* and *trouble* are inevitable.

We use *and* only once now—before the last item in the *series*—and we use a comma to separate the items. That punctuation is standard: commas between items in a series.

Some editors, however, drop the last comma from the series. They believe we don't need both the comma and the *and*. But to leave out that last comma can sometimes cause the reader to assume that the final two items are teamed up—or mixed like coffee and cream—rather than separately balanced with each other item in the series. "Sandwiches, salad, pie and ice cream" means that the ice cream and the pie are together as one dish—so that the series really has only three items: (1) sandwiches, (2) salad, (3) pie and ice cream. In the same way "Bob, Carol, Ted and Alice" suggests that Bob and Carol are separate, but Ted and Alice are a couple. Clarity calls for the final comma in a series if we intend to separate the last two items:

The nursery sells *roses, violets,* and *orchids*.

But we may leave the comma out if we want the last two items understood as one unit:

The delicatessen sells *pickles, sardines, bagels and cream cheese*.
When we were kids, we played *kickball, hospital, cops and robbers*.

Longer Pairs and Series

We've been looking at pairs and series of single-word items. But *and* is used also to join and balance *groups* of words:

Gary loved *hearing the engines* and *smelling the gasoline*.
They danced *through the night* and *into the morning*.
Our tools have been *carefully cleaned* and *safely stored*.

Of course such word groups may be linked in series of three or more:

Every hamburger sold by our company is *generously cut, deliciously cooked,* and *carefully seasoned*.
The shipping company saved thousands of dollars by *recovering the craft, floating it again,* and *tugging it back to port*.
We're still dedicated to government *of the people, by the people,* and *for the people*.

Such word groups are treated the same way as one-word items in pairs or series.

Time for Review

And may be used to link three or more items in a *series*.

Items in a series are separated by commas unless *and* is used between each two of the items.

The last comma in separation of a series (before the *and*) may be left out—but only if the last two items are to be considered as a unit: *coffee and cream, ham and eggs*.

Items in a series may be words or word groups.

Do-It-Yourself Exercise

Write in the blanks some appropriate items in series:

If you liked _____ and _____ and _____ , you'll probably love the summer.

6   Chapter One

The most popular sports in this area are _football_, _basketball_, and _tennis_.

My friends _Jeff_, _mike_, and _Steve_ have formed a new club dedicated to protecting the environment.

Since I was in training then for the football season, I spent every day _lifting_, _running_, and _eating_.

The engine _choughed_, and _hummed_, and _purred_; then it gave up altogether.

Checking up: Be sure that the items in each series are properly balanced. You shouldn't try to write "*basketball, football,* and *we swim*"; after all, *we swim* is not really the name of the sport.

Continue by writing in each blank an appropriate series—with proper punctuation:

Our college observes four holidays, including _Thanksgiving, christmas, Easter, and summer_.

Rita had three coins in her purse: _A quarter, A penny, and A dime._

There is a lot of talk these days about pollution of _Air, water, and noise_.

If I had a chance to travel, I'd like to see _the beach, the lake, and the mountains_.

Checking up: Again, be sure your items in each series are in *balance*. It would not do to write, " . . . pollution of *rivers, lakes,* and *the air is bad*"; since *the air is bad* could be a sentence by itself, it doesn't balance with *rivers* and *lakes*.

Parallelism

We have been insisting that items in pairs and in series should be in *balance*; that is, that all the items linked by *and* be similar in their relation to something else in the sentence. When the items in a pair or series are not in balance, the result will sound awkward—and will probably cause the reader some trouble in understanding. The principle of balancing items linked by a coordinator is *parallelism*.

Consider the faulty parallelism in these sentences and see the effects of proper parallelism in the revisions:

Faulty	Parallel
We really enjoyed *our summer* and *visiting with you!*	We really enjoyed *our summer* and *our visit* with you!
My new shoes are *brown* and *squeak*.	My new shoes are *brown* and *squeaky*.
Cindy hasn't enough time *for studying* and *to work*.	Cindy hasn't enough time *for studying* and *for working*.

Usually the sentence whose pairs or series have items in parallel form will be smoother and easier to read than the one that violates parallelism.

Time for Review

And may be used to link items in a series of three or more: *spring* and *summer* and *fall*. When *and* separates all items, no commas are used.

In a series *and* may be omitted entirely: *spring, summer, fall*; or *and* may be used only once (before the last item): *spring, summer,* and *fall*. In these cases the items are separated by *commas*.

In a series the comma before the *and* may be omitted—if the last two items are to be considered as a unit: His face looked *red, yellow, black and blue*. (*Black and blue* is a mixture forming just one color.)

Parallelism is the principle of using the same form (or grammatical function) for all items in a pair or series.

Do-It-Yourself Exercise

Rewrite each of these passages to give all the same information in *one* sentence:

The boss tore up the envelope. He scrawled on the letter. He handed it to me.

Rewrite as *one sentence* with three actions in series:

_____

_____

Chapter One

Lorelei's Department Store sells ladies' clothing. It also sells children's wear. One department of the store sells all kinds of leather goods.

Rewrite as *one sentence* with items in series:

<u>Lorelei's Department Store sells ladies' clothing, children's wear, and all kinds of leather goods.</u>

We are against organized crime. We don't want our air polluted. Also we don't want a corrupt government.

Rewrite as *one sentence* with items in series:

<u>We are against organized crime, air pollution, and corruption in government.</u>

The mountain road was craggy. It was very steep too. It seemed to have no end.

Rewrite as *one sentence* with items in series:

<u>The mountain road was craggy, very steep, and endless.</u>

The night watchman opened the warehouse door. He snapped on his flashlight. He yelled, "Who's there?"

Rewrite as *one sentence* with actions in series:

<u>The night watchman opened the warehouse door, snapped on his flashlight, and yelled, "Who's there?"</u>

Checking up: Review each of your entries to be sure it is just *one* sentence but tells the whole of the information. Check for *parallelism* in each series. It would be faulty to write, "The mountain road was *craggy*, *steep*, and *had no end*," since *had no end* is not parallel to *craggy* and *steep*; probably *endless* would be the best word to complete the series. Be sure that you have used commas to separate the items in each series.

Suggestions for Writing

A. Write down the names of two well-known people. In about 100 words tell why you think those two people deserve to be famous. Use *and* at least six times, forming several pairs and series in your passage. Underline *and* each time you use it.

B. If you could repaint your college buildings using three colors, what would those colors be? Write about 100 words naming the colors and telling why you would choose them. Use *and* at least six times, forming pairs and series. Underline *and* each time you use it.

C. If you could own two entirely different vehicles of transportation other than an automobile (such as a boat and a pickup truck), which two would you choose? Write about

100 words telling what they are and why you would choose them. Use *and* at least six times, forming pairs and series. Underline *and* each time you use it.

After Writing: Reread your work to be sure it fulfills the assignment. Check for proper punctuation: *comma* to separate the items in series; *period*, of course, to end each sentence.

Using Correlatives

When we use *both* with *and*, we make a slightly different sort of pair:

The President has visited *both* China *and* Russia.
Bud is one guy who can *both* eat a lot *and* lose weight.
A good politician has to be *both* honest *and* popular.

In this pattern *both* works with *and*. The word *both* provides some emphasis; otherwise the structure is much like a pair formed with *and* alone:

Iowa farmers produce wheat *and* corn.
Iowa farmers produce *both* wheat *and* corn.
Music *and* art are popular night-school courses.
Both music *and* art are popular night-school courses.
Can the Dodgers win the league pennant *and* the World series?
Can the Dodgers win *both* the league pennant *and* the World Series?
This old blouse is wrinkled *and* torn.
This old blouse is *both* wrinkled *and* torn.
Bob and his date had a snack before *and* after the show.
They shared a hot dog *both* before *and* after the show.
The path goes around the house *and* around the barn.
It goes around *both* the house *and* the barn.

Using Pairs as Subjects

Paired items (joined by *and* or *both-and*) may be used as the subject in a sentence. A *subject* is the person or thing said to do or be something:

The *tree* grows. The *shrub* grows.
Saturday is Lincoln's birthday.

The words *tree*, *shrub,* and *Saturday* are subjects. Since each is just *one* thing or *one* day, the subjects require verbs that go with the singular of that sort: *grows, is,* or some other form ending in *-s.* But if we use *and* to form pairs of subjects, we must change the verb form:

> The tree and the shrub *grow*.
>
> Saturday and Monday *are* holidays.

Since the sentences are now talking about subjects that are *more than one* thing, we use the verb forms *grow* and *are* (without *-s* endings).

This principle of *one* (singular) or *more than one* (plural) is easy to overlook as we write, so we have to give it special attention when we reread our writing to check effectiveness.

Watch the changes as we join single items into *pairs*:

> Pat *has* a big smile. Ginny *has* a big smile too. Pat and Ginny *have* big smiles.
>
> The house *needs* cleaning. The garage *needs* a new roof. Both the house and the garage *need* paint.
>
> Your brother *astonishes* me. Your sister also *astonishes* me. Both your brother and your sister *astonish* me.

But sometimes we form a pair that names just *one* thing, as *coffee and cream* is just one drink. If we are thinking of the pair as *one,* we use an action or being word with *-s* ending:

> Ham and eggs make*s* a great American breakfast.
>
> July and August i*s* a long time to be away.
>
> *War and Peace* i*s* a memorable book.
>
> Scrimping and saving tire*s* us out.

Occasionally, with *each* and *every,* we form a pair but nevertheless think of the items as separate—as *one*. Then we use the action or being word with *-s* ending:

> Each man and woman ha*s* rights.
>
> Every nook and cranny deserve*s* to be kept clean.

Time for Review

> **Both** works with *and* to form pairs: *both* you *and* I; *both* in the morning *and* in the afternoon.
>
> *Both-and* is a type of conjunction—a *correlative.*
>
> Paired items are usually thought of as *two*. When the pair is used as the

subject in a sentence, the verb (action or being word) will usually not have an -s ending: *are, have, seem, run, go.*

When a pair of items is thought of as *one* (as in *ham and eggs* or *bread and butter*) and is used in a sentence as subject, the verb (if in the *present*) will usually have an -s ending: *is, has, seems, runs, goes.*

Each-and or *every-and* may be used to link items in a pair. The items in such a pair are thought of as separate and singular. When such a pair is used as the subject in a sentence, the verb (if in the *present*) will usually have an -s ending: *takes, plays, sleeps, works, dances.*

Do-It-Yourself Exercise

Write in each blank an appropriate word to complete these sentences:

Both the __truck__ and the __bus__ were speeding when they collided.

Nowadays some very good clothing fabrics contain both __cotton__ and __silk__.

Every pot and pan __has__ to be washed right now before we eat.

The wind blew so hard that the windows both __squeeked__ and __broke__.

When each __tree__ and __bush__ in the yard __has__ been trimmed, we can go ahead to mow the lawn.

Next month *Better Homes and Gardens* __is__ going to give my fish tank a seal of approval.

My friends __Tommy__ and __Bill__, although they __have__ looked both __hard__ and __long__, just can't find the little beagle in either place.

The garage man says every __wheel__ and __axle__ in my car __has__ something wrong with it now.

Checking up: Be sure you have written only *one* word in each blank. Check for *parallelism* in each *pair*. Possible appropriate verbs: *has* or *is* to be washed; windows both *rattled* and *broke* (in the *past*); *has* been trimmed; *is* going to give . . . .

Suggestions for Writing

D. Some people eat ketchup on almost anything. Write about 100 words telling what things you like to eat ketchup with—and why. Use *and* and *both-and* to form several pairs. Underline *both* and *and* each time.
E. If you could give an award to two television newscasters, who would they be? Write about 100 words telling who they are and why you would honor them. Use *and* and *both-and* to form several pairs and series. Underline *and* and *both* each time.
F. How would you arrange to make big industries avoid polluting America's air and waterways? Write about 100 words telling what measures you would take to protect the environment from such industries. Use *and* and *both-and* several times to form pairs and series. Underline *and* and *both* each time.

After Writing: Recheck your work to be sure it fulfills the assignment. Is every pair or series properly formed? What about the *parallelism*? Recheck your use of commas; have you used the comma before *and* in every *series*? You should *not* use a comma before *and* when writing a *pair*.

And 13

QUIZ 1

Using "And"

This quiz asks you to work with *and, both-and, each-and,* and *every-and* in forming pairs and series. On the blank within each sentence write the item that you think most appropriately completes the sentence with proper *comma* usage and *parallelism*. Then mark the *letter* of your choice on your answer blank. After marking your choice, briefly explain why you chose it (*Because:* . . .).

Example: One of the counselors told us the gang would camp and ___fish___

_____ in the mountains for a week.

(a) hiking   (b) usually   (c) fish   (d) horseback riding   (e) to go fishing   Ex _c_

(*Because:* ___Verb "fish" forms pair with verb "camp"___)

1. Both math and science _____ now required for graduation.

(a) is   (b) are   (c) has been   (d) was   (e) seems   1 _b_

(*Because:* ___Plural verb_____.)
   (*Question:* Which verb is plural to match the paired *math and science*?)

2. The United States and Japan _____ made new trade agreements.

(a) have   (b) has   (c) was to have   (d) seems to have   (e) appears to have   2_____

(*Because:* _____.)
   (*Question:* Which verb is plural to match the paired *United States and Japan*?)

3. Careless and _____ work cannot earn respect.

(a) clumsily   (b) sloppiness   (c) thoughtlessly   (d) untidy   (e) haste   3 _d_

(*Because:* _____.)
   (*Question:* Which completion is a descriptive word to form a proper pair with *Careless*?)

4. The art museum has a new display of paintings and _____.

(a) by famous artists   (b) sculptures   (c) expensive   (d) popular
(e) with some sculptures   4 _b_

(*Because.* _____.)
   (*Question:* Which completion is the *name* of something to form a proper pair with *paintings*?)

14   Chapter One

5. If I take the job and _____, I can buy a car.

(a) earning money   (b) to earn money   (c) earn some money   (d) eagerly
(e) with my skill

5. _c_

(*Because:* _____.)
    (*Question:* Which completion contains a verb to form a pair with *take the job*?)

6. Men's clothes these days are colorful and _____.

(a) boldly   (b) shocking people   (c) plenty of imagination   (d) durability
(e) stimulating

6. _e_

(*Because:* _____.)

7. When the time comes for a vacation, working people really need it and _____.

(a) deserving   (b) deserve it   (c) worthy of it   (d) looking ahead
(e) wanted it

7. _b_

(*Because:* _____.)

8. Maybe I can both join the team and _____.

(a) get good grades   (b) making the honor roll   (c) without shirking my study
(d) that church group   (e) can keep up my classes

8. _A_

(*Because:* _____.)

9. Would you like riding this motorbike and _____?

(a) test its speed   (b) to own it   (c) testing it out   (d) approval of it
(e) see how to own it

9. _C_

(*Because:* _____.)

10. According to the newspaper, jobs are becoming easier to get and _____.

(a) to keep   (b) pay well   (c) with good pay   (d) having fringe benefits
(e) hanging onto

10. _d_

(*Because:* _____.)

11. The United States has always been both challenged and _____ by attempts to achieve equality for all its citizens.

(a) disturbing   (b) has been driven   (c) violently   (d) disrupted
(e) embarrassment

11. _d_

(*Because:* _____.)

And 15

12. If you went to get a drink and _____,
the fountain spurted out a stream six feet high.

(a) to the main building (b) without great care (c) in a hurry
(d) out in the hall (e) you weren't careful

12. __A__

(*Because:* _____.)

13. In her campaign speech Ivy said she would devote herself to equality, to fair

play, and _____.

(a) find better jobs for all (b) freedom of speech (c) what the students want
(d) to free tuition (e) honesty

13. _____

(*Because:* _____.)

14. Highway signs are exposed to weather, accidental _____
vandalism.

(a) damage and (b) damage, and (c) damage, and subject to
(d) damage and are subject to (e) damage, and are subject to

14. __b__

(*Because:* _____.)

15. All this year's new car models feature durable nylon upholstery, plush

carpeting _____.

(a) and vinyl trim (b) , and glareproof chrome (c) and with stereo radio
(d) , and all luxurious (e) , and have reclining seats.

15. _____

(*Because:* _____.)

16. Jerry loves to watch the roller-derby _____.

(a) and having a sandwich (b) , and the late show (c) , the news and the fights
(d) and the fights (e) , and horror movies

16. __d__

(*Because:* _____.)

17. Every office and classroom _____ a "no smoking" sign.

(a) bear (b) displays (c) exhibit (d) have (e) show

17. __d__

(*Because:* _____.)

18. Once the main switch is off, unscrew the burned-out fuse, replace it with a new

one of the same _____ restore the main switch to *on*.

(a) amperage and (b) amperage, and to (c) amperage, and remembering to
(d) amperage, and (e) amperage and,

18. __d__

(*Because:* _____.)

16   Chapter One

19. The old man had led a life of daring and danger and disappointment _____.

(a) and despair   (b) , and despair   (c) and desperate   (d) , and difficult
(e) and desperately   19. A

(Because: _____.*)*

20. Every officer and sergeant who shouted at the men _____

(a) were disliked   (b) have admitted it   (c) was sure to be hated
(d) are being criticized   (e) receive bad publicity   20. A

(Because: _____.*)*

But 2

How to work with ... more coordinators
more correlatives
other uses of *but* and *yet*

How to avoid ... faulty parallelism
faulty verb agreement

18 Chapter Two

CONSIDERING THE COORDINATOR *and* as a key to better writing, the first chapter introduced the use of the coordinator to link items in pairs or series and balance them with parallelism. This second chapter will introduce three other coordinators that work something like *and*; they are *but, or,* and *yet*:

>The fighter was young *but* careful.
>Has anybody seen Pete *or* Clara?
>Our team fumbled three times *yet* won the game.

Two of these coordinators, *but* and *yet*, indicate a contrast between the items they join. We expect a young fighter to be careless, but this one is *careful*; there is a contrast between the two words that describe him: *young* and *careful*. And we don't expect a team to fumble three times and still win; there is a contrast between the two words joined by *yet: fumbled* and *won*.

Time for Review

>*But, or,* and *yet* are coordinators. Like *and* they can be used to link items in pairs or series.
>
>*But* and *yet* usually indicate some contrast between the items that they link in a pair.

Do-It-Yourself Exercise

Write in the blanks some words that will be properly linked by *but* or *yet*. Remember that the items in pairs must be in *parallel* form:

>The climbers inched up the cliff ___steadly___ but ___surety___. (Tell *how* they climbed.)
>
>Last weekend was ___quite___ but ___happy___. (Describe the weekend.)
>
>A ___quite___ yet ___mean___ growl came from the little watchdog. (Describe the growl.)

The alley behind Yancey street is ___big___ but ___dirty___.
(Describe the alley.)

Many ___fans___ but only a few ___millionaires___ come to the stock-car races. (What kinds of people?)

Pete enters every race; he ___runs___ well yet ___looses___ every one.

I ___cut___ the tree but ___clean___ the lamppost.

Peralita ___wanted___ to keep the kittens but ___had___ to give them away.

After the argument was over, Gilbert was ___angry___ yet ___lonely___.

Kitty, who owned the saloon, always spoke _____ yet _____ about Sheriff Dillon.

Checking up: Review each of your pairs for parallelism. Are both items in each pair equally related to the rest of the sentence? It would be awkward to write, "Last weekend was *sunny* but *without friends*," since *sunny* describes the weekend, but *without friends* apparently describes a person. It wouldn't be effective to write, "Kitty . . . spoke *critically* yet *was crazy* about Sheriff Dillon," because *critically* describes how she spoke, but *was crazy* does not. Recheck your pairs to be sure that the items linked by *but* or *yet* are in contrast with one another. In the first sentence of the exercise *slowly but surely* would do very well, but there would be no contrast between such items as *slowly but carefully*.

How "Or" Works

The coordinator *or* may show contrast: *whisper* or *shout*, *up* or *down*, *eat* or *starve*, *dead* or *alive*. But *or* indicates that only one item in the pair, not both items, is to be considered:

Will you have coffee *or* milk?
Students may write the exam with pen *or* pencil.
Did the truck hit the tree *or* the fence?

It is obvious, then, that *or* does not work quite the way *and* works. It would be quite different to write:

Will you have coffee *and* milk?
Did the truck hit the tree *and* the fence?

With *and* both items in the pair are considered; with *or*, only one of them.
   When a pair is used as the subject in a sentence, again *or* differs from *and*:

Elena *and* Sylvester *live* here.
Elena *or* Sylvester *lives* here.

Both Elena and Sylvester are included with *and*, but with *or* linking the pair, only one of them is included. When a pair is formed with *or*, the one item nearer to the verb will determine whether that verb (in the *present*) has an *-s* ending added:

Berries or *ice cream is* served as dessert.
Salad or *fried potatoes come* with the hamburger.
The battery or the *sparkplugs have* gone bad.
The sparkplugs or the *battery has* gone bad.

If the subject nearer to the verb is *singular*, the verb (in the *present*) will take the *-s* ending: ice cream *is*, battery *has*.

Time for Review

The coordinator *or* indicates that only one item in the pair, not both items, is to be considered.

When a pair linked by *or* is used as the subject in a sentence, the verb should (in the *present*) match the nearer item in the pair: potatoes or *bread is*; bread or *potatoes are*.

Do-It-Yourself Exercise

Write in the blanks some items that will form *pairs* linked by *or*:

Should a beginner use __A worm__ or __A bug__ to bait his fishhook?

My watch is never on time; it is always __ahead__ or __behind__.

Jerry learned never to argue about __rules__ or __regulations__.

Whether you are __happy__ or __sad__, it's nice to have money.

Let's find out whether the bus is due __at two__ or __at three__.

Every winter my __toe__ or my __fingers__ are frostbitten.

Several __donuts__ or some __cake__ is usually on the coffee-shop menu.

Two __hamburgers__ or a __steak__ comes with the main course at the cafeteria.

Checking up: Most of the pairs are easy enough to supply: *worms* or *flies*, *politics* or *religion*, *rich* or *poor*, *now* or *later*, *at noon* or *at 1 p.m.*—or any that you found appropriate. But take special care to check the pairs in the last three sentences. You can write, "*ears* are frostbitten," but not "*nose* are frostbitten"; "some *meat* is on the menu," but not "some *vegetables* is . . ." (The last of the two items must name just *one* thing if the being word ends with *-s* here.) And "two *muffins* or one *roll* comes," but not "two *rolls* or two *muffins* comes . . . ."

Forming Series

Just as *but, yet,* and *or* can be used to link pairs, so can they be used to form a *series* of three or more items:

The story's hero is young, handsome, fun-loving, *but* arrogant.
After graduation Eddie got a job, saved his money, *yet* did have fun.
My fishing hat is old, torn, faded, dirty, *but* perfect in every way.
Have you ever known one of those students who never listen, never read, never study, *yet* always manage to make the dean's list?
The little pup didn't seem to know whether to go ahead, to turn back, *or* to stand still.
Al didn't show up for breakfast, for lunch, *or* for dinner.

Again, when a series is formed with commas separating the items, there should be a *comma* before the coordinator.

Suggestions for Writing

A. Even a friend may not seem friendly at every moment. Write a passage of about 100 words, telling about a person who is usually friendly, though not always. Use *but, yet,* and *or* to form pairs and series.
B. Women's hair styles change with the decades. Why do some like hair long and others like it short? Include the preferences of men as you write a passage of about 100 words on the topic. Use *but, yet,* and *or* to form pairs and series.

C. If the nation has excess tax money, how should that money be spent? Defense? Education? Ecology? Highways? Write your ideas in a passage of about 100 words. Use *but, yet,* and *or* to form pairs and series.

After Writing: Reread your passage to check the punctuation of series. Items in pairs should not be separated by a comma; items in series (with coordinator used once) should be separated by a comma, including a comma before the coordinator.

"Not-But" and "Not only—But Also"

Often the word *not* is used with *but* to form pairs:

It's possible to be in love *not* wisely *but* furiously.
Freddie is *not* tall *but* short.
Greet us *not* with a frown *but* with a smile.
Handling a tractor was *not* difficult *but* easy.

This *not-but* pattern emphasizes a contrast: The items in the pair are usually strongly opposed, like *tall-short, frown-smile, difficult-easy.*

The correlative *not-but* indicates that only one of the two items, not both of them, applies to the situation. Freddie is not *both* tall and short; he is only short. Carla doesn't greet the world with *both* frown and smile, but only with a smile.

Another correlative pattern, however, indicates that *both* items in the pair apply to the situation. This pattern uses *not only–but also*:

People should try to hear *not only* what is said *but also* what is meant.
Uncle Dan *not only* saves string *but also* hoards it.
The country will *not only* enjoy this new game *but also* profit from it.

There is no special *contrast* between two items paired by *not only–but also*. There's very little contrast between *what is said* and *what is meant*, between *saves* and *hoards,* or between *enjoy* and *profit from.*

Pairs linked by *not-but* and *not only–but also* will usually be awkward unless they are made with items in parallel:

Faulty	Parallel
Victor should *not* speak his report *but* in writing.	Victor should *not* speak his report *but* write it.
The Dallas Cowboys are *not only* heavier *but also* have speed.	The Dallas Cowboys are *not only* heavier *but also* faster.

But 23

Time for Review

But is used in two correlative patterns: *not-but* and *not only–but also*.

When items are linked by *not-but*, only one of the items applies to the situation.

When items are linked by *not only–but also*, both items apply to the situation.

Items paired by *not-but* or by *not only–but also* should be parallel in form and function.

Do-It-Yourself Exercise

Write in the blanks some appropriate words or word-groups to form pairs:

In the next ten years we hope to find our nation not only _____ but also __richer__.

In my family not the __men__ but the __dogs__ are in favor of women's lib.

When Mr. Hirami gets home from work, he is not only __tired__ but also __upset__.

The coach says our swimmers will not __practice__ but __rest__.

Checking up: Are the items *parallel* in each pair? It would be awkward to write "not only *peaceful* but also *prosperity*," since *peaceful* would balance with *prosperous* but not with *prosperity*. Sometimes faulty parallelism in such pairs will be easy to spot if the writer reverses the order of items: " . . . to find our nation not only *prosperity* . . . " would make the faulty structure obvious.

Continue by writing appropriate correlatives to link the items that are in *italics*:

High-speed driving is __not only__ *wasteful* __but also__ *dangerous*.

The girl wearing the yellow suit is __not only__ *my sister* __but also__ *my cousin*.

The women of the island _**not only**_ cook with sea water _**but also**_ wash with it.

**Not only** the Senate _**but also**_ the House of Representatives has passed the ecology bill.

News of the earthquake in Chile _**not only**_ shocked us _**but also**_ stirred us to helpful action.

Checking up: When there is contrast between the items in a pair, you should not use *not only–but also*. It would be ridiculous to write "The girl . . . is *not only* my sister *but also* my cousin."

"Either-Or" and "Neither-Nor"

Or also appears in correlative patterns: *either-or* and *neither-nor*:

It didn't make sense to sit around doing nothing. Sid decided he would *either* fish *or* cut bait.

The customer didn't seem to like *either* the white shoes *or* the green ones.

Don't just stand around! *Either* rake some leaves *or* go home.

Neither the hot dog *nor* the hamburger has enough mustard.

The coyote's voice is *neither* soft *nor* pleasant.

Again, of course, the items paired by the correlatives would be awkward if they were not in parallel form. It would not do to write, "The customer didn't seem to like either *the white shoes* or *satisfied with the green ones.*" The describing word *satisfied* is not parallel with *the white shoes*.

Or, whether used alone or in a correlative pattern (*either-or, neither-nor*), indicates that only one of the paired items applies to the situation. Sid will not both fish and cut bait; he will do only *one* of those things.

When *either-or* or *neither-nor* links items that are used as subjects in a sentence, the verb (in the *present*) will match the nearer of the two items:

Either Sam or *Phil cuts* the bait.

Neither the cornbread nor the *beans* cooked long enough.

Either *the beans* or *the cornbread was* undercooked.

Time for Review

Or appears in two correlative patterns: *either-or* and *neither-nor*.

When a pair linked by *either-or* or by *neither-nor* is used as the subject in a sentence, the verb should (in the *present*) match the nearer of the two items: either the cat or the *mice are* hiding; neither the mice nor the *cat is* hiding.

Items paired by correlatives should be parallel in form and function.

Do-It-Yourself Exercise

Write in the blanks some appropriate words or word groups to complete these sentences:

Mr. Paciorek told his wife that she was neither __expecting__ nor __pregnant__.

Either __the Smiths__ or __the Jones__ are always late.

Neither the __government__ nor the __state__ has full control of the company funds.

Don't worry; I will neither __hide__ your money nor __spend__ it unwisely.

I'm not sure, but I think his girlfriend's birthday is either __today__ or __tomorrow__.

Neither __Kent__ nor __Kelly__ is as old as I am.

Why do some people think that in politics you have to be either __honest__ or __rich__?

Checking up: In the first three sentences be sure you have used items that fit properly; in the second and third sentences the items must produce proper use of the verbs *are* and *has* (see p. 24). It would be wrong to write "Either you or *Joe are* always late"; the subject nearer to *are* must be something that goes with that verb, such as "Either the professor or *the students are* always late."

Continue this exercise by writing appropriate correlatives (*either-or* or *neither-nor*) to complete these sentences:

All of us hate to breathe ——————— smog ——————— dust.

If I were you, I would ——————— waste my money ——————— be stingy with it.

Will the fellow who left the radio blaring please ——————— turn it off ——————— turn it down!

I'd get married, except that all my friends are ——————— too young ——————— too old.

Checking up: The appropriate correlatives are almost obvious in those sentences. Notice that the items they join are, in each case, parallel.

Other Uses of "But"

But is often a handy substitute for other words, such as *except, only, just,* or (in the expression *all but*) *almost:*

Sally has *all but* finished the sweater she's been knitting. (*almost*)
Everybody *but* the chairman has taken a seat. (*except*)
Life is *but* a dream! (*only*)
The shop has been open *but* a few minutes. (*just*)
His convictions left him no choice *but* to run for office. (*except*)
The hour was *all but* over. (*almost*)

In these uses, of course, *but* is not a coordinator; it is working as a synonym for *except, only, just,* or *almost.*

Time for Review

But is often used as a substitute for other words, such as *except* (nothing *but* bread), *only* (take *but* one), and *almost* (It's *all but* finished).

Do-It-Yourself Exercise

Write a completion for each of these sentences, using *but* in each as called for:

I've finished washing everything _____.
                                                (meaning *except*)

Sam has repaired his car _____.
                              (meaning *just*)

Last season the team was _____.
                              (as correlative with *not*)

The den mother has a noisy _____ group of Cub Scouts on her hands.
                                  (as coordinator)

At first I thought your idea was _____.
                                  (meaning *only*)

I can't give you anything _____.
                                (meaning *except*)

When Hank slid into the base, he _____.
                                    (meaning *almost*)

We looked around the neighborhood, checked out the playground, visited the fire station, _____.
                              (as coordinator)

Checking up: As a coordinator *but* appears alone. As a correlative it appears with *not*. When *but* means *except*, *only*, or *just*, it appears alone; when it means *almost*, it appears with *all* (He *all but* broke his ankle).

Suggestions for Writing

D. "Required" courses in a college curriculum are supposedly those that every graduate should know something about if he is to be "educated." What specific courses do you believe should be required in college, and what courses should not? Write your ideas in a passage of about 200 words. Use as many different *correlatives* as you can.
E. Noticeable habits of behavior are part of what makes a "personality." Describe a teacher you have known who had some special habits in the classroom (such as losing her glasses, getting chalk all over his clothes). Write your description in a passage of about 200 words. Use *but* in as many different ways as you can.
F. Most people seem to believe that college studies increase a person's earning power,

qualifying the student for better jobs. In what ways is that belief true, and in what ways it is untrue? Write your ideas in a passage of about 200 words. Use as many *correlatives* as you can.

After Writing: Reread your passage to be sure that all items you have used in pairs or series are in parallel form. Be sure you have used commas to separate items in series, including a comma before *and, but, or,* or *yet*.

Other Uses of "Yet"

As we have shown, *yet* often works as a coordinator:

Our team fumbled three times *yet* won.

Kitty, who owned the saloon, always spoke critically *yet* admiringly about Sheriff Dillon.

Yet can also be used, like *but*, to coordinate items in a series:

Uncle Ziff is lazy, good for nothing, *yet* fun to have around.

A small, light, *yet* nourishing lunch kept her going for the afternoon.

When *yet* works to form pairs or series, it has the meaning of *but, although,* or *eventually*. Sometimes *yet* has other meanings. It may mean *besides, still,* or *eventually*:

There is much work *yet* to be done.

No doubt he'll win a scholarship *yet*.

I have *yet* to meet a really unfriendly person.

And sometimes *yet* is used to mean *now, even now,* or *until now*:

Don't leave *yet*; we haven't finished the game *yet*.

She has never *yet* disappointed me.

Time for Review

Yet has several meanings when it is not used as a coordinator: *still* (Are you here *yet*?), *eventually* (We'll do it *yet*), *even now* (Don't go *yet*), and *until now* (We've haven't quit *yet*).

Do-It-Yourself Exercise

Write an appropriate completion for each of these sentences, using *yet* in each as called for:

The detective looked around the house thoroughly _____.
(meaning *but*)

Luckily the summer is not _____.
(meaning *even now*)

Richard knew he would _____.
(meaning *eventually*)

A young _____ driver sat behind the wheel.
(meaning *but*)

The Expos and the Giants have _____.
(meaning *still*)

Snoopy will get his dinner, all right; he has never _____.
(meaning *until now*)

The lesson we all started yesterday has not _____.
(meaning *now*)

Checking up: Be sure that you have written what seem to be natural sentences. It would not do to write something awkward like "The detective looked around the house *thoroughly* yet *unsatisfied*." The items linked by *yet* (as coordinator) should be in parallel form.

Suggestions for Writing

G. When working as a member of a group or a team, do you find it more satisfying to be a leader or to be a follower? Write a passage (about 150 words) telling which would be your choice—and why. Use each of these at least once: *yet, neither-nor,* and *all but*.

H. If you had to live either where there are frequent earthquakes or where there are frequent tornadoes, which place would you select? Write a passage (about 150 words) defending your selection. In developing the passage use each of these at least once: *either-or, but* meaning *only,* and *not-but*. Underline those words in your passage.

I. If you suddenly found yourself in a place where no one speaks any language you know, how would you start to communicate with those people you met? Write a passage (about 150 words) telling how you would go about it. In developing the passage use each of these at least once: *not only-but also, either-or, yet,* and *or*. Underline those words in your passage.

After Writing: Recheck your work for parallelism. Be sure that you have used commas properly in series.

QUIZ 2

Using But, Or, and Yet

This quiz asks you to work with *but, or, yet,* and the correlatives *not-but, not only-but also, either-or,* and *neither-nor*. On the blank within each sentence write the item that you think completes the sentence most appropriately. Then mark the **letter** of that item on your answer blank. After marking your choice, briefly explain why you chose it *(Because:* . . .).

Example: Peggy's long week of waiting was ___all but___ over.

(a) yet   (b) not but   (c) either today or   (d) all but   (e) or   Ex _d_

(Because: "all but" means "nearly"; no other item has meaning that makes good sense.)

1. Either Raquel or her _____ have to accept the prize.

(a) brother   (b) friend   (c) parents   (d) teacher   (e) mother   1 _c_

(Because: _____.)
   (Question: Which of the italicized words provides a proper *either-or* pair to go with the verb *have?)*

2. It is obvious that Sal has talent but _____.

(a) money   (b) dances well   (c) training   (d) no ambition
(e) no laziness   2 _d_

(Because: _____.)
(Question: Which completion should be used after *but* for proper contrast and parallelism?)

3. My friend Tony is not only a good singer but also _____.

(a) plays guitar   (b) a great drummer   (c) he plays the accordion
(d) without lessons   (e) well trained   3 _b_

(Because: _____.)
   (Question: Since *a good singer* follows *not only*, which completion should follow *but also* for proper parallelism?)

4. My term project is _____ completed but also turned in.

(a) but   (b) yet   (c) not only   (d) either   (e) or   4 _c_

(Because: _____.)
   (Question: What goes properly with *but also?)*

32   Chapter Two

5. Neither snow nor _____ has ever bothered our messengers.

(a) floods   (b) wind   (c) rainstorms   (d) frozen roads   (e) gloomy nights   5. _b_

(*Because:* _____.)
   (*Question:* With the *neither-nor* pair, which completion will properly match the singular verb, *has*?)

6. _____ potatoes or rice have the more protein?

(a) Does   (b) Do   (c) Neither   (d) Does either   (e) Both   6. _d_

(*Because:* _____.)

7. Relations between our country and yours have been friendly, productive, yet _____.

(a) lasting   (b) which proved insincere   (c) are unappreciated   (d) costly
(e) have been difficult   7. _d_

(*Because:* _____.)

8. Hardly anyone _____ the blonde student asked a question.

(a) but   (b) yet   (c) or   (d) but also   (e) nor   8. _A_

(*Because:* _____.)

9. We like lectures either short or _____.

(a) keeping us amused   (b) to amuse us   (c) we get bored   (d) funny
(e) very informatively   9. _d_

(*Because:* _____.)

10. Our city neither attracts new industries nor _____.

(a) professional athletic teams   (b) our county   (c) encourages old ones
(d) does our state   (e) new population   10. _A_

(*Because:* _____.)

11. Your paper on "The Fuel Shortage" is rather short yet _____.

(a) an excellent one   (b) very informative   (c) accurately   (d) a good grade
(e) written it carelessly   11. _b_

(*Because:* _____.)

But   33

12. The accused has _____ to be found guilty.

(a) either confessed or   (b) neither been tried nor   (c) not denied it but
(d) not only being arrested but also   (e) yet

12. e

(Because: _____.)

13. Every student must enroll in a gym course, an English course, or _____
_____.

(a) sign up for science   (b) be on the basketball team
(c) forget about graduating   (d) a music course   (e) have a good excuse

13. d

(Because: _____.)

14. Have America _____ Germany signed the new treaty?

(a) or   (b) and   (c) yet   (d) not only   (e) all but

14. b

(Because: _____.)

15. One reviewer says the latest record by the Hootin' Owl group is not _____
_____ excitement.

(a) only good but also   (b) only fine but   (c) noisily but
(d) only entertainment but also   (e) either successful or

15. d

(Because: _____.)

16. Concerning the tax cut, should the news make citizens feel pleased or _____
_____?

(a) suspicious   (b) with fear   (c) cautiously   (d) the mayor
(e) unhappily

16. A

(Because: _____.)

17. This class, the professor says, is not _____ superior.

(a) either good but   (b) only good but   (c) either perfect yet   (d) bad nor
(e) only good but also

17. C

(Because: _____.)

34　Chapter Two

18. This traffic is heavier than usual, but we will get to the campus _____
_____.

(a) neither late nor get a ticket　(b) yet　(c) not only on time but have coffee
(d) either early or all be late　(e) not early but have an excuse

18. _b_

(Because: _____.*)*

19. After all, not the students but the _____ are to be awarded the trophy.

(a) coach　(b) college　(c) president　(d) dean　(e) parents

19. _e_

(Because: _____.*)*

20. Can you remember a story that you have heard _____?

(a) yet exciting　(b) or years ago　(c) not lately but a surprise ending
(d) but once　(e) but not reading it

20. _d_

(Because: _____.*)*

A Touch of Grammar

3

How to work with . . . the "rules" of grammar
subject and predicate
the "parts of speech"
word groups as units

GRAMMAR IS A SET OF LANGUAGE PATTERNS that people use to talk with one another. It is not a system that somebody sat down and made up; rather, its patterns grew through centuries of actual talking and writing.

What we usually call "grammar," in the schoolbook sense, is a description of that set of language patterns, an analysis of how they work. Of course, the patterns do not remain the same at all times. The grammar of today is not the same as the grammar of centuries ago. Nor is grammar the same in all places. Yet there is a basic grammar used by people who speak English.

What we call "good grammar" is what most of the people who use the language do with it when they are communicating most effectively. That doesn't mean what they do all the time, but what they do as a rule.

There is the key to grammar: what is done by effective speakers and writers *as a rule*. The expression "as a rule" means almost exactly what we mean by it in the phrase "rule of grammar." A rule of grammar is a description of what most of the effective speakers and writers of English seem to do *as a rule*: most of the time, but not always.

Making Sense in Patterns

Rules of grammar are not invented; they are discovered. They are found by studying what people really do when they put words together to make sense. Does this arrangement of words make sense?

Snore very sleeping often people soundly and dogs.

That arrangement is a jumble of nonsense. We have already seen (in Chapter 1) that the word *and* is normally used to join two things that are somewhat alike. In that group of words *and* could not naturally join any two words other than *people* and *dogs*. It is obvious that *people and dogs* is a grammatical way of putting words together in English: a pattern that makes sense. Suppose we begin the arrangement with that pattern:

People and dogs snore very sleeping often soundly.

It is getting clearer, but *snore very sleeping* is still a jumble; people just don't put words together that way. And *very snore often* wouldn't be likely either, though *very often snore* would. *Very often snore* is a grammatical way of putting words together. And *sleeping soundly* is another arrangement that would be familiar to most native speakers of English. Now we can put these grammatical groups together:

People and dogs sleeping soundly very often snore.

What was a jumble has become a sentence. Now that we have put it together, we can take it apart to discover the system of its grammar.

Most sentences have two basic parts. If we divide our sample sentence into two parts, the natural place to divide is after the word *soundly*:

People and dogs sleeping soundly   very often snore.

The first part is what is being talked about: *people and dogs sleeping soundly*. That word group is the *subject* of the sentence. The second part is what is said about the subject: *very often snore*. That word group is the *predicate* of the sentence. The two basic parts of the sentence are *subject* and *predicate*.

To review: The *subject* of a sentence is *what is talked about*; the *predicate* is *what is said or asked* about it.

The shortest possible full sentence would have just two words, subject and predicate:

Subject - Predicate
Brakes   fail.
Tires   skid.
Drivers   crash.

Brakes, tires, and *drivers* are what are talked about *(subjects). Fail, skid,* and *crash* are what is being said *(predicates).*

"Parts of Speech"

The elements of sentence structure have traditionally been called the eight "parts of speech." Five of them are these:

Conjunctions.   These are *connectors,* used to join elements within sentences. In *people and dogs* the word *and* connects the words. Chapter 1 introduced the uses of *and* to link items in pairs and series. There are four kinds of conjunction: coordinators (see Chapters 1 and 2), correlatives (see Chapters 1 and 2), conjunctive adverbs (see Chapter 5), and subordinators (see Chapters 6, 11, 12, and 15).

Nouns.   These are *names*. Words or word groups that name persons (such as the word *people*), animals (such as *dogs*), places (such as *town*), things (such as *tires*), or ideas (such as *freedom*)—any of these—are *nouns*. (See Chapter 7.)

Verbs.   These are *action* or *being* words. In *People often snore* the word *snore* indicates the action; *snore* is a verb, telling what the people *do*. In *The dog is asleep* the word *is* indicates a state of being; *is* is a verb. (See Chapters 8, 9, and 10.)

Adjectives.   These are *describers of nouns*. In *The dog is asleep* the word *asleep* describes the dog; *asleep* is an adjective. (See Chapter 11.)

38 Chapter Three

Adverbs. These are *describers* of elements other than nouns. In *People often snore* the word *often* describes the verb *snore*; *often* is an adverb. In *The dog is always asleep* the word *always* describes the adjective *asleep*; *always* is an adverb. (See Chapter 12.)

The sample sentence *People and dogs sleeping soundly very often snore* combines these five "parts of speech":

```
People     and        dogs   sleeping   soundly        very     often    snore.
  |         |          |        |          |             |        |        |
 noun   conjunction   noun ←adjective ← adverb        adverb → adverb → verb
              SUBJECT                                        PREDICATE
```

Time for Review

Grammar is a set of language patterns that people use to talk with one another.

"Good grammar" is what is done with the language by people when they are communicating effectively; it is not the same in all times or in all places.

A "rule" of grammar is a description of what most of the effective users of the language do with it *as a rule*; that is, most of the time, not necessarily always.

The rules of grammar are not invented; they are discovered by studying what users of language really do when they put words together to make sense.

The elements of sentence structure include eight "parts of speech." Five of them are (1) conjunctions (connectors), (2) nouns (names), (3) verbs (action or being words), (4) adjectives (describers of nouns), and (5) adverbs (describers of elements other than nouns).

Every sentence has two basic parts: (1) the *subject* (what the sentence is about) and (2) the *predicate* (what is said about the subject).

Do-It-Yourself Exercise

Write in each blank an appropriate word as called for to complete these sentences:

The __wAiter__ filled our __glass__ with __wine__ .
       (noun)   (noun)   (noun)

Wheat farmers __hArvest__ their wheat in the fall and __send__
                  (verb)   (verb)
it to market.

That morning some _____ clouds were hiding the sun's
                    (adjective)

_____ smile.
  (adjective)

Most _____ good books have interesting people doing
     (adverb: how good?)

exciting things; the plots move _____ .
                                (adverb: move how?)

A driving course can teach you what to do in case of breakdown _____
                                                              (conjunction)
collision.

Stormy _____ ordinarily _____ in the
         (noun)   (verb)

_____ .
   (noun)

Saturday _____ Sunday _____ beautiful
          (conjunction)   (verb)

days last week, and the _____ was _____ .
                          (noun)   (adjective)

Checking up: Be sure that the words you have supplied will make good sense in their sentences. If you had trouble thinking of appropriate words, try some nouns like *rain, water, wind, leaves, weather, spring, winter, temperature,* verbs like *happens, were, harvest, take,* adjectives like *dark, heavy, black, warm, excellent,* and adverbs like *really, quickly, fast, very.*

Continue this exercise by writing the "parts of speech" as they appear in these sentences. Use arrows to show how the adjectives and adverbs work (as on p. 38):

Drivers	speeding	wildly	quite	often	crash.
_____	_____	_____	_____	_____	_____
Brakes	adjusted	badly	very	soon	fail.
_____	_____	_____	_____	_____	_____
Tires	worn	through	too	easily	skid.
_____	_____	_____	_____	_____	_____

40 Chapter Three

Checking up: All three sentences have the same pattern, nearly the same as that of the *people and dogs* sentence on p. 38: noun ← adjective ← adverb adverb → adverb → verb.

Not all sentences have the same order, of course. Often an adjective comes before the noun it describes, and adverbs may come after the verbs they describe:

        Little   Nancy   ran   away.

        adjective → *noun*   *verb* ← *adverb*

Continue this exercise by writing the "parts of speech" as they appear in these sentences:

    Really   good   athletes   exercise   regularly.

    _____   _____   _____   _____

    Skilled   mechanics   perform   best.

    _____   _____   _____   _____

    Shiny   bubbles   floated   around.

    _____   _____   _____   _____

Checking up: The first of the three sentences begins with an adverb and ends with another adverb. All three sentences have the same basic pattern: adjective→ noun verb← adverb.

Modifiers

We have seen that an adjective describes a noun. We often say instead that the adjective *modifies* the noun. *Modify* means *limit, change,* or *describe.* Since an adjective does not always describe but sometimes limits or changes the meaning of a noun, the term *modifies* is most often used to suggest the function of an adjective.

We have seen also that an adverb describes a verb or an adjective or an adverb. In other words, an adverb *modifies* any of those elements.

Adjectives and adverbs are the two kinds of *modifier.*

Suggestions for Writing

A. Purses and wallets are often remarkable for the number of things they contain. Write a passage of about 100 words, telling of some of the essential things and some of the "junk" things that purses and wallets often carry. Underline every *noun* that you use.
B. Policemen in most cities today have many jobs to do other than writing tickets and arresting wrongdoers. Write a passage of about 100 words telling some of the things that policemen do as part of their jobs. Underline every *verb* that you use.
C. Because Monday is the first day of the work week, the day of getting back to routines, that day has come to be known as "blue." What does *blue* mean? What are some other color-words that are often used to describe things that really do not have those visible

colors? Write your ideas in a passage of about 100 words. Underline every *adjective* that you use.

After Writing: Reread your passage to be sure that it is as clear as you can make it. Now circle every word that you have used as an *adverb* in the passage. Draw an arrow from each adverb to the word that it modifies.

Word Groups as Units of Meaning

When we put words together in a meaningful group, the group works as a unit. There are three kinds of such word groups:

Sentences.   These are full statements or questions, each with a subject-predicate combination. The shortest possible full sentence is a two-word group, subject and predicate, such as "Drivers crash."

Clauses.   These are subject-predicate combinations *not* used as full sentences by themselves. In "Tires skid, and drivers crash" the two subject-predicate combinations are joined by *and*. Each of the combinations is a *clause*.

Phrases.   These are groups that do not contain a subject-predicate combination:

Noun phrases.   A noun with its modifier (such as *fast drivers*) is a noun phrase.

Verb phrases.   A verb with its modifier (such as *often crash*) is a verb phrase.

Adjective phrases.   An adjective with its modifier (such as *really good*) is an adjective phrase.

Adverb phrases.   An adverb with its modifier (such as *very often*) is an adverb phrase.

Time for Review

Meaningful *word groups* are of three kinds: (1) sentences, (2) clauses, and (3) phrases.

A word with its modifier may form a phrase. Among phrases are these four kinds: (1) noun phrase, (2) verb phrase, (3) adjective phrase, and (4) adverb phrase.

Do-It-Yourself Exercise

Write in each blank an appropriate *two-word* group to complete each sentence as called for:

When I tell my dog to sit, _____(clause)_____ .

Before dawn every morning _____(noun phrase)_____ roll out to deliver copies of the big city newspapers.

The dentist pointed to his big chair, so I _____(verb phrase)_____ .

Danny told us about a _____(adjective phrase)_____ movie that he saw last week.

"Sorry," said the shoe repair man, "but your sandals are _____(adverb phrase)_____ ready."

Grandpa says coffee makes him _____(adjective phrase)_____ .

Grandpa _____(verb phrase)_____ so shaky that he spills more coffee than he drinks.

Some people get homesick whenever they _____(verb phrase)_____ .

All the newspapers these days are noticing the _____(noun phrase)_____ of living.

The sky suddenly grew dark, and _____(clause)_____ .

Checking up: Remember that a clause must be a subject-predicate combination. "Hank Aaron took a swing at a curve ball, but *he missed.*" The words *missed it* wouldn't be a clause, since they are not subject-predicate combination. Either *big trucks* or *small boys* might roll out to deliver newspapers. When the dentist pointed, perhaps I *sat down, cried out,* or *ran away.* Coffee might make Grandpa either *very nervous* or *really happy* —but you can't write *stay awake,* since *stay* would be a verb in that sentence, not an adjective. Check each of your entries to be sure it is a two-word group that works as called for.

Other "Parts of Speech"

Three more "parts of speech" fill out the traditional eight:

Pronouns. These are *substitutes for nouns.* Examples are *I, you, she, they, it, some, everybody, this, theirs, who, himself.*

Prepositions. These are *relationship words;* they show relationships between two things. For example, the word *in* shows a relationship between a bird and a tree; a bird *in* a tree. Prepositions may also show relationships between actions and things. For example, the word *to* shows a relationship between the action *(return)* and the car; return *to* the car.

Usually a preposition begins a word group that ends with a noun: *to town, in the tree, for lunch.* The group is a *prepositional phrase.*

Prepositional phrases are most often used as modifiers:

Shop *at a store* — prepositional phrase used to
verb ← adverb   modify the verb *shop*

bird *in a tree* — prepositional phrase used to
noun ← adjective   modify the noun *bird*

lady *with a baby* — prepositional phrase used to
noun ← adjective   modify the noun *lady*

Interjections. These are words "thrown in among" other elements in a sentence but not directly related to those other elements. For example, the word *say* does not relate grammatically to the rest of the sentence in "*Say,* I like those shoes!" The words in italics are interjections:

Wow! Did you see that? It was, *oh,* about a mile high, *huh*? *Gee,* that was something else!

Time for Review

The eight traditional "parts of speech" are *nouns, adjectives, adverbs, verbs, conjunctions, prepositions, pronouns,* and *interjections.*

A *pronoun* replaces, or stands for, a noun.

A *preposition* shows a relationship between two things—or between an action and a thing.

An *interjection* is an expression not functionally related to the other parts of a sentence.

Do-It-Yourself Exercise

Write in the blank an appropriate word to complete each sentence:

Josie was ready to leave _____ the concert. With all the
                          (preposition)

excitement _____ had not had much sleep for _____
              (pronoun)   (adjective)

44 Chapter Three

days. _____ (interjection) , how she was looking forward _____ (preposition)

playing the guitar _____ (preposition) the group. Would _____ (pronoun)

really think she was ready _____ (preposition) the competition?

_____ (interjection) , at least she would try. _____ (pronoun) would all

be great experience, although winning was _____ (preposition) her wildest

dreams.

Checking up: Among useful pronouns: *she, they, it;* prepositions: *for, to, in, at, with, beyond, from;* interjections: *oh, boy, well, gee, anyhow.*

Suggestions for Writing

D. Write a brief personal letter (about 150 words) to a friend who has never seen a football game. Telling what the game is like, try to convince that friend that you should go see a game together. Use as many pronouns, prepositions, and interjections as you can—and underline each of them.
E. If you have never ridden a motorbike, imagine what it would feel like to ride one from your house to the college campus on a cool morning. Write a description (about 150 words) of the feelings, using as many pronouns, prepositions, and interjections as you can. Underline each of them.
F. Imagine that a friend has just asked you to go along to a movie on Friday night. You can't go, because you have a date—and you don't want this friend to know about that date. How are you going to turn down the movie? Write it down (in about 150 words), using as many pronouns, prepositions, and interjections as you can—and underlining each of them.

After Writing: A preposition shows a relationship between two things. Reread your passage and circle, for each underlined preposition, the two words that the preposition relates. Look again at the *interjections* you have used in your passage; be sure that you have used a comma (or a pair of commas) to set off each interjection, as shown in the examples on p. 43.

QUIZ 3

The Basics of Grammar

Write in the blank within each sentence the most appropriate of the offered completions. Then mark the *letter* of that completion on your answer blank.

Example: The "power plant" of a sentence, the part that indicates action or state of being, is the ___verb___ .

(a) subject   (b) modifier   (c) conjunction   (d) verb   (e) preposition

Ex. _d_

(Reference: See p. 37.)

1. A rule of grammar describes the pattern used by effective speakers and writers for putting certain words together to make sense: it is what those users of the language do _____ .

(a) all the time   (b) very seldom   (c) because they must   (d) as a rule
(e) only when in English class

1. ___

(Reference: See p. 36.)

2. Rules of grammar are _____ .

(a) unnatural   (b) invented   (c) perfect
(d) the same for all times and places   (e) discovered

2. ___

(Reference: See p. 36.)

3. Nouns are _____ .

(a) connectors   (b) predicates   (c) names   (d) clauses   (e) action words

3. ___

(Reference: See p. 37.)

4. In a two-word sentence (like "Babies cry") one word is the predicate, the other the _____ .

(a) adjective   (b) adverb   (c) subject   (d) conjunction   (e) pronoun

4. ___

(Reference: See p. 37.)

5. A word that replaces or stands for a noun is _____ .

(a) a pronoun   (b) an adjective   (c) an adverb   (d) a conjunction
(e) an interjection

5. ___

(Reference: See p. 42.)

6. A noun and its modifier (such as "angry tiger") form _____ .

(a) an adjective phrase   (b) a pair   (c) a clause   (d) a noun phrase
(e) a verb phrase

6. ___

(Reference: See p. 41.)

46   Chapter Three

7. A subject-verb combination (such as "angels wept") that appears in a sentence with another such combination is _____.

(a) a noun phrase   (b) a verb phrase   (c) a clause   (d) a modifier
(e) an interjection
   (*Reference:* See p. 41.)

7.____

8. A word that shows a relationship between two things (such as *on* in "butter *on* toast") is _____.

(a) an adjective   (b) a preposition   (c) a pronoun   (d) an adverb
(e) a conjunction
   (*Reference:* See p. 42-43.)

8.____

9. A prepositional phrase begins with a preposition and ends with a _____ _____.

(a) predicate   (b) verb   (c) conjunction   (d) noun   (e) modifier
   (*Reference:* See p. 43.)

9.____

10. A word "thrown in" without direct connection with other parts of a sentence (such as *oh, anyhow, well*) is _____.

(a) a conjunction   (b) an adverb   (c) an interjection   (d) a preposition
(e) a modifier
   (*Reference:* See p. 43.)

10.____

11. A word that links two verbs (such as *or* in "sink *or* swim") is a _____ _____.

(a) pronoun   (b) conjunction   (c) noun   (d) modifier   (e) preposition
   (*Reference:* See p. 37.)

11.____

12. A word that modifies an adverb (such as *quite* in "*quite* often") is _____ _____.

(a) an adjective   (b) an adverb   (c) a preposition   (d) a noun   (e) a verb
   (*Reference:* See p. 38.)

12.____

13. A verb and its modifier (such as "think fast") constitute a _____.

(a) verb phrase   (b) pair   (c) prepositional phrase   (d) clause
(e) modifier
   (*Reference:* See p. 41.)

13.____

14. Both adjectives and adverbs function as _____.

(a) interjections (b) nouns (c) verbs (d) pronouns (e) modifiers   14_____
   (*Reference:* See p. 40.)

15. Every sentence has two basic parts; they are _____.

(a) noun and conjunction   (b) verb and adverb   (c) subject and modifier
(d) subject and predicate   (e) preposition and noun   15_____
   (*Reference:* See p. 37.)

16. A word that modifies a noun is _____.

(a) an adverb   (b) a verb   (c) a preposition   (d) an adjective
(e) a conjunction   16_____
   (*Reference:* See p. 37.)

17. A word group that does not have a subject-verb combination is _____
_____.

(a) nonsense   (b) a clause   (c) a phrase   (d) a sentence
(e) an interjection   17_____
   (*Reference:* See p. 41.)

18. A word that modifies a verb is _____.

(a) a preposition   (b) an adverb   (c) an adjective   (d) a conjunction
(e) an interjection   18_____
   (*Reference:* See p. 38.)

19. An adjective with its modifier (such as "really beautiful") forms _____
_____.

(a) a prepositional phrase   (b) an adjective phrase   (c) a clause
(d) a noun phrase   (e) a sentence   19_____
   (*Reference:* See p. 41.)

20. Conjunctions are _____.

(a) modifiers   (b) subjects   (c) predicates   (d) connectors
(e) verb phrases   20_____
   (*Reference:* See p. 37.)

Sentences 4

How to work with . . . subject-predicate combinations
independent clauses
subordinate clauses
subordinators
four kinds of sentence

How to avoid . . . choppy sentences

A SENTENCE IS THE MOST FULLY MEANINGFUL kind of word group. It introduces a subject and says (or asks) something about that subject:

Subject	Predicate
(what is talked about)	(what is said about it)
Glass	breaks easily.
Wind	shook the trees.
A hurricane	is a windstorm.
Basketball players	are usually tall.

The subjects of those sentences *do* something or *are* something. The predicates tell us what the subjects do or are.

Time for Review

A sentence is a meaningful word group with two essential parts: *subject* and *predicate*.

A sentence completes a statement, a command, or a question.

Do-It-Yourself Exercise

Draw a line to separate the two essential parts of each of these sentences. Underline the subject part:

Most excuses are unbelievable.
None of my friends understands Hungarian.
A huge grizzly bear stared blankly at us.
The cost of living almost never goes down.
Four men raised the front of the old car.
Everybody was late for work that day.

Checking up: In all those sentences the subject part comes first. The line between subjects and predicates: excuses/are, friends/understands, bear/stared, living/almost, men/raised, Everybody/was.

Of course, a subject does not have to come before its predicate. Continue by drawing a line to separate the two essential parts of each of the following sentences, underlining the subject part:

There were no telephones.
Where is the bus station?
So goes the news of the world.
But now comes the scary part of the story.
There stands the famous statue of General Lee.

Checking up: In those sentences the predicates come *before* the subjects. The line between the two elements: were/no, is/the, goes/the, comes/the, stands/the.

The Simple Sentence

All the sentences considered so far in this chapter have just one subject-predicate combination. They are *simple sentences*. The *combination* of subject and predicate is what counts here; that is, a sentence may have several subjects and several predicates and yet have only one subject-predicate combination. Some examples:

George and Larry eat a lot but don't work much.
His books and papers spilled out and fell to the ground.
The man and the boy jogged and puffed around the track.

The subjects in those sentences are pairs formed with *and*. The predicates are also pairs—pairs of verbs linked by *and* or *but*. Nevertheless, each sentence has only one subject-predicate *combination*; there is only one place of separation between the basic elements of subject and predicate:

George and Larry / eat a lot but don't work much.
His books and papers / spilled out and fell to the ground.
The man and the boy / jogged and puffed around the track.

Since each sentence has but one subject-predicate combination, each is a *simple sentence*.

Time for Review

The subject in a sentence may be a pair or a series of nouns.

The predicate in a sentence may be a pair or a series of verbs.

A sentence with but one subject-predicate combination is *a simple sentence*.

Do-It-Yourself Exercise

Draw a line to separate the two essential parts of these simple sentences. Underline the subject parts:

Both cities and states have money problems and need tax reforms.

Math and science are difficult but seem useful.

All officers and men must either shape up or ship out.

Checking up: Since each of the sentences has but one *combination* of subject and predicate, each is a simple sentence. The line between the basic elements: states/have, science/are, men/must.

Making Compounds

When two or more subjects are linked in a pair or series, they form a *compound subject*. The subjects *cities and states, math and science, drivers and crews,* and *officers and men* are all compound subjects.

When two or more verbs are linked in a pair or series they form a *compound verb* or *compound predicate*. The verbs *have and need, are but seem, check in and report,* and *shape up or ship out* are all verbs in compound predicates.

The sentences in the exercise just above are all simple sentences, each with a compound subject and a compound predicate.

Time for Review

When two or more subjects are linked in a pair or series, they form a *compound subject*.

When two or more verbs are linked in a pair or series, they form a *compound predicate*.

A *simple sentence* may have a compound subject.

A *simple sentence* may have a compound predicate.

A *simple sentence* may have both compound subject and compound predicate.

Do-It-Yourself Exercises

Write in each blank an appropriate word or word group as called for to complete these sentences:

_____ had drawn a picture on the sidewalk.
        (subject)

The picture _____ a child carrying a bouquet of roses and daffodils.
                (verb)

In the picture _____ were both yellow.
                    (compound subject)

The artist _____ colored chalk and _____ the picture
              (verb)   (verb)
very large.

All day people on the sidewalk _____ .
                                    (predicate)

That night a hard rain _____ the picture away.
                         (compound verb)

In the morning _____ wished that we knew who the artist was.
                (compound subject)

Checking up: All are *simple sentences,* since each has but one subject-predicate combination. Go back and draw a line between the two essential parts of each sentence.

The Compound Sentence

We have seen that two subjects linked by a coordinator will form a compound subject, and that two predicates linked by a coordinator will form a compound predicate. It is also possible to link two subject-predicate *combinations* by using a coordinator:

   It was after three o'clock, *and* the bank had closed.
   The lady ran for the bus, *but* she missed it.
   We should stop for lunch, *or* I'll starve.
   The gang went to the pool, *yet* nobody dived in.

Each of the sentences has two subject-predicate combinations. Each of the combinations, since it could have been a sentence by itself, is an independent clause.

When two or more independent clauses are linked by a coordinator, they form a *compound sentence.* The coordinators *and, but, or,* and *yet* link the two clauses in the sentences above. Each of the sentences is a *compound sentence.*

Time for Review

A coordinator may be used to link two subject-predicate combinations.

When two or more subject-predicate combinations (independent clauses) are linked by a coordinator, they form a *compound sentence.*

54   Chapter Four

Do-It-Yourself Exercise

Write in each blank *one or two words* (not more) that will complete the kind of sentence called for:

(Simple Sentence) Pets are fun _____ have to be cared for.

(Compound Sentence) The country seems rich _____ go hungry.

(Simple Sentence) Money is the fruit of labor _____ doesn't grow on trees.

(Compound Sentence) Clouds are gathering _____ looks like rain.

(Compound Sentence) You must read the assignment _____ must guess at the answer on the test.

(Simple Sentence) Voters are intelligent _____ can't be fooled forever.

(Compound Sentence) Today's pace of living is fast _____ is getting faster.

Checking up: Each blank should contain one word or two words, not more. In the simple sentences you need just one word—a coordinator—to form a *compound predicate*. In the compound sentences you need two words—a coordinator and a subject for the verb that follows. Each compound sentence should have a comma between the clauses (before the coordinator); if you did not put the necessary commas in, do so now.

More Sentence Coordinators

Two more coordinators (in addition to *and, but, yet,* and *or*) are used to link independent clauses in compound sentences. The two are *for* and *so*:

Steve slept well, *for* he had worked hard all day.

The mail arrived, *so* they stopped to read it.

Photos are usually less imaginative than paintings, *for* the camera usually shows only what is really there.

Mario felt hungry, *so* he fixed a salami sandwich.

As a coordinator *for* means something like "because"; *so* means something like "therefore." Again, the comma is used to separate the clauses in each compound sentence.

Time for Review

The words *for* and *so* may be used as coordinators to link independent clauses in *compound sentences*.

As a coordinator *for* implies cause; *so* implies result.

A comma is used before the coordinator to separate the clauses in a compound sentence.

Do-It-Yourself Exercise

Write *for* or *so* in each blank to complete these compound sentences appropriately:

Time flies _____ make the most of it.

Aunt Sarah lost a lot of friends _____ she refused to compromise.

The road was closed _____ the bridge had been washed out.

The book was very long _____ I just skimmed it.

Jake will never change _____ you must love him anyway.

The bridge had been washed out _____ the road was closed.

Checking up: Did you remember to put in a comma before the coordinator in each compound sentence? If not, go back and write the commas in now.

Suggestions for Writing

A. News reports occasionally tell of people who say they have seen "unidentified flying objects" from outer space. Write *three simple sentences* telling what you believe about such "objects."
B. Millions of people believe that astrology is a science; millions of others think it is just fun. Write *three simple sentences* telling what you think about it.
C. Most people would rather tell a secret than keep one. What sort of thing do you believe should be kept secret? Write your answer in *three simple sentences*.

After Writing: Every simple sentence has just one combination of subject and verb. Revise your passage into *two* sentences, one *simple* and one *compound*. Underline the coordinator that you use to make the compound sentence. Remember to use a comma before the coordinator.

The Complex Sentence

Not every subject-predicate combination makes a full sentence:

Full Sentence	Not a Full Sentence
We were happy.	*if* we were happy
The weather was cold.	*when* the weather was cold
It was Friday.	*because* it was Friday

56 Chapter Four

Full Sentence	Not a Full Sentence
The water pipes froze.	*after* the water pipes froze
The family ate dinner.	*while* the family ate dinner
Mother turned off the TV.	*although* Mother turned off the TV

Obviously the difference between the full sentence and the nonsentence is (in each case) the word in italics. Those words (and others like them) are used to make a clause less important than some other clause in the same sentence:

We were happy *because* it was Friday.

The independent clause *We were happy* is more important in the sentence than *because it was Friday*. The *because* clause is just an explanation of the independent clause and is subordinated to it.

Words like *because* (as well as *if, when, after, while, since,* and *although*) are subordinators. A clause introduced by a subordinator is a *subordinate clause*.

When a sentence contains a subordinate clause as well as the essential independent clause, the sentence is *complex:*

When the weather was cold, the waterpipes froze.

Mother turned off the TV *while* the family ate dinner.

We were happy, *although* Mother turned off the TV.

Each of those sentences contains at least *two* subject-predicate combinations, at least one of them introduced by a subordinator. Each is a *complex sentence*.

Time for Review

A sentence that contains a subordinate clause as well as one independent clause is a *complex sentence*.

Do-It-Yourself Exercise

Write in each blank a subordinator *(if, because, before, when, after, since, while, although)* to form a complex sentence:

We slept outside _____ the moonlight cast shadows of our picket fence.

We awoke _____ the birds started singing.

I cannot buy the set of tools _____ I don't save some money.

Uncle Jeff decided to retire, _____ he wasn't yet of retirement age.

_____ the exam was over, I knew I shouldn't have gone to that party the night before.

The painter gets his pay _____ he finishes the job.

Birds fly south in the winter _____ in cold weather they can't find enough to eat.

Motorists will have to take the north detour _____ the bridge is washed out.

Checking up: Notice that a subordinate clause, which begins with a subordinator, may appear at the beginning of a sentence or at the end of a sentence.

Suggestions for Writing

D. Some people are "night people," and others feel best in the early morning. Write a passage of about 150 words, telling what part of the day you like best—and why. In writing the passage, use at least two *complex sentences*.
E. Telephones are convenient, but they are often demanding. Write a passage of about 150 words, telling what you think is good or bad about telephones—and why. In writing the passage, use at least two *complex sentences*.
F. The United States switched some time ago from a military draft system to a "volunteer army" system. Write a passage of about 150 words, telling whether you think the volunteer system can work adequately to keep the nation's defenses strong. In writing the passage, use at least two *complex sentences*.

After Writing: Reread your passage and underline each *subordinator* that you have used. Be sure that the subordinator begins a clause—that is, a subject-verb combination in a group of words. Since each sentence must have at least one independent clause (in this exercise only *one*), circle the word that begins the independent clause in each of your sentences.

The Compound-Complex Sentence

We have used sentences with *coordinators* joining clauses, and we have used sentences with *subordinators* joining clauses. But a sentence may contain both:

The weather was cold, *but* we were happy *because* it was Friday.

The moon cast shadows, *and* we slept, *although* birds awakened us before dawn.

After the waterpipes froze, Mother expected a power shortage too, *so* she turned off the TV.

Chapter Four

Each of those sentences has two or more independent clauses and one or more subordinate clauses. Each contains both coordinator *(and, but, so)* and subordinator *(because, although, after)*. Each of the sentences is a *compound-complex sentence*.

Time for Review

A sentence that contains both coordinators and subordinators linking clauses is a *compound-complex* sentence.

A compound-complex sentence contains at least two independent clauses and at least one subordinate clause.

Do-It-Yourself Exercise

Write in each blank an appropriate conjunction (coordinator or subordinator) to link the three clauses into one *compound-complex* sentence:

Some people don't like movies _____ the films are too violent, _____ those same people go to see the pictures.

Joe whistles _____ he works, _____ he likes to compete with the recorded music.

_____ he finished lunch at the truck stop, a rainstorm had come up, _____ he drove on in spite of it.

Save some of the money, _____ you won't have enough to spend _____ it's time for a vacation.

We keep a dog, _____ cats are too independent, _____ fish are too expensive.

Hitchhiking is free of charge, _____ it isn't free of danger, _____ you never know who may pick you up.

Water-safety training is essential _____ you want to become a lifeguard, _____ you'd better sign up for a course at the YMCA.

_____ the store manager opened his door, a crowd of women stormed in, _____ nobody bought anything.

Checking up: Each sentence should contain one subordinator *(if, because, when, after, since, while, although)* and one coordinator *(and, but, yet, or, for, so)*. Be sure that each one you have used is really appropriate to its sentence.

Recognizing Sentence Structures

When the writer knows how the conjunctions work to link clauses, he can choose the sentence structures that are most effective for what he has to say. The same knowledge helps him to read better, because the conjunctions "stand out" as key words showing how ideas are related.

One of the first steps, of course, is to recognize the conjunctions and know which of them is a coordinator and which is a subordinator. We have already shown that *six* of them are coordinators: *and, but, yet, or, for, so*. That list of six is easy to memorize. All the rest on the following list are subordinators. Now try to write each under its proper heading:

for	if	but	before
while	and	since	yet
as	although	so	because
as if	after	when	until
once	unless	till	wherever

    Coordinators   Subordinators

_____ _____ _____

_____ _____ _____

_____ _____ _____

_____ _____ _____

_____ _____ _____

_____ _____ _____

_____ _____ _____

Do-It-Yourself Exercise

Each of the items below represents a sentence. Only the conjunctions have been shown; they mark the links between independent clauses (coordinators), or they introduce subordinate clauses (subordinators). By recognizing the conjunctions and how they work, you should be able to identify the kind of sentence that each item represents. (If there are no conjunctions, of course, the sentence is *simple*.) On the blank at the right mark what kind of sentence is represented:

                                                                        Kind of
                                                                         Sentence

(a) ---------------------- , *and* ------------------ . _____
(b) ---------------------- , *because* ------------- . _____
(c) ----------------------   ------------------------ . _____

Checking up: In (a) the coordinator *and* is a signal that the sentence is probably made of two independent clauses, so the sentence is *compound*. In (b) the subordinator *because* must begin a subordinate clause, so the sentence is *complex*. In (c) there are no conjunctions, so the sentence is *simple*. Continue by identifying the kind of sentence in each of these:

(d) ------------------------, *for* ------------------ . _____
(e) *Since* ---------------, ------------------------ . _____
(f) ------------------------, *while* ---------------- . _____
(g) *When* ---------,------, *yet* ------------------- . _____
(h) ------------------------   ------------------------ . _____
(i) *If*------------------, --------- *unless* ------ . _____
(j) ---------------------- , *but* ------------------- . _____
(k) ------------------------ *before* --------------- . _____

Checking up: The way to recognize sentence structures is to recognize conjunctions and know what they do to link clauses. The key is this: no conjunctions—*simple*; coordinator—*compound*; subordinator—*complex*; both coordinator and subordinator—*compound-complex*. If a sentence has two or more subordinators (as sentence (i) does), the sentence is complex. Recheck your answer list against this key: (d) compound, (e) complex, (f) complex, (g) compound-complex, (h) simple, (i) complex, (j) compound, (k) complex.

Revising Sentence Structures

    A writer who is familiar with the conjunctions and how they link clauses can control his sentences. He can use the structures that best fit what he has to say. He may for example, write a brief report of an incident:

    My sister Mara loves to cook. She invited three friends to dinner the other night. Her green salad was sensational. Her dessert fell flat.

The incident is told in four simple sentences. The writer, when he rereads the passage, may decide that the effect is too choppy; the sentences do not give a smooth effect to the whole report. He may decide to put all four of those sentences into one, using coordinators to form a compound sentence:

My sister Mara loves to cook, *so* she invited three friends to dinner the other
night, *and* her green salad was sensational, *but* her dessert fell flat.

Perhaps the writer feels the effect is still a bit rough. He may try another pattern, using subordinators to form a complex sentence:

When my sister Mara invited three friends to dinner the other night *because* she loves to cook, her green salad was sensational, *although* her dessert fell flat.

The writer doesn't have to be satisfied with the first version—or with the last, either. He can control the effects he wants by knowing how to use conjunctions to tie clauses into differing patterns.

Do-It-Yourself Exercise

After reading the following incident told in simple sentences, supply appropriate conjunctions that will tell the whole of it in one sentence as directed:

Manuel Muleta was a matador. He was renowned in all of Spain. One day he stumbled over his own cape. He was seriously injured.

Rewrite the passage as one *compound* sentence by supplying appropriate coordinators (like *and, but, yet, or, for, so*). Don't use the same coordinator twice:

Manuel Muleta was a matador, _____ he was renowned in all of

Spain, _____ one day he stumbled over his own cape, _____ he was seriously injured.

Rewrite the passage as one *complex* sentence by supplying appropriate subordinators (like *when, although, because, since*):

Manuel Muleta, _____ he was a matador renowned in all of Spain,

was seriously injured one day _____ he stumbled over his own cape.

Rewrite the passage as one *compound-complex* sentence by supplying one coordinator and one subordinator:

Manuel Muleta, a matador, was renowned in all Spain, _____ he

was seriously injured one day _____ he fell over his own cape.

Checking up: Decide for yourself which of the three revised passages seems most effective. Do you think you would prefer to use *two* sentences rather than one to tell the incident? If you do, rewrite the passage here as *two* sentences—one simple and one complex:

_____

_____

_____

_____

The next step—and the most difficult one—is to combine *all* the ideas of the incident into one *simple* sentence. The simple sentence, of course, must have only *one* subject-predicate combination—and no connectives at all.

To achieve the *simple* sentence, the writer must reduce the number of subject-predicate combinations. He must eliminate some of those elements, or he must change some of them by turning verbs into adjectives. For example, the verb *stumbled* becomes an adjective if *-ing* is used: *stumbling*. Since *he* merely repeats the man's name, the pronoun can be eliminated; and the verb *was* can be eliminated at least twice.

What words can be crossed out or changed slightly to transform the passage into a single *simple* sentence?

> Manuel Muleta was a matador. He was renowned in all of Spain. One day he stumbled over his own cape. He was seriously injured.

Checking up: The passage might be edited like this: "Manuel Muleta, a matador renowned in all of Spain, stumbling over his own cape one day, was seriously injured." Note that moving the phrase *one day* has helped make the sentence smooth.

Suggestions for Writing

G. Girl-watching is a famous pastime for men, young and old. But what about boy-watching for girls and women? Write a passage in *three simple sentences* telling whether you think girls watch men—and how.

After Writing: Revise the passage, putting all three clauses into one *compound* sentence. Then revise again, putting all three clauses into one *compound-complex* sentence.

H. Hunting for wild game has long been a pastime in America, but lately it has been criticized because many animal species have been endangered. Write a passage in *three simple sentences* telling whether you are for or against game hunting—and why.

After Writing: Revise the passage, putting all three clauses into one *complex* sentence. Then revise again, putting all three clauses into one *simple* sentence.

I In many cities pedestrians usually have the right of way on the public streets. At uncontrolled intersections drivers must stop to let pedestrians cross, but pedestrians need not give drivers the right of way except at a red light. Write a passage in *three simple sentences* telling which you think should have the right of way—and why.

After Writing: Revise the passage, putting all three clauses into one *compound-complex* sentence. Then revise again, putting all three clauses into one *compound* sentence.

After Writing: Reread all three versions of your passage. Which do you think is most effective? If you think none of the versions is as good as you'd like it to be, try writing a fourth version—using sentences of *two* different kinds to develop the passage.

QUIZ 4

Recognizing Sentence Structures

The exercise on p. 60 has prepared you for this quiz. By recognizing the kinds of conjunction, quickly determine whether the represented sentence is apparently *simple, compound, complex,* or *compound-complex.* (If you use a form answer sheet, mark according to this key: (a) simple, (b) compound, (c) complex, (d) compound-complex.)

1. ------------------, but -------------------.   1_____

2. Since -------------, -------------.   2_____

3. -------------------------------------.   3_____

4. If ------------------, -----------------.   4_____

5. ------------------, or ------------------ when ------------------.   5_____

6. ------------------, because ------------------.   6_____

7. ------------------, yet ------------------.   7_____

8. Unless ------------------, ------------------, although------------------.   8_____

9. ------------------, for ------------------ after ------------------.   9_____

10. Once ------------------, ------------------, but ------------------.   10_____

11. ------------------ while ------------------.   11_____

12. -------------------------------------.   12_____

13. *As* the plane came down, lights on the field blazed the landing strip, *and* -------------------------------------.   13_____

14. ------------------, *but* it was soon over, *and* we breathed deeply again.   14_____

15. *When* the patient regained consciousness, ------------------.   15_____

16. Life in the big city is all right if you don't breathe the air.   16_____

17. With a long blast from her funnel, the great ship steamed out toward the middle of the river.   17_____

18. Miss Lavery sings like a canary, but we simply cannot have birdseed all over the stage. 18._____

19. Student newspapers are responsible publications, and they neglect their duties unless they are interested in all student concerns. 19._____

20. If the conservationists had been more successful, perhaps we could have got along without the ecologists. 20._____

Therefore 5

How to work with ... conjunctive adverbs
the semicolon
other uses of *therefore*

OUR FIRST TWO CHAPTERS showed how *and, but,* and the other coordinators are used to link items in pairs or series. Chapter 4 showed a further use of the coordinators and correlatives: to link independent clauses and form compound sentences:

> John does hard work, *and* he gets tired.
> Rita told her joke, *but* nobody laughed.
> I was very careful, *yet* I made a mistake.
> The light was red, *so* they stopped.

In each of those sentences, two independent clauses have been tied together by a coordinator to form a compound sentence.

We can also form such sentences by using words like *therefore, nevertheless, however,* and *accordingly:*

> John does hard work; *therefore,* he gets tired.
> Rita told her joke; *however,* nobody laughed.
> I was very careful; *nevertheless,* I made a mistake.
> The light was red; *accordingly,* they stopped.

These words are *conjunctive adverbs.* Not only do they serve as conjunctions (coordinating the independent clauses), but also they serve as adverbs (modifying the verbs in the clauses they introduce.

One important difference between the conjunctive adverbs and the coordinators appears in the examples above. The sentences formed with conjunctive adverbs have a distinctly different punctuation. When a conjunctive adverb like *therefore* is used to link two independent clauses, the clauses are separated by a semicolon (;) rather than a comma (,). And the conjunctive adverb itself is followed by a comma. In other words, a conjunctive adverb like *therefore* usually has a semicolon before it, a comma after:

> ; *therefore* ,

Another important difference between the conjunctive adverb and the coordinator is that a word like *therefore* can be moved to a different position in the second clause:

> Haste makes waste; we, *therefore,* work slowly.
> Oscar enrolled late; he was, *however,* able to catch up with the class work.
> He studied all night; he was fresh and alert, *nevertheless*.

We certainly would not move *and* or *but* (or any other coordinator) to a position other than between the two independent clauses that it joins. These sentences would be wrong:

> John does hard work, he *and* gets tired.
> The light was red, they stopped *so*.

That is why we must distinguish the conjunctive adverbs from the coordinators, although both do the job of linking independent clauses to form compound sentences.

Time for Review

Words like *therefore, however, nevertheless,* and *accordingly* are conjunctive adverbs.

Conjunctive adverbs are used to link independent clauses and form compound sentences.

When a conjunctive adverb is used, the independent clauses are separated by a semicolon (;), and the conjunctive adverb is set off by a comma (or a pair of commas).

A conjunctive adverb may be moved to a position other than directly between the two clauses. It may be placed within or at the end of the second independent clause.

Do-It-Yourself Exercise

In the blank write an appropriate conjunctive adverb *(therefore, however, nevertheless,* or *accordingly)* to replace the suggested coordinator. Change or add punctuation appropriately in each sentence:

I love hard work, _____ I can sit and watch it all day.
(so)

This may be our lucky day, _____ we'd better not depend on that.
(but)

Pete has a good job, _____ he is always broke.
(yet)

My calendar shows a red number, _____ this must be a holiday.
(so)

Sally lost her car keys today, _____ she had to walk home.
(and)

Checking up: Be sure that you have changed the comma to a semicolon between clauses—and that you have added a comma just after each conjunctive adverb. Were you able to use all four of the conjunctive adverbs we have so far discussed?

Other Conjunctive Adverbs

Several other words in addition to the four we have shown may be used as conjunctive adverbs. And certain phrases also work in the same pattern:

> A population boom may overcrowd the cities; *on the other hand,* many people have begun to move away from the big towns.
>
> Some people seem always far away in thought; *of course,* they may be only thoughtless.
>
> A new supermarket is planned for the midtown area; *in addition,* a car wash is being built.
>
> I burned out the transmission in my car yesterday; *as a consequence,* I'm feeling rather shiftless today.

Notice that the phrases used as conjunctive adverbs require the same standard punctuation as shown with *therefore*.

For reference, this is an alphabetical list of words and phrases that are often used as conjunctive adverbs:

accordingly	finally	moreover
after all	for example	namely
also	for instance	nevertheless
anyway	furthermore	of course
as a consequence	hence	on the other hand
as a matter of fact	however	still
as a result	in addition	that is
at least	indeed	therefore
besides	in fact	thus
consequently	later	to be sure

Do-It-Yourself Exercise

In each blank write an appropriate *conjunctive adverb* (either word or phrase) to complete the sentence. Remember to provide appropriate punctuation:

Sid has a new motorbike _____ it isn't paid for.

Typing helps Eddie write faster _____ he may get his papers in on time.

Katherine sings beautifully _____ she has had years of training.

I don't care much for sad music _____ I don't like it at all.

We haven't time to stop for lunch _____ we ate a very big breakfast.

Your sister seemed happy about the gift _____ she seemed almost ecstatic.

This isn't the best book I ever read; it is _____ better than the last one.

Friends, these vitamin pills may not make you strong _____ they will make you *feel* strong.

It may rain before the track meet tomorrow; we're planning to be there _____.

Aurelio's bank account is empty _____ he doesn't have a bank account.

Three streets on the north side have to be repaved _____ some sidewalks have to be repaired.

Checking up: Be sure your conjunctive adverbs show a meaningful relationship between the ideas of the sentence. It would not make good sense to write "Sid has a new motorbike; consequently, it isn't paid for" or "Katherine sings beautifully; on the other hand, she has had years of training." Review all punctuation to be sure you have followed the standard pattern (see *Time for Review* above).

Other Uses of "Therefore"

Such words as *therefore* and *however* are sometimes not used as coordinators but as *adverbs*; that is, they do not always link independent clauses to form a compound sentence. Consider these:

The summer air was sultry and *therefore* maddening.
However much it costs, that suit is for me!
John Kennedy, *still* a senator, drew international attention.
My friend, *as a matter of fact,* has never been in New Orleans.
Two thousand is *indeed* a lot of money for a secondhand car.

Do-It-Yourself Exercise

Choosing words from the list of conjunctive adverbs, use them as *adverbs* to fill the blanks in these sentences:

The good seats in the stadium _____ will be taken before noon.

Martha answered every question _____ difficult.

Dave's recovery has been miraculous ⸺!

Checking up: A phrase like *of course* is usually set off between commas, but there is no firm rule for punctuating such adverbs. Use the commas if you feel that a brief pause would add to the effectiveness of the sentence.

Suggestions for Writing

A. "What the World Needs Now Is Love, Sweet Love," said the lyrics of a popular song a few years ago. Are there some other things the world needs today? Write your answer, giving some reasons, in a passage of about five sentences. Use at least two *conjunctive adverbs*.
B. Perhaps for centuries children have repeated the jingle, "Sticks and stones will break my bones, but words will never hurt me." But, of course, words *can* hurt. Write a passage of about 200 words telling how you have known words to hurt someone, perhaps yourself. Use several *conjunctive adverbs* in your passage.
C. Some things, though difficult to learn at first (such as walking, tying shoes, or multiplying small numbers) are almost never forgotten. What are some other things that a person "never forgets"—and why do you think they are so firmly remembered? Write your answers in a passage of about 200 words. Use several conjunctive adverbs in your passage.

After Writing: Reread your passage and underline every *conjunctive adverb* you have used. Check the punctuation: Have you used a semicolon before each conjunctive adverb, a comma after? Have you written any *complex* sentences? (See p. 56 if you are not sure what a complex sentence is.) What are some of the words that begin subordinate clauses? (See pp. 55-56.)

Therefore 73

QUIZ 5

Using Conjunctive Adverbs

On the blank within each sentence write the item that you think most appropriately completes the sentence; then mark the *letter* of that item on your answer blank. Don't overlook the punctuation included in some of the offered alternatives. After marking your choice, explain briefly why you chose it (*Because:* . . .).

Example: Punctuation may affect meaning __;__ therefore, it should be handled with care.

(a) ,   (b) .   (c) ;   (d) :   (e) ,   Ex. *c*

(*Because:* Semicolon is needed before Conjunctive adverb.)

1. Employees submitted many suggestions for change _____ however, the board rejected most of the suggestions.

(a) —   (b) ,   (c) .   (d) ;   (e) :   1._____

(*Because:* _____.)
   (*Question:* What punctuation goes properly between clauses linked by *however*?)

2. Warren writes good Spanish; he is _____ furthermore, fluent in French.

(a) ;   (b) .   (c) —   (d) ;   (e) ,   2._____

(*Because:* _____.)
   (*Question:* What punctuation sets off a conjunctive adverb used *within* an independent clause?)

3. Science stimulates reasoning; art, _____, stirs the senses.

(a) as a matter of fact   (b) indeed   (c) furthermore   (d) as a result
(e) on the other hand   3._____

(*Because:* _____.)
   (*Question:* Which conjunctive adverb appropriately indicates the *contrast* shown in the clauses?)

4. Harvey sprained his ankle in practice; _____ he won't run in the finals.

(a) consequently   (b) thus   (c) consequently,   (d) nevertheless
(e) besides,   4._____

(*Because:* _____.)
   (*Question:* Which offered item shows both the appropriate meaning and the proper punctuation?)

74 Chapter Five

5. The boss is not in his office; he hasn't been in all week _____.

(a) however   (b) indeed   (c) , in fact   (d) besides   (e) , therefore

5._____

(*Because:* _____.)
   (*Question:* Which offered item shows both the appropriate meaning and the proper punctuation?)

6. I don't think I'll ever climb Mount Whitney; _____ I'd like to see it from afar.

(a) therefore,   (b) still,   (c) however   (d) in fact   (e) consequently

6._____

(*Because:* _____.)

7. Make sure that Mrs. Irving takes her medicine _____ much she may protest.

(a) ; still   (b) , thus   (c) ; however,   (d) , however   (e) in consequence

7._____

(*Because:* _____.)

8. Despite his age the former admiral runs a mile a day, plays vigorous handball, wins at tennis, and swims _____ he keeps in excellent physical condition.

(a) on the other hand   (b) ; still,   (c) ; as a consequence,   (d) , of course,
(e) ; nonetheless,

8._____

(*Because:* _____.)

9. My friend Cheryl gets top grades; last semester _____ she made the dean's list.

(a) in fact   (b) , nevertheless,   (c) however   (d) on the other hand
(e) , as a matter of fact,

9._____

(*Because:* _____.)

10. The governor said no argument could dissuade him from presenting a tax-reform bill. He did _____ promise such a bill during his campaign.

(a) , after all,   (b) consequently   (c) furthermore   (d) nevertheless,
(e) , additionally

10._____

(*Because:* _____.)

11. Sidney really believes no modern President, ———————————, will ever be so great as Lincoln.

(a) wherefore   (b) still   (c) however, brilliant   (d) however brilliant
(e) therefore, well liked   11_____

(Because: ————————————————————————.)

12. Rainfall in this region is an almost year-round phenomenon ————— it has rained every day since we arrived.

(a) ; nevertheless,   (b) ; for example,   (c) , accordingly,   (d) indeed,
(e) ; still   12_____

(Because: ————————————————————————.)

13. Your friend writes the best songs I've ever heard ————— a genius.

(a) , he is indeed   (b) he is; indeed,   (c) , he indeed is   (d) ; to be sure he is
(e) ; he is, indeed,   13_____

(Because: ————————————————————————.)

14. There were no real knights-in-armor in Don Quixote's time ————— to be foolish.

(a) he thus appeared   (b) ; he appeared thus,   (c) ; hence, he appeared
(d) of course,   (e) ; therefore he seemed   14_____

(Because: ————————————————————————.)

15. Very few genuine cowboys live in this area————— I never heard of one here.

(a) ; at least,   (b) ; still,   (c) ; on the other hand,   (d) ; however,
(e) in fact   15_____

(Because: ————————————————————————.)

16. The test was very difficult; some of the questions were —————.

(a) impossible in fact   (b) impossible; on the other hand   (c) , indeed, impossible   (d) impossible, nevertheless   (e) besides impossible   16_____

(Because: ————————————————————————.)

76   Chapter Five

17. Organizing a campaign really takes time ———————— Sally spent almost all of Saturday on the telephone.

(a) ; still,   (b) ; nevertheless,   (c) ; for instance,   (d) , of course,
(e) ; at least;   17_____

(Because: ————————————————————————.*)*

18. Mrs. Spalding had four children ———————————— she adopted two others.

(a) , of course,   (b) , nevertheless,   (c) , besides;   (d) ; as a consequence
(e) ; in addition,   18_____

(Because: ————————————————————————.*)*

19. The trucking company has been extremely successful; it has ———————— hundreds of drivers.

(a) hired, nevertheless   (b) , however,   (c) , as a matter of fact, hired
(d) ; at least,   (e) ; therefore,   19_____

(Because: ————————————————————————.*)*

20. We do believe our plan is the one most likely to succeed; we cannot be absolutely sure ————————————————————.

(a) ; nevertheless   (b) , of course   (c) ; still   (d) furthermore
(e) moreover   20_____

(Because: ————————————————————————.*)*

If, While, Until 6

How to work with . . . subordinators
adverb clauses
incomplete clauses
restrictive clauses
nonrestrictive clauses

How to avoid . . . danglers
fragments

THAT LITTLE WORD "IF" is one of the biggest words in the language, perhaps because it so often suggests wishful thinking: "*If* only . . . "—a wish for what is not.

> *If* I had a million . . .
> *If* Tony were taller . . .
> *If* it hadn't rained . . .

All of those "if's" set up conditions under which something else might be true. But none of those word groups completes a statement; the word *if* keeps each group from being a full sentence.

If is one of the *subordinators* that we saw used in Chapter 4. While introducing the complex sentence (see p. 56), that chapter showed that the word *if* can change a full sentence (such as "We were happy") into a nonsentence ("*If* we were happy . . .). Used to introduce the subject-verb combination, *if* subordinates that word group, making it a subordinate clause—one structurally less important or less complete than it was before.

This chapter will discuss in more detail how *if* works and will introduce some other words and phrases that work in similar ways. Like *if*, all these words are subordinators when they begin clauses; that is, they introduce *subordinate clauses*.

Since a subordinate clause is not itself a complete sentence, such a clause must always have an independent clause to go along with it:

> *If* I had a million friends, I'd be rich.
> *If* Tony were taller, he could touch the ceiling.
> *If* it hadn't rained, the hills wouldn't be so green.

In each of those sentences the *if* clause is subordinate; the other clause (such as *I'd be rich*) is the independent clause needed to complete the sentence.

To see the difference between an independent clause and a subordinate clause, compare these two sentences:

> Sammy will drive his car, and Pat will buy the gas.
> Sammy will drive his car *if* Pat will buy the gas.

In the first one, a compound sentence with two independent clauses, it is said that Sammy *will definitely drive* his car. But in the second sentence the subordinator *if* has changed the whole idea; Sammy will drive *only under a certain condition*.

The Pattern of Subordination

If differs from *and*, then. With *and* the two ideas are independent of one another, both equally true. With *if* the one idea is true only *if* the other is true—only under the condition suggested in the *if* clause.

If differs from *and* in another way, too. We could not reasonably put *and* anywhere but between the two clauses:

Sammy will drive his car, *and* Pat will buy the gas.

We could not properly write:

And Pat will buy the gas, Sammy will drive his car.

But *if* is a different sort of conjunction; it could reasonably appear in either position:

Sammy will drive his car *if* Pat will buy the gas.
If Pat will buy the gas, Sammy will drive his car.

A subordinator (like *if*) may begin a sentence and imply that a main idea is to follow; but a coordinator (like *and*) always implies that a main idea has gone before, even if in a different sentence:

Sammy will drive, *and* Pat will buy the gas.
Sammy will drive. *And* Pat will buy the gas.

Time for Review

If is a subordinator, a conjunction that introduces a subject-predicate combination but keeps that combination from being a sentence by itself.

Words that work like *if* introduce *subordinate clauses*.

A subordinate clause may *begin* a sentence or may *end* a sentence—or may even appear *in the middle* of a sentence. But a subordinate clause cannot be a sentence by itself. The possible patterns include these:

If the bakers strike, the bakery will close.

The bakery will close *if the bakers strike.*

The bakery, *if the bakers strike,* will close.

Since a subordinate clause is not a sentence, it must not be written as if it were. Such a clause, if written alone as a sentence, is a *fragment*—and is considered a serious fault in writing.

Do-It-Yourself Exercise

In each blank write a subordinate clause beginning with *if*:

Food will not spoil so fast _____.

Phil will be very late to the meeting _____.

_____, the parade will start at noon.

_____, stop at the store and bring home some milk.

Anyone who will be frightened _____ should not watch the show.

Checking up: Be sure that each of your completions starts with *if* (using a capital when it begins a sentence). And be sure that each contains a subject-verb combination.

Some Other Conditionals

If implies a condition under which something is true, is not true, or may be true:

If you wear tight shoes, you may ruin your feet.

Some other *subordinators* work like *if*, to indicate a *condition* under which something may happen or be true:

When the snow falls, visibility is limited.
As things are now, we don't expect too much of the team.
Since the sun is down, the temperature must be cooler.
Although Ken can play the piano, he does so only for his friends.
Though the hour is late, we'll finish the game.
Unless we get some rain, fire hazards will be great.
Provided that our information is correct, the plane is passing over the island right now.
As long as the fire lasts, we can go on roasting hot dogs.
Now that the rain has stopped, let's start the game.
Except that I'm broke, I have plenty of money.

In each sentence the subordinator (word or phrase in italics) is the mark of a subordinate clause.

Time for Review

If indicates that a condition is to be presented in a *subordinate clause*— a condition under which some other idea may be true or may happen.

Other subordinators that work like *if* include *although, as, as long as, except that, now that, provided that, since, though, unless,* and *when*.

If, While, Until **81**

Do-It-Yourself Exercise

Write an appropriate *subordinate clause* to complete each sentence. Use as many subordinators as you can:

Harry can't have breakfast _____.

Why don't you get me a drink of water _____.

Physical strength develops naturally _____.

Doctors say people can help prevent cancer _____.

_____, the engine can be started.

The searchers could find no trace of the missing hikers, _____
_____.

With the new Polamatic camera you will always get a perfect picture,_____
_____.

Checking up: Do your completions begin with *if, although, though, when, unless, provided that, as, since, except that, now that, as long as*? Does each completion contain a subject-predicate combination?

Some Other Subordinators

We have seen that *if* (and the other subordinators listed above) are used to indicate a *condition* under which something happens or is true. Subordinators may also indicate other relationships, such as those of *time*, *place*, *cause*, and *manner*.

Indicating Time:

After the fog clears, the plane will take off again.
As she was sweeping up, she noticed a coin on the floor.
While the weather is good, let's stay outdoors.
As long as you need help, we'll be here.
Before you leave, have another cup of coffee.
Once the crowd quiets down, the game can go on.
Now that you've seen the show, tell me about it.
Until we get some furniture, we don't have a place to sit down.

Indicating Place:

>An old man stood *where* the pigeons had been eating.
>*Wherever* you are, have a good holiday!

Indicating Cause:

>Get out the shovels, *because* it snowed last night.
>*Since* she had gone out with no coat, she got soaked in the downpour.
>Pick up your feet *so* you won't stumble.
>*In order that* traffic may proceed, please move that truck.

Indicating Manner:

>Do you intend to get there *as* the crow flies?
>Roger looked *as if* he had lost a friend.
>
>We hope we can do *as well as* our grandfather did.
>Crummies taste good, *like* a breakfast food should.

For years there has been some controversy over whether *like* should be used as a subordinator (as in the last sentence above). Many have preferred to use *like* only as a preposition (*like a bird, like them, like me*). But the question is one of popular taste: *Like* is very popularly used as a subordinator today.

All the subordinate clauses in the example sentences shown above are working as *adverbs*. That is, each subordinate clause—taken as a unit—is working as a modifier for the verb in the independent clause. "After the fog clears" modifies the verb phrase "will take off"; "As she was sweeping up" modifies "noticed," telling *when* she noticed. All these subordinate clauses are *adverb clauses*.

When an *adverb clause* begins a sentence in writing, it is usually set off by a comma:

>*When the package arrived,* Sherry opened it eagerly.
>*As the sun went down,* wisps of color painted the horizon.
>*Now that it's over,* I can see what we should have done.

Time for Review

>*Subordinators* introduce clauses that may indicate the *condition, time, place, cause,* or *manner* that modifies a verb in an independent clause.
>
>When a subordinate clause is so used, it is an *adverb clause*.
>
>When an *adverb clause* begins a sentence, the clause is set off by a *comma*.

Do-It-Yourself Exercise

Write an appropriate *adverb clause* to fill each blank. Use as many subordinators as you can:

I wouldn't waste my time ―――――――――――――――――.
(condition)

Mrs. Hoberman cannot read the newspaper ―――――――――――,
(cause: *why?*)

Send in the coupon, and we'll see that our product is mailed to you ―――――

―――――――――――――――.
(place: *where?*)

―――――――――――― I just couldn't resist buying one.
(time: *when?*)

There stood the little pup, barking ―――――――――――――――.
(manner: *how?*)

Have you noticed that the telephone never rings ―――――――――――,
(time: *when?*)

Hand me that hammer ―――――――――――――――――.
(cause: *why?*)

Harvey's wagon crashed into the haystack ―――――――――――.
(manner: *how?*)

Checking up: Each adverb clause should begin with a subordinator, and each must contain a subject-predicate combination. If an adverb clause begins a sentence the clause must be set off by a comma.

Suggestions for Writing:

A. In many states hitchhiking is legal, provided that the hitchhiker does not stand in the roadway to do his thumbing. Write a passage (about 250 words) stating some of the advantages and some of the disadvantages of hitchhiking. In developing the passage use at least *five adverb clauses* and underline them.
B. Airlines people often say that air travel is even safer than travel by automobile. Write

a passage (about 250 words) in which you defend or attack that belief. In developing the passage, use at least *five adverb clauses* and underline them.
C. Most Americans love sports, yet many are watchers rather than doers. Write a passage (about 250 words) in which you show your own attitude toward the do-or-watch controversy. In developing the passage, use at least *five adverb clauses* and underline them.

After Writing: Reread your passage to be sure that it clearly expresses your beliefs. Since you were directed to write at least *five adverb clauses*, your passage should contain at least five *subordinators;* circle them. Check to be sure that you used a *comma* after any adverb clause that begins a sentence.

Incomplete Clauses

Often a writer may "shorthand" an adverb clause by omitting its subject and verb:

Max will probably be here by noon; *if not*, we'll go ahead without him.

In that sentence *if not* means "if *he is* not." The subject and verb have been left out, yet the meaning is clearly understood from the rest of the sentence. Some more *incomplete clauses*:

If possible, the exam will start on time. (If *it is* possible *to do so*, . . .)
Start your engine *when ready*. (. . . when *you are* ready.)
The minutes are approved *as read*. (. . . as *they were* read.)
Although dangerous, my work pays well. (Although *it is* dangerous, . . .)

These incomplete clauses are perfectly natural and are proper means of saving words in both speech and writing. But, if the writer is careless with them, they may lead to awkward and misleading sentences:

Unless properly planted, you may have to call in a professional gardener.

Unless *what* is properly planted? The incomplete clause, since it leaves out its subject and verb, fails here to communicate clearly. It appears to apply to what closely follows—*you*. But certainly the writer could not have meant "Unless *you are* properly planted . . . ." The clause misleads the reader. It is necessary, then, for the writer to write a full adverb clause:

Unless your lawn is properly planted, you may have to call in a professional gardener.

The misleading incomplete clause produces a *dangler*, a word or word group whose relationship to the rest of the sentence is unclear. To avoid such danglers, the writer must use care with every incomplete clause. If the incomplete clause leaves an unclear idea, the writer should revise it. (For more on *danglers* and how to rephrase them see pp. 295-297.)

Time for Review

An *incomplete clause* is one whose subject and verb are left out: *when arriving* (meaning *when the ship is arriving*).

An *incomplete clause* is usually understood easily because its missing elements are made clear in the rest of the sentence.

A *dangler* may occur if an incomplete clause is not really made clear by the rest of the sentence: *"When drunk,* accidents may occur." Who is drunk—accidents?

Danglers should be revised so that the subject and verb of the clause are expressed: "When *drivers are* drunk, accidents may occur."

Do-It-Yourself Exercise

On the blank write a revision of each *dangler*, supplying subject and verb to make a full *adverb clause* and complete the sentence appropriately:

_____, the owner must take the engine block to a
     (If cracked)
reputable repair shop.

_____, Miss Corrella could not make her voice reach
     (While very high)
the soprano range.

_____, Brad's tongue is always twisted,
     (When shooting free throws)
apparently to help him concentrate.

_____, the convention session was resumed.
     (After eating)

_____, the firemen believed they could save the
     (Although out of control)
building.

_____, the driver lets the engine idle quietly.
     (Until in gear)

Checking up: Each adverb clause should be completed with a subject-verb combination to make clear *what* was cracked, high, shooting, eating, out of control, or in gear. Be sure that the completions you have written to rephrase the danglers will make sense in the full sentence.

Restrictive or Nonrestrictive?

If an adverb clause can be removed from a sentence without changing the basic idea of that sentence, the clause is nonrestrictive:

The mayor signed the ordinance, *although he disliked it*.

The basic idea is expressed in the independent clause: *The mayor signed the ordinance*. That idea would remain true even if the *although* clause were removed. The adverb clause, then, does not in any way affect the basic idea or restrict it to any condition. The clause is *nonrestrictive*.

But if an adverb clause is essential to preserve the basic idea of a sentence, the clause is restrictive:

Half the village will be washed away *if the dam breaks*.

The basic idea, *half the village will be washed away*, is not true except under the condition expressed in the *if* clause. The adverb clause, then, could not properly be removed from the sentence; it is a *restrictive* clause, for it restricts the main idea to a special condition.

Which of these adverb clauses is *restrictive*?

My sister never eats sweets, *because she wants to stay slim*.

This program will not succeed *unless we give it our full support*.

My little brother speaks three languages, *although he is only six years old*.

The adverb clause in the *second* sentence is restrictive. The clause could not be removed from the sentence without making the main idea ("This program will not succeed") untrue. The writer clearly intended to say that the program might succeed under a special condition (that "we give it our full support"). The adverb clauses in the other two sentences are nonrestrictive; they could be removed from their sentences without changing the basic ideas.

Punctuating the Nonrestrictive

Look once more at the two nonrestrictive clauses in the sample sentences just above. Each of them was set off by a *comma*. But the restrictive clause ("unless we give it our full support") was not set off. That pattern of punctuation is standard: the *nonrestrictive clause is set off by a comma*. If it appears in midsentence, a nonrestrictive clause is set off by a *pair of commas*:

The mayor, *although he disliked the ordinance,* signed it.

My sister, *because she wants to stay slim,* never eats sweets.

My little brother, *although he is only six years old,* speaks three languages.

The *restrictive* adverb clause is not set off:

The mayor will sign the ordinance *if he likes it*.

I'm always angry *when I see someone cheating*.

I'll stop loving you *when the ocean goes dry*.

When it appears at the beginning of a sentence, an adverb clause is always set off by a comma, whether it is restrictive or not:

If the mayor likes the ordinance, he will sign it.

Time for Review

An adverb clause that is not essential to the meaning of the main idea of its sentence is a *nonrestrictive* clause.

An adverb clause that is essential to the meaning of the main idea of its sentence is a *restrictive* clause and could not be removed from the sentence without changing the meaning.

A *nonrestrictive* clause is set off by a *comma*—or, if it appears within the main clause, it is set off by a pair of commas.

A *restrictive* clause is *not* set off by a comma.

An adverb clause that begins a sentence is set off by a comma.

Do-It-Yourself Exercise

Write an appropriate *adverb clause* or *incomplete clause* for each blank. Observe proper punctuation—and avoid danglers. See p. 81 for suggested subordinators.

We shall send you a check _____.
                              (time: when?)

I'll never ask for help _____.
                       (under what condition?)

The water supply has disappeared _____.
                                 (place: where?)

Always hold your breath _____.
                       (under what condition?)

I forgot my books _____.
                  (cause: why?)

_____ Sheri dances beautifully.
(under what condition?)

Perhaps fish live in water _____.
                          (cause: why?)

Jerry looked at the professor _____.
                              (manner: how?)

Sam sprang from his seat ─────────────────────────────
           (time: when?)

───.
      (manner: how?)

Checking up: Each of the *adverb clauses* (or *incomplete clauses*) should begin with a *subordinator* (such as *when, while, if, because, although, as, until, before,* and so on). The first four sentences should not have commas to set off the adverb clauses you have written; those clauses are *restrictive*. "I forgot my books" is presented as true regardless of time, place, manner, or condition; therefore, your adverb clause is *nonrestrictive* and should be set off by a comma. "Jerry looked at the professor" could take either a *restrictive* or a *nonrestrictive* clause; which did you write? Your final sentence in the exercise could present a difficulty of placement. If the adverb clause specifying manner is intended to modify *sprang*, you must be sure that it doesn't appear to modify something else. Consider this possibility:

 Sam sprang from his seat when the bell rang *as if stung by a bee*.

Does *as if stung by a bee* (an incomplete clause) modify *sprang*? Since the clause is closer to *rang*, it may appear to modify that nearer verb—saying that *the bell rang as if stung by a bee*. Of course, if a full adverb clause were used, the intention could be clearer:

 Sam sprang from his seat when the bell rang *as if he had been stung by a bee*.

But the placement is still not without possible confusion, so it would be best to write such a sentence like this:

 When the bell rang, Sam sprang from his seat *as if stung by a bee*.

(For more detail on *misplaced modifiers* see pp. 220-221.)

Suggestions for Writing

D. Suppose you have a good friend who is very popular and would probably win votes easily if he went into politics. Would you advise him to run for public office or to "stay away" from politics? State your position and give your reasons in a passage of about 250 words. Use as many *subordinators* as you can.

E. "I never win anything in those sweepstakes." That widely voiced complaint reflects the fact that only a few can win while many do not. Would you advise your friends to enter give-away programs when they have to buy something to enter? State your position and give your reasons in a passage of about 250 words. Use as many *subordinators* as you can.

F. Some people say that "you can't beat city hall," that it doesn't pay to contest a traffic ticket even when you know that you were not in the wrong. What do you think about the possibility of getting justice under the traffic-court system? Write your ideas in a passage of about 250 words. Use as many *subordinators* as you can.

After Writing: Reread your passage. Does it sound convincing enough to make readers agree with you? Underline each *subordinator* that you have used. As a special practice try rewriting one or two of your adverb clauses (each beginning with a subordinator) as *incomplete clauses*. Have you written a dangler? If so, how can you revise it?

Is It a Full Sentence?

Remember that a subordinate clause is *not* a full sentence. Its subordinator (such as *if, unless, because*) has removed it from the full-sentence category and reduced it to a dependent *portion* of a sentence.

Standard practice calls for a subordinate clause to be treated as a *portion* only, a portion that must be attached to or included within a main clause:

Faulty: Helen lost her job. *Because she couldn't type.*

Proper: Helen lost her job *because she couldn't type.*

In informal writing (or for special effect such as emphasis) a subordinate clause or other *fragment* of a sentence is sometimes written as if it were a full sentence. Contemporary advertising, for instance, makes much use of the emphatic, deliberate *fragment*:

You'll love renting one of our cars. *When you need it.*
Where you want it. Try us. *Because you'll like us.*
Hallmark cards. *When you care enough to send the very best.*
Zowie Aftershave. *If you're man enough.*

If, While, Until 91

QUIZ 6

Using Adverb Clauses

On the blank within each sentence write the item that you think most appropriately completes the sentence; then mark the *letter* of that item on your answer blank. Don't overlook punctuation included in some of the offered alternatives. After marking your choice, explain briefly why you chose it (*Because:* . . .).

Example: While ___*I was typing*___, my lamp suddenly burned out.

(a) studying   (b) reading   (c) I was typing   (d) taking a nap
(e) working on the term paper

Ex *c*

(*Because:* ___*Any other would produce a dangler*___.)

1. When time _____ we shall return.

(a) allows,   (b) slows down   (c) permits   (d) is ripe   (e) is available   1_____

(*Because:* _____.)
    (*Question:* Should a comma be used after an introductory adverb clause? See p. 83.)

2. My pet parakeet sings very loud _____ he is hungry.

(a) , if   (b) , while   (c) , when   (d) , although   (e) , as long as   2_____

(*Because:* _____.)
    (*Question:* Since no comma is used to set off a restrictive adverb clause, which completion would provide a *nonrestrictive* adverb clause?)

3. Intoxicants should never be taken _____.

(a) if driving   (b) when driving a car   (c) while at the wheel
(d) if a person expects to drive   (e) driving

_____

(*Because:* _____.)
    (*Question:* Would an *incomplete* clause create a dangler?)

4. After I get a good job and _____, I'll start thinking about marriage.

(a) with a good salary   (b) when I save some money   (c) settled down
(d) a couple of years   (e) without worries   4_____

(*Because.* _____.)
    (*Question:* Which completion provides an adverb clause for parallelism after *and*?)

92 Chapter Six

5. We knew the captain was afraid _____
he had been through a mortar shelling before.

(a) . Because   (b) . Since   (c) . Probably   (d) . Although   (e) . As

5._____

(*Because:* _____.)
  (*Question:* Can an adverb clause properly be written as a sentence by itself? See p. 80.)

6. Since Ned is late _____ assume he missed the bus.

(a) today, we   (b) this morning I   (c) for work let's   (d) now we have to
(e) we can

6._____

(*Because:* _____.)

7. Since _____ grades have improved.

(a) selling my car, my   (b) the coach put me on the team, my
(c) getting glasses, my   (d) meeting Helen, my   (e) I started studying my

7._____

(*Because:* _____.)

8. It is virtually impossible to pick your career freely. _____
_____ you have an adequate education.

(a) Unless   (b) If   (c) Although   (d) Not before
(e) But you may do so if

8._____

(*Because:* _____.)

9. Ursula's husband is perfectly happy _____ long as dinner is served on time.

(a) with her as   (b) at home, as   (c) about everything, so
(d) in marriage, just so   (e) now, as

9._____

(*Because:* _____.)

10. Students are seldom honestly satisfied with their papers when _____
_____.

(a) written carelessly   (b) turned in late   (c) the style is wordy
(d) done hurriedly   (e) full of errors

10._____

(*Because:* _____.)

If, While, Until   93

11. One magazine article says there can be no special progress in _____ _____ the people are in poverty.

(a) countries, if   (b) cities while   (c) this land, when
(d) the world, as long as   (e) India,

11.____

(Because: _____*.)*

12. We dare not ignore the water-pollution _____ it become worse.

(a) menace lest   (b) problems, lest   (c) menace, lest   (d) problems lest
(e) threats lest

12.____

(Because: _____*.)*

13. It is difficult to find a good mechanic when you need him and _____ _____.

(a) nearby   (b) on duty   (c) fully qualified   (d) where you need him
(e) not too expensive

13.____

(Because: _____*.)*

14. In a television commercial one young couple promised "to use no mouthwash _____ breath do us part.

(a) , if   (b) till   (c) , until   (d) but   (e) yet

14.____

(Because: _____*.)*

15. Rhonda has never had a traffic citation _____ she is a very careful driver.

(a) ,   (b) although   (c) because   (d) , since   (e) , that proves

15.____

(Because: _____*.)*

16. The rookie outfielder had never felt elated about his batting average _____ _____ over .320.

(a) although it was   (b) since climbing   (c) until it climbed
(d) , when it was   (e) until suddenly

16.____

(Because: _____*.)*

94 Chapter Six

17. Surely we will _____ the time comes what we should do.

(a) know when (b) be told, when (c) not forget, when
(d) understand, whenever (e) learn, as   17_____

(Because: _____.*)*

18. No spectator admits hoping to see a crack-up on the _____

_____ the anticipation of danger is clearly what draws many to the races.

(a) track if (b) track although (c) track unless (d) track, although
(e) track, because   18_____

(Because: _____.*)*

19. My sister, Ellen, although she enrolled in home ec _____ never cooked an egg.

(a) courses, had (b) courses had (c) this year (d) almost (e) had   19_____

(Because: _____.*)*

20. It really wasn't polite to _____ you'd never seen a panda before.

(a) stare, as if (b) stare as if (c) make jokes although (d) laugh, unless
(e) be rude, when   20_____

(Because: _____.*)*

George, The Cherry Tree, and Truth

7

How to work with . . . nouns
number: singular and plural
possessives: the apostrophe
appositives
noun clauses
verbal nouns
capitals

How to avoid . . . faulty possessives
faulty capitalization
faulty use of *a* and *an*

96   Chapter Seven

THIS CHAPTER DOES NOT DISCUSS HISTORY, not even the question of whether George Washington really chopped down a cherry tree and confessed. Instead, the chapter is about the *names* in its title.

Those *names* are *nouns*. The title is a series of nouns of several sorts:

1. *George* names a *person*. George is a *proper* noun. All proper nouns are written with first letter capitalized.
2. *Tree* names a *thing*. *Tree* is a *common* noun, so called because it does not name a *specific* thing; rather *tree* names a general *class* of things. There are millions of things in that class; in other words, *tree* names a group of things that have much in *common*. Common nouns are written without capitals except when they begin a sentence.
3. *Truth* names an *idea*. Truth is not something that anyone can see or hold in his hand; it can't be heard, smelled, or tasted. Truth "exists" only in the mind; it is an abstraction. The word *truth* is an *abstract* noun.
4. *George* and *tree* are names of things in the real world outside the mind; they can be seen and touched. They have concrete reality. *George* and *tree* are concrete nouns.

These four sorts of noun (proper, common, concrete, and abstract) overlap in some ways. For example, *George* is both a proper noun (since it names a specific person) and a concrete noun (since it names something that we can see and touch). *Truth* is both a common noun (since there are many examples of truth) and an abstract noun (since truth cannot be seen or touched in the physical world). Some other nouns and their overlapping sorts:

Concrete-common nouns: *pen, cloud, rabbit, wall, hat.*
Abstract-common nouns: *freedom, love, encouragement, honesty.*
Concrete-proper nouns: *Washington, Lake Erie, Hawaii, The Miami Dolphins.*
Abstract-proper nouns: *God, the Angel Gabriel, Uncle Sam, Santa Claus* (and other "persons" or "places" that do not have physical reality).

Time for Review

Nouns are *names*—of persons, places, things, or ideas.

Proper nouns are names of specific persons, places, things, or ideas.

Common nouns are names of general things or classes of things.

Concrete nouns are names of things that exist in the physical world—things that can be seen, heard, touched, tasted, smelled.

Abstract nouns are names of things that exist only in the mind.

Some of these kinds of noun may overlap: concrete-common *(house, man, bird, paper)*, abstract-common *(friendship, error, success)*, concrete-proper *(Oregon, the Mississippi River, Senator Baker)*, or abstract-proper *(the Land of Oz, Jack Frost)*.

Do-It-Yourself Exercise

Write in each blank an appropriate noun of the sort called for:

Every summer the _____ shines on the _____.
　　　　　　　　(concrete)　　　　　　　　　　(concrete)

Pick up your _____ before you go to _____.
　　　　　　　(concrete)　　　　　　　　　　(concrete)

To tell the _____ , my _____ is older than he looks.
　　　　　　(abstract)　　　　　(concrete)

If we're going to the _____ , we have no _____ to waste.
　　　　　　　　　　(concrete)　　　　　　　　(abstract)

One of our favorite _____ has a quarter-pound of _____
　　　　　　　　　(common)　　　　　　　　　　　　　(common)
between two slices of _____ .
　　　　　　　　　(common)

Joe's campaign for student office was a big _____ .
　　　　　　　　　　　　　　　　　　　　　(abstract)

I was born in _____ , a city in _____ .
　　　　　　(proper)　　　　　　　(proper)

Checking up:　Be sure that each completed sentence makes good sense. Words like *scarcely* and *swam* and *gives* just wouldn't fit; nouns must be *names*. For extra practice in the sorts of nouns, recall that *truth* is both abstract and common. Write beneath each of your nouns a second classification. For instance, in the first sentence, if you wrote *sun*, the noun is *concrete-common*; in the last sentence, if you wrote *Texas*, the noun is *concrete-proper*.

Singular or Plural?

Nouns in English often change according to *number*; that is, according to whether they name a *single* thing or *several* things. The noun that names one thing is a *singular* noun; the noun that names more than one is a *plural* noun.

There are several ways of forming the plurals of nouns. Some examples:

Singular	Plural
seat	seats
engine	engines
coach	coaches
class	classes
mouse	mice
woman	women
sheep	sheep
deer	deer
Kennedy	Kennedys
Jones	Joneses
Smith	Smiths

Those examples show that one way of forming the plural of nouns is to add *-s* to the singular *(seat, seats; Kennedy, Kennedys)*. Another way is to add *-es* to the singular *(class, classes; Jones, Joneses)*. Still another way is to change the sound (and spelling) of the singular *(mouse, mice; woman, women)*, and another is to make no change at all *(sheep, sheep; deer, deer)*.

Can You Count It?

Another way of considering nouns is according to whether the things they name can be counted. *Trees* and *persons* can be counted; they are *count nouns*. But *air* and *sunshine* cannot be counted; they are *mass nouns*. To put it another way: We may see *six trees* and *three persons*, but we can't see *six airs* or *three sunshines*.

This matter of *count noun* and *mass noun* is useful when we begin to write about such things in groups. Since the word *number* indicates counting, we can use that word with count nouns: "a *number* of trees." But we cannot say, "a *number* of sunshines." And we cannot say, "an *amount* of people," since people are in countable numbers, not in amounts. The same applies when we use the words *fewer, less, many,* and *much*. We use *fewer* and *many* only with count nouns; we use *less* and *much* only with mass nouns:

Count Nouns	Mass Nouns
a number of *friends*	an amount of *sand*
a number of *dollars*	an amount of *money*
fewer *houses*	less *confusion*
fewer *hours*	less *time*
many *mountains*	much *land*
many *gallons*	much *water*

George, The Cherry Tree, and Truth 99

Time for Review

Count nouns name things that can be counted *(chairs, days, streets)*. We may write of a *number* of them, *fewer* of them, or *many* of them.

Mass nouns name things that cannot be counted *(dirt, travel, courage)*. We may write of an *amount* of it, *less* of it, or *more* of it.

A noun that names a single thing is a *singular* noun.

A noun that names several things is a *plural* noun.

Plural nouns are formed by (1) adding -s, (2) adding -es, (3) changing the sound (and spelling) of the singular, or (4) making no change at all.

Do-It-Yourself Exercise

In each blank write *a number of, an amount of, many, much, less, few,* or *fewer*. Be sure the one you choose is appropriate to the following noun. Use *an amount of, much,* or *less* only in reference to things that cannot be counted:

Two hours before the parade _____ spectators had already lined the street.

Carmelita wants a small wedding, but she wants to invite _____ guests.

She will probably have _____ guests than Linda had for her wedding.

A customer came into the bank with _____ checks and walked out with _____ cash.

Do you think _____ errors will be made after we adopt the new system?

Have we _____ lumber sufficient to build _____ rooms?

I wish our town had _____ people and _____ traffic.

Checking up: Use *a number of, many, few,* or *fewer* with the countable things like *spectators, guests, checks, errors, people*. Use *an amount of, much,* or *less* with *cash, lumber, traffic*.

Chapter Seven

Forming the Possessive

George is related to his father. We may write that relationship in two different ways: *the father of George* or *George's father*. Since George is a person, we will usually write the shorter form, the one with the apostrophe-*s*: *George's father*. Some other examples:

a *lady's* shoes a *teacher's* class
the *officer's* badge my *brother's* car

When the noun does not name a person, it is more common to use the longer form, the one with *of*: the teacher *of the class*, the owner *of the car*, a door *of the library*. But there are some nouns whose possessive forms may be written either way:

a *day's* work the work *of a day*
the *road's* surface the surface *of the road*
the *sky's* color the color *of the sky*
time's flight the flight *of time*

The relationship between the two nouns is not always one of ownership. A lady may own her shoes, but George certainly does not own his father, and the day doesn't own the work. Nevertheless, the *'s* or *of* form is usually called the *possessive*.

The *'s* ending is standard for the possessive of virtually every *singular* noun in English, even including those that end with an *s*:

Doris's hobby the *hostess's* request
Jess's restaurant *Douglas's* book

Notice that the *'s* form of the singular possessive may sometimes produce three *s*'s, as in *Jess's*. But that is the usual form and should be written except when only one *s* sound is made in the pronunciation of the phrase. If you *say* two *s*'s, write *'s*: *Dr. Thomas's office, Keats' poetry*.

Do-It-Yourself Exercise

Write the *possessive* form of the *singular noun* indicated:

Our professor answered _____ question by quoting from
(Marty)

the _____ preface.
(book)

Did you hear the _____ shout of joy when the ball fell right
(coach)

into _____ hands?
(Milo)

The _____ brilliance tonight is remarkable!
   (moon)

There was a clatter as a _____ purse spilled its contents on
                         (girl)
the stairs.

The _____ announcement of the class party is posted on
  (chairman)

the _____ door.
   (professor)

Tom has a job at _____ meat market.
                  (Lacy)

The city _____ plan for a new park has been submitted for
        (council)

the _____ signature.
   (mayor)

The _____ estimate was that the installation of the pipeline
   (boss)

would take a _____ work.
              (week)

Checking up: Singular nouns all take the *'s* ending for the possessive: *Marty's, book's, coach's, Milo's, moon's,* and so on. All your entries should have that ending.

Plurals are something else. Many plurals of nouns end in something other than *s*: *children, sheep, deer, alumni, media,* and *people*. Such plural nouns take the same *'s* to form the possessive: *children's, sheep's, deer's, alumni's, media's, people's*. But most nouns in English form the plural by adding an *-s* or *-es*, as in *friends, churches, brushes*. The plural nouns that end in *-s* form the possessive by adding only an apostrophe: *friends' houses, teachers'* meeting, *ladies'* shoes.

Time for Review

To simplify the rule for forming the possessive of nouns: If the noun is plural and ends with an *s*, add only an apostrophe; for all other nouns, add *'s*.

Chapter Seven

Do-It-Yourself Exercise

Write in the blank the appropriate possessive of the indicated noun:

Ask _____ friend whether he'll give you a ride to the
     (Fred)

_____ gym.
(men)

Tom is selling _____ shoes at Martin _____
     (ladies)   (Dodge)
new shoe store.

The _____ organization of the _____ club
    (parents)   (boys)
will meet Tuesday night at _____ house.
                           (the Wilsons)

The _____ plan for a _____ park seems to
   (city)   (children)
have the _____ approval.
        (citizens)

Crews will start building the _____ facilities in about three
                           (park)

_____ time, according to the _____ report.
(months)   (superintendent)

Yesterday the _____ representatives met in closed session
        (workers)
with their _____ attorneys.
      (employers)

Some say the American _____ most troublesome problems
              (cities)
lie in their _____ failure to provide housing and transporta-
    (leaders)
tion for the poor.

If the liberation movement succeeds, the _____ success
(women)

may be their _____ gain.
(husbands)

Checking up: The plural nouns that do not end in *s (men, women, children)* and all of the singular nouns *(Fred, Dodge, city, park, superintendent)* should have the *'s* ending added for the possessive. All the plural nouns that do end in *s (ladies, parents, the Wilsons, citizens, months, workers, employers, cities, leaders, husbands)* should have *only the apostrophe* added.

Suggestions for Writing

A. Perhaps you sometimes ask "Why don't they" questions. Why don't they make power lawnmowers silent? Why don't they breed cats that won't eat pet fish? What are some of the things you think "they" should invent to make life better? Write your ideas in a passage of about 200 words, being sure to use full sentences.
B. Gambling is an ancient pastime that continues to be popular in spite of how few people win at it. Why do people gamble? Write your answer in a passage of about 200 words, being sure to use full sentences.
C. Why do some people believe in ghosts, although others believe such things are only imaginary? Write your ideas in a passage of about 200 words, being sure to use full sentences.

After Writing: Reread your passage and underline every *common noun*. What is an *abstract* noun? (See p. 97.) Read your passage again and circle any *abstract* noun that you have used. Below your passage make a separate list of the *possessive* nouns in your passage.

Using Appositives

When one noun is set beside another as in "my *friend Joe,*" the second noun is an *appositive*. The noun *Joe* renames the noun *friend*. Here are some more examples of appositives:

Our northernmost state, *Alaska,* is also our biggest.
One vehicle, a huge *van,* was blocking the highway.
From his deepest pocket the boy drew a single coin, a worn *nickel*.

Each of the appositives is a renaming of a noun earlier in the sentence: *Alaska* renames *state; van* renames *vehicle; nickel* renames *coin*.

In all three of those sentences the appositives are added information; they could be removed without changing the sense of the main idea. They are *nonrestrictive*. Every nonrestrictive appositive is set off by a pair of *commas* (or, at the end of a sentence, by one comma).

Some appositives, however, cannot be removed from the sentence without leaving the idea incomplete or vague. In the phrase *my friend Joe,* the name *Joe* could not be removed without leaving the thought that the writer has but one friend—an unlikely idea. In that phrase *Joe* is a *restrictive* appositive and is *not* set off by commas.

Time for Review

An *appositive* noun is a noun that follows another (not always immediately) and renames or classifies it: Mike, the *barber*; our brother *Rudy*.

A *nonrestrictive* appositive is set off by a pair of commas (or, if it ends a sentence, by one comma). A *restrictive* appositive is not set off.

Do-It-Yourself Exercise

Write in each blank an appropriate *appositive* to rename or classify the noun printed in italics. Use appropriate punctuation:

Our town's biggest *newspaper* _____ has funny news and unfunny comics.

One of television's best actors _____ has a show that is on every week.

The governor lives in the state *capital* _____ .

My *friend* _____ was born in the shortest *month* _____ .

The best *sport* _____ is played mainly during one *season* _____ .

Our favorite *uncle* _____ drives the best small *car* on the road _____ .

Sal's *hobby* _____ has turned out to be pretty expensive.

One famous *American* _____ said, "Give me liberty, or give me death!"

Checking up: Most of the appositives in these sentences should be *nonrestrictive*; they should be set off between a pair of commas. Perhaps the only exception is the one renaming *friend*. The one famous American in the final sentence was Patrick Henry, and his name should be set off between commas.

Collective Nouns

A noun that names a *group* of people or things is a *collective noun*. Of course, the word *group* is a collective noun—and the word *collection* is another. Here are some more:

team	faculty	public	mob
committee	family	orchestra	jury
audience	class	army	band
council	crowd	choir	gang

Sometimes collective nouns are used as singular, to name the collection of things as a unit:

My *family is* proud of Uncle Jim.

The whole *crowd has* been here today.

Has the *jury* delivered a verdict?

But the collective nouns may also be thought of and used as plural:

The *family are* proud of Uncle Jim.

The *crowd have* been walking out one by one.

Have the *jury* agreed on a verdict?

The writer may use a collective noun as either singular or plural, but effective writing demands consistency within a passage, which should stick to the singular if that is what it has started with. It would be ineffective to shift from singular to plural, as in "The *committee is* meeting and *are* going to make a decision today." (For more on collective nouns and their use, see pp. 131–132.)

The Verbal Nouns

Two kinds of noun are made by adding *to* or *-ing* to basic verb forms. Consider a two-word sentence with subject (noun) and predicate (verb):

Children swim.

The sentence makes a complete statement. But it will no longer make a complete statement if we put *to* before the verb:

Children to swim

That combination does not complete an idea. The experiment shows that *to swim* is not a verb, for a verb in that position would make the sentence complete: *Children swim*. And what of adding *-ing* to the verb?

>Children swimming

Again, the combination does not complete a sentence. The experiment shows that *swimming* is not a verb. If we want to produce full sentences of these combinations with *to swim* and *swimming*, we have to add some other verb:

>Children *like* to swim.
>Children *like* swimming.

Now the verb *like* makes the combinations into sentences. But *to swim* and *swimming* appear in the sentences as nouns—as *names* of what children like.

Since *to swim* and *swimming* are made from the verb *swim*, they are verbals—elements derived from verbs. Since in those sentences the two verbals work as nouns, they are *verbal nouns*.

The form made with *to* is the *infinitive*. An infinitive is often used as a noun, the name of an act or state of being:

>*To lose* is unthinkable. (subject of sentence)
>Everybody wants *to talk*. (object of verb)
>His intention *to return* is well known. (appositive renaming *intention*)

The form made by adding *-ing* is a *gerund*. A gerund is also used as a noun:

>Your *hammering* is too noisy. (subject of sentence)
>Liza studies *dancing*. (object of verb)
>One popular habit, *smoking*, is losing its popularity. (appositive renaming *habit*)

Time for Review

A *collective noun* names a group of people or other things: *team, troop, flock, jury, family*.

A collective noun may be used either as singular or as plural, but must be used consistently throughout a passage.

A *verbal noun* is made by adding *to* or *-ing* to a basic verb form: *to leap, to examine; leaping, examining*.

The verbal noun beginning with *to* is the *infinitive*.

The verbal noun made by adding *-ing* is a *gerund*.

George, The Cherry Tree, and Truth   107

Do-It-Yourself Exercise

Write in each blank an appropriate verbal noun: an *infinitive* or a *gerund:*

My hope is _____ some money for a car.

Deanna wants _____ a course in music.

I tried _____ the boat.

_____ is not Kelly's favorite sport.

The most dismal thing we did all week was _____ the garage.

_____ a mountain takes plenty of stamina.

My brother has never liked _____ .

I think Mother has a secret desire _____ Frank's motorcycle.

Checking up: Infinitives are introduced by *to: to earn, to save, to take, to steer, to sink.* Gerunds end in *-ing: hiking, climbing, fishing.* Notice that in the sentences of the exercise all the verbals work as *nouns,* the names of things.

Suggestions for Writing

D. When there's something to be done, people often put it off even though they believe they should "do it now." What sort of thing do you think should be done immediately, and what sort should be put off? Write your answers in about 200 words, being sure to use full sentences.

E. There are a number of ways of becoming famous—some of them bad. Write a passage of about 200 words on whether becoming famous is good or bad. Be sure to use full sentences.

F. Some things are worth memorizing. Write a passage of about 200 words, telling what sort of thing you believe is or is not worth memorizing. Be sure to use full sentences.

After Writing: Reread your passage and underline every *gerund.* Check carefully to be sure that the *-ing* word is used as a noun, not as an adjective; if it is an adjective, it should not be underlined. Read once more and circle any *collective nouns* that you have used. See p. 105 for a reminder on what a collective noun is.

Noun Phrases

A word group that does not contain a subject-verb combination is a *phrase* (see p. 41). If such a word group is used as a noun in its sentence, it is a *noun phrase*. A noun phrase is formed by a noun with its modifier (or several modifiers):

Good brakes are essential for auto safety.

Jack's tennis shoes are covered with mud.

The candidate has *great popular appeal*.

In the italicized phrases *good* modifies *brakes*; the noun with the modifier forms a noun phrase. *Shoes* and *appeal* also appear as nouns with modifiers.

When a verbal noun appears with a modifier, the word group also works as a noun phrase:

Jake's ambition was *to move to a farm*.

Reading faster saves a lot of time.

The infinitive *to move* is modified by *to a farm*; the entire word group, then, is an *infinitive phrase* (used, in the example sentence, as a *noun*, renaming Jake's ambition). The gerund *reading* is modified by *faster*; the word group *reading faster* forms a *gerund phrase* (used as the subject of the sentence).

Time for Review

A *noun phrase* is formed by a noun with its modifier (or modifiers).

An *infinitive phrase* may be formed by an infinitive with its modifier.

A *gerund phrase* may be formed by a gerund with its modifier.

An infinitive phrase or a gerund phrase may be used in a sentence as a *noun phrase*.

Do-It-Yourself Exercise

Write in each blank a *noun phrase*, an *infinitive phrase*, or a *gerund phrase* as indicated. Remember that each such phrase should contain a modifier for the noun, the infinitive, or the gerund:

With _____ on his back, Gilbert hitchhiked from Texas to
      (noun phrase)
Georgia.

While you're in the kitchen, get me a _____ .
                                          (noun phrase)

I wonder what it's like _____ on the ocean?
                      (infinitive phrase)

_____ will probably get your feet wet.
  (gerund phrase)

When I saw _____ with you, I knew that _____
           (noun phrase)   (gerund phrase)
would be impossible.

Stop trying _____ when your mouth is full of bubble gum.
            (infinitive phrase)

Checking up: Remember that a phrase must be at least two or three words (an infinitive phrase always at least three words). Did you begin each infinitive phrase with *to* and each gerund phrase with an *-ing* word? Each of your phrases works as a *noun* in its sentence. For examples, *a pack* might be what Gilbert carried on his back; *drink of water* might be used in the second sentence. Infinitive phrases that might be appropriate: *to ride a raft, to whistle a tune.* Possible gerund phrases: *Walking in the snow, talking with you.* (For full introduction to *gerunds* see Chapter 16; for full introduction to *infinitives* see Chapter 18.)

Noun Clauses

A word group that *does* contain a subject-verb combination is a clause (see p. 41). If it is introduced by a subordinator, such a group is a subordinate clause—and a subordinate clause may be used in a sentence as a *noun*:

What some people say doesn't worry me. (subject of sentence)
Tell us *how you liked the festival.* (object of *tell*)
Does anyone know *where the fish are hiding?* (object of *know*)
I just discovered *that ice is good for burns.* (object of *discovered*)

Each of the italicized groups is a subordinate clause that works as a noun in its sentence—as the *name* of an idea. A *noun clause* usually begins with one of these words: *what, where, why, when, that, how,* or *which.* The clause must contain a subject-verb combination.

Do-It-Yourself Exercise

Write in each blank a *noun clause*—a word group containing a subject-verb combination and beginning with *what, where, why, when, that, how,* or *which*:

This morning's news report says _____

110   Chapter Seven

Suddenly I remembered _____

_____.

The employment questionnaire asks _____

_____.

The textbook tells the student _____.

Some knowledge of _____ may be needed if the expedition is to find its way through the jungle.

_____ has great importance for me.

The owner of the house told us _____

_____.

Before you borrow these tools, please explain _____

_____.

Checking up: Reread each of your *noun clauses* to be sure that it begins with one of the words listed in the directions just above. To be sure that each clause has a subject-verb combination, write "S" above the subject and "V" above the verb in each (but remember that an infinitive, such as *to write* or *to leave* is not a verb).

Much more about *noun clauses* appears in Chapter 15, pp. 273-276.

Using Capitals

One special problem for writers is when to use a capital letter to begin a word. In general, writers of English do not capitalize a noun unless they have specific reason for doing so. What is capitalized is a matter of long-established practice by writers and printers. These are the ways capitals are used *as a rule*:

1. Capitalize the first letter of every sentence.
2. Capitalize the first word and all other words (except conjunctions and prepositions shorter than four letters and except *a, an,* and *the*) in titles of publications and works of art: *The Adventures of Huckleberry Finn, New York Times,* "Yankee Doodle."
3. Capitalize initials used for proper nouns: *J. P. Morgan, NATO, U.S.*
4. Capitalize the geographical areas *North, East, South,* and *West*—but not the directions (*north, east, south, west*).

5. Capitalize the pronoun *I*.
6. Do *not* capitalize the names of the seasons: *spring, summer, fall, autumn, winter*.
7. Capitalize *proper nouns:*
   a. names of persons
   b. names of specific places: *New Orleans, Alaska, South America,* and so on.
   c. names of institutions: *the United Nations, Northern Arizona University, the National Broadcasting Company,* and so on.
   d. names of languages and nationalities: *English, Spanish, Indian,* and so on.
   e. names of historical events: *the Revolutionary War, Custer's Last Stand,* and so on.
   f. names of centuries, eras, days of the week, and months: *Twentieth Century, the Renaissance, Tuesday, September,* and so on.
   g. names of historical documents: *the Declaration of Independence, the Constitution,* and so on.
   h. names of specific buildings, brand names, and ships: *the Empire State Building, Coca-Cola, the USS Ticonderoga,* and so on.
   i. names of school and college courses when they have special letters or numbers: *History 7, Philosophy 1, Math A* (but not when they name general study fields: *history, philosophy, mathematics*).

Do-It-Yourself Exercise

Using either fact or imagination, write in each blank the information called for. Be sure to use capitals according to the "rules" shown above:

_____ was born in _____ , _____ ,
(Name of person)   (name of city)   (name of state or country)

on a _____ in _____ . _____
     (name of day of week)   (name of month)   (Name or pronoun)

learned to speak _____ as a native language. While living in
                 (name of language)

_____ , _____ went to _____
(name of place)   (name or pronoun)   (name of high school)

_____ , taking special interest in _____ .
                                                (name of subject or activity)

Now _____ , enrolled in _____ , will be
    (name or pronoun)   (name of college)

taking courses (in addition to this _____ course) in
                                    (name of study)

_____ . So far, _____
(name of one or two other courses or studies)   (name or pronoun)

cannot boast enough fame to have been praised in the _____ ,

(name of newspaper)

but, after all, the _____ isn't over yet.

(name of century)

Checking up: Most of your entries should be capitalized. If you used a pronoun such as *he* or *she*, it should be capitalized only if beginning a sentence. Names of general studies are not capitalized, but the names of languages and specific courses (usually numbered, as in *History 1*) are capitalized.

Using "A" or "An"

Nouns in English are often introduced by *a* or *an*:

A person who applies for *a job* is often asked to fill out *a form* that asks for *a reference*, such as *a name* of *a friend* or *an employer* who might give him *a recommendation*.

It is important to notice that *an* is usually used when the following word begins with a *vowel sound*. It is *sound* that is important here, not letter, for some letters like *h* may be pronounced (or *not* pronounced) like vowels:

a hammer	*an hour*	*a happy girl*
an honest man	*a peach*	*an apple*

Do-It-Yourself Exercise

In each blank write *a* or *an* appropriately to introduce a noun phrase:

When _____ person has _____ unreasonable prejudice against _____ race or _____ religion, he usually cannot make _____ judgment on the basis of _____ fact. Rather he will be guided by _____ emotion, although he may have _____ clear mind and reach _____ unbiased opinion on _____ different subject. That is why _____ opinion should always be checked to determine whether it is based on _____ assumption or on _____ honest observation.

Checking up: Before a vowel sound use *an: an* unreasonable prejudice, *an* emotion, *an* unbiased opinion, *an* opinion, *an* assumption, *an* honest observation.

Suggestions for Writing

G. Nearly everyone is deeply influenced by others in his life. Who are the people (parents, friends, teachers, or others) who have most influenced you? Where did they associate with you (name the places, including schools, churches, and so on)? Write your passage in about 300 words.
H. Taking short cuts can save time—but can also create some embarrassments and regrets. Write a passage of about 350 words telling how taking a short cut (or several of them) got you into some embarrassment.
I. In a crowd some people stand out, while others get lost or stay in the background. Which sort of person are you—usually? Write a passage of about 350 words, telling why you stand out (or do not) in a crowd.

After Writing: Reread your passage to be sure that you have properly capitalized (1) the first word of every sentence, and (2) every proper noun. If you have used any infinitives (such as *to fight, to shout*), underline the ones used as *nouns* in your passage. Also underline any *noun clause* you have used (after seeing p. 109 for a reminder on what a noun clause is).

George, The Cherry Tree, and Truth 115

QUIZ 7

Using Nouns

On the blank within each sentence write the item that you think most appropriately completes the sentence; then mark the **letter** of that item on your answer blank. Don't overlook punctuation included in some of the offered alternatives. After marking your choice, explain briefly why you chose it (*Because:* . . .).

Example: No matter what happens, no amount of ___*money*___ can make my brother change his mind.

(a) arguments   (b) people   (c) experiences   (d) offers   (e) money   Ex _e_

(*Because:* "*Amount of*" *requires the mass noun*.)

1. Our good _____ Dr. Williams has agreed to lead the Red Cross drive this year.

(a) friend,   (b) neighbor   (c) member,   (d) neighbor,   (e) associate,   1_____

(*Because:* _____.)
   (*Question:* Is *Dr. Williams* used as a restrictive or as a nonrestrictive appositive? See pp. 103–104.)

2. It seems that the _____ have lost their enthusiasm.

(a) coach   (b) family   (c) player   (d) student   (e) child   2_____

(*Because:* _____.)
   (*Question:* Which noun would be a proper subject to agree with the verb, *have*? See p. 105.)

3. Billy didn't expect any reward for returning the _____ purse.

(a) girls'   (b) ladies'   (c) women's   (d) lady's   (e) womans   3_____

(*Because:* _____.)
   (*Question:* Which is the proper possessive form to go with the obviously singular *purse*?)

4. One of the most popular studies on American college campuses is _____

_____.

(a) Political Science   (b) Mathematics   (c) Psychology   (d) economics
(e) Chemistry   4_____

(*Because:* _____.)
   (*Question:* When should the name of a college course be capitalized? See p. 111.)

116   Chapter Seven

5. What the nation's highways need today is less _____
behind the wheel.
(a) careless drivers   (b) drunks   (c) carelessness   (d) speeders
(e) showoffs

5.____

(Because: _____.*)*
    (Question: Can *less* be used to modify a count noun?*)*

6. Our team captain has always shown a _____
that we admire.
(a) outward calm   (b) instinctive judgment   (c) average   (d) understanding
(e) leadership

6.____

(Because: _____.*)*
    (Question: Can *a* be used just before a noun that begins with a vowel sound?*)*

7. It is obvious that the professor enjoys _____.
(a) teaching english   (b) our friday classes   (c) driving a old car
(d) owning a new car   (e) Philosophy

7.____

(Because: _____.*)*

8. Many young people these days do not go along with the old struggle to keep up

with the _____.
(a) Joneses   (b) Jones   (c) Jones's   (d) Joneses'   (e) Jone's

8.____

(Because: _____.*)*

9. Dr. Bilsky's history class is writing a special report on _____.
(a) the Bill of Rights   (b) the U.S. constitution   (c) the Civil war
(d) the eighteenth century   (e) the old west

9.____

(Because: _____.*)*

10. The newest store on the block specializes in _____
clothes.
(a) mens   (b) teenager's   (c) girls'   (d) babies   (e) ladys

10.____

(Because: _____.*)*

11. What time we leave depends on whether all of the _____
are ready.
(a) luggage   (b) family   (c) bus   (d) lunch's   (e) bag's

11.____

(Because: _____.*)*

12. Any team that expects to get into the playoffs will have to win a certain amount of _____ during the season.

(a) games (b) fans (c) series (d) support (e) events

12._____

(Because: _____.*)*

13. The council has decided to set aside a _____ for observance of the celebration.

(a) afternoon in May (b) April day (c) evening next month
(d) week in June (e) hour on Tuesday

13._____

(Because: _____.*)*

14. My _____ and I are the only girls in our family of seven.

(a) sister Carmen (b) sister, Alicia, (c) sister, Ann (d) sister Jane,
(e) Sister Greta

14._____

(Because: _____.*)*

15. Most of the local _____ have large memberships.

(a) club's (b) church's (c) organization's (d) troops (e) groups'

15._____

(Because: _____.*)*

16. We hope _____ all the profits for betterment of the community.

(a) spend (b) using (c) to invest (d) setting aside (e) to spending

16._____

(Because: _____.*)*

17. Five of us have organized a study group to visit the _____ of the Southwest.

(a) Indian Pueblos (b) indian villages (c) Indian settlement's
(d) indian reservations (e) Indian pueblos

17._____

(Because: _____.*)*

18. Leaders of the movement have just signed an _____ with their foreign competitors.

(a) new contract (b) agreement (c) treaty (d) long-term contract
(e) bargain

18._____

(Because: _____.*)*

118   Chapter Seven

19. My friend Dave recovered quickly from his illness, mostly because of the

_____.

(a) doctors treatment   (b) nurse's smile   (c) greeting card's he received
(d) attention's of the nurses   (e) advance's of science   19_____

(Because: _____.*)*

20. Maybe we got lost because the directions said we should turn _____

_____.

(a) to the east   (b) to the Southward   (c) North   (d) Southwest
(e) Westward   20_____

(Because: _____.*)*

Run, Fly, Sail 8

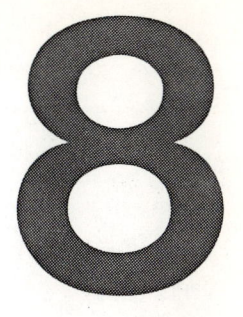

How to work with . . . verbs
tenses: past and present
regular and irregular verbs
transitive and intransitive verbs
person
verb agreement
six troublesome verbs

How to avoid . . . faulty verb forms
faulty verb agreement

VERBS ARE THE POWER PLANTS of sentences. In any sentence, the verb is the happening:

>   Horses *run*.
>   Birds *fly*.
>   Boats *sail*.

The words *run, fly,* and *sail* are verbs. They indicate the happenings in the sentences.

Happenings, of course, are not always actions. The verbs *run, fly,* and *sail* do show action; but other verbs may show status rather than action. For example, *are, seem,* and *sound*:

>   Sunsets *are* beautiful.
>   The days *seem* too short.
>   You *sound* happy today.

The verbs *are, seem,* and *sound* in those sentences do not show action; the subjects, rather than doing actions, are shown in states of being beautiful, short, or happy.

In this chapter we discuss action verbs only, including how they change their forms to show difference of time and to show agreement with their subjects. At the end of this chapter you should be able to work easily with action verbs and their forms.

Happening When?

Is the happening now, in the present? Was the happening before now, in the past? These concepts of past and present show themselves in certain changes in verb form—changes of *tense*.

Many verbs show the change from present tense to past tense by adding *-ed*:

Present tense	Past tense
We *play* soccer.	We *played* soccer.
The boats *sail* lazily.	The boats *sailed* lazily.
You *snore*.	You *snored* all night.
The exams *start* at noon.	The exams *started* at noon.
Miners *work* below ground.	Miners *worked* below ground.
They *reach* the first level.	They *reached* the first level.

These verbs that form the past tense by adding *-ed* are *regular* verbs.

Time for Review

Verbs are the *happening* words of sentences.

Verbs may show *action,* or they may show *state of being;* this chapter deals only with the action verbs.

Verbs usually change their form to show difference of time. What happens now is in the *present tense;* what has happened before now is in the *past tense.*

Many verbs indicate a change from present tense to past tense by adding *-ed.*

Verbs that add *-ed* to form the past tense are *regular* verbs.

Do-It-Yourself Exercise

Write in each blank an appropriate *regular* verb in the past tense. (The verbs shown in parentheses are suggested possibilities, but you must change their form to the *past tense*):

The clock _____ midnight before Pete had _____ the lesson.
       (show, indicate)   (learn, finish)

The investigator _____ how far the boys _____ before they _____ at the boathouse.
      (ask, wonder)   (walk, row)   (arrive, dock)

As the men _____ down the tunnel, they _____ that the cave-in _____ none of their friends.
     (crawl, move)   (realize, hope)   (trap, bury)

Checking up: All of your past-tense verbs in this exercise should end in *-ed,* since all the suggested verbs are regular verbs. Even if you wrote your own verbs instead, be sure that you used only regular verbs with *-ed* endings. Notice that a final *-y* (as in *study* or *bury*) must be changed to *i* before *-ed* is added. A final *e* (as in *indicate, move, realize, hope*) must be dropped before *-ed* is added.

Irregular Verbs

Many verbs form the past tense not by adding *-ed* but by making some other kind of change. They are *irregular* verbs:

Present Tense	Past Tense
We *see* the problem.	We *saw* the problem.
You *go* first.	You *went* first.
Puppies *sleep* soundly.	The puppies *slept* soundly.
I *run* along the shore.	I *ran* along the shore.
Don't *sing* too loud.	You *sang* too loud.

Most speakers of English learn these irregular-verb forms by long practice, imitating what they hear in conversation. Though some variations are heard in spoken English, writers usually avoid confusing the past-tense forms (like those just above) with the past-participial forms (see p. 308).

Time for Review

Regular verbs form the past tense by adding *-ed: play, played.*

Irregular verbs form the past tense by making some change other than adding *-ed: drink, drank.*

Do-It-Yourself Exercise

Write in each blank an appropriate *irregular* verb in the past tense. (The verbs shown in parentheses are suggested possibilities, but you must change their form to the past tense.)

Some kids _____ with some skill even before they _____
               (swim, write)   (take, begin)
special classes.

I always _____ a good breakfast at home, but I often _____
        (eat, get)   (buy, drink)
coffee at the cafeteria.

We _____ the cold, crowded bus in the morning and _____
     (catch, ride)   (shake, freeze)
all the way to town.

I usually _____ while my friends _____ off to sleep.
         (drive, sing)   (go, fall)

We _____ our support to whatever our candidate _____
    (give, lend)   (stand, speak)
for.

Checking up: The appropriate past-tense forms for the suggested verbs are *swam, wrote, took, began, ate, got, bought, drank, caught, rode, shook, froze, drove, sang, went, fell, gave, lent, stood,* and *spoke.* Be especially aware of *swam* and *began.*

A Problem With "-ed"

In speech, especially rapid speech, some sounds are lost (or omitted) when they occur near other sounds if the two are difficult to say together. For instance, we may say or hear:

I once *suppose* Tuesday was my lucky day. (The final *d* sound of supposed is "swallowed up" by the following *t* sound of Tuesday.)
When I was younger, I *use* to study piano. (The final *d* sound of used is swallowed up by the following *t* of *to*.)

This final *-d* or *-ed* is often omitted improperly even when there is no "swallowing up" by a following sound:

My early life *prejudice* me against water, so now I have *miss* some of the water sports that my friends have *experience*.

Especially in writing, the missing *-d* or *-ed* must be supplied:

My early life prejudic*ed* me against water, so now I have miss*ed* some of the water sports that my friends have experienc*ed*.

Verbs With Objects–or Without

When an action is done to someone or something, the action verb is *transitive*:

Bert *saw* a mouse.
Quickly Bert *grabbed* a broom.
Nevertheless, the mouse *stole* the cheese.

The actions *saw, grabbed,* and *stole* are transitive; the actions are *done to* things—to the *mouse,* the *broom,* the *cheese.* In those sentences the mouse, the broom, and the cheese are the *objects* of the transitive verbs. A *transitive verb,* in other words, is a verb that *takes an object.*
But action verbs may indicate actions that are not done to anything:

The mouse *ran.*
Suddenly the creature *stopped.*
It *looked around* in fright.

The actions *ran, stopped,* and *looked* are done by the mouse, but they are not *done to* anything. The verbs take no objects; they are *intransitive verbs.*

Chapter Eight

Every action verb is transitive or intransitive. But some verbs may be either, depending upon their usage:

Intransitive	Transitive
Jim *dropped* out.	Jim *dropped* his book.
They *will stand* up.	They *will stand* their ground.
Her mother *cried*.	Her mother *cried* huge tears.
The bear *stole* away.	The bear *stole* our breakfast.

Used as transitive verbs, *dropped, will stand, cried, stole* (and many other verbs, of course) take objects, such as *book, ground, tears,* and *breakfast.*

Time for Review

A *transitive* verb shows action done to someone or something; it takes an *object*.

An *intransitive* verb shows action not done to anything; it takes *no object*.

Every action verb is *transitive* or *intransitive* as it appears in a sentence.

Many verbs are either *transitive* or *intransitive*, depending upon whether they take objects in the sentences they are used in.

Do-It-Yourself Exercise

Write an appropriate verb (*transitive* or *intransitive* as directed) to fill each blank and complete the sentence:

Huntley _____ the rifle.
          (transitive)

The story _____ suddenly without any point.
          (intransitive)

My engine _____ badly; it _____ a tune-up.
     (intransitive)   (transitive)

Johnny _____ as he _____ what a fine job he had done.
     (intransitive)   (transitive)

Apparently some rain _____ during the night.
                        (intransitive)

The thief _____ the purse and _____ .
          (transitive)   (intransitive)

If you _____ carefully, you often _____ birds
       (intransitive)   (transitive)
chirping in the distance.

Always _____ your neighbor with his problems.
       (transitive)

Suggestions for Writing

A. If you had to teach a beginner how to drive a car around the block, you would have to specify every move to make. Write a passage of about 300 words, giving such directions from the very beginning (from opening the car door) to the end (to setting the hand brake). Use as many action verbs as you can.
B. Recall a time when you were really frightened by an experience. Tell about the experience in a passage of about 300 words, using as many action verbs as you can.
C. Imagine being taken for a ride in a flying saucer by apparently friendly visitors from outer space. Relate the experience in a passage of about 300 words, using as many action verbs as you can.

After Writing: Reread your passage, underlining every action verb. Then reconsider each verb: Is it transitive or intransitive? Circle each transitive verb and draw an arrow from it to its object.

Checking up: Remember that transitive verbs indicate action *done to* something: *fired* the rifle, *needs* a tune-up, *grabbed* the purse, *hear* birds, and so on. Intransitive verbs indicate action not done to an object: *ended* suddenly, *runs* badly, Johnny *smiled*, rain *fell,* and so on.

Person: Writer, Reader, and Topic

Verbs in the present tense usually change their form according to who or what is used as subject:

I *see* Tony.
You *see* George.
George *sees* both Tony and me.

The change from *see* to *sees* occurs only when the subject is not the speaker or writer himself and not the person being addressed. The *-s* ending (as in *sees*) is used only when the subject of the verb is someone or something being talked *about*.

This principle of speaker-listener-topic (or writer-reader-topic) is referred to as *person*. The writer himself is the *first person*, usually named as *I, me, we, us, myself,* or *ourselves*:

> *I* was just asking *myself* what *we* might do if anyone saw *us* helping *ourselves* to the cake.

Every reference to the writer or to his group is a *first-person* reference.

The listener or reader is the *second person*, usually named as *you, yourself,* or *yourselves*:

> Where will *you* look for a new job when *you* have earned *yourself* a college diploma?

The topic, or what is being talked or written about, is the *third person*, usually referred to by name or by *he, she, they, it, him, her, them,* or the appropriate *-self* words:

> *Tony* and *George* spoke to *her* about *it*, but *she* wouldn't tell *them* about *herself*.

To put the principle of *person* in another way:

> *I* (first person) tell *you* (second person) about *him* (third person).
> *He* (third person) tells *me* (first person) about *you* (second person).
> *We* (first person) have seen *you* (second person) with *them* (third person).
> *They* (third person) cannot hear *us* (first person) talking about *you* (second person).

(For more about the principle of person see pp. 240-241.)

Verbs in Third-Person Singular

When the subject of a present-tense verb is someone or something in the third-person singular, the verb usually has an *-s* or *-es* ending:

> Sam play*s* right guard.
> He go*es* fishing every Saturday.
> She like*s* folk dancing.
> It seem*s* cool this afternoon.
> The news reach*es* us too late.

The only verbs that do not take this *-s* or *-es* ending for the present third-person singular are the auxiliary verbs other than *have* and *do*:

> Sam *can* play right guard.
> He *will* go fishing every Saturday.

She *may* like folk dancing.
It *should* seem cool this afternoon.
The news *must* reach us too late.

Note carefully that the *-s* or *-es* ending forms the *singular* of a verb, not the plural. It is not to be confused with the *-s* or *-es* ending that forms the plural of a noun.

Time for Review

The principle of *person* concerns whether what is named by a noun (or pronoun) is the speaker *(first person)*, the listener *(second person)*, or the topic being discussed *(third person)*.

The *-s* or *-es* ending is used for a verb only when the subject of that verb is in the third-person singular—and only when the verb is in the present tense.

Auxiliary verbs other than *do* and *have* do not take as *-s* or *-es* ending even for the third-person singular.

Do-It-Yourself Exercise

Write in each blank an appropriate verb in the third-person singular to complete each sentence:

We start work at 10 o'clock, but Phil _____ at noon.

I say it is still early, although he _____ it's late.

When we want the clock to go fast, it _____ slow.

You write your letter after she _____ hers.

They wash the pots and pans, but Mother _____ the glassware.

Everybody _____ his own work around here.

Each of the newspapers _____ the same story.

One of the men _____ a star on his hat.

If *he* _____ late, you may sleep late too.

I have a sister, and *she* _____ a friend you'd like to meet.

It _____ a lot of courage to take a walk in the dark street after midnight.

Checking up: The verbs you have written in the blanks should all be in the third-person singular, present tense, with *-s* or *-es* endings. Compare each of them with the other verbs shown in the sentence whose subjects are plural *(we, they)* or first person *(I, we)* or second person *(you)*. Your verbs might be these: *starts, says, goes, writes, washes, sleeps, has, takes.*

Verb Agreement

When the writer uses the *-s* or *-es* ending on a verb with a third-person singular subject, he follows the principle of *verb agreement*. That is, the verb *agrees* (in person and in number) with its subject. Verb agreement gives the writer very little problem except in the present or present perfect tense, since the other tenses do not make the change of verb form for the third-person singular. But when using the present tense, the writer faces some verb-agreement problems. For examples:

    You and Mother . . . (*has* or *have*?) eyes.
    The children, not the dog, . . . (*cry* or *cries*?).
    He is one of those workers who . . . (*loaf* or *loafs*?).

These are problems that bother nearly everyone who speaks English. Often the verb choice will not be noticed in conversation, even if it is not the "proper" one. Writing, however, calls for greater precision than is necessary in ordinary conversation, and the proper verb agreement is necessary for most college-level writing.

These are some of the verb-agreement problems and their solutions for writing:

Subjects in Pairs or Series.   When two subjects are linked by *and*, the pair forms a plural and requires the plural verb:

    You and he *have* all the luck. (But "He *has* the luck.")
    He *reads*. She *reads*. He and she *read*.
    The man *sleeps*. The boy *sleeps*. The man and the boy *sleep*.
    The grass *grows*. The flower *grows*. The grass and the flower *grow*.

But when a pair linked by *and* is introduced by *each* or *every*, the items in the pair are considered separately. Then the singular verb form is used:

    Each village and town *has* one representative.
    Every bus and taxi *was* full.

The question of verb agreement is less simple when pairs and series of subjects are formed with *or* as coordinator. *Or* indicates that only *one* of the subjects, not both of them, will be considered:

    You or your brother *carries* the lunch every day.
    His head or his hand *has* been hurt.

If *or* links two subjects, one singular and one plural, the verb agrees with the subject nearer the verb:

> The eggs or the *coffee has* always been boiled too long.
> *Has the scoutmaster* or the boys shown up yet?
> *Have the boys* or their scoutmaster shown up yet?

The same rule applies when the subjects are paired with the correlative *either-or;* the verb agrees with the nearer subject:

> Either you or *Tom carries* the water.
> Either the cat or the *dogs have* been tied up.
> Either the dogs or the *cat has* been tied up.
> Either the house or the *gardens* always *need* maintenance.
> Either the gardens or the *house* always *needs* maintenance.

Nouns Between Subject and Verb.   Sometimes the subject and the verb are separated by word groups containing other nouns.

> The *girl* with the *skis* . . . (*has* or *have*?) fallen down.
> *Clouds* over the *bay* . . . (*float* or *floats*?) by.
> *Government* by the *people* . . . (*demand* or *demands*?) involvement.

In those sentences the first noun, not the second one, is the subject of the verb. The second noun follows a preposition, a word that shows a relationship between the two nouns. A noun following a preposition like *with, over,* or *by* cannot be the subject of a verb. The subjects of those three sentences, then, are *girl, clouds,* and *government:*

> The *girl* with the skis *has* a big smile.
> *Clouds* over the bay *float* by.
> *Government* by the people *demands* involvement.

Time for Review

A *verb* must *agree* (in person and in number) with its *subject.*

If the subject is third-person singular, the verb will also be in the third-person singular.

Most verbs form the third-person singular (in the present tense) with an *-s* or *-es* ending. (Exceptions: *can, may, shall, will, must.* See p. 146.)

Subjects in pairs or series with *and* form a plural and require a plural verb.

Subjects in pairs with the correlative *both–and* form a plural and require a plural verb.

Chapter Eight

Subjects in pairs or series with *or* require that the verb agree with the nearer (or nearest) subject.

Subjects in pairs with *either–or* or *neither–nor* require that the verb agree with the nearer subject.

Nouns that appear *between* subject and verb do not affect the verb. A noun following a preposition cannot be the subject of a verb.

Do-It-Yourself Exercise

Write in each blank an appropriate present-tense verb to agree with the subject and complete the sentence; underline the subject:

The new quarterback for the Dolphins _____ an outstanding pass-completion record.

Elegance in automobile styles _____ always been sought by fine-car buffs.

Gretchen and Mary _____ taken the sewing course.

Company managers considering a wage increase _____ not yet agreed among themselves.

The newscasters usually _____ to be careful about gathering facts.

The secretaries around this office _____ too much time at the water cooler.

Neither the president nor the students of this college _____ anything about the student council's work.

Ernie or Jim _____ more money than you have ever earned.

Both the elected officer and the private citizen _____ the respect of the law.

_____ Ruth, Freda, Valerie, and Irene been here for every meeting?

Either the 100-yard dash or the 220-yard hurdles race _____ a lot of speed.

_____ Henry, Wally, Charles, or Pete want to run for the team managership?

It seems that either the men or the captain _____ a difficult decision to make.

Let's hope that either the captain or the men _____ the right decision.

Checking up: Can you explain why you wrote the singular or the plural verb in each sentence? If not, reread the *Time for Review* section just above the exercise and identify the item that governs the verb choice in each of these situations. The most probable appropriate choices: *quarterback* (not Dolphins) *has; elegance* (not styles) *has; Gretchen and Mary have; managers* (not increase) *have; newscasters try* or *have; secretaries* (not office) *spend; students* (not president) *know, say,* or *care; Ernie or Jim earns; officer and citizen have; have Ruth, Freda, Valerie,* and *Irene* been; *dash or race requires; does Henry, Wally, Charles, or Pete; captain* (not men) *has; men* (not captain) *make* the right decision.

Suggestions for Writing

D. Some people say that the school of experience is the best teacher. Benjamin Franklin said that the school of experience is tough and costly, but that "a fool will learn in no other." Write a passage (about 300 words) telling what you think about the school of experience. Use *both-and, either-or,* and the coordinators *and* and *or* at least once each in your passage.

E. The old saying that "crime doesn't pay" refers, of course, to something other than *pay* in terms of money. Write a passage (about 300 words) telling in what ways crime may not pay even for a criminal who gets away with it. Use *both-and, neither-nor,* and the coordinators *and* and *or* at least once each in your passage.

F. It has been said that "a friend in need is a friend indeed." Write a passage (about 300 words) telling why friends seem more important when we are in need—and why we often ignore our friends when we are not in need. Use *both-and, either-or,* and the coordinators *and* and *or* at least once each in your passage.

After Writing: Reread your passage to be sure that every *verb* you have used *agrees* with its *subject.* Underline each subject and circle each verb; then draw an arrow from each subject to its verb. Can you explain in each case why you chose the singular or the plural verb form?

Collective Nouns as Subjects. Such nouns as *family* and *jury* and *team* name groups (or collections) of people or things. They are *collective nouns.* In using collective nouns as subjects of verbs, the writer has a choice: He may consider the jury as a unit, singular, or he may think of the jury as twelve individuals, plural:

Today the jury *returns* its verdict. (Singular.)

The jury *agree* on their verdict. (Plural.)

In the second of those sentences apparently the writer is thinking of the jury *members,* not of the jury as a unit, so he uses *jury* as a plural subject and makes the verb agree with that plural.

Though the writer has a choice of singular or plural for the collective noun and its verb, he must stick to that choice once he has made it. His work becomes inconsistent and perhaps confusing if he shifts from singular to plural in the same passage:

>The jury *meets* in secret and *decide* upon their verdict.

Using the verb *meets* (with its *-s* ending), the writer signals that he thinks of the jury as a unit, singular; by later switching to *decide* and using the pronoun *their* he shows inconsistency of thought. He must revise:

>The jury *meets* in secret and *decides* upon *its* verdict.

Or, if he decides to make the collective noun plural, he may write:

>The jury *meet* in secret and *decide* upon *their* verdict.

Other *collective nouns* that may be treated as either singular or plural include *class, group, couple, trio, audience, crowd, herd, board, committee, council, gang, squad, assembly, senate, congress,* and so on.

Indefinite Pronouns as Subjects. Indefinite pronouns are words that allow us to name without naming specifically. The word *somebody,* for example, does not name any specific person; the word *many* does not name specific things. When a writer uses an indefinite pronoun as the subject of a verb, he must know whether that pronoun names *one* thing or *more* than one.

Most of the indefinite pronouns are *singular,* even when we may think they are naming *more* than one. For example, *everybody* is normally treated as a *singular.* We always say, "Everybody *has* an opinion," rather than, "Everybody *have* an opinion," and "Everybody *does* his own thing," rather than, "Everybody *do* . . . ."

The *indefinite pronouns* in these sentences are *singular* and, when they are used as subjects of verbs, must take the third person singular verb:

>*Each* of the announcements *has* been heard.
>*Either* of the contestants *knows* he may win.
>*Everybody* with itchy feet *has* to report to the doctor.
>*Someone* from the East *was* among the delegates.
>Hardly *one* of the actors *has* learned his lines.
>*Neither* of them *takes* much time.

(Notice that the nouns *between* the subjects and verbs follow prepositions *(of, with, from)* and therefore do not affect the verb. The subject is *each,* not *announcements; either,* not *contestants; everybody,* not *feet*—and so on.)

Some *indefinite pronouns* are plural and require the plural verb:

>*Both* of the tickets *appear* to be valid.
>*Many* of the candidates *have* already signed up.

Few animals *come* out of the cages on rainy days.

Some *indefinite pronouns* are either singular or plural, depending upon what they refer to:

Some of the children *have* to ride in back. (*Some* refers to *children*.)
Some of the sand *has* spilled on the sandwiches. (*Some* refers to *sand*.)
All of your day *has* been wasted. (*All* refers to *day*.)
All of the votes *have* gone to the same candidate. (*All* refers to *votes*.)
Most of the passengers *have* claimed their baggage.

(For more on *indefinite pronouns* see pp. 248-249.)

Negatives as Subjects. When two subjects are joined as a pair and *not* (or some other negative) is applied to one of them, the verb must agree with the *affirmative* subject, not with the negative one:

The *manager* but not the employees *counts* the cash.
The *children* but not their mother *do* the dishes.
The *clowns* rather than the elephant *have* the biggest ears.
Many *shells* but never a rock *have* appeared on this beach.

Time for Review

Collective nouns may be either singular or plural. If the writer uses a collective noun as a singular, he must continue to use it as singular throughout his passage; he should not shift from singular to plural or plural to singular.

The indefinite pronouns *each, either, everybody, somebody, everyone, someone, neither,* and *one* are singular; they require a third person singular verb.

The indefinite pronouns *both, many,* and *few* are plural; they require a plural verb.

The indefinite pronouns *all, most,* and *some* may be used as either singular or plural, depending upon what they refer to. For example, *all of the paper* uses *all* as singular; *all of the books* uses *all* as plural.

When subjects are used in a pair or series and one of them is negative (as in *not the books but the paper*), the verb should agree with the *affirmative*, not with the negative subject.

Chapter Eight

Do-It-Yourself Exercise

Write an appropriate *present-tense* verb to agree with the subject and complete the sentence:

When Arthur and Bob apply for a job, both _____ the test, but neither usually _____ the job.

My family always _____ the products that they see advertised on television.

Do you suppose the committee _____ considered its choices yet?

Each of my classes _____ a lab session twice a week.

The twins but not their father _____ desserts after all their meals.

Some of the milk but none of the fruit juices _____ spoiled.

If the jury _____ back to the courtroom early, they usually _____ an unfavorable verdict to report.

Many _____ into athletics hoping for a career, but few _____ a successful one.

When Sam talks, the whole gang _____ and usually takes his advice.

None of the clocks _____ the right time, but some _____ to be closer than others.

Everybody _____ that the board _____ mistakes now and then.

All of the stores _____ opened early today, but all of the expensive material _____ unsold.

Checking up: Be sure that you have used only *present-tense* verbs in the exercise. Can you explain in each case why you used the singular—or why you used the plural?

Some appropriate possibilities: both *take*, neither *gets*; family *buy* or *use* (plural, since the *family* are later referred to as *they*); committee *has* (singular, since the committee is later referred to as *it*); each *has*; twins (not father) *eat* desserts; some of the milk (not juices) *has* spoiled; jury *come* back (plural, since jury is later referred to as *they*); they *have*; many *go*; few *have*; gang *listens* (singular, since the next verb is *takes*); none *has* or *shows*; some *seem* or *appear*; everybody *knows* or *thinks*; the board *makes* or *make* (since the collective noun could be either singular or plural); all (stores) *are* or *have*; all (material) *is* or *remains* unsold.

Suggestions for Writing

G. Some people are "joiners"; they love to be members of groups. Even people who think of themselves as "loners" are often members of groups of many sorts. Write a passage (about 300 words) telling what groups you have been a member of—and why. Use as many different *collective nouns* as you can, telling what those groups had to offer you.

H. Behind the wheels of American cars are thousands of different kinds of people with interesting habits of driving. Write a passage (about 300 words) describing several types of driver. Use as many different *indefinite pronouns* as you can in telling how these drivers differ.

I. A group of cattle form a *herd*, but a group of sheep form a *flock*. These words are *collective nouns*. Write a passage (about 300 words) telling what activities are characteristic of these: a *herd*, a *mob*, an *audience*, a *troop*, a *battalion*, a *team* (of animals), a *flock* (of church members).

After Writing: If you used past tense, revise your passage and use only present-tense verbs. Reread to be sure you have used proper *verb agreement* in every sentence. Can you tell why the singular is required for each of your singular verbs and plural for each of your plural verbs?

Six Troublesome Verbs

Few action verbs present so many difficulties for speakers of English as do these six: *lie, lay, sit, set, rise,* and *raise*. In conversation the difficulties are often ignored, but writers must avoid the mistakes in usage that often pass unnoticed in speech.

Three of these verbs *(lie, sit,* and *rise)* are intransitive; they never take objects:

The lions *lie* quietly in their cages tonight.
Harry *sits* dejectedly in the corner.
Most of us *rise* eagerly every morning.

Though the lions *lie*, they do not do the action *to* anything. Harry *sits*, and most of us *rise*, but those actions are not *done to* anything. They are *intransitive* verbs.

The other three "most troublesome verbs" are used as transitive verbs; they do take objects:

> Jack *lays* his tools beside him. (The action is done to an object, *tools*.)
> Carefully he *sets* his wrench on a fender. (The action is done to an object, the *wrench*.)
> He *raises* the hood. (The action is done to an object, the *hood*.)

These three verbs always take objects; they are *transitive* verbs.

The greatest difficulty with these six verbs is that the transitive *lay, set,* and *raise* can be so easily confused with the intransitive *lie, sit,* and *rise*. And the difficulties can seem even greater when we see that the intransitive *lie* has the word *lay* as its past-tense form. The careful writer must give extra attention to these six verbs to sort them out for appropriate usage.

These are the forms of *lie, sit,* and *rise*—the intransitive ones; they *never* indicate action done to an object:

	Present	Past	Present Perfect
I, you, we, they	lie	lay	have *lain*
it, she, he	lies	lay	has *lain*
I, you, we, they	sit	sat	have *sat*
it, she, he	sits	sat	has *sat*
I, you, we, they	rise	rose	have *risen*
it, she, he	rises	rose	has *risen*

The *present perfect* tense is formed with *have* or *has* as a helper. This tense indicates past time that extends up to the present. (For a more thorough understanding of the present perfect tense see pp. 146-147. For now, remember that these forms are used with *have* or *has* as a helper.)

Time for Review

Lie, sit, and *rise* are intransitive verbs; they do not take objects.

Lay, set, and *raise* are transitive verbs; they always take objects.

Do-It-Yourself Exercise

Write in each blank an appropriate form of *lie, sit,* or *rise* to complete these sentences:

I often _____ in bed and listen to music.

Run, Fly, Sail   **137**

Last night I _____ up watching television.

When Sam is called upon, he always _____ to the occasion.

Sometimes the sun _____ before I have awakened.

Whenever I've felt too tired to study, I _____ full length on the floor to rest.

The moon _____ , and I could see it shining through my window.

While I _____ at my desk studying, my dog _____ at my feet. He was snoring.

The poor pup _____ there like that every night for a month now.

Checking up: Present—*lie, rises, have lain, has lain;* past—*sat, rose, lay.* Whether the sentence is in past tense or present tense is shown clearly by some other part of the context, so recheck each of your verbs to be sure that it matches the tense. Be especially sure that you have not used *laid,* which is not a form of *lie* and can be used only when the action is *done to* something: "I *laid* my glasses aside."

These are forms of *lay, set,* and *raise,* which are *transitive* verbs (always indicating an action *done to* something):

	Present	Past	Present Perfect
I, you, we, they	lay	laid	have laid
it, she, he	lays	laid	has laid
I, you, we, they	set	set	have set
it, she, he	sets	set	has set
I, you, we, they	raise	raised	have raised
it, she, he	raises	raised	has raised

Write in each blank an appropriate form of *lay, set,* or *raise* to agree with the tense suggested by the context:

Every time I _____ the scissors down, I can't find them again.

This morning she _____ the table for breakfast; then she poured the coffee.

No matter how difficult things are, Professor Johanssen never _____ his voice in class.

Let's see whether we can _____ a little money for our favorite charity.

Last year we _____ about two hundred dollars.

You _____ the brake when you parked the car, didn't you?

There I go! I have _____ those scissors down again!

Checking up: Present—*lay, raise, can raise;* past—*set, raised;* perfect—*have set* or *have laid.* Be especially careful with the spelling of *laid;* there is no *y* in *laid.*

QUIZ 8

Using Action Verbs

On the blank within each sentence write the item that most effectively completes the sentence; then mark the *letter* of that item on your answer blank. After marking your choice, explain briefly why you chose it (*Because:* . . .).

Example: Willie never gets discouraged, even when ___most___ of his ideas go wrong.

(a) either   (b) one   (c) most   (d) each   (e) every one   Ex _c_

(*Because:* _Verb "go" requires plural subject here_.)

1. When my friend Gilbert was younger, he _____ sense of responsibility.

(a) use to have no   (b) used to have no   (c) never develop any
(d) doesn't have any   (e) miss developing a   1_____

(*Because:* _____.)
   (*Question:* Which item is in past tense consistent with the verb *was*?)

2. Is _____ his friends here yet?

(a) both Bob and   (b) either Bob or   (c) not Bob but
(d) neither Bob's parents nor   (e) some of Bob's relatives or   2_____

(*Because:* _____.)
   (*Question:* Which item provides a singular subject in affimative form to agree with the verb *Is*?)

3. The poor turtle just _____ there on its back.

(a) lay   (b) lays   (c) laid   (d) lain   (e) lying   3_____

(*Because:* _____.)
   (*Question:* Which completion is a verb in the third-person singular to agree with the subject, *turtle*?)

4. Fire but not earthquakes really _____ me.

(a) worry   (b) scares   (c) do frighten   (d) bother   (e) have an effect on   4_____

(*Because:* _____.)
   (*Question:* Should the verb agree with the affirmative or with the negative subject?)

140 Chapter Eight

5. Neither the jury members nor the judge ―――――――――― much patience with the bickering of attorneys.

(a) have shown   (b) ever display   (c) displaying   (d) has had
(e) are in possession of

5.―――――

(Because: ――――――――――――――――――――――.)
   (Question: When subjects are joined by *neither-nor,* which subject governs the verb agreement?)

6. Once when I was a sophomore in high school, the teacher asked for a volunteer to erase the blackboard. I still don't know why I ―――――――― from my seat.

(a) risen   (b) raised   (c) had rose   (d) rose   (e) rised

6.―――――

(Because: ――――――――――――――――――――――.)

7. Chick got up, went to the living room, and set ――――――――――.

(a) the TV dial   (b) down   (c) around all evening   (d) quietly
(e) in his big chair

7.―――――

(Because: ――――――――――――――――――――――.)

8. If the applicant's response to the questions ――――――――――, we'll hire her.

(a) seem proper   (b) turn out right   (c) pleases us   (d) have good form
(e) win approval

8.―――――

(Because: ――――――――――――――――――――――.)

9. Does ―――――――――――――――――― carry the heavy pack?

(a) the scouts or the leader   (b) the horse or the mules   (c) the man and his wife
(d) the camels or the elephant   (e) my brother and I

9.―――――

(Because: ――――――――――――――――――――――.)

10. Some of my ―――――――――――――――― have gone down the drain.

(a) hard-earned money   (b) best rubber ducks   (c) drink   (d) lunch money
(e) business

10.―――――

(Because: ――――――――――――――――――――――.)

11. Mr. Borish's basset hound paddled ashore and laid _____

(a) down at the hunter's feet   (b) on the weeds, exhausted
(c) the wounded bird down on the grass   (d) exhausted on the grass
(e) there without a sound

(*Because:* _____.)

12. Either John or his parents _____ for the dented fender.

(a) agrees to pay   (b) pays   (c) has to pay   (d) offers payment
(e) want to pay.

12_____

(*Because:* _____.)

13. The nurse couldn't rise _____.

(a) the bed   (b) the patient's arm   (c) a pulse   (d) to the occasion
(e) the patient to the bed

13_____

(*Because:* _____.)

14. Freedman sat _____.

(a) his book down   (b) down on his book   (c) a candle on the table
(d) down his glass   (e) a fire in the fireplace

14_____

(*Because:* _____.)

15. Last summer I _____ so much that I can hardly look at water now.

(a) drunk   (b) swum   (c) fish   (d) drink   (e) swam

15_____

(*Because:* _____.)

16. It seems that most of your _____ brings good results.

(a) statistics   (b) good works   (c) early investments   (d) confidence
(e) studies in college

16_____

(*Because:* _____.)

17. The only one of the coach's decisions that _____ us restricts the training diet.

(a) affect   (b) bother   (c) disturb   (d) concerns   (e) trouble

17_____

(*Because:* _____.)

142   Chapter Eight

18. The senator's involvement in the clean-environment movement really _____

_____ me in his favor.

(a) push   (b) encourage   (c) prejudice   (d) biased   (e) win   18._____

(*Because:* _____.)

19. In case _____ of the guests arrive early, have something ready to serve.

(a) either   (b) one   (c) most   (d) each   (e) every one   19._____

(*Because:* _____.)

20. Only my brother, none of my sisters and neither of my parents, _____ sports.

(a) enjoys   (b) love   (c) take interest in   (d) have fun in   (e) watch   20._____

(*Because:* _____.)

Have Done, Will Do

9

How to work with ... auxiliary verbs
the future tense
the perfect tenses
sequence of tenses
consistency of tenses

How to avoid ... faulty auxiliaries
faulty sequence of tenses
shifts of verb tense

IN THE COURSE OF A DAY the average person will serve in many different capacities. According to the time and place, the person may be a student, a driver, a radio listener, a reader, a clerk, a writer, a sports fan. Like people, words change their functions as they appear in different environments.

Have and *do* are sometimes transitive verbs. That is, *have* and *do* may sometimes be used in sentences with objects—receivers of action:

> We *have* a new job.
> *Have* you a car?
> I *have* an early class this morning.
> Most students *do* very good work.
> I always *do* my chemistry first.
> *Do* the job carefully.

In those sentences *job, car, class, work, chemistry* are objects of the verbs *have* and *do*. The verbs are transitive.

But consider another way of using *have* or *do*:

> We *have* worked late today.
> I *have* run too fast.
> Most people *do* try hard.
> What *do* you think?

In those sentences the verbs *have* and *do* take no objects; rather, they are used to show some special shade of meaning in the other verbs that follow them: *worked, run, try, think*. Used in this way, *have* and *do* are *auxiliary* verbs.

An *auxiliary* verb is a helper. It works with another verb in a phrase like *have worked, have run, do try,* or *do think*.

Time for Review

Have and *do* may be used as transitive verbs, as in "I *have* a friend" or "They *do* some harm."

When used in a phrase as helper to another verb, *have* and *do* work as auxiliary verbs, as in "*have* seen" or "*do* take."

Do-It-Yourself Exercise

Using *have* or *do* as an auxiliary verb, write an appropriate verb *phrase* to complete each sentence:

According to claims, quite a few people _____ flying saucers.

Very few of our friends _____ prizes in give-away contests.

Some professional basketball stars _____ for many years with major teams.

At last I _____ my career in business.

If you ever _____ the assignment, be sure that you _____ all the errors.

We certainly _____ some new furniture.

When you _____ the neighbors, please tell them that we _____ to call them.

Checking up: Every completion should begin with *have* or *do*: *have seen, have won, do play, have played, have begun, have started, do finish, have corrected, do like, do need, do visit, have tried,* or any other verb phrases beginning with *have* or *do*.

Other Auxiliary Verbs

The verb *be* (in any of its forms, such as *am, is, are, was, were,* and so on) sometimes works as an auxiliary. Used before an *-ing* word, *be* helps to form the *progressive tense* in a verb phrase that indicates action or being that is or was *in progress*:

I *am doing* well.
She *is resting* quietly this morning.
They *were asking* questions yesterday.

Used before words like *played, taken,* or *lost*, any form of *be* helps to form the *passive voice:*

The rest of the game *was played* in silence.
The medicine *was taken* regularly.
My keys *were lost* in the gym.

(These forms, the progressive tense and the passive voice, lend themselves to a different sort of analysis as well. See Chapter 10 on *be* as a *linking verb*.)

Nine other verbs are used as auxiliary verbs: *can, could, may, might, shall, should, will, would, must*. Unlike *have* and *do*, these verbs are never used as transitive verbs; they are always auxiliaries. They work with other verb forms to form verb phrases:

> We *can say* that we *shall attend* the ceremonies.
> The early morning *should bring* cooler weather.
> If you *would write* down your address, then I *could send* you a card now and then.
> Pete says that he *may go* with us to the game.
> Surely they *will agree* that we must leave on time.

These nine auxiliary verbs differ from most other verbs in one way: These auxiliaries do not add *-s* to form the third-person singular, but remain the same for all persons:

> I *may* go; he *may* go.
> You *will* stay; she *will* stay.

The Future Tense

We have earlier distinguished the *present* and *past* tenses. The *future tense* of verbs is usually formed with the auxiliary *shall* or *will*:

Present Tense	Past Tense	Future Tense
We *enjoy* the game.	We *enjoyed* it.	We *shall enjoy* it.
She *wears* shoes.	She *wore* shoes.	She *will wear* shoes.
I *go* barefoot.	I *went* barefoot.	I *will go* barefoot.

In the future tense *will* is much more popular than *shall*. The auxiliary *shall* is used mostly in formal situations and usually only with the first person.

The Perfect Tenses

As used in grammar, the word *perfect* means "finished, completed." The *perfect tenses*, then, indicate action that is, was, or will be completed. These tenses are formed with the auxiliary verb *have:*

Present Perfect	Past Perfect	Future Perfect
We *have voted* today.	We *had voted* earlier.	We *shall have voted*.
Who *has won* a prize?	Who *had won* a prize?	Who *will have won*?
Snow *has fallen*.	Snow *had fallen*.	Snow *will have fallen*.

When the perfect tenses are used in questions, the verb phrase is often split by placement of the subject right after the auxiliary:

Have you *seen* the button that fell off my shirt?
Where *have* I *met* you before?
Had Ralph *bought* the groceries before coming home?

In forming the perfect tenses the auxiliary *have* may itself be "helped" by other auxiliary verbs:

You *may have finished* before the hour was up.
They *could have taken* the bus.
By next summer I *will have saved* enough for expenses.

When two auxiliaries are used in a verb phrase in a question, the subject is often placed between the two:

When *will* you *have completed* the job?
How *could* anyone *have forgotten* the assignment?
Should I *have recognized* your brother?

Time for Review

In addition to *have* and *do,* nine other words work as *auxiliary* verbs: *can, could, may, might, shall, should, will, would,* and *must.*

Other than *have* and *do,* the auxiliary verbs do not have special -*s* endings for the third-person singular

The *future tense* is usually formed with the auxiliary verb *shall* or *will; will* is used more often.

The *perfect tenses* indicate action that is, was, or will be completed.

The perfect tenses are formed with the auxiliary verb *have: have* seen, *has* taken, *had* gone, *will have* shown.

In questions a verb phrase is often split by placement of the subject just after *have*—or, when two auxiliaries are used, placement of the subject between the auxiliaries: "When *had* you *seen* him?" or "When *will* you *have seen* him?"

Do-It-Yourself Exercise

Write an appropriate verb in the perfect tense (as indicated) to complete each sentence:

Chapter Nine

All the supermarkets _____ their prices.
                    (present perfect)

Some companies _____ new employees.
               (present perfect)

After I _____ the doctor's office, I felt much better.
        (past perfect)

The judge couldn't read the verdict until he _____ his glasses.
                                              (past perfect)

By the time we _____ lunch, most of the good seats in the
                (present perfect)

stadium _____ with people.
         (future perfect)

What _____ you _____ since I saw you last?
      (present . . . . perfect)

Before I could run to the corner, the bus _____.
                                           (past perfect)

_____ they _____ the movie
(future . . . . perfect)

before we find a place to park the car?

Checking up: Remember the forms for the present perfect *(have* or *has)*, the past perfect *(had)*, and the future perfect *(will have)*. Check each of your completions to be sure it fits the specified perfect tense. Take special care never to write "of" when you mean "have." Quick pronunciation sometimes makes us think we are hearing "of" when the word is really "have."

Suggestions for Writing

A. Having to face a new situation can bring on fear or anxiety. Most people have at some time known what it feels like to be the new kid on the block, the new employee on the job, the new arrival in school. Tell about such feelings as you have known them, writing a passage of about 300 words and using as many *auxiliary verbs* as you can.

B. A friend of yours who is taking a course at night school has left the campus late one night and has walked to his car, where he discovers that he has lost his keys. By now the classrooms and offices are all locked up. He has only a dime in his pocket. What can he do? Advise him in a passage of about 300 words, using as many *auxiliary verbs* as you can.

C. In most places for many years young men under age 25 have been charged higher auto-insurance rates than those paid by other groups of drivers. Try to suggest some reasons why that has been so, writing a passage of about 300 words and using as many *auxiliary verbs* as you can.

After Writing: Reread your passage, circling every *transitive* verb that you have used. Draw an arrow from each circle to the object of that verb. Remembering that an irregular verb is one that forms its past tense by some means *other than* adding *-ed*, underline each *irregular* verb in your passage (even if it does not appear in the past tense in your passage).

Tenses of Auxiliaries

The tense forms of auxiliaries are rather loosely observed in conversational English, but in writing (whose purposes are usually less informal than those of speech) these forms are used:

Present Tense	Past Tense
can	could
may	might
shall	should
must	must have
will	would
have, has	had
do, does	did

Although *will* and *shall* are *present-tense* forms, they are most often used to express the future. *Must* is the *present* form but expresses the past when used with *have*: "She *must have* seen us."

Sequence of Tenses

When a sentence contains a subordinate clause, the writer must consider time sequence. Can the verb in the subordinate clause indicate a tense different from that of the verb in the independent (or main) clause? For example:

The clerk *said* that the mail *has* arrived.

That sentence would "feel" wrong to most users of English because *said* is past tense and *has* shifts into the present. Most writers take care to use the same tense in both clauses:

She *says* that the mail *has* arrived.
She *said* that the mail *had* arrived.

As a rule writers observe these patterns of sequence:

1. If the main verb is in the *present*, any tense may follow unless the happenings are clearly at the same time:

He *knows* that we *try* our best.
        that we *have tried* our best.
        that we *tried* our best.
        that we *had tried* our best.
        that we *will try* our best.
        that we *will have tried* our best.

2. If the main verb is in the *past*, only *past* tenses may follow:

She *thought* that you *went* swimming.
        that you *had gone* swimming.
        that you *might have gone* swimming.

We *had understood* that you *fell* from the bike.
        that you *had fallen* from the bike.
        that you *could have fallen* from the bike.

3 If the main verb is in the *future*, only *present* or *future* tenses may follow; the *past* cannot follow:

They *will realize* that we *have studied*.
        that we *may study*.
        that we *will study*.
        that we *will have studied*.

Do-It-Yourself Exercise

Write in each blank the appropriate form of the verb indicated in parentheses. Complete the sentence, using proper sequence of tenses:

The newspaper *reported* that a riot _____ out following the
                                                        (break)
meeting.

The crowd *will cheer* wildly when their hero _____.
                                                                (arrive)

Surely you *knew* that Frank _____ Spanish.
                                      (speak)

Most of the class *will have finished* before I _____.
                                                               (begin)

No one *had discovered* where she _____ the money.
                                             (hide)

You *might have done* some exercises while you _____.
                                                    (wait)

The counselor *thanked* Larry for all the help the club _____
                                                              (give)
to the college.

Although I _____ the picture once I _____
              (see)   (want)
to see it again.

Checking up: Since there are several appropriate completions in some of the sentences, try writing a second version that would be equally good for each sentence. Refer to the patterns cited and illustrated just above this exercise. Can you tell in each of your exercise sentences why the sequence of tenses is proper? Remember that one *past tense* (or *past perfect tense*) verb requires another *past* (or *past perfect*) verb in the sequence. But after a *future* (or *future perfect*) verb the *past* cannot be used.

Consistency of Tense

In writing a passage that develops a single train of thought with many sentences, a writer produces some confusion if he shifts unnecessarily from one tense to another. Consider how the train of thought is jolted when such a shift occurs:

> We *bought* a ticket and *were* about to get on the bus. Then Uncle Jack *remembered* that he *had left* his glasses at home. Naturally, without his glasses Uncle Jack *will have* a terrible trip, so we *turn* around and *go* home again. There *were* the glasses, right where he *had left* them.

Most of the verbs in the passage are in the *past*, but without need or warning the reader is suddenly bounced into the future (*will have* a terrible trip) and then into the present (*turn* around and *go* home). The writer needs to revise, using past tense verbs all the way through the passage:

> . . . Naturally, without his glasses Uncle Jack *would have* a terrible trip, so we *turned* around and *went* home again. There *were* the glasses, right where he *had left* them.

Time for Review

When a sentence contains a subordinate clause, a proper *sequence of tense* must be followed:

If the main verb is in the *present,* any tense may follow, unless the happenings are clearly at the same time.

Chapter Nine

If the main verb is in the *past*, only *past* tenses may follow.
If the main verb is in the *future*, only *present* or *future* tense may follow.

In a passage containing several sentences the verbs should not shift unnecessarily from one tense to another.

Do-It-Yourself Exercise

Write in each blank the appropriate *past-tense* form of each suggested verb, being sure to maintain a proper consistency of tense throughout this passage:

On the Halloween of 1970 my medical corps unit _____ (receive) a shipment of hot pumpkin pie from Da Nang. When the helicopter _____ (have) gone, and the dust from the chopper _____ (settle), we suddenly _____ (hear) the crack of rifle fire. "Incoming!" somebody _____ (shout). Then I _____ (see) our lieutenant face-down in the dirt. A little pool of blood _____ (grow) below his jaw, where the sniper fire _____ (have) hit. I _____ (run) to him. I _____ (know) he _____ (can) not breathe. Hardly thinking, I _____ (pull) a sterile knife from my pack and quickly _____ (make) a small incision in the lieutenant's throat. He _____ (can) breathe again, but the blood still _____ (flow) from his wound. We _____ (can) not evacuate him to the field hospital; the 'copter _____(will)_____ not land again, because the sniper

fire _____(turn)_____ our area into a "hot" zone. In a couple of hours

the lieutenant _____(go)_____ into shock and _____(die)_____

with me at his side. I nearly _____(choke)_____ with anger,

and I _____(wonder)_____ whether I _____(do)_____ the

right thing as a corpsman. I _____(feel)_____ depressed for the next week.

But one day the lieutenant's parents _____(call)_____ me, all the way

from the States. They _____(say)_____ the chaplain _____(tell)_____

them I _____(have)_____ tried to save their son's life, and they _____(want)_____

to thank me. Nothing _____(can)_____ bring the lieutenant back, but

after that phone call my depression _____(leave)_____, and I _____(don't)_____

worry any more about being a medical corpsman.

Checking up: All the verbs of the passage should be in the past tense: *had, saw, grew, ran, could, would, went, felt,* and verbs ending in *-ed: received, settled, flowed, died, called,* and so on. Could the passage be revised in the *present* tense? What forms would be used in the present-tense version for the verbs *have, shout, grow, go, flow, turn, die*?

Continue this exercise by writing *present-tense* forms of the suggested verbs in this passage, maintaining a proper consistency of tense throughout:

It's hard for a person not to move fast when everything is moving fast around him. If he _____(move)_____ slower, he _____(see)_____

more, _____(hear)_____ more, and _____(enjoy)_____ more; still

he _____ slow down, because the world _____
   (cannot)   (whirl)

around him, and he sort of _____ caught up. Then one day
                              (get)

he _____ around him and _____ where he
   (look)   (find)

and the crowd _____ gone: nowhere. Then he
                 (have)

_____ that he _____ to slow down.
  (know)   (have)

Checking up: Since the subject of most verbs in the passage is *he*, the verbs will be in the *third-person singular* forms: *moves, sees, hears, enjoys,* and so on. But "he and the crowd" is a paired subject forming a plural; therefore, "he and the crowd *have* gone."

Continue this exercise with one more passage, this time writing appropriate *future-tense* verbs, maintaining a proper consistency of tense throughout:

Soon the dawn _____, and the first rays of the sun
                 (break)

_____ through the cracks in my curtains. My
   (shine)

dog _____ at my door and _____ to push
     (scratch)   (manage)

it open. I _____ bacon frying, and the aroma of coffee
              (smell)

_____ into my room. The dog _____
   (drift)   (jump)

up beside me, and of course he _____ that he _____
                                  (think)   (bring)

me back to life. But I _____ my new day on the sun and the
                          (blame)

smells from the kitchen. Anyway, neither of us _____ the
                                                  (refuse)

meeting.

Checking up: Most of the verbs in the passage should be formed with the auxiliary *will: will break, will shine,* and so on. The subordinate clause beginning with *that* may take the present-perfect tense: " . . . of course he will think that he *has brought* me back to life."

Suggestions for Writing

D. Imagine yourself observing what happens in a hospital when a major disaster has occurred in the city. Tell about the imaginary experience in a passage of about 300 words, using as many *auxiliary verbs* and *perfect tenses* as you can.
E. Recall (or imagine) an experience in which a person undergoes the stress of extreme cold (as in a northern winter out of doors) or extreme heat (as in a tropical desert) for several days without shelter. Write a passage of about 300 words relating what that person does to keep himself alive. Use as many *auxiliary verbs* and *perfect tenses* as you can.
F. What will city life be like as the 20th century comes to its conclusion with 2001? Write a passage of about 250 words telling what your life or that of your friends might be then. Use chiefly the *future tense*.

After Writing: Reread your passage and underline every *verb phrase*. Has each sentence followed a proper sequence of tenses? Check the entire passage for consistency of tense. For extra practice, revise the passage into a different tense, such as the *past* or the *present*.

QUIZ 9

Using Auxiliary Verbs

In the blank write the item that most effectively completes the sentence; then mark the *letter* of that item on your answer blank. After marking your choice, explain briefly why you chose it (*Because:* . . .).

Example: Until now the paying of bills *has not played* a big part in my life.

(a) had not played   (b) has not played   (c) does not play   (d) do not play
(e) have not played

Ex. *b*

(*Because:* "*Now*" *requires present tense;* "*has*" *agrees with paying*.)

1. One of my closest friends has _____ drums since he was a kid.

(a) play   (b) a set of   (c) practice   (d) had a set of   (e) took lessons on

1. _____

(*Because:* _____.)
    (*Question:* Which completion will go with *has* and also be consistent with the past-tense *was*?)

2. After the drudgery of the week the average office worker _____ the weekend of fun that is coming.

(a) would enjoy   (b) might look forward to   (c) will probably delight in
(d) have to relish   (e) couldn't relax for

2. _____

(*Because:* _____.)
    (*Question:* Which auxiliary verb agrees with the subject, *worker*, and is consistent with the future tense suggested by *is coming*?)

3. When Alicia was a child, her father _____ her to her first Mardi Gras.

(a) must take   (b) will have taken   (c) has taken   (d) took   (e) may take

3. _____

(*Because:* _____.)
    (*Question:* Which verb is consistent with the simple past-tense *was*?)

4. If you will pick me up early enough, we _____ make it to class on time.

(a) could   (b) may   (c) would   (d) have   (e) might

4. _____

(*Because:* _____.)
    (*Question:* Which auxiliary verb goes with *make* and is consistent with the future "*will pick* me up"?)

158 Chapter Nine

5. Mary _____ the shopping by the time we get home.

(a) will have done (b) had finished (c) might do (d) shall have done
(e) could have done

5.____

(*Because:* _____.)

   (*Question:* Which verb phrase is consistent with the suggested future tense of "by the time we *get* home"?)

6. What time _____ the assignment?

(a) you finished (b) she did finish (c) does the professor announce
(d) had he did (e) must we of done

6.____

(*Because:* _____.)

7. The college president or our sponsors usually _____ at the club meetings.

(a) has appeared (b) does speak (c) have supervised (d) will spoken
(e) have showed up

7.____

(*Because:* _____.)

8. Before the trial opened last week, the judge _____ reporters from the courtroom.

(a) had barred (b) has banned (c) may ban (d) can bar
(e) will exclude

8.____

(*Because:* _____.)

9. Even if you have tried the soup, you _____ know for sure that the sandwiches aren't good.

(a) must have (b) couldn't (c) can't (d) might not (e) cannot have

9.____

(*Because:* _____.)

10. Felix, but not his friends, _____ us when we start our new organization.

(a) have joined (b) had joined (c) has joined (d) will joined
(e) may join

10.____

(*Because:* _____.)

11. Dina probably _____ any job she wants after she graduates from business school.

(a) might get (b) could get (c) can get (d) will have get
(e) have gotten

11.____

(*Because:* _____.)

Have Done, Will Do   159

12. When the sun comes up tomorrow, you and I ——————————— been up for two hours.

(a) could have (b) will have (c) might of (d) might have (e) must of   12_____

(*Because:* ———————————————————————————.)

13. ——————————— either of the players know the rules yet?

(a) Has (b) Do (c) Does (d) Might (e) Shall   13_____

(*Because:* ———————————————————————————.)

14. When ——————————— expect to receive the shipment?

(a) may I (b) I may (c) might I (d) I must (e) shall they   14_____

(*Because:* ———————————————————————————.)

15. The team have packed their gear and now ——————————— to meet the bus.

(a) has (b) do (c) must go (d) could of gone (e) shall go   15_____

(*Because:* ———————————————————————————.)

16. ——————————— go with us when we tour the plant?

(a) He can (b) He might (c) May he (d) Shall she (e) She must   16_____

(*Because:* ———————————————————————————.)

17. Mrs. Valera announced that the new shipment of supplies ——————————— arrived from the city.

(a) has (b) could (c) cannot have (d) had already (e) might of   17_____

(*Because:* ———————————————————————————.)

18. The whole family was glad that ——————————— new neighbors next door.

(a) it has (b) they have (c) they will have (d) it had (e) it could of had   18_____

(*Because:* ———————————————————————————.)

19. Some of the recent news ——————————— us that times are sure to improve.

(a) has convince (b) do convince (c) does convince (d) must shown
(e) had proved to   19_____

(*Because:* ———————————————————————————.)

20. We ——————————— gone away without locking our doors.

(a) cannot (b) will not (c) never had (d) shouldn't of (e) couldn't   20_____

(*Because:* ———————————————————————————.)

Be, Seem, Sound   10

How to work with . . . linking verbs
noun complements
adjective complements
active voice
passive voice

How to avoid . . . faulty verb agreement
overuse of passive voice

WE HAVE CONSIDERED action verbs and auxiliary verbs, showing that *have, do, will, can, may, shall,* and *must* are often used as auxiliaries, or helpers, to form verb phrases. We now turn to the verb *be*.

The verb *be* is one of the most irregular in English; that is, *be* has more changes of form than most verbs have:

	Present	Past	Future	Present Perfect	Past Perfect
I	am	was	will be	have been	had been
you, we	are	were	will be	have been	had been
it, she, he	is	was	will be	has been	had been

In any of these forms the verb *be* may be used as an auxiliary verb, forming a verb phrase with an *-ing* word:

The flowers *are blooming* in the fields.

Rain *has been falling* during the night.

You *were telling* me about your work.

Those verb phrases indicate actions that are or were in progress. They form the *progressive* tenses.

The *be* verbs also may be used with *-ed* forms:

Concerts *are played* here every Friday.

When our friends appeared, our work *was shoved* aside.

Most of the words *had been erased*.

Those verb phrases (the auxiliary *be* with an *-ed* form) produce the passive voice, a form in which the subject does not do the action but is acted upon. (For more on the passive voice, see pp. 172–175.)

Time for Review

The verb *be* is an irregular verb; its forms include *am, is, are, was, were,* and the verb phrases beginning with auxiliaries: *will be, have been, can be, should be,* and so on.

Forms of *be* may be used as auxiliaries.

As an auxiliary with an *-ing* word, a *be* form is used to make the progressive tense: *is giving, are speeding,* and so on.

As an auxiliary with an *-ed* word, a *be* form is used to make the passive voice: *am urged, is replaced,* and so on.

Do-It-Yourself Exercise

Write in each blank a verb phrase with *be* as an auxiliary:

Having escaped from its owner, the old dog _____ at a passing truck.

Although the weather is cold, I _____ no coat.

When only 12 years old, my father _____ his own money by selling newspapers.

During the show she noticed that her friends _____ in the front row.

While the Martins were at work one day, their house _____, and they lost most of their belongings.

An egg is hard boiled if it _____ five minutes.

Checking up: Every phrase you have written in this exercise should begin with a form of *be* and end with an *-ing* or *-ed* word. You may have written such phrases as *was barking, am wearing, was earning, were seated, was burglarized, has been boiled.*

Other Uses of "Be"

The forms of *be* do not always appear as auxiliaries. Consider these sentences:

My aunt *is* a nurse.
Lewis and Ben *were* friends.
Sid *may be* eligible, although he *is* overweight.

The words *nurse* and *friends* are nouns, not verbs. The words *eligible* and *overweight* are adjectives, not verbs. Thus the *be* verbs in those sentences are not auxiliaries, since they do not begin verb phrases. They are used, rather, to link the subject to a noun or adjective, and they are called *linking verbs*.

Linking verbs work to form two special patterns, the *noun complement* pattern and the *adjective complement* pattern.

The Noun Complement Pattern

A noun complement is a noun that either renames the subject (as in "Millie is *my aunt*") or names a class that the subject is a member of (as in "My aunt is *a nurse*"). *Millie* is another name for my aunt; *a nurse* names a class of which my aunt is a member.

Consider these noun complements:

> The winner is *Secretariat*. (Renames the subject.)
> Secretariat is *a horse*. (Classifies the subject.)
> Next Friday is *my birthday*. (Renames the subject.)
> My cousin is *a mechanic*. (Classifies the subject.)
> This building is *the gym*. (Renames the subject.)
> You really are *a friend*. (Classifies the subject.)

Time for Review

The verb *be* is not always an auxiliary verb.

When followed by a noun structure or by an adjective, *be* is a *linking verb*.

A *linking verb* is used to link a subject to a noun complement or to an adjective complement.

A *noun complement* is a noun structure that renames or classifies the subject.

Do-It-Yourself Exercise

Write in each blank an appropriate *noun complement* to rename or classify the subject and complete the sentence:

My best *friend* is _____.
                 (renames the subject)

The *Daily Times* is a _____.
                 (classifies the subject)

One well-known athlete is _____.
                 (renames the subject)

Many American voters are _____.
                 (classifies the subject)

George Washington was the first _____.
                 (renames the subject)

Cardinals are _____.
                 (classifies the subject)

Checking up: Be sure that each completion is a *noun* and that it does appropriately rename or classify the subject. The final sentence may say that Cardinals are *birds, priests,* or *ballplayers*. Some possibilities for the other *noun complements:* Mike (or any other name), *newspaper, Hank Aaron* (or any other athlete), *Democrats* or *Republicans*, *President*.

The Adjective Complement Pattern

The verb *is, are, was, were,* or any other form of *be* may be followed by a different sort of complement:

> The skies are *blue*.
> The sun is *bright*.
> We are *happy*.

The words *blue, bright,* and *happy* are not nouns but *adjectives*; they are describers. In these sentences those words describe the subject and serve as complements following *be* verbs. The words *blue, bright,* and *happy* in these sentences are *adjective complements*.

An adjective complement is a *describer* of the subject. It is linked to the subject by a verb like *is, are, was, were*. Consider these adjective complements:

> After football practice my shirt is *dirty*. (Describes the subject, *shirt*.)
> Your music is too *loud*. (Describes the subject, *music*.)
> Every window in the place is *broken*. (Describes the subject, *window*.)
> The answer to your question is *obvious*. (Describes the subject, *answer*.)

Noun or Adjective?

It is important to distinguish the noun complement from the adjective complement. Which of these sentences contains an *adjective complement*?

> Sally is beautiful.
> Sally is a beauty.
> Sally is a beautiful girl.

Of course, *beautiful* is an adjective. In the first of those sentences it appears as an adjective complement describing the subject, Sally. In the third of those sentences *beautiful* describes *girl*, not Sally; the sentence contains a noun complement but not an adjective complement. The second sentence also has a noun complement pattern, since *a beauty* is a noun phrase. Consider a few other sentences:

> Theo is inexperienced. (Adjective complement.)
> Theo is an inexperienced player. (Noun phrase as noun complement.)
> This book is heavy. (Adjective complement.)
> This is a heavy book. (Noun phrase as noun complement.)

The thing to recognize is whether an adjective appears as a complement modifying the subject—or merely as a modifier for a noun complement.

Adjective or Adverb?

An adjective complement must be an *adjective*, not an adverb. Consider these sentences, which show an awkward use of an adverb in place of an adjective complement:

I feel *badly* today.
This milk has turned *sourly*.
This coffee tastes very *well*.

The adverbs *badly, sourly,* and *well* cannot properly be used to describe the subjects *I, milk,* and *coffee*. The adverbs, awkwardly used after linking verbs, should be revised as adjective complements:

I feel *bad* today.
This milk has turned *sour*.
This coffee tastes very *good*.

On the other hand, it would be awkward to use adjectives if the verbs were not linking verbs but action or process verbs instead:

I performed *bad* today.
The doctor talked *excited*.
The coffee splashed *sloppy* into her lap.

The adjectives *bad, excited,* and *sloppy* cannot properly be used to describe the actions *performed, talked,* and *splashed*. The adjectives, awkwardly used after action or process verbs, should be revised as adverbs:

I performed *badly* today.
The doctor talked *excitedly*.
The coffee splashed *sloppily* into her lap.

Time for Review

The *be* verbs (*is, are, were, was, have been,* and so on) are usually followed by *complements*.

The two sorts of complement are the *noun complement* and the *adjective complement*.

An *adjective complement* is an adjective that describes the subject after a linking verb.

An adjective that appears in a noun phrase cannot be used as an adjective complement; the noun phrase, however, may be used as a *noun complement*.

An adverb properly modifies a verb and cannot be used as an adjective complement.

An adjective properly modifies a noun and cannot be used to modify a verb.

Do-It-Yourself Exercise

Write in each blank an appropriate *adjective complement* to describe the subject and complete the sentence:

The moon is very _____ tonight.

Friday morning I was _____ for my math test.

I thought the book about whales was _____. (Describe the *book*.)

The voters are _____ enough to make good choices most of the time. (Describe the subject, *voters*.)

The salami sandwich I had for lunch was _____. (Describe the subject, *sandwich*.)

Nobody is _____. (Describe the subject, *nobody*.)

The dentist said he felt _____ about having to remove my baby tooth. (Describe the subject, *dentist*.)

Rita's new dress looks very _____ on her. (Describe the subject, *dress*.)

Checking up: Some possible adjective complements appropriate to these sentences: *fascinating, intelligent, perfect, excellent, tasty, bright, beautiful, excited, anxious, funny, informed*. Be sure you have not used adverbs; the dentist felt *bad* or *sorry*, not *badly* or *sorrily*; Rita's dress looks *great* or *beautiful* or *charming*, not *greatly, beautifully,* or *charmingly*.

The Linking Verb

Because the forms of *be* are used to link a subject and its noun complement or adjective complement, the *be* verbs are *linking verbs*:

Chapter Ten

>I *am* curious.
>Who *was* first?
>This steak *is* really tough.
>Some of his comments *were* ridiculous.
>Those apples *are* delicious.
>You *will be* sorry tomorrow.

Certain other verbs sometimes mean almost the same thing as *is, are, was,* or *were*:

>Nothing in the world *remains* unchanged.
>Suddenly the lights *turned* green.
>All your answers *seem* perfect.
>Enemies sometimes *become* friends.
>The guests *appear* pleased.
>You *seem* tired.
>He *has grown* taller since I saw him last.
>Today everything *goes* right!
>The show *proved* especially exciting.
>My brother *acts* ridiculous.
>The liquid *gets* dark during the experiment.
>Something about her *rings* true.
>I *stand* corrected.

Try rereading each of those sentences using *is, are, were, was,* or *has been*. Such verbs are in a sense interchangeable with *be* verbs; all are *linking verbs*, used to link complements with their subjects.

Another set of verbs also may work as *linking verbs*. They are the *sense* verbs, those associated with the five senses:

>Your hair *looks* shiny.
>The siren *sounds* shrill.
>Velvet seldom *feels* rough.
>This drink *tastes* sour.
>My bouquet *smells* beautiful.

Time for Review

All of the *be* verbs may be used as *linking verbs*.

Verbs used as synonyms for *be* verbs may also be *linking verbs*.

The *sense* verbs *(look, sound, feel, taste, smell)* are often *linking verbs*.

Linking verbs are used to link a subject and its *noun complement* or *adjective complement*.

Do-It-Yourself Exercise

Write an appropriate *linking verb* to fit each blank. Do not use the same verb twice:

No doubt the air _____ cold when you stepped out.

My grandmother _____ forgetful in her last years.

Little Gary _____ such a genius when he recites!

If the apple _____ bitter, wait till it _____ ripe.

Oh, rock _____ good music, but it _____ too loud.

What shall we do if something _____ wrong?

A certain air about the man _____ phony; he _____ an impostor.

You can tell autumn is coming when the leaves _____ brown

I _____ calm in spite of the excitement.

"Hey, man, _____ cool!" the suspect said to the officer.

Checking up: You should have used thirteen different *linking verbs* to complete the sentences, including *be* verbs, sense verbs, and other such synonyms as *grew, seems, gets, goes, appears, turn, remain, stay, keep, proves*.

Verb Agreement

Like most other verbs, the linking verbs should agree with their subjects in person and in number; that is, a singular subject requires a singular verb, and a plural subject requires a plural verb:

His *friend is* a newcomer.
His *friends are* musicians.
The election *was* close.
The elections *were* always close.
I *am* a football fan.
We *have been* football fans for years.

Since the noun complement renames or classifies the subject in a sentence, the subject and the complement are often interchangeable:

His *friend* is a *newcomer*.
The *newcomer* is his *friend*.

In a noun-complement sentence the linking verb always agrees with the subject, not with the noun complement:

My mother's *specialty is* pancakes.
Pancakes are my mother's specialty.
Bud's *hobby is* coins.
Coins are Bud's hobby.

A special agreement problem appears when the subject in a noun-complement sentence is a subordinate clause, a word group with its own subject-verb combination:

What I like best is hotdogs.
What she asked for was two eggs.
Why you jumped is a mystery to me.
What disturbs me is your tapping feet.

As those examples show, the linking verb agrees with the subject (the subordinate clause), which is considered singular. The verb does not agree with the noun complement.

Another agreement problem may occur when the word *there* is used before a linking verb. *There* is used only for the sake of rhythm in such a sentence; it does not serve as a subject. The linking verb will agree with the real subject, which usually follows the verb:

There *is* a *cloud* in the sky.
There *are* two *sandwiches* in the refrigerator.
There *has been* no *sunshine* all week.
Suddenly there *appeared* (or *appears*) a *dragon*.
Yes, there *seem* to be several *nicks* in the handle.

Time for Review

All forms of *be (am, is, are, was, were, have been,* and so on) may be used as *linking verbs*.

Other verbs that mean almost the same thing as *be* verbs may be used as linking verbs, including *seem, appear, become, go, get, grow, prove, turn, remain, continue, keep, stay, act, ring, stand*.

The *sense* verbs (associated with the five senses) may also be used as linking verbs: *look, sound, feel, taste, smell*.

A *linking verb* is used to join a subject to its noun complement or adjective complement.

A linking verb *agrees* (in person and in number) with the *subject*, not with the noun complement.

When a subordinate clause (such as *What I like* or *What you saw*) is used as a subject, it is considered singular; the verb should agree with the *singular*.

When *there* is used before a linking verb, the verb agrees with the real subject, which usually follows the verb.

Do-It-Yourself Exercise

Write in each blank an appropriate *linking verb* to agree with the subject and complete the sentence; use *present* tense:

The topic of today's lecture _____ roses.

Roses _____ the topic for the week.

I _____ a good swimmer since my childhood.

Norton's girlfriend _____ an excellent swimmer too.

My order _____ three hotdogs and an ice cream cone.

Three hotdogs and an ice cream cone _____ my order.

What happens now _____ a surprise to me.

Chapter Ten

When she ——————— a famous dancer, we'll applaud.

There ——————— very few hippies in barber shops.

What I want to know ——————— the dates of the two World Wars.

Tomorrow's assignment ——————— three pages in the blue book.

Six pages in the red book ——————— the assignment for Thursday.

No matter how bad times get, Sheila ——————— a good friend.

When there ——————— gray skies, these indoor games ——————— a great pastime.

Checking up: Be sure that your linking verbs agree with their *subjects*, not with the noun complements. The subordinate clauses as subjects *(What happens now, What I want to know)* are considered *singular* and should take singular verbs. The word *there* is not a subject; when that word appears before a linking verb, the subject follows the verb.

Suggestions for Writing

A. Many health experts have pointed to exercise as the road to good health. But *why* is exercise good for the body? What happens to the muscles, the heart, the blood vessels when the body gets too little exercise? Write your answers in a passage of about 300 words, using as many *linking verbs* as you can. Underline each linking verb.
B. Exercise is just as important for the mind as it is for the muscles. What happens to a person's mind when it is inactive? Write your answer in a passage of about 300 words, using as many *linking verbs* as you can. Underline each linking verb.
C. The five senses help people to know that they are alive. How do sights, sounds, smells, tastes, and textures keep us from boredom and protect us from danger? Write some answers in a passage of about 300 words, using as many *linking verbs* as you can. Underline each linking verb.

After Writing: Reread your passage to make sure that your *linking verbs* (including *sense* verbs) agree with their subjects. Circle every noun complement or adjective complement. Can you properly label each of them as NC or AC?

Active and Passive Voice

One sort of adjective complement is the adjective made from a verb, such as *played, brought, taken,* and so on. Such adjectives often appear in sentences like these:

The game was *played* at night.

Our furniture was *brought* from our old house.

Three plates were *taken* off the table.

When these verbal adjectives (formed from verbs) are used in such sentences, the subjects are not *doers* but *be-ers*. That is, the *game*, the *furniture*, and the *plates* do not do anything in those sentences; rather, they have something *done to them*. The subjects are not active, but passive.

When the subject of a sentence does not do anything but has something done to it, the sentence is in the *passive voice*. Notice how a sentence in the passive voice can be rewritten in the *active voice*:

Passive	Active
The apple pie was baked by Dan's wife.	Dan's wife baked the apple pie.
New economic controls were announced by the President.	The President announced new economic controls.
All the seats have been taken by spectators.	Spectators have taken all the seats.
Stella's bracelet was given to her by her mother.	Stella's mother gave her the bracelet.

Consistency of *voice* helps the writer avoid awkwardness. If two or more ideas are used in a sentence, it is usually best to write them both in the active voice or both in the passive voice—unless there is clearly good reason for shifting from one to the other. Consider the awkwardness in these sentences:

We received our paychecks, and they were deposited in the bank immediately.

After Luisa's phone rang, it was answered by her.

The class came to attention, and a notebook was opened by each student.

Revision might improve those sentences; the writer might keep the active voice throughout:

We received our paychecks, and we deposited them in the bank immediately.

After Luisa's phone rang, she answered it.

The class came to attention, and each student opened a notebook.

Active voice emphasizes the *doer* in a sentence, but *passive voice* emphasizes the *receiver* of the action:

Someone kicked me in the shin.

I was kicked in the shin by someone.

Across the street a *policeman* was giving a driver a ticket.

Across the street a *driver* was being given a ticket by a policeman.

Obviously it takes more words to write a *passive voice* sentence than it does to write an *active voice* one.

Chapter Ten

Time for Review

A sentence whose subject *does* the action is in the *active voice*.

A sentence whose subject *receives* the action is in the *passive voice*.

Active voice emphasizes an action or the *doer* of the action.

Passive voice emphasizes the *receiver* of the action.

Passive voice requires more words than does active voice.

Do-It-Yourself Exercise

Using the content suggested as *doer, action,* and *receiver*, write a sentence in the active voice or in the passive voice (as called for) for each group:

Doer: *ten students*   Action: *achieved*   Receiver: *scholarships*

(Passive Voice) _____

_____

Doer: *coach*   Action: *criticized*   Receiver: *quarterback*

(Active Voice) _____

_____

Doer: *most Americans*   Action: *read*   Receiver: *newspapers*

(Passive Voice) _____

_____

Doer: *prisoners*   Action: *dynamited*   Receiver: *cell-block doors*

(Passive Voice) _____

_____

Doer: *capacity audience*   Action: *gave ovation*   Receiver: *speaker*

(Active Voice) _____

_____

Doer: *FBI agents*   Action: *arrested*   Receiver: *kidnaper*

(Passive Voice) _____

_____

Doer: *unjust penalties*   Action: *discouraged*   Receiver: *our team*

(Active Voice) _____

(Passive Voice) _____

_____

Doer: *thieves*   Action: *steal*   Receiver: *500 cars a week*

(Passive Voice) _____

_____

Checking up: Passive-voice sentences usually have *be*-verbs in phrases like *were achieved, are read, were dynamited, was arrested, are stolen*. The final item (about the 500 cars) probably doesn't need a *by thieves* phrase; if the action is stealing, we don't need to be told it was by thieves. When you can save words without sacrificing an idea, do so.

Suggestions for Writing:

D. If you have never received a ticket for illegal parking, speeding, or running a red light, perhaps someone you know has had that experience. In a passage of about 300 words tell how it happened. Use *passive voice* as much as you can in the passage.
E. The struggle against "red tape" in the world seems never to end. Filling out application forms and other kinds of questionnaires is part of that struggle. Describe one such experience, writing a passage of about 300 words. Use the *passive voice* as much as you can.
F. A person who "blows his top" in anger usually wishes later that he hadn't. Write a passage of about 300 words, telling of such an experience. Use the *passive voice* as much as you can.

After Writing: Reread your passage to be sure that all verbs agree with their subjects. Are you satisfied that the passive voice tells the story as well as you can tell it? Try revising the passage, using only the *active voice*. Then compare the two versions. Which version takes more words? Which version seems more interesting in style?

QUIZ 10

Using Linking Verbs

In the blank write the item that most effectively completes the sentence; then mark the *letter* of that item on your answer blank. After marking your choice, explain briefly why you chose it (*Because:* . . .).

Example: My favorite food ____*is*____ potatoes and gravy.
(a) were   (b) have been   (c) are   (d) is   (e) seem to be   Ex *d*
(*Because:* Singular "is" agrees with subject, "food".)

1. There _____ three good ways to avoid a collision.

(a) was   (b) were   (c) am   (d) is   (e) appears   1_____

(*Because:* _____.)
(*Question:* Which verb agrees with the plural subject, *ways*?)

2. Thanks for the bouquet of roses; they smell _____ here in my hospital room.

(a) marvelously   (b) well   (c) delightful   (d) especially nicely
(e) exquisitely   2_____

(*Because:* _____.)
(*Question:* Which completion forms a proper *adjective* complement?)

3. What I want _____ some new answers to old questions.

(a) was   (b) is   (c) were   (d) was   (e) seem to be   3_____

(*Because:* _____.)
(*Question:* Which linking verb agrees with the subject, *What I want* and is in proper sequence with the present-tense *want*?)

4. None of the cornstalks _____ taller than any other.

(a) seems   (b) appear   (c) grow   (d) are   (e) get   4_____

(*Because:* _____.)
(*Question:* Which linking verb agrees with the subject, *None*? The plural *cornstalks* is not the subject.)

5. The doctor took out his stethoscope. I opened my shirt, and _____.

(a) he listened to my heartbeat   (b) my heartbeat was listened to
(c) my heart was examined   (d) the examination was begun   5_____
(e) I was thoroughly examined

Chapter Ten

6. The singing star waved from the car, and all the girls said he looked _____

_____ in his mod suit and cowboy hat.
(a) really good (b) very well (c) so sharply (d) handsomely
(e) real nicely

6._____

(*Because:* _____.)

7. Jake's pants or his coat invariably _____ too long.
(a) look (b) seem (c) are (d) was much (e) were

7._____

(*Because:* _____.)

8. Everybody with a passport to the Asian nations _____ subject to customs inspection.
(a) were (b) becomes (c) have to be (d) seem (e) are now

8._____

(*Because:* _____.)

9. What I would like to see _____ more open parklands.
(a) was (b) have been (c) is (d) are (e) were

9._____

(*Because:* _____.)

10. The number of applicants for each available job _____ very large.
(a) prove to be (b) were usually (c) seem to be very (d) are remarkably
(e) appears to be

10._____

(*Because:* _____.)

11. After all those weeks that I had spent living on nothing but jungle food, that hamburger really tasted _____.
(a) well (b) lusciously (c) deliciously (d) good (e) marvelously

11._____

(*Because:* _____.)

12. This group of films _____ by the distributor.
(a) rate X (b) were rated X (c) have been rated X (d) was rated X
(e) rating X

12._____

(*Because:* _____.)

13. Usually there _____ a polar bear and her cubs frolicking in a tank at the zoo.
(a) was (b) were (c) seems to be (d) has been (e) is

13._____

(*Because:* _____.)

14. Whenever I went to visit my grandfather, _____ fishing on the lake.

(a) I was taken   (b) he took me   (c) fun was had   (d) I would be taken
(e) we could be found

14._____

(Because: _____.*)*

15. We learned that butter would _____ if kept in a bucket submerged in the stream.

(a) stay purely   (b) keep freshly   (c) remain fresh   (d) get hardly
(e) taste more sweetly

15._____

(Because: _____.*)*

16. My favorite dish _____ strawberries in cream.

(a) have always been   (b) turn out to be   (c) were   (d) now is   (e) are

16._____

(Because: _____.*)*

17. There _____ birds in the tree at our corner.

(a) was always lots of   (b) always seems to be   (c) never has been any
(d) was a nest of   (e) does not seem to be any

17._____

(Because: _____.*)*

18. What the assignment calls for _____ five paragraphs about money.

(a) is   (b) are   (c) were   (d) have been   (e) seem to be

18._____

(Because: _____.*)*

19. You can see by Terry's eyes that she does not feel _____.

(a) happily today   (b) well about the exam   (c) very good   (d) perfectly
(e) sadly about it

19._____

(Because: _____.*)*

20. After the flowers wilted, they didn't smell _____.

(a) very well   (b) so sweetly   (c) fragrantly   (d) so good
(e) so beautifully

20._____

(Because: _____.*)*

Which 11

How to work with . . . adjectives
determiners
comparatives and superlatives
compound adjectives
adjective phrases
adjective clauses

How to avoid . . . faulty parallelism
danglers
misplaced modifiers

GOOD READERS USUALLY ASK QUESTIONS as they read. They want to know details, at least enough details to make them see, hear, taste, and touch things with their imagination. Good writers try to supply those details by answering the readers' questions in advance.

One of the ways of satisfying a reader's curiosity about details is to use descriptive words and phrases. If the writer mentions *houses*, the reference may be too general; the reader will want to know *which* houses, *how many, how big, where, what kind, what color*. Words and phrases that supply those descriptive details are *adjectives:* "I had always wondered about *those curious old brownstone* houses *rising four stories above the streets of uptown Manhattan*."

The adjectives in that sentence answer questions: Which houses?—*those*. What sort of houses?—*old, brownstone*. How big?—*rising four stories*. Where?—*above the streets of uptown Manhattan*. Such *adjectives* are the topic of this chapter, which deals with several different kinds of adjectives and how to use them effectively.

Questions About Nouns

Although adjectives do answer questions about nouns, not every answer to such a question is an adjective. The answer to "Which man?" may be "Tom Jones." The name is a proper noun, not an adjective. The answer to "Which country?" may be "China"—a proper noun, not an adjective. So when we say that adjectives answer questions, we do not mean to say that they are the *only* way to answer questions about nouns.

Consider a few possible ways to use adjectives to answer a *which* question:

Which man?

that man
the man *in the blue shirt*
the man *with the dark hair*
the man *standing by the door*
the man *followed by autograph hunters*
the *worried* man
the *angry* man
the man *who just slammed the door*

All the italicized words and word groups are *adjectives*. Each of them modifies the noun *man*, supplying descriptive detail.

Time for Review

Words, phrases, and clauses that describe nouns are *adjectives*.

Adjectives supply descriptive detail, providing answers to possible questions, such as *which?*

Do-It-Yourself Exercise

Answer these questions by writing in each blank an *adjective* (in a word or word group) that will describe the noun:

Which picture? The _____ picture.

Which child? The child _____ .

Which house? The _____ house.

Which freedom? The freedom _____ .

Which sweater? The _____ sweater.

Which street? The street _____ .

Which flag? The _____ flag.

Which song? The song _____ .

Checking up: As your completed phrases probably show, one-word adjectives usually go before the noun, and word-group adjectives usually go after the noun. Such adjectives as *square* or *first* may tell which picture. Other possible adjectives to answer these questions: *yellow* house, child *with the dog*, freedom *of speech*, *torn* sweater, street *where I live*, *American* flag, song *that we sang*. Are your entries similar to these?

More Adjective Questions

Of course, *which?* is not the only question that can be answered by an adjective. Given a noun like *shoes,* we might ask for some other details:

Whose shoes?
What sort of shoes?
What color shoes?
What shape shoes?
Where?
Made of what?
How many?
How big?

And those are not all of the possible questions about the *shoes*. The point here is that the answers to such questions may be supplied by adjectives:

Darlene's shoes—the *two little pointed, narrow, white canvas* shoes *in her closet.*

In one phrase we have told whose, how many, how big, what color, what shape, what the shoes are made of, and where they are. The italicized words are adjectives or adjective phrases.

The Possessive Adjectives

In the example shown above, the question *whose?* was answered by *Darlene's*. That word, with the *'s* added to a noun, is an adjective indicating possession. Such possessive noun forms are used as adjectives to tell *whose*. The possessive pronouns (*my, your, his, her, its, our,* and *their*) are also used as adjectives; in fact, they are not truly pronouns, since they cannot be used to name things; they are *possessive adjectives:*

My house is near the corner.
Your dog is bigger than *our* cat.
His mother told *Linda's* aunt about *their* vacation.

The possessive adjectives in those sentences tell *whose* are the house, the dog, the cat, the mother, the aunt, and the vacation.

Time for Review

Adjectives answer many questions that may be asked about nouns—questions of size, shape, color, number, ownership, place, age, and many more.

The question of ownership—*whose?*—may be answered by a *possessive adjective* like *Darlene's* or *your*.

Do-It-Yourself Exercise

Write an adjective (word or word group) appropriate to answer the question asked (in parentheses) about one of the nouns in each sentence:

Visitors in _____ states are often impressed
                (which?)

by the _____ rivers and _____ valleys.
      (what size?)   (what color?)

Some of the beaches _____ attract _____
                (where?)   (how many?)

vacationers _____ .
          (who do what?)

Usually the tourists _____ carry _____
              (from where?)   (what sort?)

cameras and come home with _____ luggage full of
                           (whose?)

_____ film.
(what sort?)

Going through customs may take _____ hours if the authorities
                           (how many?)

suspect smuggling _____ .
               (what sort?)

Checking up: Don't assume that anything that could be put into the blanks would be adjectives. It would be possible to write "*crossing* rivers and *admiring* valleys," but *crossing* and *admiring* would not describe the rivers and valleys and would not be adjectives. Some of the adjectives don't have to be exact answers to the questions; for example, you could write *many* in answer to "how many?" What sort of film?—*color* film, *exposed* film, or *precious* film. What sort of smuggling?—smuggling *of jewels*, smuggling *by tourists*, smuggling *from Europe*.

Determiners

One class of adjectives includes *a, an,* and *the*. These words always indicate that a noun is soon to follow; that is, they predict or determine that a noun is coming. They are often referred to as *determiners*, or noun markers.

A, an, and *the* are sometimes called *articles. The* is the *definite article* because it suggests a particular or specified thing: not just any dog, but *the* dog. *A tree* or *an apple* are not particular; *any* tree or *any* apple may be indicated; so *a* and *an* are the *indefinite articles.*

Also among determiners are the words *this, that, these,* and *those.* Since these words seem to point at the nouns they modify, as if demonstrating, they are *demonstrative adjectives. This chair* seems to demonstrate the chair, *those countries* to point out the countries. *This* and *that* are singular; *these* and *those* are plural. *This* and *these* imply something near by; *that* and *those* imply something at a distance from the speaker.

Still others among the determiners are adjectives that suggest quantity or order: *few* people, *some* money, *five* centers, *third* day, *both* girls. These are limiting adjectives, or *limiters.*

Last among the determiners are the *possessive* adjectives: *my* house, *your* friend, *its* completion, *whose* brother, *their* cat, *our* country, *her* application, *his* necktie. The possessive adjectives are spelled *without apostrophes* in these forms.

Time for Review

Determiners are adjectives that always indicate that a noun is soon to follow. They introduce noun phrases.

Among determiners are these:

Articles (a, an, the).

Demonstrative adjectives *(this, that, these, those).*

Limiters (such as *few, some, many, both, each, every, either, all, most, one, two, first, second,* and all other numbers).

Possessive adjectives *(my, your, his, her, its, our,* and *their).*

Do-It-Yourself Exercise

Write determiners (of the kinds indicated in parentheses) to begin the noun phrases in these sentences:

Today _____ treasurer, in _____ report to
            (article)   (possessive)

_____ board, has cited _____
  (demonstrative)   (limiter)
points that must directly concern us.

After studying _____ problem at _____ end
              (limiter)   (article)

of _____ assignment, read the _____
    (possessive)   (limiter)
chapter again.

Has _____ newspaper reported _____ facts
     (article)   (limiter)

about _____ friends who took _____ hike
   (possessive)   (demonstrative)

during _____ storm?
    (article)

Congressman Phelps is _____ man _____
                         (limiter)   (possessive)

record in _____ session is unquestioned.
     (demonstrative)

There are _____ things that _____ animal
      (limiter)   (article)

can do better than _____ man, and _____ of
        (article)   (limiter)

_____ things is to see in _____
 (demonstrative)   (article)
dark.

Checking up: Possible appropriate articles: *the* treasurer, *the* end, *the* newspaper, *an* animal, *a* man (notice that *an* must be used rather than *a* before a vowel sound); possible limiters: *some* points, *many* points, *six* (or any number) points; *third* (or any number) chapter, *any* facts, *one* problem, *one* man, *several* (or *many* or any number) things; possible demonstratives: *this* board, *that* hike, *this* session, *those* things; possible possessives: *his* report, *your* assignment, *our* friends, *whose* record.

Descriptive Adjectives

To describe something is to present a mental picture of it by means of language. The most obviously descriptive sort of language is the adjective.

But the *determiners* do not describe things. *An* tells us nothing of what *an elephant* looks like, and *those* tells us nothing of the qualities of *those children*. To reveal qualities of things, we need *descriptive* adjectives: "those *noisy* children," "an *aging* elephant."

Adjectives in Pairs or Series

When adjectives are used in pairs, they may be joined by a coordinator: "A *large* and *heavy* package," "a *short* and *simple* note." But the coordinator may often be omitted, in which case the two adjectives are usually separated by a comma: "a *large, heavy* package," "a *short, simple* note."

But not all adjectives used in pairs or series can be properly coordinated. It would be awkward to write, "an *old, American* custom"; it would be better to omit the comma: "an *old American* custom." To test whether the comma should or should not be used, try thinking *and* between the two adjectives; if *and* sounds proper, then use the comma when omitting *and:*

> He saw a *long, narrow* passage ahead. (The passage is long *and* narrow.)
>
> We walked down a *long dirt* road. (It would be awkward to say "a long *and* dirt road," so use no comma.)
>
> The baby had a *round, chubby* face. (The face was round *and* chubby.)
>
> She is a *fascinating young* lady. (It would be awkward to say "a fascinating *and* young lady," so use no comma.)

Time for Review

Descriptive adjectives modify nouns by suggesting details of size, shape, substance, purpose, color, or other *quality*.

Adjectives in *pairs* or *series* are joined by a coordinator or (when the coordinator is omitted) separated by a comma. When it would be awkward to use *and*, it would also be awkward to use a comma.

Do-It-Yourself Exercise

In each blank write a *pair* of *descriptive adjectives* to modify the noun in italics. Do not use a coordinator, but use a comma when it is appropriate:

All the kids laughed when a _____ bird flew through the
(size? shape?)
classroom window.

Everybody applauded when the _____ girl won the beauty
(height? nationality?)
contest.

It's going to be a _____ winter.
(length? weather?)

After staying up all night to study, he couldn't keep his _____
(condition? color?)
eyes open in class.

A pyramid is an _____ tomb where a Pharaoh, or king, is buried.
(age? nationality?)

Mr. Potter was wearing his _____ suit and his _____ necktie.
(age? color?) (condition? made of what?)

My _____ shoes aren't broken in yet.
(age? purpose?)

Checking up: The questions in parentheses suggest the *qualities* that your descriptive adjectives should reveal, such as *big, fat* bird; *tall Brazilian* girl; *long, rainy* winter; *tired blue* eyes or *old, red* eyes; *old Egyptian* tomb; *new green* suit; *dirty silk* necktie; *new tennis* shoes. Where the commas are not used, notice that it would be awkward to say, "tall *and* Brazilian girl," "tired *and* blue eyes," or "dirty *and* silk necktie," and so on. If *and* would be awkward, use no comma.

Suggestions for Writing

A. What is the most unusual piece of furniture in your home? Write a passage (about 200 words) describing it, answering at least 10 questions about it, such as: whose? where? what sort? what size? what shape? what color? made of what? how good? expensive? how old? Answer the questions by using adjectives or word groups used as adjectives.

B. What was the biggest meal you can remember eating? Write a passage (about 200 words) describing that meal, reporting the kinds of food it contained. Answer at least 10 questions about the meal (or about the separate dishes), such as: how many? where? what sort? what size? what color? made of what? how good? expensive? what shape? Of course you should describe the odors and tastes too. Answer the questions by using adjectives or word groups used as adjectives.

C. Who was the most memorable teacher you ever knew? Your impression may be either favorable or unfavorable as you write a passage (about 200 words) describing that teacher and answering at least 10 questions about the person: where? man or woman? height? hair color? weight? age? personality traits (helpful? grouchy? friendly? humble? easygoing? stern?). Answer the questions by using adjectives or word groups used as adjectives.

After Writing: Underline the words or word groups you have used as *adjectives*. Are you able to give each of those adjectives a label: *article, demonstrative, limiter, possessive, descriptive?*

Making Comparisons

A handy way to reveal the qualities of things is to compare them to other things:

Razors are usually *sharper* than knives.

This is the *earliest* snow we've had in years.

My sister is *younger* than I am.
Which car is the *fastest* on the track?

These adjective forms are the *comparative* (ending in *-er*) and the *superlative* (ending in *-est*). The *-er* form is used when only two things are involved in the comparison:

Pete is the *older* of the two brothers.
The grass is *greener* on your side of the fence.

The *-est* form is used when three or more things are involved in the comparison:

Olivia was the *youngest* of six children.
Rhode Island is the *smallest* of the 50 states.

When the *-er* or *-est* ending would produce an awkward word, the comparative is formed with *more* or the superlative with *most:*

The eggs are *more* burned than the toast. (Not *burneder.*)
She is the *most* beautiful of all. (Not *beautifulest.*)

The *more* and *most* forms are almost always used with words of three or more syllables.

Parallelism in Comparisons

Careful writers avoid producing unintended comparisons. Suppose you were to be told:

Stan's voice is *louder than* his sister.

Would you think it awkward to compare the *voice* with the *sister?* The writer apparently intends to say instead:

Stan's *voice* is louder than his sister's *voice* (or, if the repetition seems unnecessary, "louder than his *sister's*").

It is usually possible to avoid awkwardness or misunderstanding by revising the faulty parallelism in comparisons:

Faulty	Parallel
Life in the country seems much slower than *the city.*	*Life in the country* seems much slower than *life in the city.*
I have a *car* much cheaper than *my father.*	I have a car much cheaper than *my father's.*
Are *skyscrapers* in New York higher than Chicago?	Are *skyscrapers* in New York higher than *those* in Chicago?

Getting out into the open air is better than *the house*.	*Getting out* into the open air is better than *staying in* the house.

The same principle of parallelism in comparisons should be followed when *more than* is used instead of *-er than:*

Life in the country seems much *more slow than* life in the city.
I have *more responsible* friends *than* my brother has. (It would be faulty to write "than my *brother*.")

Avoiding Danglers and Misplaced Adjectives

Adjectives are normally placed near the nouns (or pronouns) they are intended to modify. But consider what can happen when an adjective is placed near some noun that it is not intended to modify:

Beautiful as always, he smiled when his girlfriend came out the door. (Who was *beautiful*—he?)
Green with the first growth of spring, the morning dew glistened on the grass. (What was *green*—the dew?)
Spotted in the parking lot, the police found my stolen car. (What was *spotted*—the police?)

Such misplaced adjectives require revision:

I smiled when my girlfriend, *beautiful* as always, came out the door.
My stolen car was *spotted* in the parking lot.
The grass, *green* with the first growth of spring, glistened in the morning dew

The adjectives are properly placed near the nouns they modify.

Time for Review

The comparative adjectives are formed by adding *-er: slower, brighter, cleaner,* and so on.

Items compared by *-er* adjectives (or by the *more-than* pattern), should be in parallel.

An adjective should be placed near the noun it is intended to modify—at least nearer to that noun than to some other that the adjective should not modify.

Chapter Eleven

Do-It-Yourself Exercise

Write in each blank a *comparative* or *superlative* adjective to complete the sentence appropriately:

The _____ of the twins was Julia.

Is the grass really _____ on our side of the fence?

Of all the cities Merton has lived in, the _____ is New York.

Which course do you think is _____: math, history, or English?

Who is _____, Mario or his sister?

April is _____ than May, but February is the _____ month of the year.

Checking up: Be sure that *-er* comparatives involve only two things and *-est* superlatives involve three or more.

In parentheses following each of these sentences are two suggested adjectives. Write in the blank the *one* of those adjectives which best completes the sentence:

Too _____ to be comfortable, Patty couldn't walk in her new shoes. *(tight/nervous)*

_____ of the team's pitchers, the manager decided to use Barney on the mound for the playoff game. *(Best/Proud)*

_____ in California, Len had never visited Mt. Whitney. *(Highest/Born)*

Utterly _____, the cafeteria sandwiches never have enough meat in them for Bob. *(tasteless/disgusted)*

Even if _____, Professor Kinney makes every lesson seem exciting. *(tired/tedious)*

Checking up: The adjective must properly modify the noun nearer (or nearest) to it: *nervous*—Patty, *Proud*—manager, *Born*—Len, *tasteless*—sandwiches, *tired*—Professor

Kinney. The other offered adjectives would produce awkward or misleading sentences with misplaced modifiers.

Compound Adjectives

A *compound adjective* is formed by two or more words written to form a unit, either by omission of space between them or by use of the hyphen; for examples: *stronghearted* man, *run-of-the-mill* product, *high-school* student, *well-known* writer.

A good dictionary is the best guide to whether these compound adjectives should be written as single words (*shoestring* catch) or as hyphenated groups (*one-in-a-lifetime* chance). To write them as separate words may produce confusion: Does *high school* student mean a school student who is high? To write *high-school* student avoids that possibility.

When the first element of a compound is an adverb that ends in *-ly,* no hyphen should be used: a *narrowly missed* opportunity, a *quickly written* note.

Other Word Groups as Adjectives

An *adjective phrase* is made of an adjective and its modifier. The adjective *clean* may be modified by the adverb *very*; thus *very clean* is an adjective phrase. Other examples:

too dark	*seldom aware*	*quite doubtful*
not beautiful	*always bright*	*never true*

A *prepositional phrase*, beginning with a preposition and ending with a noun, may be used as an adjective:

This shirt has a ring *around the collar*.

He serves a great drink called a Niagara; it's straight water *over the rocks*.

Do you have a notebook *with a lock?*

This is a day *for celebration*.

The nouns *ring, water, notebook,* and *day* are modified by the prepositional phrases used as adjectives.

A *subordinate clause*, beginning with a word like *who, which,* or *that* and containing a subject-verb combination, may be used as an adjective:

The student *who sits in the back row* often hopes to be ignored.

Police science, *which is my major,* offers an exciting career.

The *Tribune-Examiner* is a newspaper *that tells it as it is*.

The nouns *student, police science,* and *newspaper* are modified by the adjective clauses.

Chapter Eleven

Time for Review

A *compound adjective* is a word group used as a unit and written either as a single word (a *newsworthy* event) or as a hyphenated group (a *drive-in* theater).

When the first element of a compound adjective is an *-ly* adverb, no hyphen should be used: a *nearly forgotten* star, a *badly worn* tire.

An *adjective phrase* contains an adjective and its modifier, such as *really good, quite true*.

A *prepositional phrase* may work as an adjective: the girl *in the bikini*, a house *on the corner*.

A subordinate clause beginning with *who, which,* or *that* may work as an *adjective clause*.

Do-It-Yourself Exercise

Write in each blank the sort of *adjective* (compound, phrase, or clause) called for in the parentheses below the blank. Be sure what you write is appropriate to complete the sentence:

I like my coffee _____.
(prepositional phrase)

Last Saturday we watched a _____ game on television.
(adjective phrase)

Harry has a new job _____.
(prepositional phrase)

Isn't this the same book _____?
(adjective clause)

Yours is one of the _____ suggestions yet to be heard from
(adjective phrase)

this group.

People _____ shouldn't throw parties.
(adjective clause)

Checking up: Some appropriate adjectives for those sentences: prepositional phrases —*with cream, without sugar, at a store, with this company;* adjective phrases—*really good, very exciting, quite boring;* adjective clauses—*that you read, that we lost, who* *live in glass houses, who hate housework*. Be sure that each adjective *clause* has a subject-verb combination and that each adjective *phrase* or prepositional *phrase* does not.

Write in each blank a *compound adjective* appropriate to complete the sentence:

José Feliciano is a _____ singer.

You now have a _____ opportunity to further your education.

A _____ person is one who is really down and really out.

A freshman is a _____ college student.

Chick's car is a _____ mess.

Checking up: These compound adjectives (or others like them) would be appropriate: *well-known, folk-rock, once-in-a-lifetime, down-and-out, first-year, worn-out, broken-down.*

Suggestions for Writing

D. Recall the stormiest day you have experienced in your life. Write a passage of about 250 words describing that day by answering such questions as when? where? weather? color of sky? appearance of water or snow? speed of wind? temperature? Answer the questions by using *adjectives, prepositional phrases,* and *adjective clauses*.
E. Recall or imagine a really "close call," a narrow escape from injury or death. Write a passage of about 250 words describing the experience by answering such questions as what sort? where? when? color of things? size of things? shape of things? Answer the questions by using *adjectives, prepositional phrases,* and *adjective clauses*.
F. Dream car, dream house, dream job—nearly everyone has such a dream. Write a passage of about 250 words describing one of your "dream" things. Describe it by answering questions about it: size? shape? color? made of what? expensive? valuable? important? Answer the questions by using *adjectives, prepositional phrases,* and *adjective clauses*.

After Writing: Reread your passage and underline each of the descriptive and determiner words or word groups. Be sure that all of your underlined elements really are used as adjectives. Each of them should modify a *noun*. If any of them describes (or otherwise modifies) a verb instead, you have written an adverb rather than an adjective. Can you identify in each case what sort of adjective you have written: determiner, descriptive, prepositional phrase, adjective clause?

(For more thorough practice with prepositional phrases see pp. 218–224. For more thorough practice with adjective clauses see pp. 265–269.)

QUIZ 11

Using Adjectives

On the blank within each sentence write the item that you think most appropriately completes the sentence; then mark the *letter* of that item on your answer blank. Don't overlook punctuation included in some of the offered alternatives. After marking your choice, explain briefly why you chose it *(Because: . . .)*.

Example: Last night a *disturbing* story appeared on the television news.

(a) exciting (b) interesting (c) disturbing (d) amusing
(e) out-of-this-world

Ex. *c*

(Because: Determiner "a" must be followed by consonant.)

1. I have always liked _____ kind of people.

(a) those (b) all (c) you're (d) that (e) these

1._____

(Because: _____.)
   (Question: Which adjective is singular to match the singular noun, *kind?* Is *you're* an adjective?)

2. Yours is the best of _____ reports read to the class so far.

(a) the two (b) several (c) the couple of (d) the pair of (e) both of the

2._____

(Because: _____.)
   (Question: Which completion properly refers to three or more things and matches the superlative, *best?)*

3. Usually college students are more serious than _____.

(a) high school (b) high-school students (c) high school-students
(d) high school students (e) high-school

3._____

(Because: _____.)
   (Question: Which completion provides proper parallelism with *college students?* Which also forms a clear compound adjective?)

4. For breakfast I often have _____ eggs.

(a) two fresh, boiled (b) two, perfect fried (c) two hard-boiled
(d) two, soft poached (e) two, medium,

4._____

(Because: _____.)
   (Question: When are commas used to separate adjectives in pairs or series?)

198   Chapter Eleven

5. Lazier than my brother, _____ doesn't interest me.
(a) his job   (b) work   (c) I won't take a job that   (d) this is a job that
(e) getting a job

5._____

(Because: _____.)
   (Question: Which completion provides a subject to be modified by *lazier* and thus avoids a dangler?)

6. Someday I want a house with _____ fireplace.
(a) a used brick   (b) an open-hearth   (c) a wood burning
(d) an old fashioned   (e) an honest to goodness

6._____

(Because: _____.)

7. Miss Meltone came home full of stories about the _____ man she had met on the ship.
(a) handsome, Italian   (b) rich, insurance   (c) interesting, young
(d) fascinating, romantic   (e) athletic, old

7._____

(Because: _____.)

8. Which of the twins is the _____?
(a) prettiest   (b) most beautiful   (c) beautifulest   (d) prettier
(e) beautifuler

8._____

(Because. _____.)

9. We have just rented a _____ apartment.
(a) new one bedroom   (b) new, one-bedroom   (c) newly-build
(d) on the third floor   (e) fourth-floor

9._____

(Because: _____.)

10. _____ of Mark Twain's books, our class is now reading *The Adventures of Huckleberry Finn.*

(a) Most famous   (b) The best   (c) Among the earliest
(d) Interested in some   (e) Not the first

10._____

(Because: _____.)

11. There on the front page was a picture of the _____ Miss Lucy Sexton, daughter of a country parson, now a glamorous star of stage and screen.
(a) fully-clothed   (b) well-known   (c) newly-arrived   (d) richly-dressed
(e) beautifully-built

11._____

(Because: _____.)

12. Our friends saw some bullfights _____ while they were on vacation.

(a) who went to Mexico (b) very exciting (c) that really excited them
(d) superb (e) very colorful   12_____

(Because: _____.)

13. Mr. Payton is supervisor of all of our _____ salesmen.

(a) over-the-counter (b) over the counter (c) dry goods
(d) antique furniture (e) high volume   13_____

(Because: _____.)

14. I understand you are writing for the _____ newspaper.

(a) local, weekly (b) on the campus (c) issued daily
(d) that comes out daily (e) collegiate   14_____

(Because: _____.)

15. Bob's baritone voice sounds _____ tonight.

(a) bad (b) poorly (c) badly (d) delightfully (e) perfectly   15_____

(Because: _____.)

16. Somehow home cooking always seems tastier than _____
_____.

(a) away from home (b) in restaurants (c) restaurant cooking
(d) anywhere else (e) when you eat out   16_____

(Because: _____.)

17. Marlene is certainly the _____ of the two contestants.

(a) most tall (b) tallest (c) more tall (d) taller (e) statuesquer   17_____

(Because: _____.)

200   Chapter Eleven

18. Yesterday morning I stopped to watch a flight of birds ―――――――――
―――――――――――――――――――――――――――――――――――――――.

(a) on the way to work   (b) walking toward the office   (c) over the parkway
(d) southwardly-bound   (e) newly-arriving   18.―――

(Because: ――――――――――――――――――――――――――.)

19. All employees who have been with the company for two years are entitled to a

――――――――――――――――― vacation.

(a) three week   (b) two-week   (c) long, European   (d) average
(e) on-the-payroll   19.―――

(Because: ――――――――――――――――――――――――――.)

20. ―――――――――――――――――――, Sam's income fell below its
usual level.

(a) Temporarily reduced   (b) Out of work   (c) Jobless for a month
(d) In the hospital   (e) Hit by illness   20.―――

(Because: ――――――――――――――――――――――――――.)

When, Where, Why, and How 12

How to work with . . . adverbs
clipped forms of adverbs
adverb clauses

How to avoid . . . misplaced modifiers
faulty adverbs

SOMETHING HAPPENS. When we are told of it, we want to know some details: *When did it happen, where, how, why, under what conditions?* Answers to those questions would help us to understand and visualize more clearly. The answers can be supplied by *adverbs*:

> Look, light snow is falling *now*. (Tells *when*.)
> Our bacon is sizzling *in the pan*. (Tells *where*.)
> Some people diet *to stay thin*. (Tells *why*.)
> I sat and cried *like a baby*. (Tells *how*.)
> We sat in the kitchen *while the water was heating*. (Tells *under what conditions*.)

The adverb may be a single word (like *now*), a phrase (like *in the pan, to stay thin*, or *like a baby*), or a subordinate clause (like *while the water was heating*). In each of those example sentences the adverb tells us something about the time, place, purpose, manner, or conditions of an action or state of being.

Adverbs are *modifiers*; they serve to describe verbs or to describe other modifiers. Observe some examples:

> The puppy sat *up*. (*Up* modifies the verb, *sat*.)
> She looked *terribly* sad. (*Terribly* modifies the adjective, *sad*.)
> She whined *so pitifully*. (*So* modifies the adverb, *pitifully; pitifully* modifies the verb, *whined*.)

Time for Review

> An *adverb* is a modifier.
>
> An *adverb* modifies a verb, an adjective, or an adverb.
>
> An adverb answers a question such as *when, where, why, how,* or *under what conditions*.

Do-It-Yourself Exercise

In each blank write an appropriate *adverb* (a word or phrase) to answer the question (asked in parentheses) about the italicized verb:

Rounding the far turn, the driver deliberately *skidded* _____.
                                                        (where?)

I *have* _____ taken an interest in ancient history.
          (when?)

Larry will *play* his guitar _____.
                             (under what condition?)

The bus driver *must hurry* _____.
                                    (why?)

Please *walk* _____.
              (how?)

You *should* _____ *disconnect* the power switch
              (when?)

_____.
       (how?)

My dog *complains* _____ _____.
                    (how?)   (under what conditions?)

Checking up: Single words or groups of words could be used to answer those questions and modify the verbs. Some possible appropriate adverbs: *across the track, if you ask him, to stay on schedule, around the flower bed, always, never, then, next, by turning the key, loudly, whenever I lock him up.* Of course, your own answers to those questions may be just as good as these, provided that they really do answer the questions and modify the verbs.

In the following sentences fill in *adverbs* to answer the questions (asked in parentheses) about the italicized adjectives:

This is a _____ *good* sandwich.
          (*how* good?)

The trouble with glass is that it can be *broken* _____.
                                                     (how?)

Those diet drinks taste _____ *sweet* to me.
                        (how much?)

Sorry, your answer was _____ *late* to win a prize.
                       (how much?)

I thought his practical jokes were _____ *funny*.
                                    (how much?)

Pete's bicycle was *built* _____.
                           (how?)

Born _____, she travels home every summer.
       (where?)

Sleepy _____, I just couldn't
         (why?)
concentrate on the job this morning.

Checking up: Whether they are word groups or single words, the adverbs should be reasonable answers to the suggested questions. Some possible adverbs: *really, too, very, extremely, not, from an old tricycle, in Canada, because I stayed up half the night.* Your own answers to the questions, of course, may be just as good as these.

In the following sentences fill in *adverbs* that modify the italicized adverbs:

Your Uncle Harry seems _____ *well* educated.

Is anyone ever _____ *much* praised for his work?

You are seated _____ *far* back in the room.

Children _____ *really* understand their parents.

This story couldn't have been _____ *excitingly* written.

The weather this morning is _____ *actually* cold.

Checking up: Some possible adverbs to fill those blanks: *quite, very, remarkably, too, never, less, more, not, hardly.*

Avoiding Misplaced Adverbs

Adverbs often are placed freely in sentences without any change in their meanings or effects:

Now we want to announce something.
We want *now* to announce something.
We want to announce something *now*.

The shifting placement of *now* does not change the meaning of the sentence; the adverb, in any of those places, modifies *want*, telling when. But sometimes the placement of an adverb can have important effect upon a difference in meaning:

Tom *only* will enroll for one course.
Tom will *only* enroll for one course.
Tom will enroll *only* for one course.
Tom will enroll for *only* one course.
Tom will enroll for one course *only*.

In those sentences the shifting adverb *only* does cause some possible misunderstanding. Is it *Tom only* who will enroll—and no one else? Will Tom *only enroll*—but never attend?

When, Where, Why, and How 205

Obviously some of the placements of *only* give the sentence a different meaning.

A writer can usually improve his work by placing adverbs where they cannot distract the reader from the intended meaning. Notice how some misleading adverbs can be rewritten:

Misleading	Improved
We decided *after the show* to gather at Fred's place.	We decided to gather at Fred's place *after the show*.
Mother dislikes my playing the trombone *very much*.	Mother *very much* dislikes my playing the trombone.
I mailed the letter I had finished reading *to my sister*.	I mailed *to my sister* the letter I had finished reading.
The newspaper printed a story that Miss Perino had been married *prematurely*.	The newspaper *prematurely* printed a story that Miss Perino had been married.

Time for Review

Effective use of adverbs calls for their being as near as possible to the elements they are intended to modify—or at least nearer than to something they might mistakenly appear to modify.

Do-It-Yourself Exercise

Each of these sentences shows more than one blank. An adverb is shown in parentheses before the sentence; write that adverb into the sentence *once*—in the blank where the adverb most appropriately completes the sentence:

(always) _____ put your brain in gear _____ before _____ engaging in an argument.

(about your wife)   Can you listen to his joking _____ and not feel embarrassed _____?

(when the time comes) _____ I'm sure that _____ Frank will make the right decision about investing _____.

(entirely)   Professor Wright was _____ wrong about my

_____ missing the point _____.

(firmly)   The lecturer held _____ to his point

_____ when he was questioned _____.

(throughout the trip)   Our guide told us _____ we

would find many souvenirs to send to friends at home _____

_____.

Checking up: Some of the adverbs could be placed in any of the blanks in the sentence, depending upon what you intended the sentence to mean. Be sure that your completed sentence does say what you think it means. If you have placed the adverb at the beginning of a sentence, be sure that you have used a capital letter.

Some Adverb Problems

Many adverbs in English end with *-ly*. The adverb is formed by adding *-ly* to an adjective: quick—*quickly*, cautious—*cautiously*, awful—*awfully*, curious—*curiously*, and so on. But conversational English often favors the adjective form, even when the adverb is intended:

He dropped that hot iron *quick! (quickly?)*

Vernon was *awful* good about washing the dishes. *(awfully?)*

Professor Overton talked very *cautious* about the rioting on campus. *(cautiously?)*

The lecture was interesting, but the air in the room was *real* stifling. *(really stifling?)*

Such "clipped form" adverbs are usually avoided by careful writers, except when they are trying to produce an informal, conversational effect. Some of these "clipped forms" have actually come to be preferred, even in writing—among them the adverbs in these phrases:

travel *light*   hang *loose*   look *straight*
stand *close*   talk *loud*   hold *tight*
cut *deep*   come *quick*   turn *wrong*
play *fair*   spread *smooth*

But these forms usually follow the verbs. If the adverb comes before the verb, the *-ly* form is used:

lightly travel   *loudly* talk   *quickly* drop
deeply cut   *smoothly* spread   *really* was
loosely hang   *tightly* hold

When, Where, Why, and How 207

Now and then it is necessary to distinguish the adverb from the adjective according to how they work in their sentences; the adverb modifies the verb or other modifier—but the adjective modifies a noun (as in the adjective complement):

Adverb (modifies verb)	Adjective (modifies noun)
Alice sings *beautifully*.	Alice sounds *beautiful*.
The mechanic worked *quietly*.	The mechanic seemed *quiet*.
He drives *perfectly*.	He's a *perfect* driver.
I don't paint *well*.	My paintings look *bad*.
We considered it *seriously*.	We considered it *serious*.
You and I work *differently*.	You and I are *different*.

Some of the clipped forms have become the only acceptable forms. Nobody today says "travel *fastly*," and even the street signs read "Slow," not "Slow*ly*." The ordinal numbers (*first, second, third,* and so on) are most often used without *-ly*, most writers avoiding the more pretentious "first*ly*, second*ly*." And "thus*ly*" is redundant, *thus* being enough.

Do-It-Yourself Exercise

Complete these sentences with appropriate adverbs. Use single words only, avoiding clipped forms (without *-ly*) except when you're sure they are appropriate to the tone and to normal usage:

Our winter sports were _____ exciting this year.

Come in! I'm _____ finished with my homework.

One passenger was thrown against the windshield when the bus stopped _____.

The star _____ forgot her lines in the third act.

Why did Mrs. Grundy speak so _____ to her daughter?

The knife cut _____ through the wood.

We'll do the job _____ next time.

This plan will _____ improve the public's chance to drive _____ on the highways.

Canadian Airlines will fly you _____ to Montreal.

Checking up: Most adverbs end with *-ly*, as all of yours should in this exercise. But now return to the exercise and try using clipped forms for some of your entries: *clear, safe, direct*. And where would some other adverbs be appropriate without *-ly*—*almost, now, much, sometimes?*

Suggestions for Writing

A. It is a long-standing principle of American law that an accused person is considered "innocent until proven guilty." To what extent is that principle understood and upheld by most people you know? Write your comment in a passage of about 200 words.
B. Research and experiment have shown that seat belts in automobiles can reduce the likelihood of serious injury or death in case of accident; yet, many drivers—and still more passengers—do not use their seat belts. Write a passage of about 200 words, telling why some people do not use seat belts.
C. The famed American humorist Will Rogers used to say, "All I know is what I read in the papers." To what extent is what we read in the newspapers (or hear on the news broadcasts) really believable? Write a passage of about 250 words, telling what you think about the believability of news reports.

After Writing: Reread your passage and underline each *adverb* that you have used, whether word, phrase, or clause. Reading the passage again, circle the verb, adjective, or adverb that is modified by each of your underlined adverbs.

Adverbs in Series

Adverbs can be paired, as in "They conferred *quietly* and *secretly*"—and they can be used in series, as in "Natural gas burns *steadily, controllably,* and *efficiently.*" As in the pairing of other elements, parallelism is a requisite. Be sure that the paired or listed adverbs are not inappropriately mixed with adjectives or nouns:

Faulty Parallelism	Effective Parallelism
The governor spoke *carefully* and *true*.	The governor spoke *carefully* and *truthfully*.
He stood *firm* and *steadfastly* upon principle.	He stood *firm* and *steadfast* upon principle.

Though some looseness may be accepted (or overlooked), it is even best to avoid mixing one-word adverbs with longer adverb forms:

Our candidate will win *easily*
   and *without sacrificing*
   honor.   . . . *easily* and *honorably*.
Computers do most jobs *rapidly*,
   without error, and   . . . *rapidly, accurately,*
   economically.   and *economically*.

The Adverb Clause

A subordinate clause used to modify a verb, adjective, or adverb is an *adverb clause*.
The adverb clause is a subject-verb combination introduced by a *subordinator*. Some examples:

     S   V
If a strike is called, Hank will be out of work.
When the buzzer sounded, the announcer jumped from his chair.
Unless you swim, don't go near the water.

Adverb clauses can often be identified by these subordinators:

Time (When?)	Place (Where?)	Reason (Why?)	Manner (How?)
when	where	because	as
while		since	as if
as		so that	
since			
before		Condition (Under What Conditions?)	
after		although	though
until		if	unless
once		provided that	as though

Do-It-Yourself Exercise

Write an appropriate adverb clause to answer the question suggested for each blank. Remember: the clause must begin with a subordinator (see list above) and must contain a subject-verb combination.

Mike broke his leg _____.
                        (when?)

The troopers sought the suspect _____.
                                  (where?)

I can't buy a new car _____.
                        (why?)

The boss said I could have the promotion _____.
                                                      (under what conditions?)

The new council will conduct its business _____.
                                            (how?)

We knew nothing about the accident _____.
                                          (when?)

Checking up: Does each of your entries begin with a subordinator *(when, where, because, if, as, until)*? Does each entry have a subject-verb combination? As a further exercise, circle the word that is modified by your adverb clause.

Time for Review

The adverb is versatile. It may modify a verb, an adjective, or another adverb.

Adverbs occasionally modify negatively: *no, not, never.*

Adverbs may be placed before, after, or in the midst of the elements they modify—but for best effect should be placed where they cannot lead to misunderstanding.

Many adverbs are formed with the suffix *-ly*. But the *-ly* is often dropped from those adverbs in conversational English *(first, fast)* and many more *-ly* suffixes are being dropped as English continues to change *(slow, quick, direct)*. The "clipped forms" are useful, but writers still use the full *-ly* forms for formal work.

When using adverbs in pairs or in series, the writer must observe *parallelism*.

An *adverb clause* is a subject-verb combination introduced by a subordinator and used to modify a verb, an adjective, or an adverb.

Suggestions for Writing

D. Benjamin Franklin said, "A penny saved is a penny earned." But a penny won't buy as much today as it did in his time—or even ten years ago. Write a passage of about 200 words, telling your attitude toward saving money.
E. Competition spurs people to achievements—or discourages them. Write a passage of about 250 words, telling your ideas on the effects of competition in our lives.
F. Much of human life depends upon trust in mankind. To what extent do you believe people in this world can be trusted (considering friendship, business, and money matters)? Write your ideas in a passage of about 250 words.

After Writing: Reread your passage and underline each *adverb* that you have used, whether word, phrase, or clause. If you have not used an adverb clause, revise the passage to include at least two of them. Then circle the subordinator (such as *if, when, because, while, as,* or *until*) that begins each adverb clause. Can you identify the word that is modified by each adverb clause in your passage?

When, Where, Why, and How 211

QUIZ 12

Using Adverbs

On the blank within each sentence write the item that you think most appropriately completes the sentence; then mark the **letter** of that item on your answer blank. Don't overlook punctuation included in some of the offered alternatives. After marking your choice, explain briefly why you chose it (***Because:*** . . .).

Example: The television movie ___*often*___ begins late because of the football broadcast just before it.

(a) usual   (b) only   (c) often   (d) occasional   (e) probable   Ex _c_

(***Because:*** *"Only" would be misplaced; a, d, and e are adjectives.*)

1. Oliver's dog doesn't eat _____ when it's tired.

(a) very eager   (b) so good   (c) so ravenous   (d) with good appetite   (e) healthy   1_____

(***Because:*** _____.)

   (***Question:*** Which word or phrase is an adverb that will properly modify the verb, *eat?*)

2. Mrs. Hammond told her bridge guests that she felt _____ about the burned dessert.

(a) bad   (b) awfully   (c) real badly   (d) miserably   (e) really badly   2_____

(***Because:*** _____.)

   (***Question:*** Should the completion modify the verb, *felt,* or the subject, *she?* Would an adverb properly modify *she?*)

3. I wanted the day to be perfect, but I feared _____.

(a) it might rain in my heart   (b) that snow would fall secretly   (c) secretly that it might rain   (d) that clouds might gather foolishly   (e) it would be a mess silently   3_____

(***Because:*** _____.)

   (***Question:*** Which completion properly places an adverb to modify the verb *feared?*)

4. To maintain good health, one should exercise regularly and _____ _____.

(a) vigorous   (b) before he needs to   (c) enthusiastically   (d) whether he is tired or not   (e) because health is precious.   4_____

(***Because:*** _____.)

   (***Question:*** Which completion provides an adverb that properly parallels *regularly* in a pair linked by *and?*)

5. The accused said he had a _____ perfect alibi.
(a) real   (b) near   (c) almost   (d) sure   (e) nearly

5._____

(Because: _____*.)*
   (Question: Which completion provides an adverb to modify the adjective, *perfect,* and to follow the determiner, *a?)*

6. Kathy spent most of the summer acquiring her _____ rich suntan.

(a) beautiful   (b) true   (c) real   (d) beautifully   (e) deeply and

6._____

(Because: _____*.)*

7. Slowly and _____ he made his way to the speaker's platform.

(a) hesitant   (b) as tears rolled down his cheek   (c) with head bowed
(d) unemotional   (e) unsmilingly

7._____

(Because: _____*.)*

8. Fred didn't know how to write the paper _____.

(a) original   (b) as his professor wanted it   (c) any different   (d) good
(e) easy

8._____

(Because: _____*.)*

9. The caravan _____ every town along the route.

(a) almost stopped at   (b) stopped almost at   (c) stopped at almost
(d) nearly made a stop   (e) stopped nearly at

9._____

(Because: _____*.)*

10. _____ led lives of affluence.

(a) All men have not   (b) Not all men have

10._____

(Because: _____*.)*

11. While we're on vacation in California we'll _____ go to Disneyland.

(a) probable   (b) first   (c) sure   (d) natural   (e) firstly

11._____

(Because: _____*.)*

12. Will anyone who has finished the test _____.

(a) silently leave the room (b) quickly turn it in
(c) raise his hand immediately (d) not submit it
(e) without delay go on to the next

12_____

(*Because:* _____.)

13. Jim's trouble is that he never takes anything _____.

(a) very seriously (b) real seriously (c) real serious (d) serious enough
(e) too serious

13_____

(*Because:* _____.)

14. Because of her training in art, Carol can hold a brush _____ than I can.

(a) steadier (b) more steady (c) more steadily (d) steadily more
(e) more steadier

14_____

(*Because:* _____.)

15. Call me _____.

(a) when you get to Dallas on the telephone
(b) when you get off the plane by long distance (c) when you arrive collect
(d) on the telephone when you arrive (e) if you want to see me on the telephone

15_____

(*Because:* _____.)

16. My girlfriend was afraid she'd get a bad grade on the term paper because she types _____.

(a) as bad as I do (b) real badly (c) awful sloppy (d) as bad as me
(e) so awkwardly

16_____

(*Because:* _____.)

17. We haven't _____ practiced enough for competition.

(a) hardly (b) scarcely (c) really (d) honest (e) like we should

17_____

(*Because:* _____.)

214 Chapter Twelve

18. The young couple decided they would get up early in the morning and drive _____ to Albuquerque.

(a) direct (b) as the sun came up (c) without saying goodbye (d) directly
(e) speedy

18._____

(*Because:* _____.)

19. It will be our pleasure to introduce the _____ president of the corporation.

(a) newly elected (b) newly-appointed (c) new-chosen (d) highly-liked
(e) well qualified

19._____

(*Because:* _____.)

20. The contractor is expected to complete the job economically and _____ _____.

(a) before the rainy season (b) as soon as he can (c) rapidly
(d) with no undue delay (e) while the weather is good

20._____

(*Because:* _____.)

Of, From, With, Between 13

How to work with ... prepositions
prepositional phrases
the long possessive
indirect objects

How to avoid ... misplaced modifiers
problems with prepositions

Chapter Thirteen

OUR STUDY HAS TAKEN US through five of the essential "parts of speech" (conjunctions, nouns, verbs, adjectives, and adverbs) with considerable practice in how they pattern into sentences. The rest of this book concerns variations on those elements in sentences, paragraphs, and essays.

Modifiers, we have seen, are of two kinds: adjectives and adverbs. In this chapter we consider a special pattern that always works as a modifier, the prepositional phrase. But first, how do we recognize a *preposition*?

A preposition is a relationship word. It links two things (such as two nouns) and suggests how those things are related:

Things	Relationships
bottle, milk	bottle *of* milk
book, history	book *of* history
man, strength	man *of* strength
composer, music	composer *of* music
city, San Francisco	city *of* San Francisco
plays, Shakespeare	plays *of* Shakespeare
Don Quixote, La Mancha	Don Quixote *of* La Mancha

The "things" listed are nouns. But actions are also things, so a preposition may show a relationship between a *verb* and a noun:

Things	Relationships
speak, love	speak *of* love
learn, the news	learn *of* the news
die, laughter	die *of* laughter

A preposition may also show a relationship between a *quality* and a thing—that is, between a *modifier* and a noun.

Qualities, Things	Relationships
hard, hearing	hard *of* hearing
beautiful, figure	beautiful *of* figure
lazy, mind	lazy *of* mind

We have used *of* as an example in all the above just to show what a variety of relationships can be indicated by that one preposition. Of course, the variety is still greater, for English uses about fifty words as *prepositions*:

aboard	as	by	near	till
about	at	despite	of	to
above	before	down	off	toward
across	behind	during	on	under
after	below	except	onto	until
against	beneath	for	over	unto
along	beside	from	per	up
alongside	besides	in	round	upon
amid	between	inside	since	with
among	beyond	into	through	within
around	but	like	throughout	without

A preposition begins a phrase that ends with a *noun* (or *pronoun*—see p. 242). The *prepositional phrase* works as a modifier. In other words, in "bottle of milk" the prepositional phrase *of milk* modifies the noun *bottle;* in "speak of love" the prepositional phrase *of love* modifies the verb *speak*. Some further examples:

Noun or Verb	Prepositional Phrase
control	*of* energy
fight	*for* freedom
women	*with* children
water	*under* pressure
rest	*after* lunch
flight	*from* Denver
disappear	*into* darkness
reach	*beyond* planets

Time for Review

A *preposition* is a word that links two elements (such as two nouns or a verb and noun) and suggests how they are related.

A *preposition* usually begins a phrase. The prepositional phrase ends with a noun.

A *prepositional phrase* works as a modifier—as an adjective or adverb.

Do-It-Yourself Exercise

Write an appropriate *preposition* (refer to the list at the top of page 217) to fill each blank and complete these sentences:

The initial piece _____ legislation is nearly ready _____ signature _____ Governor Martin. It extends full rights _____ adulthood _____ persons _____ 18 and 21 years _____ age. No doubt _____ it, young people _____ America already are making a contribution that is rivaled _____ the youth _____ few other nations _____ the globe. This state wisely places its trust _____ them.

Checking up: The passage clearly requires such prepositions as *of, for, by, to, between, about, in,* and *around*.

Longer Prepositional Phrases

So far we have considered prepositional phrases consisting of only two elements—the preposition and its noun. The noun that ends a prepositional phrase is the *object* of the preposition:

Preposition	Object
of	*legislation*
to	*persons*
in	*America*
for	*signature*
about	*it*
by	*few*

In the Do-It-Yourself exercise, however, one of the prepositional phrases was longer. In "*between* 18 and 21 years" (or "*of* 18 and 21 years") the noun *years* was expanded to include its modifiers, *18* and *21*. The object of the preposition, then, was a *noun phrase* rather than a one-word noun. The object of a preposition may be a one-word noun, a noun phrase, or a noun clause; or it may be any of those elements in a pair or series:

at *home*	(one-word noun)
beyond *the old bridge*	(noun phrase)
near *where they live*	(noun clause)
between *brother and sister*	(pair of nouns)
for *the man and his wife*	(pair of noun phrases)

Of, From, With, Between   **219**

When the objects of a preposition are *pronouns* in pairs or in series, a problem of parallelism arises. That problem is discussed in detail in the chapter on pronouns (see p. 244).

Time for Review

The noun that ends a prepositional phrase is the *object* of the preposition.

The *object* of a preposition may be a one-word noun, a noun phrase, or a noun clause; or it may be any of those elements in a pair or series.

Do-It-Yourself Exercise

Write in each blank an appropriate noun, noun phrase, or noun clause to serve as the *object* of the italicized preposition:

The key *to* _____ is kept *in* _____.
              (noun phrase)   (noun phrase)

During _____ I swallowed my coffee too fast.
       (noun)

She usually does her studying *at* _____ *after* _____.
                                 (noun)   (noun)

What's a little argument *among* _____?
                             (noun)

If you are suffering *from* _____, take one of these aspirin
                           (noun phrase)

tablets *per* _____.
        (noun)

We were sitting *around* _____ telling stories *about*
               (noun phrase)

_____.
(noun clause)

The crew is expected to be *aboard* _____ *by* _____.
                                    (noun phrase)   (noun)

We shouldn't get *into* _____ *between* _____.
                    (noun phrase)   (pair of nouns)

She swept everything *under* _____ *except* _____.
                           (noun phrase)   (noun phrase)

You may walk *along* _____ (noun phrase), but don't go *near* _____ (noun phrase).

The sun has moved *behind* _____ (pair of noun phrases).

Sally doesn't want to go *through* _____ (noun phrase) *without* _____ (pair of proper nouns).

During _____ (noun phrase) the professor did not go *into* _____ (noun phrase).

Checking up: Recheck each of your entries to be sure that it is really a noun, noun phrase, or noun clause as called for. If you aren't sure what a noun clause is, remember that a clause must contain a subject-verb combination. For a discussion of noun clauses and how they work, see Chapter 15, especially p. 274.

Suggestions for Writing

A. In a police report an auto accident is seldom referred to as *an accident*; it is, instead, a *collision*. The report will probably not say that Car A "ran into" Car B, but that Car A "collided with" Car B. Is it a good thing that police reports use such careful language? Write your ideas in a passage of about 200 words. Underline every prepositional phrase.
B. Looking ahead is a pastime for all people, though some do it through rose-colored glasses and some do it through the gray-toned spectacles of doom. Write a passage of about 300 words telling what kind of world you see ahead in the next 20 years. Underline every prepositional phrase.
C. Why should private citizens be allowed to own and carry guns—or why not? Write your reasons in a passage of about 300 words, considering both individual freedom and public safety. Underline every prepositional phrase.

After Writing: Since every prepositional phrase is a modifier, you should know what is being modified by each of your prepositional phrases. Reread your passage and draw an arrow from each preposition to the word that the prepositional phrase is intended to modify. Can you also tell whether each phrase is an *adjective* or an *adverb*? Remember that adjectives modify *nouns;* adverbs modify other elements.

Placement of Prepositional Phrases

When it works as an adjective, a prepositional phrase usually follows the noun that it modifies:

house *on the corner*
children *with clean hands*

room *for my books*
clerk *at the library*
grease *under the car*
secrets *between friends*

When it works as an adverb, the prepositional phrase usually follows the verb (or other element) that it modifies—though not necessarily immediately:

drive *across town*
write *to the editor*
hidden *inside the box*
swimming *around the tank*
guilty *of certain errors*

Other elements may be used between the verb (or modifier) and the prepositional phrase:

heard the traffic cases *in the morning*
shoved the laundry *under the bed*
offer a gift *to an old friend*
sent whatever we could *to the treasury*
written very rapidly *without a typewriter*

The placement of a prepositional phrase is important to smoothness and clarity. Consider the possible misunderstanding of these:

I didn't know you had been at the bank *until now*.
She hid the note she had written *under her pillow*.
He cracked the walnut he had stolen *between his teeth*.

Would the ideas be clearer if the prepositional phrases were placed more carefully?

Until now I didn't know you had been at the bank.
Under her pillow she hid the note she had written.
Between his teeth he cracked the walnut he had stolen.

Sometimes a whole new sentence structure is needed if the writer is to avoid misplacement of a prepositional phrase:

Dad shot the gopher that had been eating our lawn *between the eyes*. (Was our lawn *between the eyes*?)
Dad shot the gopher *between the eyes* that had been eating our lawn. (Had *the eyes* been eating our lawn?)
Dad shot *between the eyes* the gopher that had been eating our lawn.

The third version, though not misleading, seems awkward. The writer would be wise to revise the entire idea:

A gopher had been eating our lawn, but Dad shot that gopher *between the eyes*.

Chapter Thirteen

Time for Review

A prepositional phrase is used as a *modifier*.

A prepositional phrase usually follows the element that it modifies, though not necessarily immediately.

Careless placement of a prepositional phrase may confuse the reader; such a misplaced modifier should be avoided.

Do-It-Yourself Exercise

In each blank write a *prepositional phrase* to complete the sentence. Avoid misplaced modifiers. Try to use as many different prepositions as you can:

Mr. Barnes has received a letter from a customer _____.

Using worms _____, Jake caught three fish _____.

Everyone _____ has plenty of enthusiasm.

The woman standing there _____ is a receptionist _____.

Don't leave your clothes _____; hang them up _____.

The runaway turned _____ and sped _____.

Seated _____, the doctor's wife was talking quietly _____.

Checking up: Remember that a prepositional phrase begins with a preposition like one of these: *from, for, with, as, in, around, by, on, down, over, toward, into, through, beside, between*. The phrase must end with a noun or pronoun. If you have used the same preposition more than once, try writing the exercise a second time, using entirely different prepositions.

Suggestions for Writing

D. Do men talk differently from women? Suppose two people, a man and a woman, have the same background and the same kind of job in the same kind of place? Will they use

the same *slang* (see p. 343) and the same *euphemisms* (see p. 347)? Which will be the more direct, which the more roundabout? Write your answers in a passage of about 200 words. Use as many prepositional phrases as you can.
E. Censorship of public information and entertainment remains an important issue, just as it has for centuries. What, if anything, should be censored (movies, television, news; violence, sex, crude language, ethnic bias)? Write your ideas in a passage of about 200 words. Use as many *prepositional phrases* as you can.
F. Look up the word *malinger* in the dictionary. Whom do you know that malingers often, or at least occasionally? When have you done some malingering yourself? Write your response in a passage of about 200 words. Use as many *prepositional phrases* as you can.

After Writing: Reread your passage and underline each prepositional phrase. Since a prepositional phrase is used as a modifier, draw an arrow from each of your prepositions to the word that the phrase modifies. Has each prepositional phrase been clearly placed? (See pp. 220–221).

Preposition or Conjunction?

A number of the words on the list of prepositions (p. 217) also appear on the list of conjunctions. How shall we be sure whether a word is working as a preposition or as a conjunction? What is the difference in these two uses of *after?*—

After the storm we'll shovel the snow.
After the storm ends, we'll shovel the snow.

The difference is the verb, *ends*. When *after* is followed by a noun (like *the storm*), the result is a prepositional phrase: *after the storm*. But when *after* is followed by a subject-verb combination (*the storm ends*), the result is a subordinate clause. Beginning a subordinate clause, *after* works as a conjunction—a subordinator.

Among the words that may work as a preposition (before a noun without verb) or as a conjunction (before a subject-verb combination) are these:

Preposition–Noun	Conjunction–Subject–Verb
After work let's relax.	*After* we work, let's relax.
As a typist he's fast.	*As* he types, he's fast.
Before you I was lonely.	*Before* you came along, I was lonely.
I drove *for* Sam.	I drove, *for* Sam was tired.
You talk just *like* Amy.	You talk just *like* Amy does.
We haven't eaten *since* lunch.	We haven't eaten *since* you left.
Let's quit *till* tomorrow.	Let's quit *till* tomorrow comes.
Rest *until* the game.	Rest *until* the game starts.

In each case the *preposition* is followed by a noun without a verb, but the *conjunction* is followed by a subject-verb combination.

Time for Review

Many words may work either as *prepositions* or as *conjunctions*.

A *preposition* is followed by a noun, noun phrase, or noun clause used as the *object* of the preposition.

A *conjunction* is followed by a subject-verb combination; the word group is a clause.

Do-It-Yourself Exercise

In each blank write a *prepositional phrase* to replace the suggested clause; thus, change the italicized word to a preposition:

The boys had to finish their work _____.
(*before* they had dinner)

We bought a new stove _____.
(*for* Mother needed one)

The professor is very effective _____.
(*as* he speaks)

The crowd hasn't stopped cheering _____.
(*since* the game ended)

A few moments _____ the air turns cooler.
(*after* the sun goes down)

Checking up: Using *before, for, as, since,* and *after* as prepositions, you should have supplied a noun or noun phrase (with no verb) as object of the preposition. For example, "*before* they had dinner" should be changed to "*before* dinner."

Suggestions for Writing

G. Newspapers, when they refer to someone who is running for elective office, will seldom refer to that person as a *politician*. In a news story the office seeker will instead be referred to as *the candidate* or *the senator* or *the incumbent*. Can you tell why newspapers avoid the word *politician*? Write your ideas in a passage of about 200 words. Underline every prepositional phrase.

H. One hundred years ago nearly every worker in American industry worked about 14 hours a day, six days a week. That made an 84-hour work week. Today the average is eight hours a day, five days a week. Some say we may soon have a four-day week.

Write a passage of about 300 words telling what you think would be the result if suddenly everyone in America had a three-day holiday every week.
I. Critics of television and movies have pointed out that there is much violence on the screen. Some say the violence reflects something in American life. Do you think violence is a part of our everyday lives? Write your ideas in a passage of about 300 words. Underline every prepositional phrase.

After Writing: Reread your passage and mark with a circle every word that you have used as a *conjunction*. Can you tell why each such word is not working as a preposition?

The Long Possessive

The prepositional phrase beginning with *of* is often used as a possessive, especially when the "possessor" is not a person or animal:

Ted and Alice met at the door *of the library*.
Our side scored in the first quarter *of the game*.
There I am at the top *of the picture*!
She appeared as a friend *of the court*.

Such possessives would seem awkward with the shorter *'s* form: the *library's* door, the *game's* first quarter, the *picture's* top, the *court's* friend—but even these shorter forms are not unknown.

When the "possessor" is a person or an animal, the *'s* form is more often used, but the long possessive (with *of*) is possible:

I have the *owner's* manual.
She took her *doctor's* advice (or the advice *of her doctor*).
We drink a lot of *cow's* milk.
He stepped on a *cat's* tail (or the tail *of a cat*).

And the *'s* form is almost always used with people's names or titles:

What caused *Mr. Eliot's* confusion?
Someone stole the *captain's* horse.

It would seem awkward to write "the horse *of the captain*," and "the confusion *of Mr. Eliot*" might mean something different from "*Mr. Eliot's* confusion."

The Indirect Object

When a *verb's* action is done *to* something, that something is the *object* of the verb:

My boss wrote a *note*.
One morning we sent *flowers*.

The objects, *note* and *flowers*, are the things acted upon. If a receiver is added for those objects, the sentences may read:

> My boss wrote a note *to his wife*.
> One morning we sent flowers *to Mother*.

The nouns in these prepositional phrases that indicate the receivers of objects are *indirect objects*. Consider a few more:

> Please buy an extra ticket *for Sandy*.
> Paul mixed a soda *for the lady*.

When the indirect object appears before the object, the preposition is ordinarily omitted:

> Please buy *Sandy* an extra ticket.
> Paul mixed *the lady* a soda.
> My boss wrote *his wife* a note.
> One morning we sent *Mother* some flowers.

But the preposition may be used even in that sort of sentence if some special purpose, such as poetic rhythm, is wanted:

> My true love sent *to me* a partridge in a pear tree.

Time for Review

A prepositional phrase beginning with *of* is often used as a possessive, especially when the "possessor" is not a person or animal.

The prepositional phrase beginning with *of* is sometimes used as a possessive even when the "possessor" is a person or animal, but then the *'s* form is more common.

The *'s* form of the possessive is almost always used with people's names or titles.

A prepositional phrase beginning with *to* or *for*, is often used to indicate the indirect object of a verb—the receiver of the thing acted upon.

When the indirect object appears before the object, the preposition is usually omitted.

Of, From, With, Between   227

Do-It-Yourself Exercise

Write in each blank the word or word group called for: a possessive (with *'s* or *of*), a prepositional phrase, or a subordinate clause:

A large piece had been cut from the center _____.
                                              (possessive)

The _____ center had been cut out.
       (possessive)

We always exercise to limber up _____.
                                    (prepositional phrase)

Exercise helps _____.
                  (subordinate clause)

We made a thorough search _____.
                              (prepositional phrase)

We had to make a thorough search, _____.
                                      (subordinate clause)

Today looks _____
               (prepositional phrase)

It looks _____ today.
            (subordinate clause)

My brother works _____ in an auto shop.
                    (prepositional phrase)

My brother usually whistles _____.
                                (subordinate clause)

Shall we go straight home _____?
                              (prepositional phrase)

Sure, we always go straight home _____.
                                     (subordinate clause)

Robert didn't listen to the advice _____.
                                       (possessive)

His _____ advice had never meant much to him.
       (possessive)

Checking up: When possessives follow the noun, they usually take the long form: center *of the cake*, advice *of his mother;* when they come before the noun, they usually take the *'s* form: the *cake's* center, his *mother's* advice. Each of the other completions should begin with *after, as, before, for, like, since, till,* or *until*. A subordinate clause must contain a subject-verb combination; a prepositional phrase contains only preposition and noun without verb. Return to the exercise and mark "V" above the verb in each of your subordinate clauses.

Preposition To End a Sentence?

Users of English have long questioned whether a preposition should be used at the end of a sentence. Are these acceptable sentences?—

This is the candidate to vote *for*.
Give me some space to work *in*.
We have very little to talk *about*.
He's the clerk that all the mail comes *to*.
No decision has been arrived *at*.

Most speakers and writers of English would say, "Yes, those are good sentences." Such sentences have been used effectively in English for centuries. They are certainly better than the rather fancy form using *whom* or *which*:

This is the candidate *for whom* to vote.
Give me some space *in which* to work.
We have very little *about which* to talk.

On the other hand, it is wasteful and awkward to use a preposition at the end if that preposition has already been used in the sentence:

We need a pail *in which* to carry water *in*.
This is the address *at which* I live *at*.

The repeated preposition ruins the sentence, and it usually would seem more natural to put the preposition only at the end:

We need a pail to carry water *in*.
This is the address I live *at*.

The usual advice now is: If the preposition seems natural at the end, put it there.

Preposition or Adverb?

Sometimes a sentence may end with what seems to be a preposition but is really an adverb:

You can't play *inside*.
Why don't you run *along*?
We're just walking *around*.

Of, From, With, Between 229

Since those sentences do not have nouns that work as the objects of prepositions, the words *inside, along,* and *around* are adverbs modifying the verb *play,* the verb *run,* and the adjective *walking.*

Is "To" a Preposition?

Since *to* does appear on the list of prepositions, it may be easy to assume that *to* is always a preposition. But a preposition must always have a *noun* or *pronoun* as its object:

We talked *to Jim* yesterday.
He gave some advice *to us.*
Drive around *to the alley.*

The nouns *Jim, us,* and *alley* are objects of *to,* the preposition. But consider some sentences that use *to* with no object:

We wanted *to tell* him *to call* home.
To release the brake, pull the handle.
I have a heavy assignment *to finish.*

The words *tell, call, release,* and *finish* are verb forms, not nouns. In such usage the word *to* is not a preposition but the marker of the *infinitive* (see pp. 325–326).

Time for Review

Prepositions are often used at the ends of sentences. Such usage is entirely proper if the sentence seems natural.

Words that appear on the preposition list (see p. 217) may sometimes be used as *adverbs.* If the word does not have a noun as its object, the word probably is used as an adverb.

When *to* is followed by a noun as its object, *to* is a preposition.

When *to* is followed by a verb form (like to *see,* to *handle*), *to* is the marker of an *infinitive* (see pp. 322–323).

Do-It-Yourself Exercise

Refer to the list of prepositions on p. 217. Using words from that list, write prepositional phrases (include their objects), adverbs, or prepositions-at-end to complete these sentences appropriately:

Chapter Thirteen

We opened the box _____ and found a small radio
                       (prepositional phrase)

_____.
       (prepositional phrase)

The captain had gone _____ to rest.
                              (adverb)

No one _____ is responsible for the safety
         (prepositional phrase)

_____.
       (prepositional phrase)

Leaning _____, the instructor glanced
         (prepositional phrase)

_____ pleasantly.
      (adverb)

There was nothing to be sorry _____.
                                (preposition)

The truck route goes _____ and _____.
                     (prepositional phrase)   (prepositional phrase)

My boss is really a great man to be working _____.
                                              (preposition)

_____ sat the very letter that we had spent all
   (prepositional phrase)

morning talking _____.
                (preposition or adverb)

Walking _____, I felt _____.
        (prepositional phrase)   (prepositional phrase)

Why don't we go _____ and talk _____.
                 (adverb)   (prepositional phrase)

I dashed _____ a note _____.
          (adverb)   (prepositional phrase)

Checking up: Does each of your *phrases* begin with a preposition and end with a noun? All the other entries should be single words. For extra understanding draw an arrow from each of your entries to the word that it modifies; for example, does your first entry in the exercise modify *box* (box *of corn flakes*), or does it modify *opened* (opened the box *with a knife*)?

Some Problems With Prepositions

Some prepositions have meanings that limit their uses. For example, *between* implies *two* things being related—never more than two. When three or more things are related, we use *among* rather than *between*: "*between* you and me," "*among* us three." Here are some of the special restrictions on how prepositions are used:

amid — denotes position but no association. If we are *amid* people, we are not really *among* them.

among — denotes active association of three or more: *among* friends, *among* brothers.

besides — denotes addition or apartness: What do you have *besides* money? Not to be confused with *beside*, which denotes nearness: She stood *beside* me.

between — relates *two* things, not more.

except — denotes exclusion; should not be confused with the verb *accept*.

in — implies enclosure; should not be confused with *into*, which implies a moving from outside to inside: We walk *into* a restaurant and eat *in* a restaurant—not the other way around.

like — implies similarity; often used also as a conjunction with informal effect.

off — implies separation from: *off* the mark, *off* schedule.

on — should not be confused with *onto*: We step *onto* a bus, but ride *on* a bus—not the other way around.

onto — implies a movement from *off* to *on*.

over — implies position; sometimes used to imply *more than* (with informal effect): He stepped *over* the rock *over* ten times.

since — should not be confused (in spelling) with *sense*.

till — usually means the same as *until*, but is spelled with two *l*'s.

toward — sometimes written *towards* (with informal effect).

unto — usually means *to*; seldom used.

Using the right preposition in the right way can often make meaning more exact. Being *annoyed by* someone isn't the same thing as being *annoyed with* someone; the taste *for* sugar isn't the same thing as the taste *of* sugar. An omitted preposition can sometimes cause an awkward sentence:

The director seemed startled and ashamed *of* the orchestra's bad performance.

Does the sentence mean to say he was "startled *of* the performance?" Startled *by* is more likely:

The director seemed *startled by* and *ashamed of* the orchestra's bad performance.

Of course, when the same preposition is appropriate to both of the paired elements, it need not be repeated:

Bud both *campaigned* and *voted for* Senator Snort.
We take *pride* and *pleasure in* this company.

Standard usage requires careful use of prepositions. These are a few misuses that may require revision:

angry at	angry *with*
cannot help but	cannot *help*
comply to	comply *with*
different than	different *from*
dissent to	dissent *from*
identical to	identical *with*
in search for	in search *of*
similar with	similar *to*

Time for Review

Many prepositions have shades of meaning that limit their uses: *amid, among, between; beside, besides; in, into; on, onto.*

Several prepositions are easily confused with other words and must be carefully distinguished from those words: *except* (not *accept*), *since* (not *sense*), *until* or *till* (not *untill* or *til*).

Standard usage requires careful application of prepositions. A thing may be similar *to* another (not similar *with*), we may dissent *from* an opinion (not dissent *with* or dissent *to*).

When two prepositions share the same object in a context, both prepositions must be expressed and appropriately used: grateful *for* and pleased *with* the gift (not grateful and pleased *with* the gift.)

Do-It-Yourself Exercise

Beneath each blank are shown two prepositions. Write in the blank the *one* of them that most appropriately completes the sentence.

The chairman stepped _____ the room and strode
                            (in, into)

_____ the platform.
     (on, onto)

Of, From, With, Between 233

Just _____ the six of us, who's going to win the election?
(among, between)

Cathy is _____ the woods, walking _____ the trees.
(in, into)   (amid, among)

I found some real friends _____ the members of the club.
(amid, among)

Will you please get _____ this lawn and comply
(off, off of)

_____ the posted sign?
(with, to)

Dean seems happy and pleased _____ his job.
(by, with)

_____ music Ralph also likes painting.
(Beside, Besides)

Stand here _____ me, not _____ your parents.
(beside, besides)   (between, among)

Checking up: Review each of your choices according to the list of prepositions and their uses (on p. 231). Can you tell why these are the appropriate choices?—*into* the room, *onto* the platform, *among* the six, *in* the woods, *amid* the trees, *among* the members, *off* this lawn, happy and pleased *with*, *Besides* music, *beside* me, *between* your parents.

Of, From, With, Between   235

QUIZ 13

Using Prepositions

Quiz 13a: Which of the lettered items is used as a *preposition?* Mark the **letter** of that item on your answer blank.

Example: Stay *inside* and don't walk *around* much, *since* you must keep your
                    (a)   (b)   (c)
temperature *down near* the normal level.
              (d)   (e)

Ex *e*___

(Because: *"Near" is the only item followed by an object*.)

1. *Unless* this shipment arrives *before* our supply gives out, we'll have *to* stand
     (a)   (b)   (c)
by for a new order.
(d) (e)

1.___

(Because: _____.)
   (*Question:* Which of the words is followed by a noun but not by a subject-verb combination?)

2. When Al is invited *to* eat *with* us, he usually waits *until* it's too late *to* come
                      (a)   (b)   (c)   (d)
over.
(e)

2.___

(Because: _____.)
   (*Question:* Is *to* a preposition when it is followed by a verb form like *eat* or *come?* Is *over* followed by a noun or pronoun?)

3. *Amid* shouts of approval the captain strode *aboard, but* he immediately went
     (a)   (b)   (c)
below till the celebration was over.
 (d)   (e)

3.___

(Because: _____.)

4. *After* her guests arrived, Mrs. Hurribon put the rolls *on* to warm, *for* she wanted
    (a)   (b)   (c)
to serve dinner almost *at* once.
(d)   (e)

4.___

(Because: _____.)

Quiz 13b: Which of these prepositional phrases is used as an *adjective?*

5. Running *across dry land* is not so difficult *for most horses* as slopping
              (a)   (b)
   through the mud on the track after a rain.
         (c)   (d)   (e)

   5._____

   (Because: _____.)
       (Question: Which phrase modifies a noun? *Running* and *slopping* are verbals and are modified by adverbs.)

6. If the defendant pleads guilty *to the charge of extortion,* he will probably be
                                  (a)   (b)
   sentenced *to ten years* and required to repay the funds *upon his release* or *within two*
            (c)   (d)   (e)
   years.

   6._____

   (Because: _____.)
       (Question: Which phrase modifies a noun?)

7. We were able to row *across the river without difficulty,* but we found that the
                      (a)   (b)
   current had carried us *about a mile* downstream *to a point near the rapids.*
                  (c)   (d)   (e)

   7._____

   (Because: _____.)

8. Attach the pulley *to the drive shaft* and slip the chain *through the pulley*
                   (a)   (b)
   before securing it *to one end of the derrick.*
       (c)   (d)   (e)

   8._____

   (Because: _____.)

Quiz 13c: Which of these prepositional phrases is used as an *adverb?*

9. The ship *at the dock* arrived *at noon of the day before the strike by union*
         (a)   (b)   (c)   (d)   (e)
   workers.

   9._____

   (Because: _____.)
       (Question: Which phrase modifies a verb?)

10. The man *behind the promotion of this plan for improvement of air safety* sits
                (a)   (b)   (c)   (d)
    here *among our members* tonight.
            (e)

    10._____

    (Because: _____.)
        (Question: Which phrase modifies a verb?)

Of, From, With, Between   237

11. The drift *toward the cities* *by farmers* *of the plains states* was obvious *to*
　　　　　　　　(a)　　　　　　(b)　　　　　(c)
authorities *within the agriculture department*.
　　　　　(d)　　　　　　(e)　　　　　　　　　　　　　　　　　　　　　　　11_____

(*Because:* _____.)

　　(*Question:* Which phrase modifies an adjective?)

12. Some *of the beaches* *along the coast* *of Florida* have been reserved *for private*
　　　　　(a)　　　　　　(b)　　　　　(c)　　　　　　　　　　　　　　　(d)
use *by residents*.
　　(e)　　　　　　　　　　　　　　　　　　　　　　　　　　　　　　　　　12_____

(*Because:* _____.)

Quiz 13d:　Some of these sentences contain prepositional phrases that are badly placed. Underline each prepositional phrase that is misplaced. On your answer blank mark each sentence as (a) if clear, (b) if not clear:

13. Sandy took a course on meat-cutting by correspondence.　　　　　　13_____
14. Experts advise us to invest the first money we earn in life insurance.　14_____
15. You will know in the morning why the judge couldn't tell us about the case.　15_____
16. Mrs. Brown went to the doctor with a pain in the elbow　　　　　　16_____
17. Any question from recruits about the camp will have to wait for tomorrow morning.　　　　　　　　　　　　　　　　　　　　　　　　　　17_____
18. Just hand your trip folder to the stewardess with the ticket inside.　　18_____
19. It's good to travel to complete your education, but not merely to get away from home.　　　　　　　　　　　　　　　　　　　　　　　　　　19_____
20. Amy swept the dust out of the sight of her guests under the couch.　20_____

Me, Myself, and I   14

How to work with . . . pronouns
person
number
case
pronoun agreement
pronoun reference
eight kinds of pronoun

How to avoid . . . faulty pronoun case
faulty pronoun agreement
faulty use of *who* and *whom*
faulty use of *whose* and *who's*

IF WE WERE WRITING A STORY about George and Martha, we might find it clumsy to keep repeating their names:

> When George had lunch with Martha, George told Martha that George liked apple pie and that Martha's was the best George had ever eaten.

To avoid that kind of repetition, we could use other words to take the places of the names:

> When George had lunch with Martha, *he* told *her* that *he* liked apple pie and that *hers* was the best *he* had ever eaten.

The words *he, her,* and *hers* are pronouns. This chapter will introduce eight different sorts of pronoun and offer practice in using them effectively in writing.

Like the nouns they replace, pronouns *name* (at least indirectly) the people, places, things, and ideas that we want to refer to as we talk or write. *He* can be used as another name for George, *she* for Martha, *they* for friends, *it* for apple pie. Pronouns allow us to refer to things with quickness and variety.

What "Person" Means

Each of us is "number one" in his own world. The *first person* in your life is the one you call "I." That is why "I" is the *first-person* pronoun. All of the words referring to the one who calls himself *I* (such words as *me, myself, mine*) and all of the words referring to that person's group (such as *we, ourselves, ours*) are *first-person* pronouns.

The "I" in any speech or writing is the one doing the talking or the writing. When he addresses his words to someone else, he talks or writes to the *second person,* his audience, who is referred to as "you." All pronouns that refer to that listener or reader are *second-person* pronouns: *you, yourself, yours,* or *yourselves.*

When the writer tells his audience *about* someone, that person talked about is the *third person,* referred to as "he" or "she"—or, in the case of animals or things, "it." All pronouns that name the *topic* of the discourse are *third-person* pronouns: *he, him, she, her, it, his, hers, its, himself, herself, itself, they, them, themselves.*

The concept of *person* applies to both nouns and pronouns. Consider some nouns and pronouns in sentences:

> **First Person:** *I, Peter Penman, author* of these words, find *myself* unable to say what troubles *me,* for *mine* are troubles too deep for words.

Second Person: When will *you,* my *friend Tom,* learn that *you* must take *yourself* seriously?

Third Person: *History* impresses *itself* upon *man* whether *he himself* knows *it* or not—and upon *woman,* too, for *she* is not alone, and *what* is *his* that is not *hers?*

One—or More Than One?

Just as nouns are *singular* when they name one thing or person and *plural* when they name more than one, so are pronouns singular or plural. The pronoun *I* names one; *we* names more than one; *this* names one, but *these* names more than one—and so on.

Doer—or One Done To?

If *bites* is the action in a sentence, the one who does the biting is the doer, or the *subject.* The one who is bitten is the receiver of the action, or the *object.* Many pronouns change their form according to whether they name the subject or the object of an action: *I* see *him,* but *he* sees *me.* The switch from *I* to *me* is the switch from subject to object. The switch from *him* to *he* is the switch from object to subject.

Personal Pronouns

One of the eight kinds of pronoun is the class of *personal* pronouns. All the pronouns of this class can be shown on a chart that brings together the concepts of *number* (singular, plural), *person* (speaker, listener, topic), and *case* (subject, object, possessive):

PERSONAL PRONOUNS

SINGULAR

	Subjective	*Objective*	*Possessive*
First person:	I	me	mine
Second person:	you	you	yours
Third person:	it	it	its
	he	him	his
	she	her	hers

PLURAL

	Subjective	*Objective*	*Possessive*
First person:	we	us	ours
Second person:	you	you	yours
Third person:	they	them	theirs

Chapter Fourteen

Time for Review

A *pronoun* is a replacement, or substitute, for a *noun*.

A *first-person* pronoun names the speaker or writer—or his group: *I, me, myself, we, us, ourselves*.

A *second-person* pronoun names the listener or reader—or group of listeners or readers: *you, yourselves*.

A *third-person* pronoun names the persons or things being talked or written about: *it, he, she, him, her, himself, herself, they, them, themselves*.

A *singular* pronoun names *one* person or thing: *I, she, itself*, and so on.

A *plural* pronoun names more than one person or thing: *we, they, ourselves, themselves*, and so on.

A *subjective* pronoun names the *subject* or *noun complement* in a sentence: *I, it, he, she, we, they*.

An *objective* pronoun names the *object* of a verb or *object* of a preposition: *me, you, him, her, us, them, myself, yourself*, and so on.

A *possessive* pronoun names a person or thing possessed or otherwise related: *mine, yours, his, hers, ours, theirs, its*. (Note that these possessive personal pronouns are *not* spelled with apostrophes.)

Do-It-Yourself Exercise

Write in each blank an appropriate *pronoun* to complete each sentence:

When _____ am happy, _____ talk a lot.

My girlfriend likes to swim, because _____ looks good in a bikini.

If _____ wish, _____ may use my math book.

My speech was longer than _____.

As Frank guided the car into the turn, _____ kept firm pressure on the accelerator.

_____ likes to watch the snow as _____ falls through the trees.

Since _____ couldn't find their own tools, _____ borrowed _____ from _____.

Checking up: Reread to be sure that each sentence seems natural. It would be awkward to write "*she* am" or "*I* likes." Any one of several different pronouns may do in some of the blanks: "If *I, you, we,* or *they* wish . . ."; " . . . longer than *yours, his, theirs*"; " . . . we, they, he, she,* or *I* borrowed *mine, his,* or *hers* from *me, him,* or *her.*"

Verb Agreement

When a pronoun is used as subject of a verb, the verb must *agree* with that pronoun; that is, the verb must be appropriate for use with the *number* (singular or plural) and the *person* (first, second, or third) of that pronoun:

I *am.* You *are.* He *is.* She *is.* We *are.* They *are.*
I *see.* You *see.* He *sees.* She *sees.* We *see.* They *see.*
I *study.* You *study.* He *studies.* She *studies.* We *study.* They *study.*

Difference of *person* is important with the *be* verbs, which change their form for the first-, second-, and third-person singular *(am, are, is)*. Difference of *number* is important with most verbs, although only the third-person singular *(he, it, she,* or any singular noun as subject) takes the verb with the *-s* or *-es* ending.

Time for Review

When a pronoun is the subject of a verb, the verb must agree with that pronoun in *person* and in *number*.

When a pronoun is used as the subject of a verb, the pronoun must be in the *subjective* form: *I, you, it, he, she, we, they.*

When a pronoun is used as the object of a verb, as indirect object, or as object of a preposition, the pronoun must be in the *objective* form: *me, you, it, him, her, us, them.*

Do-It-Yourself Exercise

Write in each blank an appropriate pronoun to agree with the verb and complete the sentence:

_____ am interested in what _____ does.

When _____ are here, _____ has plenty to talk about.

I think _____ have what _____ takes to become a qualified secretary.

If _____ doesn't arrive on time, _____ is sure to miss the performance.

Checking up: The *-s* or *-es* verb endings require third-person singular pronoun subjects: *it, he,* or *she*. Of course, *am* requires the first-person singular, *I*. The other verbs may take subjects like these: *we* are, *they* are, *you* are, *I* have, *you* have, *we* have, *they* have.

Pronouns in Pairs

When *and* links a noun and a pronoun in a pair, as in *Tommy and I,* the pair forms a plural. The verb then must be in the plural:

Tommy and I *are* ready for the game.
Georgette and I *have* a date for tonight.

When *and* joins two pronouns, again the result is plural and a plural verb is required:

You and she *are* not twins, *are* you?
He and they *do* not agree on everything.

Pronouns in Parallel

Using a pronoun in a pair with a noun, a speaker may produce some awkwardness:

Tommy and *me* played marbles all afternoon.
There was nothing else for Tommy and *I* to do.

Those inappropriate pronouns produce an awkwardness that would be immediately obvious if the pronoun were used alone:

Me played marbles all afternoon.

There was nothing else for *I* to do.

Almost no one who speaks English would say sentences like those. Certainly such inappropriate usage should always be avoided by a writer.

One way to check the pronoun for appropriate usage in such a pair as "Tommy and *I*" or "Tommy and *me*" is to consider how the sentence would sound with the pronoun alone. Such a check for appropriateness is called the "leave out" test.

Time for Review

Pairs of nouns or pronouns linked by *and* form plurals. When such a pair is used as the subject of a verb, the verb must be plural.

When a pronoun is used in a pair linked by *and*, its appropriateness of form may be tested by considering the pronoun without the other item in the pair. Such a check is called the "leave out" test.

Do-It-Yourself Exercise

Applying the "leave out" test, consider how the sentence would sound without the first item in the pair—that is, with the pronoun alone. Then write an appropriate *pronoun* to complete each sentence:

Harry's remarks made Jake and _____ angry.

The ordeal was enjoyable for nobody but Vera and _____.

When the children and _____ arrived, the party began.

It was Molly and _____ who finished the dishes.

Why don't you visit Dolores and _____ some weekend?

Teasing my friend and _____ won't get you anywhere.

For you and _____ this kind of work is not profitable.

There was always plenty for my brother, my sister, and _____ to eat.

Checking up: Leaving out the "Jake and" or "the children and" will probably lead to the appropriate pronouns. No one would be likely to say, "Teasing *I* won't get you anywhere"; better make it, "Teasing my friend and *me* . . . ." One of the sentences is a special problem: "It was Molly and *I*" is the appropriate form in writing, although "It was Molly and *me*" might be used in informal speech.

The Reflexives and Intensives

A reflex camera is called that because it reflects an image off a mirror. A *reflexive pronoun* is called that because it *reflects* an action or a state of being—reflects it so that the one who *does* is also the one who *receives:*

Henry struck *himself* on the shin.

Henry *did* the action—and Henry also *received* the action. The reflexive pronoun, *himself,* is used to name Henry as the *object.*
 Reflexive pronouns are those with -*self* or -*selves* as ending. They are used only as objects when the subject and object are the same person or thing. The forms of the reflexive pronouns:

	Singular	Plural
First person:	*myself*	*ourselves*
Second person:	*yourself*	*yourselves*
Third person:	*himself*	
	herself	*themselves*
	itself	

It is not standard to use the reflexive as a subject. We do not write, "*Myself* am learning to write" or "*Yourself* are my friend." The reflexive is not used when some different subject does the action. We do not write, "He saw Jim and *myself*" or "They sent a gift to Mary and *myself.*"
 The -*self* and -*selves* pronouns also have another use. Consider these sentences:

Yes, I wrote the paper *myself.*
Are you *yourselves* on the dean's list?
The list *itself* is not complete.

Those -*self* pronouns are not reflexive; they do not serve as objects of an action reflected upon the doer. Rather, they are used to emphasize, or intensify, a noun or pronoun already used in the sentence. They are *intensive pronouns*.

Time for Review

A *reflexive pronoun* (with a *-self* or *-selves* ending) is used as the object when an action is reflected upon the doer. It indicates that the object is the same person or thing as the subject.

An *intensive pronoun* (with a *-self* or *-selves* ending) is used to emphasize, or intensify, a noun or pronoun already expressed.

Do-It-Yourself Exercise

Write in each blank an appropriate *intensive* or *reflexive* pronoun:

The Olsens have bought _____ a new wagon.

The judge _____ didn't think the defendant was guilty.

It never occurred to us to ask _____ whether the clock

_____ might be wrong.

Helen knew that she _____ had won the prize.

I think only you _____ can solve the problem.

Why shouldn't I treat _____ to a hot dog with mustard and onions?

Checking up: Be sure that each intensive or reflexive pronoun agrees with what it names—in person and in number: the Olsens, *themselves;* the judge *himself;* us, *ourselves;* the clock *itself;* she *herself;* you *yourself;* I *myself.* Which of the pronouns is used as *intensive*, and which as *reflexive?* Write "R" above each *reflexive* pronoun.

Demonstrative Pronouns

To *demonstrate* is to show or point out. The *demonstrative pronouns* are used to point out something that is already in evidence or clearly understood:

This is my two-year-old beagle.
What shall we do about *that?*
Are *these* good enough for you?
Give me two more of *those.*

The demonstrative pronouns *this* and *that* are singular; *these* and *those* are plural. In usage *this* and *these* refer to things that are near at hand, while *that* and *those* refer to things that are farther away from the speaker. These demonstrative pronouns are of course meaningless unless the listener or reader sees or knows clearly the things they stand for; if he does not, the pronouns cannot be understood. Consider the possible confusion in these sentences:

> Unleaded gasoline helps reduce air pollution, and *this* has certain advantages.
>
> Bob had trouble with spelling in his term paper; *that* discouraged him.

What has certain advantages—unleaded gasoline, air pollution, or the reduction of air pollution? What discouraged Bob—trouble, spelling, or the term paper? It would be wise to avoid the unclear demonstrative pronoun in such sentences and use, instead, nouns that clearly name what is meant:

> *Unleaded gasoline,* since it helps reduce air pollution, has certain advantages.
>
> Bob had trouble with spelling in his term paper, and *the trouble* discouraged him.

Indefinite Pronouns

What is indefinite is uncertain—not defined. Sometimes a writer does not want to be definite in reference to things. He does not want to mention every person in a group, so he writes *everybody;* he doesn't want to specify Mr. Jones, so he writes *someone.* These words are *indefinite* pronouns; they name unspecified persons, things, or groups:

> *Many* are concerned about rising prices.
>
> *Somebody* has answered the call for help.
>
> *None* of the remedies is good for *everyone*.
>
> If *each* takes *more* than his share, there won't be *any* for the *others*.

In those sentences we won't know exactly who are the *many*, who is the *somebody,* who is the *each,* what is the *more*—and so on. But it would be unnecessary, even ridiculous, to specify in every such case. The *indefinite pronouns* are handy devices when the specific nouns would be cumbersome.

Some *indefinite pronouns* work as plurals, some as singulars, and some as both:

Singular		Plural	Both Singular and Plural
another	everybody	both	all
anybody	everyone	few	any
anyone	everything	many	some
anything	little	most	
each	much	some	
either	neither	others	
one			

This matter of singular or plural is important when we use an *indefinite pronoun* as subject of a verb, since the verb must agree in number:

Everybody *is* ready.
Most of the decorations *are* ready.
All of the guests *are* ready.
All of the gifts *are* ready.
Both of us *are* ready.
All of the dinner *is* ready.
Some of the music *is* ready.

Time for Review

A *demonstrative pronoun* names a person or thing that is demonstrated (or clearly in evidence): *this, that, these, those.*

The demonstrative pronouns should not be used unless what they stand for is entirely clear in the context.

An *indefinite pronoun* names an unspecified person, thing, or group.

Do-It-Yourself Exercise

Write in each blank an appropriate *demonstrative* or *indefinite* pronoun, being sure that each such pronoun (if used as a subject) agrees with the verb:

If _____ agrees, _____ are going to be the next contestants on the show.

I am sure that _____ of us knows _____ who needs help.

Very _____ bothers Joe when he's asleep.

Are there _____ who want to try _____?

We didn't have _____ for breakfast, so _____ of us are hungry.

Isn't _____ your pencil over there on the floor?

A lot of people bought tickets, but _____

didn't use them; in fact, a _____ were returned for refund.

Will _____ who expect to join the group please form a line?

_____ are excellent buttered peas; won't you try _____ ?

Checking up: Agreement and consistency are the standards in this exercise. Does each of your pronouns agree with the verb? (The final pronoun in the exercise, of course, is used as *object* of the verb *try,* and does not need to agree.)

Suggestions for Writing

A. One of life's common problems is that of meeting a person for the first time, hearing that person's name, and then realizing two minutes later that the name is forgotten. Recall or imagine such an embarrassment and tell about it in a passage of about 250 words. Use as many pronouns as you can.
B. To see yourself as others see you is no easy thing, but to do so has great possible benefits. Imagine that you are your own mother or father, husband or wife, sister or brother. Describe yourself from the point of view of that relative, using the *third-person* approach. Write the description in a passage of about 250 words. Use as many pronouns as you can.
C. Recall a time when you missed a class, an appointment, or a date because something happened to you unexpectedly. Write the incident in a passage of about 250 words. Use as many pronouns as you can.

After Writing: Reread your passage and underline each pronoun you have used. If you have not used any *reflexive, intensive, demonstrative,* or *indefinite* pronouns, revise the passage so that it contains at least one of each of those kinds of pronouns. Read again to be sure that every verb agrees with its subject (as singular or plural). Remember that a reflexive or intensive pronoun cannot properly be used as a subject.

Interrogative Pronouns

When we use a pronoun as a question, it is an *interrogative pronoun.* Most such pronouns are *wh-*words: *who? what? which? whom? whose? whatever? whoever?*

Who wants another slice of pie?
Which is the best of the films?
Whose are the books on the floor?
Whom did you see today?
What are you doing here?
Whatever happened?

Relative Pronouns

Some pronouns do two jobs at once, working as both pronoun and conjunction:

Every runner *who* is eligible should report to the starter.
Dottie loves swimming, *which* she learned as a child.
The problem *that* troubles me most is saving money.

Each of those pronouns, *who, that,* and *which,* works also as a conjunction introducing a subordinate clause. The clause begun by the *relative pronoun* works as a modifier—an adjective modifying the noun before it, *runner, swimming,* or *problem.*

A *relative pronoun* stands for a noun that appears earlier in its sentence, as *who* stands for *runner, which* stands for *swimming,* and *that* stands for *problem.*

Time for Review

An *interrogative pronoun* is a *wh*-word *(who, what, which, whom, whose, whatever, whoever)* that is used to ask a question.

A *relative pronoun* works as pronoun and conjunction at once, standing for a noun already used in the sentence and introducing a subordinate clause that modifies that noun.

The *relative pronouns* are *who, that, which,* and *whom.*

Do-It-Yourself Exercise

Write in each blank an appropriate *interrogative* or *relative* pronoun to complete the sentence:

Near Tulsa we found an old barn _____ was so picturesque we couldn't resist painting it.

_____ spilled the ink here?

Is the person _____ spilled it still here?

One of these wrenches is the right one, but _____ ?

Our geology class, _____ has been studying the rock formations of the Southwest, is going to take a trip to the Grand Canyon.

The man _____ she married is still in the navy.

_____ is the dress _____ you like best?

Is this _____ you really want?

Checking up: Among the relative pronouns, *who* and *whom* are used to refer to persons; *that* and *which* are usually used to refer to animals and things. Some appropriate possible completions for the exercise: an old barn *that, Who* spilled, person *who*, but *which?* class, *which;* man *whom; what* or *whose* is the dress; is this *what* you really want?

Who or Whom?

One of the most troublesome things in English usage is the problem of when to use *who* and when to use *whom*. The matter is easier than it is often assumed to be: *Who* is used as a subject, *whom* as an object. *Whom* is never used to name a subject. Consider these sentences:

There goes the lady *who* called us. *(Who* is subject of the verb *called.)*
There goes the lady *whom* we called. *(Whom* is object of the verb *called.)*
Did you vote for the candidate *who* was elected? *(Who* is subject of the verb *was.)*
Did you vote for the candidate *whom* we elected? *(Whom* is object of the verb *elected.)*

"Who's" or "Whose"?

The *-'s* in *who's* forms a *contraction,* or drawing together, of the two words *who* and *is*. In this word the *-'s* has nothing to do with forming a possessive. The possessive word is *whose*. Like all the other possessive pronouns, *whose* is *not* spelled with an apostrophe.

Time for Review

As a relative pronoun *who* is used as the *subject* in a clause.

As a relative pronoun *whom* is used as the *object* of a verb or of a preposition.

Whose is a possessive.

Who's is the contraction of *who is*.

Do-It-Yourself Exercise

Write in each blank the appropriate one of these words: *who, whom, whose,* or *who's:*

Isn't she the girl _____ won the homemaking contest?

_____ old boots are these?

_____ will the mail be delivered to?

Can you guess _____ going to be there?

_____ the man _____ you introduced?

The people _____ attended were not the ones _____ were invited.

Nobody _____ we recognized was there.

Where is the lady _____ expected to address the crowd today?

Checking up: Remember that *who* is always a subject, *whom* always an object. *Who's* means *who is*. Some appropriate completions for the sentences: girl *who* won, *whose* are these, *who's* going, *Who's* the man, *whom* you introduced, people *who* attended, ones *who* were invited, Nobody *whom* we recognized, lady *who* expected or lady *who's* expected.

Pronoun Agreement

Since a pronoun stands for a noun, the pronoun agrees with that noun. That is, the pronoun should be the same in *number* (singular or plural) as the noun it stands for:

Our dog barks, but *it* doesn't bite. (Stands for *dog,* singular.)

When leaves turn color, *they* are about to drop off. (Stands for *leaves,* plural.)

Whenever anyone rings this bell, *he* gets a surprise. (Stands for *anyone*, singular.)

If a person wants anything, *he* should ask for it. (Stands for *a person*, singular.)

Pronouns must also agree in *person* with the nouns they stand for:

The professor asked *me* whether *I* wrote *mine* by *myself*. (All have reference to the *first person* or his possession.

The day was cool as *it* dawned and began making a life for *itself*. (Both refer to *day, third person.*)

Sweetheart, *you* have to give *yourself* credit. (Both refer to *sweetheart, second person.*)

Pronouns also agree in *gender* (masculine or feminine or neuter) if they stand for nouns in the third-person singular:

> My mother is happiest when *she* has friends around *her*.
> Each man in his time learns that *he* must trust *himself*.
> The giant tree, as *it* fell, crashed cleanly between the smaller ones around *it*.

The *indefinite pronouns* present some agreement problems. Since the indefinite pronouns do not clearly refer to specific nouns, the writer may be unsure about the number, person, or gender of those pronouns. Does *everybody* mean just one person, or more? Does *all* mean just men, just women, or both men and women? The answers, of course, depend upon the context in which the words are used.

Since a writer is composing his own context, he can decide whether his indefinite pronouns are masculine or feminine. But he should observe the standard usage of such pronouns as singular or plural (see p. 248). When an indefinite pronoun like *everybody* (singular) or *all* (plural) is later referred to by another pronoun, the later pronoun must agree

> *Everybody* may have a second serving if *he* wants it.
> *Each* of the girls may help *herself*.
> *All* may do what *they* want.
> *Some* have introduced *themselves* already.
> *Nobody* seems tired unless his eyes betray *him*.
> *Somebody* said that *he* would help.

It is important not to be distracted by words that come between the noun (or pronoun) and the pronoun that renames it.

Pronoun Reference

The writer should not make his reader guess at what a pronoun stands for. Consider the reader's puzzlement as he reads sentences like these:

> Linda called, and when Alice answered, *she* wouldn't speak to *her*.
> These songs come from the islands where *they* do those backbreaking limbo dances.
> I tried swimming in the ocean once, but I didn't like *it*.

Was it Linda or Alice who wouldn't speak? Do the *songs* do those dances? What didn't I like—the swimming, or the ocean? The reader may have some difficulty trying to decipher those pronouns because of their inexact or *faulty reference* to the nouns they should stand for.

Me, Myself, and I 255

Among the most troublesome of pronoun-reference problems for a reader (and therefore for the careful writer) are those involving the relative pronoun *which*. In conversation *which* is often used to refer hazily to a whole idea that has previously been mentioned.

> The Grunbergs had an auto accident during their vacation, *which* was a terrible shock.
> Elmore fell to the floor as he tried to steal the ball, *which* brought a roar from the crowd.
> Muriel smiled when Rich mentioned studying together for the exam, *which* made his heart jump.
> Tomorrow is expected to be sunny, *which* will bring crowds to the resorts.

Listeners may grasp the intended meanings. But readers expect greater clarity; if they are forced, even momentarily, to wonder whether the Grunbergs' *vacation* was a shock, whether the *ball* or the *steal* or the *fall* brought a roar, or whether the *exam* made Rich's heart jump, the writer has lost their attention. Since the pronoun *which* does not refer clearly to one of the nouns in such a sentence, the writer must avoid faulty reference by revising:

> During their vacation the Grunbergs had an auto *accident* that was a terrible shock.
> As he tried to steal the ball, Elmore fell to the floor; the *fall* brought a roar from the crowd.
> When Rich mentioned studying together for the exam, Muriel's *smile* made his heart jump.
> Tomorrow's expected *sunshine* will bring crowds to the resorts.

Time for Review

Pronouns must *agree* in number, in person, and in gender with the nouns they stand for.

Pronouns should be clear in *reference*, so that the reader can see easily what each pronoun stands for.

Do-It-Yourself Exercise

Write in each blank a *noun* or *pronoun* to replace the faulty one shown in parentheses. Be sure that the pronoun you write agrees with what it stands for—and that it clearly stands for a noun. If no pronoun would be clear, write a noun instead:

I wanted to play musical *works*, not just study _____.
(it)

At last I got my chance when _____ gave me a job in a
(they)

dance band. I knew that _____ would require practice, so
(it)

I went at _____ enthusiastically; _____
(it)   (which)

led, of course, to neglect of my studies; _____ led to trouble.
(which)

I knew I would have to choose between college and music or forget _____

_____. I chose _____, and
(it)   (one)

I have never regretted _____. My counselor knows
(that)

_____, and _____ have
(it)   (they)

helped me a lot in the music department, too. The dance-band leader told

me to do one thing at a time and not try to mix _____.
(them)

Checking up: It doesn't matter whether your version indicates choosing music or choosing college. All that matters is whether you have written nouns and pronouns that make the passage clear. The faulty agreement or faulty reference must be eliminated. Perhaps your final version reads something like this: "I wanted to play musical works, not just study *music*. At last I got my chance when *friends* gave me a job in a dance band. I knew that *playing* would require practice, so I went at *the practice* enthusiastically; *practicing* led, of course, to neglect of my studies; *the neglect* led to trouble. I knew I would have to choose between college and music or forget *both*. I chose *college,* and I have never regretted *the choice.* My counselor knows *my problem,* and *professors* have helped me a lot in the music department, too. The dance-band director told me to do one thing at a time and not try to mix *activities.*

Time for Review

There are eight kinds of pronoun: *personal, possessive, reflexive, intensive, demonstrative, indefinite, interrogative,* and *relative.* The *possessive* pronouns are sometimes classed among the *personal* pronouns.

Suggestions for Writing

D. First impressions are sometimes accurate, but still more often those impressions have to be revised. Write a passage of about 300 words, telling about some person you had a wrong first impression of. What happened to make you change that impression? Use as many pronouns as you can, including especially *relative* pronouns.
E. Some people believe everyone has a right to privacy, yet modern life is full of things that deny that right. Who really has a right to privacy, and what limits upon privacy are necessary? Write your ideas in a passage of about 300 words. Use as many pronouns as you can, including especially *relative* pronouns.
F. Democracy is based upon the principle of majority rule. Yet America today seems intensely conscious of minority rights. When the will of a majority conflicts with the right of a minority, who is to prevail? Write your ideas in a passage of about 300 words. Use as many pronouns as you can, including especially *relative* pronouns.

After Writing: Reread your passage and underline every pronoun. Then circle the noun (or pronoun) that each pronoun refers to. If you have trouble finding what should be circled, perhaps you have written a pronoun with *faulty reference* (see p. 254) and will have to revise. Check for agreement of verbs with their subjects. Be sure you have not used *who* for *whom* (see p. 252).

Me, Myself, and I 259

QUIZ 14

Using Pronouns

On the blank within each sentence write the item that you think completes the sentence most effectively; then mark the **letter** of that item on your answer blank. After marking your choice, explain briefly why you chose it (**Because:** . . .).

Example: There is still time for Arnold and ____*me*____ to finish work.

(a) she   (b) myself   (c) I   (d) me   (e) we   Ex. *d*

(**Because:** *"Me" is a proper object of the preposition "for"* .)

1. Ralph and _____ will be here at 8 o'clock.

(a) them   (b) us   (c) her   (d) him   (e) she   1._____

(**Because:** _____.)
    (**Question:** Which pronoun is appropriate as the *subject* in a pair with *Ralph*?)

2. The trouble with Terry and _____ is that we can't be sure we really love each other.

(a) myself   (b) me   (c) she   (d) I   (e) we   2._____

(**Because:** _____.)
    (**Question:** Which pronoun makes a proper pair with *Terry* as object of *with*?)

3. In South Polynesia _____ eat a lot of papaya.

(a) they   (b) most   (c) the natives   (d) those   (e) everybody   3._____

(**Because:** _____.)
    (**Question:** Would any pronoun provide clear reference?)

4. I forgot to ask about _____ took you to the party.

(a) who   (b) whom   (c) who's   (d) he   (e) them   4._____

(**Because:** _____.)
    (**Question:** Which pronoun can properly serve both as subject of *took* and as subordinator?)

5. As for _____, I don't expect anything but success.

(a) I   (b) myself   (c) our's   (d) me   (e) we   5._____

(**Because:** _____.)
    (**Question:** Which pronoun provides a proper object of the preposition *for*? Does the verb action seem to be reflected upon *I*?)

Chapter Fourteen

6. We suppose that _____ are going to win.

(a) none (b) everybody (c) each (d) nobody (e) both

6._____

(*Because:* _____.)
 (*Question:* Which indefinite pronoun matches the plural verb, *are*?)

7. _____ will the city government accept as its labor representative?

(a) Who (b) Whom (c) Who's (d) That (e) Either

7._____

(*Because:* _____.)
 (*Question:* Which pronoun provides a proper *object* of the verb? Are *that* and *either* interrogatives?)

8. Uncle Sam informed Jimmy that _____ was not ready for involvement in Europe.

(a) they (b) neither (c) he (d) the nation (e) it

8._____

(*Because:* _____.)

9. The old lady's shoe obviously had a hole in _____.

(a) both (b) her (c) them (d) it (e) him

9._____

(*Because:* _____.)

10. My hose are ruined! Has one of you girls found a run in _____ too?

(a) her's (b) theirs (c) hers (d) their's (e) our's

10._____

(*Because:* _____.)

11. My term paper is not finished. _____ is?

(a) Who (b) Whose (c) Who's (d) Whom (e) Your's

11._____

(*Because:* _____.)

12. Nothing really bothers my brother and _____ except seeing people go hungry.

(a) me (b) I (c) we (d) myself (e) he

12._____

(*Because:* _____.)

13. Nick's cousin always seems to be hurting _____.

(a) hisself (b) herself (c) her's (d) whom (e) we

13._____

(*Because:* _____.)

14. _____ is your favorite date this year?

(a) Who (b) Whom (c) Who's (d) Her's (e) These

14_____

(*Because:* _____.)

15. Losing your girlfriend's car keys is likely to be embarrassing to _____

_____.

(a) herself (b) oneself (c) one (d) both you and she
(e) both you and her

15_____

(*Because:* _____.)

16. People who destroy _____ with drugs always arouse society's anger as well as pity.

(a) them (b) both (c) theirselves (d) themselves (e) their

16_____

(*Because:* _____.)

17. Life is not consistently good to my family and _____.

(a) I (b) your's (c) hers (d) we (e) they

17_____

(*Because:* _____.)

18. The puppy looked lovingly at _____.

(a) hisself (b) me (c) our's (d) themselves (e) whom

18_____

(*Because:* _____.)

19. _____ who will take money for nothing has very little integrity.

(a) All (b) Some (c) Most (d) Anyone (e) Few of us

19_____

(*Because:* _____.)

20. Somehow I can't get friends to do things for _____.

(a) myself (b) theirself (c) us (d) you and I (e) she and me

20_____

(*Because:* _____.)

Who and What 15

How to work with ... interrogative pronouns
relative pronouns
adjective clauses
who and whom
noun clauses
appositive clauses
incomplete clauses
commas with nonrestrictive clauses

How to avoid ... misplaced adjective clauses
danglers
commas with restrictive clauses

NEWS REPORTERS LOOKING FOR THE FACTS of a story are trained to "get the five W's"—*who, what, when, where,* and *why*. The core of the story is often in those first two, *who* and *what:*

What happened?
Who did it?

What stands for a thing or an action. *Who* stands for a person. These two words, then, take the place of *nouns;* they are *pronouns*.

Interrogative Pronouns

When *who* and *what* appear in *independent* clauses (as in the "What happened?" and "Who did it?" above), they usually ask a question. In such sentences they are *interrogative pronouns:*

Who's there?
What's the score?
Who plays the violin for the philharmonic?
What are the business opportunities today?

Other words that work as interrogative pronouns are *whom, which,* and the *-ever* words: *whoever, whomever, whatever.*

Whom do you prefer among the candidates?
Which is your favorite team?
Whatever have you done?
Whoever took my chair?

Time for Review

Who and *what* are pronouns.

Used in an independent clause, *who* or *what* usually asks a question; these words are *interrogative pronouns.*

Other interrogative pronouns are *whom, which,* and the *-ever* words: *whoever, whomever, whatever.*

Do-It-Yourself Exercise

Write in each blank an appropriate *interrogative pronoun* to complete each sentence:

_____ seems to be leading the race?

_____ is the date of the election?

_____ of the propositions shall we vote for?

_____ was the outcome last time?

_____ in the world is wrong with this system?

_____ should I vote for?

Checking up: *What* will probably be used in two of those sentences. If you have used any other interrogative pronouns more than once, repeat the exercise and use each only once.

"Who" as Subordinator

When the pronoun *who* or *whom* appears to stand for a noun that has already been used in the sentence, a different pattern occurs:

It was Larry *who* picked up the ball.

In that sentence *who* stands for Larry. But *who* also has other functions in the sentence: *who* is the subject of the verb *picked up,* and *who* is a subordinator introducing the clause *who picked up the ball.*

The words *whom, which,* and *that* can work in that same way—as *pronoun* renaming a noun, and as *subordinator* introducing a subordinate clause:

She is the girl *whom* we nominated.

Those tires, *which* are worn thin, should be replaced.

Show us the trophy *that* you won.

The Adjective Clause

When a subordinate clause is used to modify a noun, it works as an adjective clause. For example, *whom we nominated* modifies *girl;* therefore, *whom we nominated* is an adjective clause. In other examples above, *which are worn thin* is an adjective clause modifying *tires,* and *that you won* is an adjective clause modifying *trophy.*

Several other words also may be used as subordinators to begin adjective clauses: *whose, where, when,* and *why.*

Jack, *whose* mother is ill, can't be here today.
That is the place *where* I was born.
I remember the day *when* the bridge fell.
There's no reason *why* we can't do the job.

Those words *(whose, where, when,* and *why)* are not pronouns—but they do work as subordinators to introduce the adjective clauses that modify the nouns *Jack, place, day,* and *reason*

Time for Review

The pronouns *who, whom, that,* and *which* may also function as subordinators at the same time.

When serving the double function of pronoun-subordinator, *who, whom, that,* or *which* introduces a subordinate clause.

A subordinate clause may work as an *adjective clause,* modifying a noun.

Some other words may begin adjective clauses: *whose, where, when,* and *why.*

Do-It-Yourself Exercise

Write in each blank an appropriate subordinator *(who, whom, whose, that, which, where, when,* or *why)* to introduce the adjective clause modifying the italicized noun:

We need a *candidate* _____ has an imaginative welfare program.

The skating *star* _____ we saw on television has won three Olympic medals.

Most drivers today want a *car* _____ has built-in safety devices.

Does your college have a *place* _____ you can study quietly?

Surely there is a *reason* _____ you missed the bus.

Is there a *time* _____ I can meet with you?

Jake is a *man* _____ friends stand by him.

The *room*, _____ was filled with people, seemed stuffy.

Coach Darcy, _____ we all respect, always gets good performance from his men.

Checking up: The subordinator should be appropriate to the noun it stands for. *Who, whom,* and *whose* are used to stand for persons; *when* refers to times, *why* to reasons, *where* to places. *Whom* should be used only in clauses that have some other subject, as in "star *whom* we saw" *(we* is the subject of the clause).

Continue this exercise by writing an entire *adjective clause* to fill each blank in the following sentences. Remember that the clause must begin with one of the subordinators *who, whom, whose, that, which, when, where,* or *why*. Each adjective clause must contain a subject-verb combination:

The editor has criticized most of the *movies* _____
_____.

A firebug is a *person* _____.

Henry has to write a term *paper* _____
_____.

Every basketball *player* _____ must keep in excellent physical condition.

Get plenty of exercise, because *muscles* _____ waste away.

There will come a *day* _____.

The market *manager*, _____, said he would keep me in mind for the job.

The committee must have a *reason* _____
_____.

New York is a *city* _____.

Checking up: Be sure that each of your adjective clauses begins with one of the subordinators listed in the directions. Reread your clauses, marking "S" above each subject and "V" above each verb; each clause must have both. The pronoun-subordinators *who, which,* and *that* may be subjects in their clauses.

Restrictive or Nonrestrictive?

When a writer uses an adjective clause, he has to consider how to punctuate. Should such a clause be set off by a comma (or a pair of commas)? His answer lies in whether the clause is *essential* in the sentence. For example:

People *who are afraid of water* shouldn't own boats.

Could the writer leave out that adjective clause without changing the meaning of his sentence? No, because the sentence would not be true without that clause: The writer surely doesn't mean to say that "People shouldn't own boats"; he means only that the certain sort of people, those *who are afraid of water,* should not own boats. The adjective clause is, therefore, necessary, for it *restricts* the meaning of *people;* it is a *restrictive clause.*

The *restrictive clause* should *not* be set off by a comma (or between commas).

On the other hand, an adjective clause that merely adds information but is not essential to the meaning of the sentence is *nonrestrictive*—and should be set off between commas:

My brother Ralph, *who drives racing cars,* loves high speed.

Senator Blaine, *who is a bachelor,* enjoys Washington parties.

Those sentences would remain fully understandable even if the adjective clauses were removed. They are *nonrestrictive* clauses.

Most contemporary writers use *that* to begin a restrictive clause, but *which* to begin a *nonrestrictive* clause:

I remember the document *that* John Hancock signed.

The Declaration of Independence, *which* John Hancock signed, is displayed at Independence Hall.

The general noun *document* needs the adjective clause to define it, but the specific noun *Declaration of Independence* does not.

Time for Review

Adjective clauses may begin with the relative pronouns *who, whom, that, which,* or with the subordinators *whose, when, where,* and *why.*

If an adjective clause is *restrictive* (needed to define or restrict the meaning of its noun), the clause is not set off by commas.

If an adjective clause is *nonrestrictive* (not needed to define or restrict the meaning of its noun), the clause is set off by a comma (or between a pair of commas).

Do-It-Yourself Exercise

Write adjective clauses (and punctuate them appropriately) to complete these sentences. Try to use a variety of *relative pronouns* and *subordinators*.

Have you been to San Francisco _____?

The party wants the conference to be held in an area _____

_____.

Because of his convictions about nonviolence Mr. McLean won't take part

in games _____.

The treasurer said that he wanted to know the reason _____

_____.

Your story about forgetting your keys reminds me of the morning

_____.

The chairman of the board spends an hour every morning poring through

The Wall Street Journal _____.

He says he likes a newspaper _____.

Checking up: Since proper nouns (naming things like *San Francisco* and the *Wall Street Journal*) do not need further definition, the clauses that modify them will probably be *nonrestrictive*—set off by commas. The other nouns *(area, games, reason, morning, newspaper)* are general; the clauses that modify them are *restrictive,* necessary to define which *area,* which *games,* which *newspaper* is meant, and such clauses are not set off by commas. If you did not use at least five different *relative pronouns* to begin your adjective clauses, you may get further practice by trying to do so.

Suggestions for Writing

A. Is a college student who is married likely to do as well in studies as one who is unmarried? Discuss that question and your answers in a passage of about 350 words. In your passage use several *adjective clauses.*

B. People often say "I think so" when they are really guessing, not thinking. What is the difference between thinking and guessing? Write a passage of about 350 words pointing out the difference and naming a few things that you *think* and a few that you only *guess*. Use as many adjective clauses as you can.

C. Some people, including many famous writers and some philosophers, believe that childhood is the best time of a person's life. Part of that view holds that adults, because of their longer contact with corrupt society, have become somehow unwholesome or "adulterated." How do you feel toward that attitude? Write your opinions in a passage of about 350 words. Use several *adjective clauses* in your passage.

After Writing: Reread your passage and underline each *adjective clause*. Then circle the noun that each clause modifies. Did you use a comma (or a pair of commas) to set off each *nonrestrictive* adjective clause? How can you be sure whether a modifying clause is *nonrestrictive?* (See p. 268.)

Verb Agreement With "Who"

When *who* introduces an adjective clause, *who* is usually the subject of the verb in that clause. Should that verb be singular, or should it be plural?

As a relative pronoun *who* stands for a noun used earlier in its sentence. *Who* should, then, be considered as having the same number as the noun it stands for:

> Gloria is the girl *who* won the lifeguard's heart.
>
> Stan has many friends *who* still call him "Stanley."

In the first of those sentences *who* stands for *girl,* so *who* is singular; in the second *who* stands for *friends,* so *who* is plural. And the *verb* in the subordinate clause agrees:

> It's always his wife who *does* the shopping. *(Does* is singular to agree with *wife.)*
>
> Are you the one who *takes* guitar lessons? *(Takes* is singular to agree with *one.)*
>
> Yes, I'm one of those who *take* lessons. *(Take* is plural to agree with *those.)*
>
> Each of the actors who *try* for the part must be able to dance. *(Try* is plural to agree with *actors.)*
>
> Each actor who *tries* for the part must be able to dance. *(Tries* is singular to agree with *actor.)*

The word *who* is used to stand for persons, groups of persons, or occasionally animals. But *that* or *which* is used to stand for most other things. Both *that* and *which,* when used as subjects, require a verb that agrees with the noun they stand for:

> Every label *that* has a skull on it indicates poison. *(That* stands for *label,* singular: *that has.)*
>
> Few of the rocks *that* are in my collection are ancient. *(That* stands for *rocks,* plural: *that are.)*

The decisions *which* have affected us most are well known. *(Which* stands for *decisions,* plural: *which have.)*

A dog or cat *that* has fleas can be protected from them by a flea collar. *(That* stands for *dog* or *cat,* singular, but not for both: *that has.)*

The court is familiar with cases of murder *which* have never been solved. *(Which* stands for *cases,* plural: *which have.)*

Time for Review

As a relative pronoun *who* introduces a subordinate clause.

In an adjective clause *who* is the subject of the verb.

In an adjective clause *who* stands for a noun used earlier in the sentence.

Who must agree in number with the noun that *who* stands for; therefore, the verb in the *who*-clause must also agree with the noun that *who* stands for.

Who is used to refer to people (and sometimes animals); *that* or *which* is used to refer to most other things.

Like *who,* the words *that* and *which* (when used as subjects in relative clauses) require verbs that agree with the nouns *that* and *which* stand for.

Do-It-Yourself Exercise

Write in each blank an appropriate verb (in the *present* tense) to agree with the italicized relative pronoun:

Most of the customers *who* _____ our product will find it superior.

Any child of wealthy parents *who* _____ more attention than they give him might as well be poor.

Kelly is one of those fellows *who* always _____ to outdo everyone else.

Our friend Lisa is one girl out of the crowd *who* _____ herself seriously.

I am the only student so far *who* _____ completed all of the assignments.

Eddie and Sal, *who* _____ been married only a week, _____ asked us to join them for dinner.

Any one of you ladies *who* _____ not like the soap may return it for refund.

This is one of those beautiful days *that* _____ us smile.

Elwood is the representative of the people *who* _____ freedom.

The *New York Times* is one of the few large daily newspapers *that* _____ _____ no comic section.

Shirley is one of the ladies *who* _____ supporting Women's Lib movements.

One of the animals, *which* apparently _____ no need for company, has broken away from the herd.

Dune-buggying and motorbiking, *which* _____ become so popular recently, can be done only in special areas.

The vote of the Supreme Court justices, *which* _____ not please all of us, may turn out to be a wise one, nevertheless.

Checking up: Draw a circle around the noun that each of the relative pronouns stands for. Be sure that the verb you have written agrees with that noun. Your circled nouns should be: *customers, child, fellows, girl, student, Eddie and Sal, one, days, people, newspapers, ladies, one, dune-buggying and motorbiking, vote.* Check your verb agreement again.

Clear Placement of Adjective Clauses

An adjective clause should be placed so that it clearly modifies the noun that the writer intends it to modify. Consider what can happen if the placement is not clear:

No girl can work for Mr. Griffin *who wears short skirts.*
He needs a truck for his job *that has a flat bed.*
How can a candidate become mayor *whom nobody likes?*

The obvious misplacements distract the reader, perhaps making him laugh. Such distraction could be avoided by more careful placement of the adjective clause in each sentence:

No girl *who wears short skirts* can work for Mr. Griffin.
For his job he needs a truck *that has a flat bed*.
How can a candidate *whom nobody likes* become mayor?

Time for Review

An *adjective clause* should be placed so that it clearly modifies the noun that the writer intends it to modify.

Do-It-Yourself Exercise

Each of the italicized clauses below should fit into the sentence shown just beneath it. Draw a line in the sentence, showing where the adjective clause should be placed:

who run away from home
  Sometimes children get sympathy from policemen.
that has wire wheels.
  I'd like to buy a car to impress the crowd.
which gave birth to a litter of kittens
  My pet cat disturbed the neighbor family during the night.
that I like to watch
  The show has great music and very funny lines.
who was passing out cigars
  The wife of one man had just presented him with a baby daughter.
whose drilling was quite painless
  My mother told a friend about a dentist.

Checking up: Do *policemen* run away from home? Does the *crowd* have wire wheels? Did the *neighbor family* give birth to a litter of kittens? Is it the *music* that I like to watch? Was the *baby daughter* passing out cigars? Check each of your decisions to be sure you have avoided a misplaced adjective clause.

The Noun Clause

When a pronoun like *who* begins a subordinate clause but does not rename a noun already used, a different pattern occurs:

I know *who wrote the note*.

Guess *whom I saw yesterday*.

She asked *whose car was available*.

In those sentences the subordinate clauses do not work as adjectives, for they do not modify any noun. Rather, the clauses are themselves used as nouns: *who wrote the note* is the name of what *I know*; *whom I saw yesterday* is the name of the thing you are asked to *guess*; *whose car was available* is the name of what *she asked*.

As *names* of things or ideas these clauses are *noun clauses*.

A *noun clause* is a subordinate clause used in a sentence as a noun. A noun clause usually begins with one of these subordinators: *who, whom, whose, what, that, where, when, why, how, whatever, which, whoever, whomever*, or *whether*.

Like other nouns, noun clauses may be used in sentences as *subjects*:

Whatever she knew was told willingly.

Why she ran from the scene remained a mystery.

That she had seen two men was beyond doubt.

Noun clauses may be used as *objects of verbs*:

The witness told *who had bribed her*.

She did not say *which man was guilty*.

She had been at the scene but didn't know *whether she had observed everything*.

or as *noun complements*:

The shooting was *what she had seen*.

The question was *who had bribed her*.

The library foyer was *where the crime occurred*.

or as *objects of prepositions*:

We asked about *how she had seen the event*.

The jury took a bus to *where the crime had occurred*.

Much depended on *whether she had seen it all*.

or as *objects of verbals*:

They heard her saying *that she had seen two men*.

The prosecutor wanted to know *whose voice she had heard*.

Jurors were told *which weapon had been used*.

or as *noun-appositives*:

It was clear *whom she had observed on the stairs*.

Her belief *that she had seen two men* was unshakable.

She never answered the question *why she ran from the scene*.

Time for Review

A subordinate clause may work as a noun: a *noun clause*.

A noun clause usually is introduced by one of the *wh-* words: *who, whom, whose, which, where, why, when, whether,* or by the word *that*.

A noun clause may be used as most other nouns are used: as *subject, object, noun complement, object of preposition, object of verbal,* or *appositive*.

Do-It-Yourself Exercise

Write in each blank an appropriate subordinator to begin the noun clause:

As the song says, love is _____ the world needs now.

Turn on the news and find out _____ won the first game.

A good road map will tell _____ is the best route to Taos from Albuquerque.

The *Times* editorial made it obvious _____ the publisher is supporting for district attorney.

Please tell me _____ you will go or not.

Did you find out _____ the roof fell in?

Salad is _____ we want for lunch.

Ask the cook _____ he made the soup.

_____ it is snowing is no surprise to me.

Checking up: These might be the appropriate subordinators to begin the noun clauses (but not necessarily in this order): *which, whom, when, who, that, whether, why, what.*

Continue this exercise by writing an entire *noun clause* to fill each blank in the following sentences. Remember that each clause must begin with one of the subordinators and must contain a subject-verb combination:

With a good view of the front door, the store manager could see _____

276 Chapter Fifteen

_____.

The other day Esther was asking about _____

_____.

When we have our party, you may bring _____

_____.

Of course, we can't be sure of _____

_____.

Can you tell me _____

_____.

What you see is _____

_____.

I like both horses and dogs, and I can't decide _____

_____.

Julie has been feeling bad, so she doesn't know _____

_____.

Checking up: Have you used a variety of the subordinators, such as *who, what, where, whether, that, why, which, whoever, whatever?* Be sure you did not use *who* in a clause that has another subject. Also be sure that each of your clauses contains a subject-verb combination. Something like *what to do* will not complete a clause, since *to do* is an infinitive and not a verb; *what he should do* has subject and verb and is a complete clause.

The Incomplete Clause

Writers and speakers often leave out part of a structure when that part can be clearly understood without being expressed. It is common, for example, to leave out the subordinator from a noun clause:

All his friends know *he likes jazz. (That* he likes jazz.)
Do you think *I am overconfident? (That* I am overconfident.)

These noun clauses, with *that* omitted, are *incomplete clauses*—but they still carry the full meaning and are quite acceptable in both writing and speaking.

Adjective clauses also may have their subordinators omitted:

The flavor *I like best* is chocolate. *(That* I like best.)

The man *we want* is Joe. *(Whom* we want.)

There's the place *I work. (Where* I work.)

The subordinator should not be omitted, of course, if any misunderstanding might result: "The library is the place *I study"* could mean that I study the library rather than that I study *in* the library.

Punctuating the Appositive Clause

When a noun clause works as an *appositive* (to rename or explain some noun already used in the sentence), it presents a problem: whether to punctuate or not to punctuate. The appositive noun clause is set off by a comma (or a pair of commas) if the clause is not essential to define or explain the noun:

Eddie's favorite topic, *how dodos became extinct,* just never seemed to come up at rap sessions.

One question, *whether the group liked him,* was never really answered.

Those noun clauses could be left out of the sentences, though the sentences would be rather uninformative without them. But some appositive noun clauses could not be left out without producing meaningless results:

It is astonishing *that porpoises are so intelligent.*

The idea *that men waste their resources* is unchallenged.

Without those noun clauses the sentences would be unclear: *What* is astonishing? *What* idea is unchallenged? The clauses present the essential information; they are *restrictive* appositives.

Restrictive appositive clauses are not set off by commas, but nonrestrictive clauses are set off.

Time for Review

An *incomplete clause* is a subordinate clause whose subordinator has been left out.

An *incomplete clause* carries the same meaning as the full clause and is acceptable in both writing and speaking—unless misunderstanding might result.

An *appositive* noun clause is used to rename or explain a noun used earlier in the sentence.

A *nonrestrictive* appositive clause, which could be left out of the sentence without great loss, is set off by a comma (or between a pair of commas).

Chapter Fifteen

Do-It-Yourself Exercise

Write in each blank an *incomplete clause* appropriate to the sentence. Remember that an incomplete clause omits the subordinator, but it must contain a subject-verb combination:

Discovering that you have lost your wallet is a crisis _____

_____.

It was a pleasure to meet the girl _____.

The government hopes to hold food prices to a level _____

_____.

At the end of our trip we spent a day in the city _____

_____.

One of the people _____ is my dentist.

Checking up: After each of your completed sentences write the *subordinator* that is meant but not expressed. To be sure you have written a clause, write "S" above the subject and "V" above the verb in each of your incomplete clauses.

Continue this exercise by writing in the blank an appropriate noun clause as an appositive for the italicized word:

It never did become clear _____.

My own *suggestion* _____ was
    received with enthusiasm.
We had to give up the *idea* _____.

Slade's *remark* _____ seemed
    a bit sarcastic.
I cannot accept the *belief* _____.

If it were not for the *fact* _____,
    I wouldn't even be here.

Checking up: Each appositive noun clause should begin with a subordinator such as *that* or *whether*, and each must contain a subject-verb combination. In the clauses you have written, write "S" above the subject and "V" above the verb.

Suggestions for Writing

D. Most people believe a great many things that they don't know for sure. What is the difference between *believing* and *knowing?* Write a passage of about 350 words, pointing out the difference and naming a few of your *beliefs* as well as a few of your bits of real knowledge. Use as many *noun clauses* as you can.
E. Some of the heartbreak in life occurs when people say things that they don't really mean. What are some of the things you have said (or things that have been said to you) that were not really meant? What trouble did the insincerity cause? Write your answers in a passage of about 350 words. Use as many *noun clauses* as you can.
F. People who are too "opinionated" often lose friends. What sorts of opinion should people avoid stating too strongly if they want to avoid alienating others? Recall some opinions that you have heard stated (or that you have stated yourself) when silence or compromise would have been better for friendships. Write about them in a passage of about 350 words. Use as many *noun clauses* as you can.

After Writing: Reread your passage and underline every *noun clause* that you have used. Circle the *subordinator* that begins each of those clauses.

QUIZ 15

Using Interrogative Pronouns, Adjective Clauses, and Noun Clauses

On the blank within each sentence write the item that you think completes the sentence most effectively; then mark the *letter* of that item on your answer blank. After marking your choice, explain briefly why you chose it (*Because:* . . .).

Example: This organization, let us admit, needs a leader whose _____

___*honesty we can trust*___.

(a) trustworthy ✓(b) deserving of trust   (c) honesty we can trust
(d) not afraid of work   (e) hard working and dynamic   Ex *c*

(*Because:* *All other items would require "who's"*.)

1. The top job usually goes to the man who's _____.
(a) qualifications are trusted   (b) wife is the boss's daughter
(c) influence is the greatest   (d) work has proven him worthy   (e) best qualified   1_____

(*Because:* _____.)
   (*Question:* Since *who's* means "who is," which completion properly follows?)

2. People _____ people are the luckiest people in the world.
(a) , which need   (b) who need   (c) , who need   (d) whom are in need of
(e) , that need   2_____

(*Because:* _____.)
   (*Question:* Can *Which* be used for people? Is *whom* a proper subject of the verb *are*? Is the adjective clause restrictive?)

3. Chuck is the only one of the players _____ fully eligible.
(a) that are   (b) , who are   (c) who is   (d) which is   (e) whom is   3_____

(*Because:* _____.)
   (*Question:* Should the relative pronoun stand for *one* or for *players*? Is *which* proper to stand for a person? Is *whom* a proper subject for *is*? Is the adjective clause restrictive?)

4. There are parks _____ that are closed during the winter months.
(a) in many states   (b) full of bears   (c) for children   (d) in Montana
(e) for mobile homes of travelers   4_____

(*Because:* _____.)
   (*Question:* Would the pronoun *that* be clear after the plural nouns? What really *are closed?*)

282   Chapter Fifteen

5. The textbook doesn't _____ Napoleon invaded Russia.

(a) tell, why   (b) explain, how   (c) deny, that   (d) report the fact that
(e) make clear, when

5._____

(*Because:* _____.)
  (*Question:* Should the noun clause, used as object of the verb, be set off by a comma? See *cf3*, p. 442.)

6. Sometimes people do not recognize the influences _____ have had the most lasting effects upon them.

(a) whom   (b) , that   (c) , which   (d) that   (e) whose

6._____

(*Because.* _____.)
  (*Question:* Which of the relative pronouns can properly stand for *influences*? Is the adjective clause restrictive?)

7. No doubt the convention will nominate _____ the standard-bearer wants as his running mate.

(a) who   (b) whoever   (c) whomever   (d) however   (e) which

7._____

(*Because:* _____.)
  (*Question:* Which of the completions could stand for the person the standard-bearer *wants*?)

8. Everyone in the office thinks Jim is the one _____ get the first promotion.

(a) who's sure to   (b) whose going to   (c) whom will   (d) , that will
(e) which will

8._____

(*Because:* _____.)

9. The crowd seemed uncertain about _____ the officials had called time out.

(a) who   (b) whom   (c) that   (d) why   (e) which

9._____

(*Because:* _____.)

10. Whomever _____ will have to merit our confidence.

(a) we elect   (b) takes the job   (c) is chosen   (d) goes to Washington
(e) he is, he

10._____

(*Because:* _____.)

11. The inventor of the cotton gin _____,
probably made very dry martinis.
(a) which appeared in the 1800's   (b) , which had immense value
(c) whose name was Eli Whitney   (d) whom died in 1825
(e) , that takes the seeds out of cotton

11_____

(Because: _____.)

12. Whose _____ one of all?
(a) the fairest   (b) girlfriend is the prettiest
(c) the girl we've named the most talented   (d) your friend, the tallest
(e) to be named the loveliest

12_____

(Because: _____.)

13. The grand prize will go to _____ achieves the highest bowling score.

(a) the man which   (b) whomever   (c) the one who's wife   (d) whoever
(e) the man, who

13_____

(Because: _____.)

14. Thomas Carlyle was a hard-working writer _____ could not be discouraged by adversity.
(a) who   (b) whom   (c) which   (d) whose   (e) , that

14_____

(Because: _____.)

15. There is one commentator _____ news program I always watch.
(a) who's   (b) whose   (c) , whose   (d) , which   (e) that

15_____

(Because: _____.)

16. Voters want an economic program designed by men whom _____

_____.

(a) are experts   (b) think conservatively   (c) they can trust
(d) never waste money   (e) have been elected openly

16_____

(Because: _____.)

17. "Was this the face _____ launched a thousand ships?"
(a) whom   (b) whoever   (c) that   (d) , which   (e) whose

17_____

(Because: _____.)

Chapter Fifteen

18. Ramon's wife said that she saw _____
_____
that was on sale.

(a) a model at the store that wore a coat (b) a store which had a coat on a model
(c) a coat at the store which was on a model
(d) a store which had a model wearing a coat   18__
(e) a coat that was on a model at the store

(Because: _____.)

19. _____ the train had been derailed was obvious because the engineer's clock had been smashed.

(a) Who   (b) What   (c) When   (d) Why   (e) How   19__

(Because: _____.)

20. The loser's only excuse _____ he had broken a shoelace.

(a) was, that   (b) was which   (c) was, how   (d) was what   (e) was that   20__

(Because: _____.)

-Ing Words 16

How to work with . . . gerunds: verbal nouns
gerund phrases
present participles: verbal adjectives
participial phrases
absolute phrases
commas with participial phrases
rephrasing danglers

How to avoid . . . danglers
faulty pronoun case with gerunds

EARLIER WE DISCUSSED VERBS, the action or state-of-being words that indicate the happenings in sentences. In every part of this book, of course, we have been using verbs. But this chapter will introduce some words that are something *like* verbs but do not work as verbs. They are words with *-ing* added.

At first thought you might call *writing* a verb, since it seems to indicate an action. But on second thought it should appear that *writing* is not a verb, although *write* is one. By adding *-ing* to the verb *write* we have changed it from verb to something else.

If *-ing* words like *writing, taking,* and *loving* were verbs, we'd be able to use them to finish two-word sentences. But compare the actual two-word sentences below with the *-ing*-word versions:

Full Sentences	Not Sentences
I *think*.	I *thinking*
Friends *talk*.	Friends *talking*
Wood *burns*.	Wood *burning*
Glass *breaks*.	Glass *breaking*

The *-ing* words leave us feeling that nothing has been said, that no sentence has been finished. It is clear, then, that the *-ing* words like *thinking, talking, burning,* and *breaking* are not verbs.

Will an *-ing* word become a verb if we use *am* or *is* before it? *I am thinking* certainly is a full sentence. But *am* is the verb—or, in another way of describing the sentence, *am thinking* is the verb. *Thinking* cannot work as a verb by itself.

If the *-ing* words do not work as verbs, then how do they work? Consider these sentences:

Thinking is difficult work, but it is often profitable.
Talking can get people into trouble.
Dancing requires grace and balance.

In those sentences the *-ing* words are *nouns*, each used as the subject in its sentence. Such *-ing* words used as nouns are *gerunds*.

Gerunds–Verbal Nouns

Since *gerunds* are made from verbs by the addition of *-ing,* they are *verbal* nouns. That means they are derived from verbs and that they have certain verb-like characteristics, although they cannot work as verbs themselves.

Verbals are similar to verbs in two ways: (1) They can be modified by adverbs, and (2) if they are made from transitive verbs, they can take objects.

Time for Review

Words with -ing endings added to them are not verbs.

When an -ing word is used as a noun, it is a *gerund*.

Gerunds are verbal nouns.

Verbals are like verbs in two ways: (1) They can be modified by adverbs, and (2) if they are made from transitive verbs, they can take objects.

Do-It-Yourself Exercise

Write in each blank an appropriate *gerund* to complete the sentence:

You need not shout at me; my _____ is perfect.

The clown's _____ amused the queen.

Jennifer has some new shoes for _____.

We like to listen to the _____ of birds.

The _____ of church bells woke him up.

I have a _____ that she likes me!

Cigaret packages warn that _____ may be injurious to health.

"Meter maids" are women traffic officers who sometimes give citations for _____ overtime.

Whatever prize you'd like is yours for the _____.

If I had to do my own _____, I'd starve!

Checking up: All gerunds should be -*ing*-ending words made from verbs. Sleep will not do, since it doesn't end in -*ing;* *king* will not do, since it doesn't derive from a verb. And *ring* will not do, since (although it may be a verb) it does not have an added -*ing* ending. Possible gerunds for the exercise are *hearing, joking, singing, dancing, ringing, feeling,* and so on. Each works as a *noun* within its sentence.

The Gerund Phrase

Although it is used as a noun, a gerund is a *verbal* and can therefore be modified by an adverb:

Dancing wildly may wear out your shoes.
Thinking about work is as tiring as work itself.
Eating fast can spoil a good digestion.

The gerund with its modifier constitutes a *gerund phrase*. The gerund phrase, as a unit, works as a noun phrase.

Since a gerund is used as a noun, a gerund can be modified by an adjective:

Most dancing requires grace and balance.
Librarians don't approve of *loud talking*.
This *constant bickering* gets on my nerves.

Again, the gerund with its modifier constitutes a *gerund phrase*.

Gerunds are made from verbs. When they are made from transitive verbs, gerunds may express action done to something or someone; that is, gerunds may take objects:

Owning a cat is an educational experience.
Chopping wood builds muscle and coordination.
Some people really enjoy *collecting stamps*.

The nouns *cat, wood,* and *stamps* are the objects of the gerunds. The gerund with its object constitutes a *gerund phrase*.

Nouns are often used in English to modify other nouns, as in *head start, ground rules, telephone book, college student*. And since gerunds are nouns, they too can be used to modify other nouns:

Put on your *swimming suit* and come on in the water.
Pete decided to take a *cooking class*.
My Aunt Irma needs a *hearing aid*.

In such phrases, of course, the gerunds are used as modifiers for nouns, so they are elements in *noun phrases*.

Time for Review

A gerund with its modifier constitutes a *gerund phrase*.

A gerund with its object constitutes a *gerund phrase*.

Since a gerund is a noun, it may be modified by an *adjective;* but since a gerund is also a verbal, it may be modified by an *adverb*.

Since nouns may modify nouns, a gerund may modify a noun (as in *flying lessons, fishing gear, drinking glass*). Such phrases are *noun phrases*.

Do-It-Yourself Exercise

Write in each blank an appropriate *gerund phrase* to complete the sentence:

Jerry broke his leg by _____.

After _____, the runner got up and finished the race.

The coach says nothing matters except _____.

If you can't swim, you can probably stay afloat by _____ _____.

_____ may cause you to catch a cold.

People who live in glass houses seem to enjoy _____ _____.

Some people get rid of hiccups by _____.

Erasers are put on pencils for people who are always _____ _____.

Checking up: A gerund phrase must contain a gerund and something more: an object or a modifier. Could you have used such phrases as *treading water, falling down, slipping on the ice, winning the game?*

Suggestions for Writing

A. Women have "come a long way" since the days when their place was "in the home." What are some of the activities that were once considered strictly for men but are now open to women as well? Write your answer in a passage of about 200 words, using as many gerunds as you can. Underline each gerund.
B. What skills should girls be taught, and what skills should boys be taught? What skills are useful to both boys and girls? Write your answers in a passage of about 200 words, using as many gerunds as you can. Underline each gerund.
C. School is not the only place for learning. What are some of the skills you learned before you ever went to school? What are some of the skills you have learned since— but outside of school? Write your answers in a passage of about 200 words, using as many gerunds as you can. Underline each gerund.

After Writing: Reread your passage. Are the activities or skills you have named expressed as *gerunds: cooking, plumbing, gardening, using* a spoon, *tying* your shoes?

Gerunds made from transitive verbs usually have objects; write "O" above the object of each transitive gerund you have used.

Possessives With Gerunds

Now and then a gerund can present a puzzle. Consider the problem of meaning in this sentence:

My girlfriend doesn't like *me sneering* at her dad.

Just what is it that the girlfriend doesn't like—*me,* or the *sneering?* It is unlikely that the writer means that the girl "doesn't like *me,*" yet the pronoun *me* is in the form of an object. To avoid that possible misunderstanding, the writer should use *my* (the possessive adjective) rather than *me:*

My girlfriend doesn't like *my sneering* at her dad.

Now there can be no mistake about what the girlfriend dislikes. That is why most careful writers and speakers use the possessive, not the objective, before a gerund:

Misleading	Revised
Do you disapprove of your *dad* running for office?	Do you disapprove of your *dad's* running for office?
We really enjoyed *you* singing.	We really enjoyed *your* singing.
Me winning the scholarship made the family proud.	*My* winning the scholarship made the family proud.
Anne hates her *husband* bringing guests home for dinner.	Anne hates her *husband's* bringing guests home for dinner.

Sometimes a gerund presents a misunderstanding that cannot be so easily cleared up:

I don't approve of my wife cooking.

To avoid having the reader assume that the writer doesn't approve of the *wife,* the possessive might be used:

I don't approve of my *wife's* cooking.

But that revision seems just as wrong, for it seems to say that the wife's *cooking* is bad. Perhaps the writer means only that he doesn't want his wife to be obligated to cook, so he revises the sentence:

I don't approve of my wife's *having to cook.*

In that version the misunderstanding is avoided.

The possessive is usually used before a gerund if the word is singular *(husband's* bringing guests, *wife's* cooking) and if the word is a pronoun *(your* singing, *their* complaining). But when the word is plural, the objective form is more often used before a gerund:

Don't interfere with the *guests* dancing.

We don't mind the *children* playing here.

People having a good time is all right with me.

And the noun before a gerund is usually in the objective form if it names an *abstract idea* or an *inanimate object:*

There's nothing more beautiful than young *love* having its way.

Was there a good reason for the *truck* running off the road?

Unless the gerund comes immediately after the noun, the noun is never in the possessive form:

We can't imagine the *candidate* of our party *losing.*

I hadn't seen the *driver* of the car *turning.*

Time for Review

A noun or pronoun used immediately before a gerund is usually in the *possessive* form—unless the noun is *plural,* or unless it names an abstract or an inanimate object.

Do-It-Yourself Exercise

Write in the blank the appropriate form of the noun or pronoun suggested in the parentheses:

Fred must know that we're irritated by _____ laughing at us.
(him/his)

The performance was interrupted by _____ falling on the
(Estelle/Estelle's)
makeshift stairway.

Young Ms. Green couldn't stand _____ nearly always having
(men/men's)
the jobs of authority.

Their friendship was not broken by their _____ ending.
(engagement/engagement's)

_____ finding the ring on the street does not mean that you
(You/Your)
will marry a cement worker.

Checking up: Your choices should be the possessives—except for the plural *(men)* and the abstract *(engagement).*

Some Other "-ing" Verbals

Though gerunds work as nouns, *-ing*-suffix words may instead be used as adjectives:

running water
tapping feet
withering plants

amusing situation
teeming crowd
oscillating beam

These *-ing* adjectives, derived from verbs, are used to modify nouns by suggesting some action that the noun (or what is named by the noun) is engaged in. The water runs, the feet tap, the plants wither. These *-ing*-suffix words are exactly like gerunds in form— but they are different in function: They work as adjectives. These words are *present participles*.

Since the *present participles* are formed exactly as *gerunds* are, by adding *-ing* to a base verb form, the two may be confused. The difference lies in how they are used in a context: gerunds as *nouns,* present participles as *adjectives*.

> Pat couldn't lift weights until he tried *drinking* Malto. (gerund, object of *tried*)
>
> You can't lead a *drinking* horse away from the water. (present participle, modifying *horse*)
>
> The busload of tourists watched the *setting* sun. (present participle, modifying *sun*)
>
> *Setting* the table is Mary's job. (gerund, subject of *is*)

Present Participial Phrases

Since the present participle is a *verbal,* it may be modified by an *adverb:*

> They saw the race cars *flashing by.*
>
> *Cursing angrily,* he handed me my package.
>
> The lady *sitting down* is my mother's aunt.

And, like other verbals, the present participle that is made from a *transitive* verb may take an *object:*

> The girls *setting the table* are Mary and Jean.
>
> Carefully *slicing the tomatoes,* we made the salad.
>
> *Missing your call,* I had to go to class alone.

The nouns *table, tomatoes,* and *call* are objects of the verbals. The present participle with its modifier or its object constitutes a *present participial phrase.*

As the examples have shown, a participial phrase may be used either before or after the noun that it modifies.

Time for Review

> A *present participle* is an *adjective* made from a verb by *-ing* added to a base verb form.
>
> A *present participle* may be modified by an *adverb*.

A *present participle,* if made from a transitive verb, may take an object.

A *present participle* with its modifier or its object constitutes a present participial phrase.

Do-It-Yourself Exercise

Write in each blank an appropriate *present participial phrase* to modify the italicized word and complete the sentence:

That *fellow* _____ looks like an old friend of mine from high-school days.

Anyone _____ should turn it in to the stadium office.

_____ , *the captain* ordered his crew to drop anchor.

My *friend and I,* _____ , heard a great noise in the street; then, _____ , *we* saw a crowd _____ .

Bobby wrote home that the mosquitoes have eaten him up, but *he* is _____ at camp.

Checking up: Most present participial phrases *begin* with a present participle—an *-ing*-ending verbal. But an adverb may be used *before* the participle: *"anxiously scurrying* to the window" or "a crowd *quickly gathering."*

Punctuating Participial Phrases

Most writers use a *comma* after a present participial phrase that begins a sentence:

Leaving the city in ruins, the tornado moved out to sea.
Picking me up at my corner, Dooley gave me a lift to the campus.
Spotting their opponents a touchdown, the 'Gators went on to win 34-7.

When a participial phrase does not begin a sentence, the writer has to consider whether to set it off with a comma (or between a pair of commas). If the phrase is *essential* to distinguish the noun that it modifies, the phrase is restrictive, and the writer does not set it off:

The lady *rocking on the porch* is my wife's aunt.
That distinguished man *wearing the white suit* is Senator Baker.
The day *following the game* is a holiday.

But if the participial phrase is not essential and could be omitted without harm to the meaning of the sentence, the phrase will be set off between commas:

Aunt Millie, *rocking on the porch,* prayed for the astronauts as well as for the Astros.
My father, *wearing the white suit,* looks uncomfortable.
Next Tuesday, *being a holiday,* is expected to bring many tourists into town.

The Absolute Phrase

When a noun is used before a present participial phrase, the noun may appear to work as subject of the verbal. The result is not a sentence; it is an *absolute phrase:*

Tuesday being a holiday, we expect many tourists.
Our truck being nearly out of gas, we decided to stop at the next station.
His arm throbbing painfully, Sal crawled behind a rock for protection.

The nouns *Tuesday, our truck,* and *his arm* serve as subjects of the participles.

The absolute phrase has no apparent grammatical relationship to the main thought, unless the phrase is seen as a substitute for a full clause such as "Since Tuesday is a holiday" or "Because our truck was nearly out of gas."

An absolute phrase is usually set off by a comma (or a pair of commas).

Time for Review

When a *participial phrase* is used to begin a sentence, it is set off by a *comma.*

Within or at the end of a sentence, a *participial phrase* is set off by a comma (or a pair of commas) only if the phrase is *nonrestrictive.*

An *absolute phrase* is formed when a noun is used as apparent *subject* of a present participle, as in *"Mother* hearing a noise" or *"His toe* catching in the door, . . . "

An absolute phrase is set off by a comma (or between a pair of commas).

Do-It-Yourself Exercise

Write—and punctuate—appropriate *present participial* and *absolute* phrases to complete these sentences.

There is a brush and timber fire _____.
                                    (participial phrase)

All the spectators _____ will
                        (participial phrase)
be asked to move to the grandstand.

_____ the young life-
    (participial phrase)
guard jumped from his perch and dived into the pool.

One of the lions _____ growled
                      (absolute phrase)
at us languidly as our car passed by on "safari."

_____ I really can't
    (absolute phrase)
compete in the swim meet today.

Our tour guide _____ told us
                    (participial phrase)
we'd have to walk the last mile _____
                                       (absolute phrase)
_____.

_____ the coach
      (participial phrase)
shouted that the men should jog around the track _____
                                                        (absolute phrase)
_____.

Checking up: Each phrase, remember, must contain an *-ing* word. Check your punctuation against the "Time for Review" section just above. Is your phrase that modifies *tour guide* set off between commas? If it is, can you tell why?

Rephrasing Danglers

Since a *present participle* works as an adjective, the writer must be sure that each of his participles clearly modifies a noun that he intends it to modify. Suppose you had written, in the exercise just above, something like this:

Gasping to catch her breath, the young lifeguard jumped from his perch and dived into the pool.

Who does the *gasping?* Apparently it isn't the lifeguard but a girl who is having trouble in the water—and she isn't clearly mentioned in the sentence.

The participial phrase that appears to modify the wrong thing, or modifies nothing at all, is a *dangler*—that is, it has no clear relationship to the rest of the sentence.

Dangling participles show that the writer, after starting out with one thought, has switched to another in midsentence:

> *Rocking on the porch,* Aunt Millie's prayer asked safety for the astronauts.
> *Hitchhiking across the country,* rides are hard to get.
> *Complaining that my luck had run out,* suddenly a big fish struck my bait.
> *Sitting in the stands,* our team looked great.

Such dangling participles can be repaired, of course. The writer can clarify his thought by using either of two methods:

    1. Converting the participial phrase to a subordinate clause (with *subordinator, subject,* and *verb):*

> Just *when I was complaining* that my luck had run out, suddenly a big fish struck my bait.
> From *where we sat* in the stands, our team looked great.

    2. Changing the subject of the sentence to a noun that is properly modified by the participle:

> *Rocking* on the porch, *Aunt Millie* prayed for the safety of the astronauts.
> *Sitting* in the stands, *we* thought our team looked great.

In each revision it is clear who complains, who sits, who rocks; the *dangling participles* have been repaired.

Time for Review

A *dangling participle* is one that does not clearly modify the noun that the writer intended it to modify.

A dangling participle may be repaired by: (1) using a subordinate clause to replace the phrase; (2) using as *subject* the noun that the phrase properly modifies.

Do-It-Yourself Exercise

Repair these *dangling participles* by either of the two methods just described.

Ringing three times, Janice finally answered.

    Revision: _____

_____

Opening at 9:30, hordes of women stormed in for bargains.

    Revision: _____

_____

Pitching six scoreless innings, a no-hitter seems to be developing for the young left-hander.

Revision: _____

_____.

Driving a car with an air-cooled engine, no water is needed.

Revision: _____

_____.

Checking up: Review the two methods for rephrasing danglers (see p. 296). Check your punctuation to be sure you have used a comma after each introductory participial phrase or adverb clause.

Is there a third method of rephrasing danglers? Return to the exercise just above and try converting each participial phrase into an *absolute phrase* (see p. 294).

Suggestions for Writing

D. Spend about fifteen minutes on a "people watching" tour of your neighborhood or your college campus. Write a passage of about 300 words describing six different people and telling what they were doing when you saw them. Use as many *present participial phrases* as you can.
E. Recall the day of a well-remembered historical event (such as a flood, an assassination, a moon landing, an inauguration, a riot). Write a passage of about 300 words telling what you and some of your friends were doing after you heard the news. Use as many *present participial phrases* as you can.
F. If all electrical power were suddenly cut off in your town for several days, how would your life be affected? Write a passage of about 300 words telling how you would have to change patterns of activity. Use as many *present participial phrases* as you can.

After Writing: Reread your passage to be sure that you have not written any dangling participles (see p. 295). If you do find a dangler in your work, revise it by using one of the methods indicated on p. 296. Have you written any absolute phrases? If not, revise one of your sentences so that it includes an *absolute phrase*.

-Ing Words 299

QUIZ 16

Using Gerunds and Present Participles

On the blank within each sentence write the item that you think completes the sentence most effectively; then mark the **letter** of that item on your answer blank. After marking your choice, explain briefly why you chose it (*Because:* . . .).

Example: Reaching for another piece of pie, _I had eyes that_ proved bigger than my stomach.

(a) my eyes (b) my appetite (c) it (d) I had eyes that (e) the anticipation

Ex _d_

(*Because:* _"I" tells who did the reaching; otherwise, danglers result_)

1. Picking up a pipe wrench, _____ the easiest way to increase plumbing bills.

(a) sloppy work is (b) Steve discovered (c) is usually
(d) the do-it-yourself method is (e) demonstrates

1.____

(*Because:* _____.)
   (*Question:* Is *picking* a gerund (subject) or a participle (adjective)? Who does the picking up?)

2. We have a receptionist with pretty legs _____ in our office.

(a) answering the phone (b) taking appointments (c) drawing attention
(d) keeping books (e) listening to complaints

2.____

(*Because:* _____.)
   (*Question:* After all, what are the pretty legs really doing?)

3. Most of the gang admire _____ singing.

(a) Sammy (b) Glen (c) José's (d) him (e) us

3.____

(*Because:* _____.)
   (*Question:* What do they admire—the singing or the singer? Remember: possessive before gerund.)

4. A flock of ducks _____ in the pond behind our cabin.

(a) quacking (b) doing their thing (c) swimming (d) swim
(e) diving for their food

4.____

(*Because:* _____.)
   (*Question:* Can an *-ing* word work as a verb to complete the sentence?)

Chapter Sixteen

5. Richard Halliburton ———————————————————— he led a charmed life, apparently died while attempting a solo voyage by sea.

(a) thinking (b) , believing (c) assuming that (d) whose believing that
(e) mistakenly assuming that

5.———

(*Because:* ————————————————————————————.)
(*Question:* Should a nonrestrictive participial phrase be set off between commas? See pp. 293–294.)

6. Overcoming great difficulties and ————————————————, the old fisherman at last made his way back to port.

(a) with a lot of grit (b) when he had a full catch (c) courageously
(d) after the storm ended (e) securing the huge fish

6.———

(*Because:* ————————————————————————————.)
(*Question:* Since a participial phrase appears before *and*, which completion will provide parallelism?)

7. Linda could reach the top shelf ———————————————— on a chair.

(a) perched (b) when she stood (c) standing (d) climbing
(e) jumping up

7.———

(*Because:* ————————————————————————————.)

8. Mr. Quiller never ———————————————————— on a couch.

(a) once dozing off (b) sitting (c) laid his notebook (d) for lounging
(e) taking a nap

8.———

(*Because:* ————————————————————————————.)

9. Coming in off the ocean, ————————————————————.

(a) our bus was delayed by the fog   (b) the fog delayed our bus
(c) we had the fog delay our bus   (d) a delay in the fog made our bus late
(e) our tardiness was caused by the fog

9.———

(*Because:* ————————————————————————————.)

10 Running in the halls———————————— got Alfie into trouble.

(a) , finally (b) , a fall (c) , a friend (d) , never (e) , usually

10.———

(*Because:* ————————————————————————————.)

-Ing Words **301**

11. Rodney earned his way through college by waiting on tables, selling shoes, and _____ in a rock band.

(a) as drummer (b) guitarist (c) was organist (d) played drums
(e) playing the guitar

11_____

(Because: _____.*)*

12. Then, seizing the first opportunity, _____ was to get away for a whole month's vacation.

(a) my doctor's advice (b) my plan (c) my dad (d) my only hope
(e) my family's dream

12_____

(Because: _____.*)*

13. _____ having announced his retirement, the entire crowd rose to shout acclaim and to protest the popular leader's decision.

(a) When (b) Upon (c) After the coach (d) The coach
(e) Just as the coach

13_____

(Because: _____.*)*

14. Summer activities at the camp include lessons in boating, hiking, _____ _____ cooking.

(a) outdoor survival, and (b) how to fish, and (c) Indian lore, and
(d) fishing and (e) fishing, and

14_____

(Because: _____.*)*

15. Your life will be more secure _____ for the future.

(a) making some investments (b) putting away money (c) if saving
(d) if you save (e) by planning

15_____

(Because: _____.*)*

16. The brunette _____ on the sand is the girl I intend to marry.

(a) , plopped out there (b) , who's lying out there (c) lying there
(d) , lying out (e) with the bikini lying

16_____

(Because: _____.*)*

17. Dr. Anderson's hobbies include _____
violin in an amateur symphony orchestra.

(a) him playing first   (b) a stamp collection and playing   (c) boating and
(d) his playing   (e) his ham radio and playing   17._____

(*Because:* _____.)

18. Most of the candidates have been asked about spending and _____

_____ funds for welfare.

(a) appropriate funds   (b) if they favor   (c) controlling
(d) how they would raise   (e) whether they approve   18._____

(*Because:* _____.)

19. Someone asked Professor Johnson about _____
saying, "The play's the thing."

(a) Shakespeare   (b) whether the playwright   (c) Hamlet's
(d) the meaning of Hamlet   (e) Hamlet's scheme and   19._____

(*Because:* _____.)

20. Frowning with disappointment and _____
into the wastebasket.

(a) anger Tom tossed the rejection slip
(b) anger, the rejection slip went immediately
(c) anger, his hopes fell with the rejection slip   20._____
(d) anger, Tom crushed the rejection slip
(e) anger, the whole manuscript was tossed

(*Because:* _____.)

Borrowed, Stolen, Lost, or Sunk 17

How to work with . . . **past participles**
past-participial phrases
restrictive modifiers
nonrestrictive modifiers
active voice
passive voice

How to avoid . . . **misplaced modifiers**
danglers
faulty use of commas

THE CHAPTER JUST BEFORE THIS ONE discussed two kinds of *verbal,* the gerund and the present participle. Both are verbals; they are made from verbs but do not work as verbs. Both are distinguished by their *-ing* endings.

Now we turn to a third sort of verbal, the *past participle.* Like the other verbals, this one is derived from a verb but does not work as a verb in a sentence. Many past participles end with *-ed:*

> The artist makes pictures in *stained* glass.
> Keith, who had a *bruised* elbow, sat on the bench.
> Some cafeteria customers won't eat *cooked* cereal.

Those *-ed* words are obviously derived from verbs. What do we get when we stain glass?— *stained* glass; when we bruise an elbow?—a *bruised* elbow; when we cook cereal?— *cooked* cereal. But the *-ed* words in those sentences are not working as verbs. They work as adjectives, since they modify the nouns *glass, elbow,* and *cereal.*

One pattern, however, does use the past participle as a verb. That pattern is a verb phrase using the auxiliary *have:*

> The artists *have stained* the glass.
> Keith *has bruised* his elbow.
> The chef *has cooked* some cereal for breakfast.

The helping verb *have* (see Chapter 9) helps the past participle to function as a verb.

Time for Review

> *Past participles* are verbals that work as adjectives except when they appear with the auxiliary verb *have.*
>
> When a past participle appears with *have,* the result is a verb phrase.
>
> Many past participles end in *-ed.*

Do-It-Yourself Exercise

As a start toward learning how past participles work, write in each blank an appropriate *past participle* to modify the italicized noun and complete the sentence:

Dad's breakfast always begins with coffee, toast, and two _____

eggs.

I really love guitar *music* if it's _____
by an expert.

After several hours of hard digging, the workmen took a break for some much

_____ *rest*.

Before you go to bed, be sure to check the _____ *door*.

The professor noticed that several _____
students were yawning during his lecture.

Checking up: Remember that a past participle often ends in *-ed* and always modifies a noun or pronoun. Some appropriate ones for the sentences in this exercise are *boiled, cooked, fried,* or *poached* (eggs); *played* or *performed* (music); *needed* or *deserved* (rest); *locked* or *closed* (door); *disgruntled* or *bored* (students).

Past Participle or Verb?

The past participle is not always easy to distinguish from a verb. Since the verb *played* (as in "He *played* the piano") has exactly the same form as the past participle *played* (as in "The piano *played* by an expert is wonderful to hear"), they can be told apart only by how they are used in phrases or sentences. When an *-ed* word like *played* is used as an adjective, the word is a *past participle*. Consider the differences:

Verbs	Past Participles
Harriet *burned* the potatoes.	We ate the *burned* potatoes.
I just *painted* my car.	The *painted* car really shines.
She *overexposed* the film.	She has lots of *overexposed* film.

As a verb the *-ed* word has a subject *(Harriet, I, she),* but as a past participle the *-ed* word modifies a noun *(potatoes, car, film)*.

Time for Review

Past participles made from *regular* verbs have an *-ed* ending. Since the past-tense form of such verbs also ends in *-ed*, the past participle can be distinguished from the verb only by its different function.

The past participle works as an *adjective*.

Do-It-Yourself Exercise

The completed sentences in this exercise show regular verbs in the past tense (ending in *-ed*). Beneath each sentence is a partial revision; complete the revision by using the same *-ed* word as a past participle (and include in your addition a noun to be modified by the participle):

They *listed* six numbers.

Revision: We saw the six _____.

Obviously the senator *rehearsed* his speech.

Revision: Listeners could tell it was a _____.

After Phyllis *combed* her hair, it looked neater.

Revision: _____ always looks neater.

Our shouting may be what *frightened* the cat.

Revision: Did you see the _____ run?

Something in this town *polluted* the air.

Revision: _____ may be unfit to breathe.

One motorist's car *stalled* during the rainstorm.

Revision: The motorist's _____ wouldn't move.

Taking the instructor's advice, I *revised* the sentence.

Revision: I'll admit that the _____ was clearer than the original.

Checking up: Of course the phrase appropriate to the first sentence in the exercise is *listed numbers.* The other revisions should be *Combed hair, frightened cat,* and so on. In each revision the *-ed* word becomes an adjective modifying a noun.

Other Past Participles

Another look at the title of this chapter can serve as a hint that not all past participles end in *-ed*. We have shown that the past participles of *regular* verbs do end in *-ed*, but what about *irregular* verbs? Consider the four words of our chapter title, this time in a sentence:

The Coast Guard did not report whether the boat had been *borrowed, stolen, lost,* or *sunk.*

Obviously *borrowed* is one of the *-ed* past participles that we have already discussed.

Borrowed, Stolen, Lost, or Sunk 307

But the three other words, *stolen, lost,* and *sunk* do not end in *-ed,* although they too are past participles. To be sure what words are past participles, we need to take note of some further characteristics of both form and usage.

Past participles can be recognized by their endings *(-d* as in *paid* or *borrowed, -n* as in *spoken* or *flown,* or *-t* as in *lost* or *brought);* or some past participles can be recognized by a change of vowel sound (as in *slid, fled, sunk, strung, done, run).*

Consider a few past participles with the *-t* ending, noting how they differ from the verbs they derive from:

Verbs	Past Participles
Dino *lost* his voice.	His *lost* voice came back.
I *bent* my knife.	A *bent* knife is useless.
Some glass *cut* the tires.	*Cut* tires can be dangerous.

The word forms are the same, but their use within the sentences differs. Always the past participles are used as adjectives; in the sentences above *lost* modifies *voice, bent* modifies *knife,* and *cut* modifies *tires.*

Past participles with the *-n* ending differ from their verbs in both form and use:

Verbs	Past Participles
Who *broke* the window?	Who will pay for the *broken* window?
She *spoke* soft words.	Words *spoken* softly may soothe us.
His tears *grew* noticeable.	A *grown* man may cry honestly.

Again the past participles are used to modify nouns.

Among past participles distinguished by a change in sound (rather than by addition of an ending), some have the same form as the past-tense verb:

Verbs	Past Participles
We *dug* a cave for protection.	*Dug* deep, the cave kept out the wind and rain.
She *stuck* the papers together.	The *stuck* papers wouldn't come apart.
The Giants *won* two games.	Two games *won* by the Giants helped to cinch the pennant.

But still other past participles of this sort are different from the past-tense verb:

Verbs	Past Participles
He awoke when the bell *rang.*	A bell *rung* softly could awaken him.
They *swam* the sprints first.	*Swum* first, the sprints were soon over.

Recognizing the Past Participle

All verbs in English (except some of the auxiliaries) have past-participial forms. Since there is such variety in those forms, it may help to have a quick way of knowing the past participle of any verb. Speakers who have used English for many years will usually have little trouble "knowing" the past participle if they apply this rule: The past participle does not end in *-ing,* but it is the form that may be used as an adjective complement after a linking verb like *was:*

The game was *played* in darkness.

Every word was *spoken* clearly.

My lunch was *brought* from home.

The lights were *strung* on the tree.

Whatever he did was *done* well.

Time for Review

Past participles of *regular* verbs end in *-d* or *-ed: said, played.*

Past participles of *irregular* verbs often end in -t: *left, caught, shot.*

Past participles of irregular verbs often end in *-n* or *-en: drawn, torn, broken, written.*

Some past participles are distinguished by a change in sound (and so a change in spelling) from the base verb: dig, *dug;* win, *won;* swim, *swum;* sting, *stung;* ring, *rung.*

The past participle (like the present participle—see pp. 292–293) is often used as an adjective complement following a linking verb like *was:* was *seen,* was *made,* were *taught,* is *torn,* seemed *forgotten,* looked *pleased.*

Do-It-Yourself Exercise

Write in each blank a *past participle* to complete the sentence appropriately:

Every *window* in the house was _____.

The *television set* worked well after it was _____.

Mary was _____ that she had received a bargain.

The long fly *ball* was _____ by the left fielder.

My *money* was _____ before the month was over.

Borrowed, Stolen, Lost, or Sunk **309**

Most of Grandpa's *savings* were _____ in his mattress.

No truer *word* was ever _____.

None of my story was _____.

The *battle* was _____ in dense jungles.

Suddenly a *picture* was _____ on the screen.

That old *song* was _____ to me by my grandmother.

Checking up: All the past participles should end in *-d, -t,* or *-n*—or should have a short *u* sound as in *done, sprung, sung*. Each past participle modifies the noun that is italicized in the sentence.

Since a past participle sometimes appears *before* the noun that it modifies (rather than after a verb like *was)*, continue this exercise by writing in each blank a *past* participle to modify the following noun in each sentence:

I had to pay for the _____ *window*.

It doesn't pay to cry over _____ *milk*.

Steve's _____ *dog* was reported wandering around miles from home.

A _____ *driver* crashed into my _____ *car*.

Gracie is a very _____ *performer*.

When Pat fell down he suffered a _____ *knee*.

Hamburger is made of _____ *meat*.

Please turn in your _____ *paper*.

I always hate to see a _____ *man* cry.

It stings when you put iodine on a _____ *finger*.

Checking up: Again the past participles should end in *-d, -t,* or *-n*—or should have a short *u* sound as in *drunk (drunken* would be better to describe a person), *shrunk*.

Past Participial Phrases

Since the past participle is a *verbal*, it may be modified by an adverb:

Mr. Dexter still drives that *broken down* car.
Immediately released, the prisoner ran in fright.
The sun, *entirely obscured*, gave us little warmth.

The past participle with its modifier constitutes a *past participial phrase*.

As the examples have shown, a participial phrase may be used either before or after the noun that it modifies.

Punctuating Participial Phrases

When a past participial phrase begins a sentence, it is usually set off by a comma:

Picked too early, an apple may be too green to eat.
Seated on the 50-yard line, Harvey's mother saw every fumble perfectly.
Grown over a weekend, Bob's mustache is hardly visible.

When a participial phrase does not begin a sentence, it is set off by a comma (or between a pair of commas) only if the phrase is *nonrestrictive*—not essential to define the noun it modifies:

This apple, *picked too early*, is too green to eat.
Harvey's mother, *seated on the 50-yard line*, had a tremendous view.
Bob's mustache, *grown over a weekend*, can hardly be seen.

But if the past participial phrase is essential to distinguish the noun it modifies, the phrase is *restrictive* and should not be set off:

Any apple *picked too early* is too green to eat.
All the fans *seated on the 50-yard line* had a tremendous view.
A mustache *grown over a weekend* can hardly be seen.

These phrases are essential, *restrictive*, because the nouns *any apple, all the fans,* and *a mustache* would not be adequately restricted without those phrases.

Time for Review

A past participle with a modifier constitutes a *past participial phrase*.

When a past participial phrase *begins* a sentence, it is usually set off by a *comma*.

When a past participial phrase does not begin a sentence, it is set off by a comma (or between a pair of commas) only if the phrase is *nonrestrictive*.

Do-It-Yourself Exercise

Write—and punctuate—an appropriate *past participial phrase* to modify the italicized word in each sentence:

Anyone _____ will be asked to move to the front of the room.

There is my *sister* _____.

Last night my *bicycle* was _____.

_____ the *fish* had to be thawed out before we could cook it.

Two aspirin *tablets* _____ will sometimes relieve a headache.

Every *letter* _____ must have sufficient postage.

Henry had to look for a new job when *he* was _____.

The batter was allowed to take first base when *he* was _____.

Connie was _____ by his compliments.

Checking up: Each blank should be filled by a past participle and its modifier. Some possible phrases: *taken with water, seated in the back, fired by his boss, hit by a ball, flattered willingly, sent by airmail, stolen from me, dressed in blue*. Three of the sentences should contain commas: a comma after *sister*, a comma before *the fish*, and a pair of commas to set off the nonrestrictive phrase after *aspirin tablets*. Can you tell why those three must be *nonrestrictive* phrases?

Misplaced or Dangling Participles

A past participial phrase must be placed near the noun that the writer intends it to modify. If it is placed near some other noun instead, misunderstanding may result:

Bathed in sunshine, everybody loved Florida.

Is *everybody* bathed in sunshine? No, the writer meant to say that *Florida* is bathed in sunshine. The misplaced participial phrase demands a revision:

Everybody loves Florida, a state *bathed in sunshine.*

Consider some other misplaced past participial phrases:

> *Shot from a cannon,* I eat Bangies every morning.
> *Written by Herman Melville,* our class really enjoyed *Moby-Dick.*
> *Turned out by his wife,* Thomas wore a gorgeous handmade necktie.
> *Forgotten in later years,* my mother taught me many delightful poems.
> *Controlled by external pressure,* the professor held a Bunsen burner at arm's length.
> *Seated far back in the auditorium,* the music was almost inaudible.

The last of those examples is a *dangler;* that is, a phrase that has no noun that it should properly modify. Certainly the *music* was not *seated;* whoever was seated is not mentioned.

Such dangling or misplaced participial phrases need revision. Each participle must have a noun to modify and must be nearer to that noun than it is to some other noun:

> *Shot from a cannon,* Bangies are my favorite cereal.
> Our class really enjoyed *Moby-Dick, written by Herman Melville.*
> Thomas wore a gorgeous handmade tie *turned out by his wife.*
> My mother taught me many delightful poems, all *forgotten in later years.*
> At arm's length the professor held a Bunsen burner *controlled by external pressure.*
> To a person *seated far back in the auditorium,* the music was almost inaudible.

The Passive Voice

As some of the examples above have shown, a past participle is often used as an *adjective complement:*

> The Mets were *defeated* in the series.

The past participle, *defeated,* is an adjective complement modifying the subject, *the Mets,* and linked to that subject by a linking verb, *were.* In such a structure the past participle helps to form the *passive voice.*

The passive voice occurs in writing or speech whenever the *subject* of a verb is not a doer, but a receiver, of the action. For instance, the Mets do not do the action in the example; they have that action done to them: They *are defeated.* Consider some other examples of *passive voice:*

> Three ships *were sighted* on the horizon.
> This dress *was sewn* by a professional.
> What *was meant* by that remark?
> The log *had been split* right down the middle.
> Every joke *was laughed at* by the audience.

By contrast the *active voice* occurs when the subject of a verb is the actual *doer* of that action. The sentences just above could be revised as *active voice* sentences:

We sighted three ships on the horizon.
A professional sewed this dress.
What did *you* mean by that remark?
Someone had split the log right down the middle.
The audience laughed at every joke.

In those versions the subjects (italicized) *do* the actions indicated in the verbs. Full-fledged *verbs* are used instead of past participles. (The *active voice* and *passive voice* are considered further on pp. 172–175.)

Time for Review

A *past participial phrase* should be placed near the noun that the writer intends it to modify.

A *dangling participle* is one whose sentence does not contain the noun that the writer really intends the participle to modify.

Misplaced and dangling participial phrases should be revised so that they clearly modify the nearest noun in the sentence.

The *passive* voice is used when a past participle follows a linking verb so that the subject of the sentence does not *do* the action but *receives* the action.

The *active voice* is used when the subject of a verb actually is the *doer* of the action.

Do-It-Yourself Exercise

Write in each blank a *past participial phrase* that appropriately completes the sentence. Use *commas* to set off every nonrestrictive participial phrase. Be careful to avoid any *misplaced* or *dangling* participial phrase:

_____ the cartoon drew much criticism from the readers.

_____ the submarine sank quickly.

Uncle Joe certainly was never _____.

I prefer movies _____ to the ones _____

_____.

My favorite candy bar has delicious peanuts _____.

314 Chapter Seventeen

Don't throw away a match unless you are sure that the flame has been _____

_____.

Checking up: Some useful past participial phrases: *Hit by a torpedo, frightened by a mouse, made in Hollywood, filmed overseas, entirely extinguished, Printed in the newspaper, dipped in chocolate, covered with cream.* Of course, you may have written others equally appropriate—each with a past participle and its modifier. But be sure that you have not written a misplaced or dangling participial phrase like *"Shocked by its violence,* the cartoon . . . ."; after all, the cartoon could not be *shocked.* Did you use a comma to set off the *nonrestrictive* phrase before *cartoon* and the one before *the submarine?*

Continue this exercise by revising the *passive voice* to the *active voice:*

My books were taken from my locker by a thief.

Revision: _____.

It is reported by the newspaper that crime rates have gone down.

Revised: _____.

A complaint has been registered by an angry customer.

Revised: _____.

Mount Everest has been climbed by only a few people.

Revision: _____.

Sports cars are driven by millions of Americans.

Revision: _____.

Coming from the apartment, the suspect was seen by an off-duty policeman.

Revision: _____.

Checking up: To write an active voice sentence, be sure that the subject *does* the action. The past participles *(taken, reported, registered, climbed,* and *driven)* should be written instead as verbs *(took, reported, registered, climbed,* and *drive),* each with its appropriate subject.

A Reminder About "-ed"

Because speech is often hasty, we sometimes do not *hear* the *-ed* endings on past-tense verbs and past participles. "Victor is *prejudiced* toward math" may sound like "Victor is *prejudice* toward math." In that situation the *-ed* sound is swallowed up by the following *t* sound of *toward.* The "swallowing up" of sounds occurs most often when the *-ed* is not a full syllable by itself:

The plate was finally *pass* to me. (*passed* to me)
My junker had to be *push* down the street. (*pushed* down the street)
He was *rush* to the hospital. (*rushed* to the hospital)

Whatever may happen in speech, the *-ed* must not be omitted in writing:

The country *used* to be united on the issues. (not *use* to be)
We are *supposed* to cheer for him. (not *suppose to*)
He was *replaced* by a substitute. (not *replace by*)

Two popular words often heard in conversation are seldom used in writing: the past participles of *drag* and *sneak* in the forms *drug* and *snuck*. The acceptable forms are:

He was *dragged* off the field. (*Drug* is wrong.)
It had to be *sneaked* in. (*Snuck* is wrong.)

Suggestions for Writing

A. Modern times, many Americans have come to believe, are *too* modern. Some even believe that the best life is to be gained only by getting away from big cities, modern dress, modern hair styles, modern gadgets, and so on. How do you feel about that attitude? Write your ideas in a passage of about 350 words. Use as many *past participles* in the passage as you can.
B. When "the environment" became a major concern of Americans in the early 1970's, many people were shocked to discover that some natural resources were in short supply. The result, of course, was shortages in many man-made products as well. What shortages would be most serious in your own life? Write your answers in a passage of about 350 words. Use as many *past participles* as you can.
C. Both comedians and psychologists are interested in the question of what people laugh at. Most who have thought seriously about that question have agreed that people laugh at *the unexpected*. When someone slips and falls, the fall is unexpected—and the first reaction, very often, is a laugh. What do you think people are most likely to laugh at? Write your ideas in a passage of about 350 words. Use as many *past participles* as you can.

After Writing: Reread your passage and underline every *past participle* that you have used. Circle the noun that each participle modifies. Which of your past participles (or past participial phrases) have you set off by commas? Can you explain why you did or did not set off each of those modifiers? Has each of your participial phrases been properly placed so that it clearly modifies the noun you intend it to modify?

Borrowed, Stolen, Lost, or Sunk 317

QUIZ 17

Using Past Participles

On the blank within each sentence write the item that you think most appropriately completes the sentence; then mark the *letter* of that item on your answer blank. Don't overlook punctuation included in some of the offered alternatives. After marking your choice, explain briefly why you chose it *(Because: . . .)*.

Example: As the Renegades' best high-jumper, Steve was *shaken* up by the college newspaper, which reported his grade average.

(a) took   (b) wrote   (c) shook   (d) shaken   (e) showed   Ex *d*

(Because: "Shaken" is the only past participle .*)*

1. Held in Atlantic City, the _____ selected Miss America, who reigned for an entire year.

   (a) girl   (b) judges   (c) pageant   (d) nation   (e) winner was   1.___

   (Because: _____ .*)*
   (Question: Which completion avoids a dangler? Who or what was really "held in Atlantic City"?)

2. Excited by the sound of the crowd's _____ through the gate into the stadium.

   (a) cheering, he had snuck   (b) applause she sneaked   (c) uproar, Jack rush
   (d) cheering, they sneaked   (e) applause, he snuck   2.___

   (Because: _____ .*)*
   (Question: Which is the right participle, *snuck* or *sneaked?* See p. 315. Should the introductory phrase be set off by a comma? See p. 310.)

3. Every week Al got a package _____ filled with cookies.

   (a) from his mother   (b) that was   (c) through the mail   (d) from the family
   (e) from an unknown admirer   3.___

   (Because: _____ .*)*
   (Question: Which completion avoids a misplaced modifier? Who or what is really "filled with cookies"?)

318   Chapter Seventeen

4. My _____ that he had been accepted at college, called home immediately.

(a) roommate, learned   (b) brother, told   (c) cousin informed
(d) best friend delighted   (e) son, found

4._____

(*Because:* _____.)
   (*Question:* Which completion includes a nonrestrictive participle? Should the completion include a verb?)

5. The employees didn't expect their cause to be understood by the obviously _____ management.

(a) prejudice   (b) confuse   (c) prejudiced   (d) bias   (e) incense

5._____

(*Because:* _____.)
   (*Question:* Which of the words is a past participle?)

6. The desert town suffered a shortage of water _____ its growing population.

(a) use to supply   (b) caused by   (c) created by   (d) brought about by
(e) piped in for

6._____

(*Because:* _____.)
   (*Question:* Should the completion modify *shortage* or modify *water*? Is *use* a proper past participle?)

7. The day's receipts have to be _____ the bank before closing time.

(a) took to   (b) rush to   (c) ran over to   (d) deposited in
(e) total up for

7._____

(*Because:* _____.)

8. Excited by his team's first win of the _____ run all the way home to tell his dad.

(a) season, Teddy   (b) series Bill   (c) year, Pete had
(d) playoffs Jimmy had   (e) month, Hank breathlessly

8._____

(*Because:* _____.)

9. Elsie couldn't bear to drink milk _____ by a cow.

(a) after she was frightened   (b) bitten   (c) that was produce   (d) frightened
(e) given a nasty look

9._____

(*Because:* _____.)

Borrowed, Stolen, Lost, or Sunk   **319**

10. Floyd just couldn't believe he had _____ the whole thing.

(a) drink   (b) ate   (c) drunken   (d) drank   (e) drunk   10_____

(*Because:* _____.)

11. Citizens who know something of propaganda techniques are not easily

_____ by demagogues.

(a) led   (b) lead   (c) leaden   (d) govern   (e) manage   11_____

(*Because:* _____.)

12. Hidden behind a _____ was not likely to be discovered.

(a) tree, my fear   (b) screen the child   (c) bush, the turtle
(d) barn our kissing   (e) book, I was sure the note   12_____

(*Because:* _____.)

13. The mail is _____ to arrive before noon.

(a) schedule   (b) suppose   (c) not supposed   (d) never knew
(e) seldom believe   13_____

(*Because:* _____.)

14. Shoved quickly into a coat _____ the tickets were lost.

(a) pocket, Tom's girlfriend thought   (b) pocket, it appeared   (c) pocket even
(d) pocket, I assumed   (e) pocket, all   14_____

(*Because:* _____.)

15. Harvey had enjoyed photographing the birds that had _____
past his little cabin that summer.

(a) flowed   (b) flew   (c) flowen   (d) flown   (e) flied   15_____

(*Because:* _____.)

16. Distinguished by his waxed _____ old ham actor had a firm reputation as a ladies' man.

(a) cane the   (b) Cadillac the   (c) mustache, the   (d) museum the
(e) manner the   16_____

(*Because:* _____.)

320   Chapter Seventeen

17. Mike, the best swimmer on our college team, became known nationally after he _____ the channel.

(a) swam   (b) swum   (c) swimming   (d) had swam   (e) swimmed

17._____

(Because: _____.)

18. Suddenly _____ by the news, burst into tears.

(a) Louise, shook   (b) Louise, disturb   (c) Louise shaken   (d) Louise hurt
(e) Louise, shaken

18._____

(Because: _____.)

19. Remodeled last year, _____ like the old city hall.

(a) I don't really   (b) the mayor says it isn't   (c) the courthouse doesn't look
(d) there's no building   (e) Sam made his office look

19._____

(Because: _____.)

20. Margaret _____ learn to dance before she tried to get into television.

(a) arrange to   (b) use to   (c) was advised to   (d) had plan to
(e) was encourage to

20._____

(Because: _____.)

To Live, To Love 18

How to work with . . . infinitives
infinitive phrases
placement of infinitives

How to avoid . . . misplaced infinitives
danglers
commas with verbal nouns

TWO CHAPTERS JUST BEFORE THIS one have introduced the *verbals,* a class of words that are made from verbs but do not do the work of verbs in sentences. After working with gerunds, present participles, and past participles, we can see the difference between those verbals and the verbs they are made from:

Verbs	Verbals
We *live* too dangerously.	*Living* dangerously keeps us on our toes.
Friends often *shake* hands.	*Shaking* hands, people show their friendship.
My order *listed* six items.	Please send me the *listed* items.

As verbals, *living, shaking,* and *listed* do not work as verbs. The gerund, *living,* works as a noun; the participles, both present *(shaking)* and past *(listed)* work as adjectives.

This chapter considers a verbal of another sort. We'll introduce it by asking a question first: What are the *verbs* in these sentences?—

A parrot learns to talk.
We need someone to lead the way.
Is it too early to go?

Each of those is a simple sentence with one subject and one verb. The subjects are *a parrot, we,* and *it.* The verbs indicate the action or state: a parrot *learns,* we *need,* and *is* it. The verbs are *learns, need,* and *is.*

Then what of *to talk, to lead,* and *to go?* Are they not verbs? That's right; they're not. When we use a subject with a verb, we produce a sentence; but what happens when we use a subject with one of those *to*-groups?—

A parrot *to talk*
We *to lead*
It *to go*

None of those is a sentence. The experiment shows that *to talk, to lead, to go,* although they may at first glance appear to be verbs, do not work as verbs at all. They are *infinitives.*

The infinitive is formed when we use *to* before a basic verb form: *to be, to ask, to travel, to delay,* and so on. Nearly every verb in English (all but some of the auxiliaries) has an *infinitive* form made with *to.*

Though they cannot work as verbs, the infinitives can work in a variety of other ways. The infinitive may be used as a *noun:*

To see is to believe.
Sally loves *to talk*.
Have you ever tried *to dance*?

In those sentences *to see* is the subject of *is; to talk* is an object: the thing Sally loves; *to dance* is also an object: the thing you may have tried. The infinitives are, then, names of things—that is, names of actions; they are *nouns*.

Time for Review

The *infinitive* is formed with *to* and a base verb-form: *to stop, to answer, to wash.*

The *infinitive* cannot work as a verb.

The *infinitive* can work as a *noun*.

Do-It-Yourself Exercise

Write in each blank an appropriate infinitive that works as a noun:

The family would like _____ a house, but all the good houses cost too much.

Last night I tried _____ a pie, but I burned it.

Our hope is _____ the trophy home.

It is never much fun _____ a game.

Maybe Myrna can get a job as a secretary if she ever learns _____.

Checking up: Each of your infinitives must begin with *to*. Each is the name of an action: the action that I tried, the action we expect to do to the trophy, the action that isn't much fun, the action that Myrna may learn. Each of the infinitives in those sentences works as a *noun*.

Infinitives as Modifiers

The infinitive may also work as an *adjective:*

Pat has a paper *to write*. (modifies *paper*)
The man *to see* is our mechanic, Mr. Adler. (modifies *man*)
Bill has some experiences *to share* with us. (modifies *experiences*)

Chapter Eighteen

Used to modify nouns, those infinitives work as *adjectives*.

The infinitive may also work as an *adverb:*

Bud goes to the track and runs *to keep* in shape.
The big box was too heavy *to carry*.
I was too excited *to sleep*.

Used to modify the verb *runs, to keep* works as an *adverb*. Used to modify the adjectives *heavy* and *excited*, the infinitives *to carry* and *to sleep* work as *adverbs*.

Of course, since an infinitive is a verbal, it too may be modified by an adverb. Therefore an infinitive may modify another infinitive:

She was forced *to run to catch* the bus.

In that sentence *to catch* modifies *to run*. Since the infinitive *to catch* modifies another infinitive, *to catch* works in the sentence as an adverb.

Time for Review

An infinitive can work as an *adjective*.

An infinitive can work as an *adverb*.

Do-It-Yourself Exercise

Write in each blank an appropriate *infinitive* that modifies the word in italics:

Your counselor is the *person* _____ if you have any questions.

I have a list of Spanish *verbs* _____ , but I am really too

tired _____ them tonight.

Most of my friends have been *able* _____ smoking.

The new highway is an obvious *attempt* _____ money from the people of this state.

Was Christopher Columbus really the first *explorer* _____ America?

All citizens should be *encouraged* _____ the nation's natural resources.

Klunky's Shoe Store has *sizes* _____ every feminine foot.

Checking up: Each infinitive must begin with *to: to protect, to study, to discover, to learn, to fit, to steal, to see,* and so on. The infinitives that modify nouns are adjectives; those that modify adjectives or adverbs or verbs are working as adverbs.

Infinitive–or Prepositional Phrase?

Like most other words, *to* has many functions in English. In another chapter we saw *to* as a preposition; now we are using it to form the infinitive. How can these functions be distinguished?

If *to* appears before a noun or noun phrase, *to* is a preposition. But if it appears before a verb form, *to* is the mark of the infinitive. Compare:

Prepositions	Infinitives
Nancy took a book *to* the class.	She took the book *to read*.
I am walking *to* my class.	I am walking *to economize*.
Take this money *to* the store.	Take this money *to buy* lunch.

The preposition *to* is always followed by a noun or noun phrase. The *to* followed by a verb form (such as *read, economize, buy*) is the mark of the infinitive.

Time for Review

When *to* is followed by a noun, pronoun, or noun phrase, *to* works as a *preposition: to them, to college, to the stadium.*

When *to* is followed by a basic verb form, *to* works as the "sign of the *infinitive": To live, to love, to laugh.*

Do-It-Yourself Exercise

Remembering the review points just above, write an infinitive phrase or a prepositional phrase (as called for) to complete each sentence:

Send me something ——————— you by.
　　　　　　　　　　(infinitive)

The child cried; it was obvious he didn't want ——————— a nap.
　　　　　　　　　　　　　　　　　　　　　(infinitive)

When she heard a knock, she went ———————
　　　　　　　　　　　　　　　　(prepositional phrase)
and opened it cautiously.

The driver said he had seen the train but was going too fast ———————.
　　　　　　　　　　　　　　　　　　　　　　　　　　　　(infinitive)

I'd really like _____ with you longer, but
             (infinitive)

I have _____, because class is about _____.
        (infinitive)   (infinitive)

On your way _____ be sure _____ my letters
            (prepositional phrase)   (infinitive)
at the post office.

Let's go _____ and get a bite _____.
         (prepositional phrase)   (infinitive)

The professor said something _____ about going _____
                             (prepositional phrase)   (prepositional phrase)
to check out some books.

Checking up: Each of your completions should begin with *to*. In the infinitive *to* must be followed by a basic verb form: *to remember, to take, to stop, to talk,* and so on. In the prepositional phrase *to* must be followed by a pronoun (as in *to me*), a noun (as in *to school*), or a noun phrase (as in *to the door* or *to the coffee shop*).

Now and then it may seem difficult to tell the difference between infinitive and prepositional phrase beginning with *to*. After all, a word like *love* may be used as a verb or as a noun. How, then, can we tell the difference between these uses:

Everyone needs somebody *to love.*

The whole world gives way *to love.*

The first of the two sentences is clear enough; it uses *to love* as an infinitive. The second is less clear; *love* may be a verb form or a noun in that usage, though it seems more likely to have been meant as a noun: *to love* is probably a prepositional phrase. The writer doesn't really have to worry about the difference unless his sentence could be unclear in meaning.

Infinitives in Pairs or Series

Like many other sentence elements, infinitives may be used in pairs or in series:

Some movies are intended *to shock* or *to disturb.*

Children need time *to play, to grow,* and *to think.*

The careful writer observes parallelism in such pairs or series. It would be awkward to switch from infinitive to prepositional phrase or gerund:

Faulty	Parallel
The ad asked for someone *to cook* and *for housework.*	The ad asked for someone *to cook* and *to do housework.*
Mountain people love *to hunt* and *fishing.*	Mountain people love *to hunt* and *to fish.*

When infinitives are used in such pairs or in series, the *to* is often omitted in all but the first:

> Where did you learn *to sing* and *dance*? (meaning *to* dance)
>
> The scholar loves *to read, observe,* and *compare*. (meaning *to* observe and *to* compare)

When infinitives are used in a pair joined by *either-or, both-and,* or any such correlative, the *to* is usually used in both (for more effective parallelism):

> Molly tried neither *to encourage* her boyfriend nor *to shatter* his hopes completely.
>
> I want not only *to welcome* you here but also *to help* you in getting started.

Time for Review

Infinitives may be used as items in pairs or series.

In a pair or series joined by a coordinator, *to* is often omitted from all but the first: *to live, love,* and *laugh.*

In a pair joined by a correlative, *to* is usually used in both infinitives for effective parallelism: either *to laugh* or *to cry.*

Do-It-Yourself Exercise

Write in each blank an appropriate *infinitive* to complete a pair or series:

Low-phosphate detergents have become the popular ones _____

and _____.

While I'm wearing this leg cast, you can't expect me _____

or _____.

Try _____ your breath and _____ under water.

My fellow citizens, vote for the clean-city candidate, the one who will work for a better city in which _____, _____, and

_____.

Many young Americans love sports, not only _____ on

television but also _____ active part in.

In what is called a "clean fight," a boxer is expected not _____,

_____, or _____.

Checking up: The word *to* begins the infinitive, but in some pairs and series *to* may be omitted after the first use. Which infinitives in this exercise did you write without *to*?

Infinitive Phrases

We saw earlier that such verbals as gerunds and participles may be modified by *adverbs*. Since the infinitive is a verbal, it too may be modified by an *adverb:*

It is wise *to drive carefully.*
We were told *never to waste.*
To eat more slowly may improve digestion.

And an infinitive that is made from a transitive verb may take an object:

Don't use your shoe *to drive nails.*
I can see you would like *to ask a question.*
To save my life, I couldn't remember his name.

The nouns *nails, a question,* and *my life* are all objects of the infinitives. The infinitive with its modifier or its object constitutes an *infinitive phrase.* Indeed, an infinitive phrase may contain *both* modifier *and* object:

To ride a horse safely may call for more than horse sense.

The infinitive *to ride* takes the object *a horse* and is modified by the adverb *safely. To ride a horse safely* is an infinitive phrase.

Time for Review

An infinitive may be modified by an *adverb.*

An infinitive that is made from a *transitive* verb may take an *object.* (For a reminder on transitive verbs see p. 124.)

The infinitive with its modifier or its object constitutes an *infinitive phrase.*

An infinitive phrase may contain both *modifier* and *object.*

Do-It-Yourself Exercise

Write in each blank an appropriate *noun* or *noun phrase* (as object of the infinitive) or an appropriate adverb or adverb phrase (as modifier of the infinitive) to complete the infinitive phrase:

Jim plans *to join* _____.
                    (object)

Next year I will be able *to buy* _____.
                                 (object)

One way *to catch* _____ is *to take* _____
                (object)   (modifier)

_____ in a rainstorm.
    (object)

After a glance at his watch *to see* _____ , the chairman started
                                         (object)

to talk _____.
        (modifier)

As he aimed for his first shot on the rifle range, the rookie wanted *to hit* _____

_____ but was secretly afraid that he was likely
     (object)

to miss _____.
       (modifier)

Banks usually charge their customers who want *to borrow* _____.
                                                (object)

Bobby knelt beside his bed *to say* _____.
                               (object)

Anyone would have *to run* _____ *to beat* _____.
                      (modifier)   (object)

Checking up: Objects are nouns or noun phrases: *the club, a new car, a cold, the time, the bullseye,* and so on. Adverbs tell *when, where, why, how;* some appropriate modifiers for the infinitives: *off, faster, entirely, badly, like a racehorse,* and so on. Be sure that you have not written a noun when a modifier is called for.

Placement of Infinitives

An infinitive will ordinarily seem to work with what is nearest to it:

Henry has a difficult job *to do*. (modifies *job*)

Henry has *to do* a difficult job. (object of *has*)
Henry is required *to do* a difficult job. (modifies *required*)

But when the sense demands, an infinitive will easily seem to work with some element not so near:

We hired Henry *to please his mother*. (modifies *hired*, telling why we *hired* him)

What the writer must consider is whether his reader may be confused by the placement. Do we expect Henry *to please his mother*? If not, it might be better to replace the infinitive phrase to make the sentence clearer:

To please Henry's mother, we hired him.

Revising Danglers

A *dangling infinitive* occurs when the verbal phrase does not clearly apply to or modify an element in the sentence:

To keep an outside job, study time must be carefully arranged.

Since the person who is *to keep an outside job* has not been mentioned, the sentence seems to imply that *study time* is *to keep* the job; but the writer could not have meant that, and his sentence must be revised:

To keep an outside job, a student must carefully arrange his study time.

Now the infinitive phrase clearly applies to the *student* and tells why he must arrange his study time.

Punctuating Infinitive Phrases

When an infinitive phrase is used as a subject, as an object, or as a noun complement, the phrase is *not* set off by a comma:

To turn the truck around was not easy. (subject)
The company guarantees *to refund your money*. (object)
The best plan is *to sit tight*. (noun complement)

When an infinitive is used as a modifier at the beginning of a sentence, the phrase is set off by a comma:

To turn the truck around, Jake grabbed the wheel.
To open the box, use a sharp knife.
To register a complaint, write to our headquarters.

When an infinitive is used as an appositive (renaming a noun), the phrase is set off between commas only if the appositive is *nonrestrictive:*

>The company's first aim, *to boost profits,* has been achieved.
>
>My only wish, *to be of service,* is known to everyone.

The *restrictive* infinitive phrase is not set off:

>My ambition *to become a fireman* faded before I was ten years old.
>
>The attempt *to fly to the moon* seemed futile to unimaginative men.

Time for Review

An *infinitive phrase* should be placed so that it does not suggest an unintended meaning.

A *dangling infinitive* occurs when the infinitive does not clearly apply to any element in the sentence.

An infinitive phrase used as subject, as object, or as noun complement is *not* set off by a comma.

An infinitive phrase used as a modifier at the beginning of a sentence *is* set off by a comma.

An infinitive phrase used as a *nonrestrictive* appositive is set off by a comma or a pair of commas; as a *restrictive* appositive, such a phrase is *not* set off.

Do-It-Yourself Exercise

Write in each blank an appropriate infinitive phrase. Add proper punctuation. Be sure to avoid any *dangler* or *misplaced* infinitive phrase:

It is always safe _____ before starting your engine and putting the car in motion.

_____ always wash the car thoroughly before applying this wax.

One of the mayor's promises _____ has already been realized.

_____ can get a deep-sea diver into serious trouble.

Earl bought a new jacket _____.

I have given up my ambition _____.

_____ you must turn in every assignment paper on time.

Joyce knew she wanted _____ while she was still only a little girl.

_____ the training course must be taken seriously.

Checking up: Check each of your completed sentences against the review section just above this exercise. Have you used commas in the appropriate places? Why should your phrase be set off between two commas in the third sentence? Why would it be wrong to use a comma after *ambition* in the sixth sentence? Did you use a comma to set off your infinitive phrase in the last sentence of the exercise? In that last sentence does your infinitive phrase really modify the *course*? (If not, your infinitive phrase may be a *dangler* and may need revision.) If any of your phrases or its punctuation does not check out against the review points above, revise appropriately.

Suggestions for Writing

A. Children often have ambitions to follow one kind of life or another—ambitions that usually change many times before the children are old enough to realize them. (See the paragraph by Mark Twain on p. 400.) Write a passage of about 250 words telling what were some of the ambitions you had as you were growing up. Use as many *infinitives* as you can.
B. What things in your life have been most difficult to learn? Write a passage of about 250 words telling about several of those things and saying why you found them difficult. Use as many *infinitive phrases* as you can.
C. The title of this chapter may suggest many things to you about how to find the "good life." Write a passage of about 250 words telling what you think a person should try to do to make that "good life" come true for himself. Use as many *infinitive phrases* as you can.

After Writing: Reread your passage and underline every infinitive phrase that you have used. Referring to the review on p. 331, check your passage for punctuation of the infinitive phrases. Can you tell the reason for setting off (or *not* setting off) each of those phrases? Is any of your infinitive phrases a *dangler*? If so, how can it be revised? Check through the passage once more to be sure that every phrase you have underlined is really an infinitive phrase and not a prepositional phrase. In the margin of your paper write (opposite each infinitive phrase) the function of that phrase in its sentence: *noun, adjective,* or *adverb.*

The Split Infinitive

When a writer puts a word like *sometimes* between *to* and the basic verb form in his infinitive, as in "to *sometimes* go," he writes a *split infinitive:*

Professor Charney tries *to* never *confuse* us.
Do you have *to* always *get* up on time?
At home we like *to* occasionally *have* a chicken dinner.

Whether a *split infinitive* is good or bad for effective writing depends upon naturalness and clarity. In the first example just above, the split infinitive isn't quite natural; it would be better not to split it:

Professor Charney tries never *to confuse* us.

And the other examples also seem less effective than they would be if the infinitives were not split:

Do you always have *to get up* on time?
At home we like *to have* a chicken dinner occasionally.

But now and then a split infinitive provides the easiest way of avoiding misunderstanding. Consider the possible confusion of meaning in placement of the word *really*:

We want *really* to beat the Cougars this week.
We want to beat *really* the Cougars this week.
We want to beat the Cougars *really* this week.
We *really* want to beat the Cougars this week.

Some of the sentences seem awkward, and each of them has a slightly different meaning. None of them will mean quite what is meant by the sentence with the split infinitive:

We want to *really* beat the Cougars this week.

On the other hand, most good writers avoid splitting an infinitive by a long phrase or clause. These would be awkward:

Be sure *to* next time you're in town *stop* in to see us.
Archie likes *to* as soon as he gets home and before dinner is ready *have* a cold beer.
I like *to* after dinner *sit* down in front of the television.

In the last example even the short phrase *after dinner* creates an awkward split. The best advice about split infinitives is: Don't split an infinitive unless the sentence can't be written clearly without the split.

Chapter Eighteen

Time for Review

A split infinitive occurs when something is used between *to* and the basic verb form of an infinitive, as in *"To* later *become* a winner."

A split infinitive should be avoided unless the sentence can't be written clearly without it.

Do-It-Yourself Exercise

If the split infinitive seems necessary in its sentence, write "OK" in the blank. If the split infinitive seems awkward, revise the sentence:

We are going *to* now *have* a few words from the boss.

Revision: _____.

The rain is expected *to* really *ruin* the crops.

Revision: _____.

The suspect was believed *to* always *have* a knife in his possession.

Revision: _____.

Jake expects *to* after graduating from junior college *start* his own photography business.

Revision: _____

_____.

Janie liked *to* while kissing her boyfriend always *keep* her eyes open.

Revision: _____

_____.

Checking up: Sometimes the attempt to revise an awkward sentence may produce another kind of awkwardness. Be sure that each of your revisions really makes the sentence clearer than it was before—and less awkward. Which of the sentences did you mark "OK"? If none, where did you place the words *really* and *always* in the second and third sentences?

To Live, To Love   335

QUIZ 18

Using Infinitives

On the blank within each sentence write the item that you think completes the sentence most effectively; then mark the **letter** of that item on your answer blank. Don't overlook punctuation included in some of the offered alternatives. After marking your choice, explain briefly why you chose it (*Because:* . . .).

Example: To turn in the money he had found on the ___*playground*___ ___*would*___ make him feel better, Joe thought.

(a) street, probably would   (b) way home, would   (c) park bench, might
(d) bus, could   (e) playground would

Ex *e*

(*Because:* ___*No comma is used between subject and verb*___.)

1. It is not our _____ the facts for general publication.

(a) intention, to release   (b) policy, to release, all   (c) obligation to, release
(d) intention to release   (e) policy, to release

1. ____

(*Because:* _____.)
     (*Question:* Since *to release* is appositive for *it*, should the phrase be set off by a comma? Is the appositive nonrestrictive?)

2. The new TV show tries _____ its audience.

(a) neither to educate nor amuse   (b) to neither educate nor to amuse
(c) neither to educate nor to amuse   (d) both to educate and amuse
(e) to not only educate but to amuse

2. ____

(*Because:* _____.)
     (*Question:* Which completion achieves parallelism in the pair joined by the correlative?)

3. Miss Hinkle said she would like _____ a gift of expensive perfume.

(a) just once to receive   (b) to just once receive   (c) just to once receive
(d) to just receive once   (e) once to just receive

3. ____

(*Because:* _____.)
     (*Question:* Which completion avoids an unnecessary split infinitive?)

336   Chapter Eighteen

4. To claim your prize, _____

_____ after the show.
(a) your token may be exchanged at the box office   (b) the box office will be open
(c) it will be waiting for you at the box office   (d) go to the box office
(e) the manager will give it to you at the box office   4____

(Because: _____.*)*
   (Question: Which completion avoids a dangler? Who is "to claim the prize"?*)*

5. The good life allows time to work, to play _____.
(a) and love   (b) and to love   (c) , and love   (d) , and to love
(e) , and time to love   5____

(Because: _____.*)*
   (Question: Which completion provides parallelism in the series of infinitives? Should the comma be used before *and* in the series?*)*

6. It certainly isn't _____ in trim without exercise.
(a) easy to, keep   (b) easy, to keep   (c) easy to keep   (d) easy to keep,
(e) easy, to keep.   6____

(Because: _____.*)*
   (Question: When should an infinitive phrase be set off by a comma? Is the infinitive phrase in this sentence a subject, an appositive, or a modifier?*)*

7. Economic theories are fine, but in actual business it is nearly impossible both to keep prices down and _____ up.
(a) to keep wages   (b) keep wages   (c) wages   (d) with wages
(e) holding wages   7____

(Because: _____.*)*

8. Do you believe Ben Franklin ever really expected _____

_____?
(a) to the lightning   (b) to discover electricity   (c) to a key to a kite
(d) to an experiment   (e) to success   8____

(Because: _____.*)*

9. To invest in a business, _____ both cash and courage.
(a) takes   (b) you'll need   (c) will require   (d) it takes
(e) success demands   9____

(Because. _____.*)*

10. Obviously running out of gas, the old bus began to chug, _____ down the road.
(a) to cough and wheeze (b) to cough and to wheeze
(c) cough, and to wheeze (d) cough, and wheeze (e) to cough, and wheeze   10._____

(Because: _____.)

11. Ralph is so conscientious that he tries to give not only at the office but also _____.
(a) give at home (b) at home (c) give when at home
(d) tries to give at home (e) for to his home   11._____

(Because: _____.)

12. Friends, I firmly believe that Sheldon Sharp is _____ election to Congress!
(a) the man to win (b) the man, to win (c) able, to win
(d) the man to without a doubt win (e) certain to this year win   12._____

(Because: _____.)

13. To hit consistently, to throw hard, and _____ are all essential to big-league play.
(a) to the best of one's ability (b) to when you're in the field catch (c) run fast
(d) speed on the base paths (e) to run fast   13._____

(Because: _____.)

14. A massive weather front is expected to move into this area tonight and _____.
(a) bring heavy rains (b) bringing thunder showers
(c) to probably in the morning rain (d) to after a long drought provide some rain
(e) at last to thank goodness bring us some rain   14._____

(Because: _____.)

15. Fred's new pocket calculator will help him to add _____.
(a) accurate (b) careful (c) speedy (d) proper (e) precisely   15._____

(Because: _____.)

16. To please _____ is our first thought.
(a) ourselves,   (b) the public,   (c) our customers   (d) you, always
(e) our clients,   16____

(Because: _____.*)*

17. The attempt _____ has clearly failed.
(a) , to save money   (b) , to lower taxes,   (c) to win public approval
(d) to control weather,   (e) to during winter reduce fuel shortages   17____

(Because: _____.*)*

18. After the day's work she was too exhausted _____

(a) to cook a big meal   (b) to if the phone rang accept a date   (c) , to go out
(d) to later that night have company   (e) , to be good company   18____

(Because: _____.*)*

19. The most effective sentence is: _____

(a) I have hours of research for my term paper to do.
(b) I have hours to do of research for my term paper.
(c) I have hours of research for to do my term paper.
(d) I have hours of research to do for my term paper.
(e) I have to for my term paper do hours of research.   19____

(Because: _____.*)*

20. The most effective sentence is: _____

(a) Drivers need seat belts to be safe.   (b) Drivers need, to be safe, seat belts.
(c) To be safe drivers need seat belts.   (d) To be safe, drivers need seat belts.
(e) To drive safely seat belts are needed.   20____

(Because: _____.*)*

A Choice of Words 19

How to work with . . . appropriate words
everyday words
exact words
concise words
fresh words

How to avoid . . . fancy words
slang words
jargon
out-of-date words
confused words
euphemisms
malapropisms
signposts
redundancies
fat phrasing
faulty comparisons
clichés

IN PUTTING WORDS ON PAPER the writer reveals himself. Whether he thinks of doing so or not, by choosing one word rather than another he tells his readers what sort of person he is. If he is straightforward, his honesty shows; if he is affected, his affectation shows too. If he is haughty or humble, bored or eager, careless or exact, his attitudes and habits of mind will show through his words.

The careful writer, of course, wants to reveal the best of himself. To do that, he must know something about how words work, how they "say" (with greatest clarity) and "show" (to best advantage) what sort of person he is.

Until now this book has focused upon the building of effective sentences. This chapter turns to the use of words. For at last, no matter how effective are the sentences he builds, the writer's work succeeds or fails because of his choice of words.

Tone: Attitudes Revealed

What the writer feels about his topic helps to determine what words he chooses to apply to it. If he finds the topic fun, his pleasure will show; if he finds the topic dull, his words will reveal that attitude; if the topic angers him, his words will convey his anger. Consider how the following passage makes an impression upon the reader:

> Upon entering my first college class, I seated myself at the rear of the huge hall and attempted to avoid being observed. However, a skinny girl who occupied the seat immediately in front of mine twisted around and grinned. She proceeded to engage me in a whispering conversation numerous times during the hour. I made a decision to change my location.

The writer's attitude toward the "skinny girl" is obvious. We are sure that she annoys the writer, who will move away from her before the next class meeting. We also gather that the writer (who uses words like *entering, seated myself, attempted, occupied, proceeded, numerous*) is a rather stuffy person who doesn't care much for people. But consider the same passage written with a different choice of words:

> When I went to my first college class, I sat in the back of the big room and tried not to be seen. But a slender girl sitting just in front of me turned and smiled. She spoke softly with me several times during the hour. I decided to change my seat.

This time we know the writer's attitude is wholly different. The "slender girl" certainly doesn't annoy him. The writer will probably change seats next time, but we're sure he will sit beside the girl. The writer (who this time "sat in the back" rather than "seated myself," who "decided" rather than "made a decision") is a much more friendly person.

Such impressions come from what is sometimes called "reading between the lines." But that familiar phrase suggests something mysterious, as if readers had strange powers of understanding. Most readers, we suspect, do not; but they do pick up impressions about the writer and his attitudes. Those impressions come from the *tone* of what he writes, and *tone* arises from the writer's choice of words.

If a writer is to convey his intended tone, he must give attention to the effects of words on paper. How *appropriate* are the words he uses? How *exact* are they in getting at his meaning? How *concise* is his use of them? How *fresh* are they in the way they say things?

Choosing Appropriate Words

Everyday words take a reader directly into the writer's confidence. They can show him warm and friendly, or they can show him harsh and angry, but they don't hide him behind a mask. Fancy words put the reader at a distance. They are more likely to make the writer seem cool and aloof. Consider the tone of this passage.

> During my extensive servitude in the Marines I suffered a greater amount of solitude than most of my associates, because I did not receive a numerous amount of communications from former acquaintances I had known in civilian life, although I did attempt to keep them regularly informed of my activities as frequently as time allowed.

The choice of all those fancy words produces a tone that reveals the writer in spite of the mask he tries to put up. We gather that his old friends may have been bored by his "attempt to keep them regularly informed." We gather also that he is a rather pretentious person, a bit self-pitying ("I suffered"), and that he is careless with words. He probably means "service" rather than "servitude," probably "loneliness" rather than "solitude," and "friends" rather than "acquaintances." We somehow feel that he caused most of his own suffering, and we do not much care about him. But the same information, with a different choice of words, would reveal quite a different writer:

> I was more lonely than most of my fellow Marines, because I didn't get many letters from friends at home, although I did try to write to them as often as I could.

This time we know that the writer is a sensitive person, but not overly sentimental or self-pitying. Certainly he is not so pretentious; he is more like someone we'd like to know. We feel that his friends at home really should have written to him more often.

Avoiding Fancy Words: In the first passage by the Marine it was the writer's choice of fancy words that betrayed him by giving us an impression that he wouldn't want us to have. In the second passage the choice of everyday words helps the writer reach his reader quite differently.

How do we know *everyday* words from *fancy* ones? Everyday words do not draw attention to themselves; they are words that people live with, familiar but never worn out. Everyday words do not send many readers running to the dictionary or, more likely, to the television. And everyday words are usually *shorter* than the fancy ones that mean much the same thing. Consider the difference between these:

Fancy words	Everyday words
She *arose* and *descended* to breakfast.	She *got up* and *went down* to breakfast.
Fred *discoursed* for *approximately* an hour.	Fred *spoke* for *about* an hour.
They *proceeded* with regular *negotiations*.	They *went about* their *business*.
I have never been *acquainted* with *numerous females*.	I have never *known many women*.
We *attended* the *festivities*.	We *went* to the *party*.

Formal words are appropriate, of course, to formal writing. But even in such serious work as the college term paper or the weightier editorials in newspapers, good writers do not overload their work with big or fancy words. The test is this: Is the word in keeping with the intended effect, and is the intended effect appropriate to the subject matter and to the audience?

Time for Review

A writer's attitude toward his topic and toward his readers will direct his choice of words.

Choice of words produces *tone* in writing.

Through *tone* the writer's personality and habits of mind are revealed to his readers.

Everyday words do not hide the writer behind a mask.

Fancy words put the writer behind a mask—but they do not hide him.

Everyday words are best for most kinds of writing.

A writer should choose words that are in keeping with his intended effect, and that effect should be appropriate to the subject matter and to the audience.

Do-It-Yourself Exercise

Write in each blank an *everyday* word or phrase that will have a meaning similar to that of the fancy words shown below the blank:

Operator, I _____ to call Philadelphia.
              (desire)

Students shouldn't talk too loud when an exam is _____ within
                                                 (proceeding)

_____ range.
(audibility)

Bob would have jumped right over the fence if he hadn't been _____
                                                              (restrained)

by the two men who _____ him.
                   (accompanied)

You'll find the library _____ the new science _____.
                        (in proximity to)   (edifice)

A good mother can tell when her children have had _____.
                                                   (a sufficiency of nutriment)

Professor Macías _____ to _____ a
                 (endeavored)   (maintain)

_____ classroom manner.
(companionable)

Shall we _____ this friendly _____ later
         (perpetuate)   (disputation)

at my _____?
      (residence)

Checking up: The fancy words shown below the blanks are useful words, but most of them are inappropriate to the tone of their context here. *Desire,* of course, means *want.* Did you use such everyday words as *going on, hearing, held back, were with* (for *accompanied*), *near, building, enough food, tried, keep, friendly, carry on* (or *continue*), *argument,* and *home*?

Avoiding Slang Words: Slang is vigorous and colorful, but it tends to have short life and limited range. Like the spoken word, it is here for a moment, then gone. The writer who uses it must be sure (1) that his audience understands it, and (2) that it is appropriate to the subject matter.

College writing topics are likely to be more serious than those that would make slang useful. Such writing, usually intended for a general readership (not merely for the instructor), may be informal; but slang goes a step beyond informality into quick-passing fancy. Some writers of earlier times did use the current slang in their work, but that work is mostly unreadable today because the slang is dead.

What are slang words? They are expressions like *cop-out, goof, hang-up, with it, blast* (for good time), *jerk* (for stupid or unfortunate person), *bomb* (for failure), *fuzz* (for police), *in* (for acceptable), and *far out* (for unusual or good).

Avoiding Jargon: Every business and profession, every social group or age group has its special words used only among those who are in that group. The social scientists talk about "peer groups" and "heterogeneous societalities." The astronauts have their "extra-vehicular activity." Medical men speak of "cardiac arrest" and "tissue infarction." But when those people want to be understood by others outside their groups, they have to put such jargon into more standard terms.

In most college writing *jargon* is out of place. It can be appropriately used if the writer is doing a paper in a special field for a specialized audience, but very little such writing is done by any but graduate students. It is best to put ideas into terms that the general reader is likely to understand without special knowledge.

Avoiding Out-of-Date Words: Language is always changing. Many words that were used by nearly everyone many centuries ago are almost forgotten today. But as we read or hear older works, we may pick up and imitate words that have long since passed into the graveyard of language. Even a word like *alas*, once much used, is seldom appropriate today in writing. Such words as *thou, methinks, lief, ye olde, ere,* and *o're* will not do well in writing today—not even in poetry.

Time for Review

Slang words, colorful while in fashion, are soon dead. They should be avoided in writing.

Jargon, the specialized terms of limited groups or studies, will perhaps not be understood outside those groups or studies. Jargon should be avoided in writing.

Out-of-date words like *thou, ere,* and *methinks* should not be used in writing.

Do-It-Yourself Exercise

Revise these sentences, changing their slang, jargon, or out-of-date words to more understandable language. Use a dictionary if you need help with any of the jargon:

Working on a wheat farm in Canada was my bag for last summer, and I'd just as lief do it again.

_____

_____

_____.

My peer group seems to have an allergenic effect upon those old broads at the public library.

_____

_____

I looked across the room, and there was Jimmy, flaked out, alas, during the sociology lecture.

_____

_____

Our society needs more severe punishment for those who drive under the influence of alcohol. The fuzz should issue a citation to every drunk driver and take his wheels away from him.

_____

_____

_____

_____

It was my first flight aboard a jet, and while flying o'er the clouds at 33,000 feet, I felt a great deal of compassion for those jerks who had to drive on the crowded freeways.

_____

_____

_____

_____

Checking up: Reread your revisions to be sure you have not used such slang as *my bag, old broads, flaked out, fuzz,* and *wheels.* Did you translate jargon terms such as *peer group* and *allergenic effect*? You should have changed *just as lief, alas,* and *o're* to everyday terms like *willingly, unfortunately,* and *above.*

Suggestions for Writing

A. Nearly everyone has a specialty (such as a job, a hobby, or a study interest) that he knows more about than most people do. That specialty probably has a jargon, a number of words and expressions used by its enthusiasts but not by the general public. Write

a passage of about 250 words, explaining some of the jargon of an activity you are especially interested in. Underline the terms you believe are *jargon*.
B. What does "far out" mean? How do you and your friends use that bit of slang? Write a passage of about 250 words, defining that term and commenting on whether to be "far out" is good or bad.
C. Many young people find that their parents and grandparents use words and expressions that seem "odd," perhaps the faded slang of earlier times. What are some expressions used by older people whom you know? Write a passage of about 250 words, pointing out some of those expressions and trying to translate them into your own language.

After Writing: Remember that you are trying to inform your reader about some special kinds of language, not to persuade him that some people are "peculiar." If your passage has a critical *tone,* how can it be revised?

Choosing Exact Words

A good writer's vocabulary does not necessarily burden itself with big or fancy words; instead, the writer finds richness of expression in using everyday words with precision. He is willing to spend time finding out the standard ways of using words that seem useful.

Recognizing Connotations: Not all of the meanings of words can be found in a dictionary. Read again the two passages on p. 340. Why was the "skinny girl" so different from the "slender girl"? Don't *skinny* and *slender* mean about the same thing? They both mean something like *thin*. But the skinny girl is not admired; the slender girl is. The difference is in the *connotations* of those two words.

A connotation is a suggestive meaning *implied,* rather than openly expressed, by a word. It is a meaning given to the word by often repeated associations. Consider the contrasting effects of the italicized words here:

His habits *differ* from the normal.	His habits *deviate* from the normal.
This is an *inactive* group.	This is a *lazy* group.
I've become a *pupil* in an art class.	I've become a *student* in an art class.
He is *renowned* as a *statesman*.	He is *popular* as a *politician*.
She *challenged* the professor's theory.	She *contradicted* the professor's theory.
My father is very *dogmatic*.	My father is very *bigoted*.

To recognize the sometimes subtle differences in the connotations of words can help the writer to avoid making an unwanted impression. If the writer does stir a word-reaction that he doesn't want, the effect of his writing may be destroyed. Consider your reaction to this:

"The focus of my campaign," said the candidate, "will be upon issues important to youth. I hope to win the support of the millions of youngsters in our colleges today."

Would that candidate get your vote? How did you feel about being referred to as a "youngster"? Are young people of voting age really "youngsters"? The outward meaning of the word, of course, is "young people"; the connotation, however, is "children." The candidate, without intending to do so, has probably lost many of the votes he hoped to win.

Recognizing Euphemisms: Language is often a shield against unpleasantness. If we are offended by an idea, we can ward off its sting by using a "nice" word for it instead of the "nasty" word for it. These "nice" words are *euphemisms*.

Euphemisms have their place in helping us to avoid cruelty. There is no profit in referring to a person as "crippled" if the word "handicapped" can avert a reminder of pain. On the other hand, there may be something dishonest about hiding certain kinds of truth behind euphemisms. How often have people been deceived by advertising like this:

> This car is *great transportation*! (a junker)
> Here's a fine *fixer-upper*. (a house in bad condition)
> We feature *self-service*. (no oil-check, no tire-check, no window washing)

Usually we see through the evasive and deceptive use of words. It is best to avoid euphemisms in writing if there is a chance that the reader will sense deception. A good writer tries to learn when to soften a crude or cruel word, but as a rule he profits most from being direct and honest.

Using Specific Words: A word like *furniture* doesn't give so clear a picture as does a word like *chair*. The word *chair* is a more specific word, since it indicates one sort of furniture. A word whose meaning includes many kinds of things is a general word; a word whose meaning includes fewer things (or even a single thing) is a specific word. Consider the greater clarity of the specific words:

General Words	Specific Words
A *relative* met me at the bus.	My *sister* met me at the bus.
Dan used a *tool* to *turn* the device.	Dan used a *wrench* to *loosen* the *pipe*.
I ordered a *sandwich* and a drink.	I ordered a *hamburger* and milk.
The burglars *entered* the *structure* through a *hole* in the roof.	The burglars *broke into* the *warehouse* through a *ventilator shaft* in the roof.

Avoiding Malapropisms: When a speaker or writer mistakes one word for another, using a word that sounds something like the right one, he uses a *malapropism*. The result may be that the writer misleads the reader or makes the reader laugh. Either way the result is bad for the writer. Consider these malapropisms:

> Zelda is in bed with a very high *temperament*. (temperature?)
> The professor seems *insulated* when students whisper during his lecture. (insulted?)

We wanted to try a zone defense for the game, but the coach wasn't *receptacle* to the idea. (receptive?)

He has dignity, and he receives the respect which he *soulfully* deserves. (so fully?)

When I was in fifth grade, I was *enarmored* of my teacher. (enamored?)

The doctor gave me a *subscription*. (prescription?)

Lester was ostracized by the group, and *desertedly* so. (deservedly?)

Such mistakes reveal a hazy awareness of words. The writer who uses a malapropism risks being laughed at by his reader, so that the intended effects are lost.

Time for Review

Most words have *connotations*, implied meanings that go beyond the dictionary senses. A writer must be aware of the connotations of his words.

A *euphemism* is a "nice" word that softens or cleans up an unpleasant idea. Effective writers use euphemisms only when occasion really demands; usually they prefer the direct and honest word.

A *specific* word gives a clearer picture than a general word does. Effective writers prefer the specific word most of the time.

A *malapropism* is a wrong or distorted word used for another that sounds something like it. Effective writers always avoid malapropisms.

Do-It-Yourself Exercise

A. Improve these sentences by replacing the suggested general words with *specific* words:

Ralph snapped his _____ strap and climbed onto his _____
                    (hat)

_____.
(vehicle)

Tony's _____ is usually unbuttoned at the collar.
     (apparel)

The _____ suddenly _____ into the street
     (child)   (went)

chasing the _____.
         (toy)

B. Improve these sentences by replacing the suggested words, using words with more appropriate *connotation:*

Bonnie eats so little that a date with her is always very _____.
(cheap)

What a secretary wears while she's on the job should be _____
(immaterial)
to her boss.

Since husbands may tire of the same old routines, wives should try to be

_____.
(contrary)

C. Improve these sentences by replacing the suggested *euphemisms,* using words that are more exact:

You'll be proud to drive one of these _____ Cadillacs.
(previously owned)

I now have a _____ as a _____ at an
(position)   (fuel-supply technician)

_____.
(auto maintenance center)

Sam told the professor: "I'm sorry, I _____ to _____
(was unable)   (complete)

the assignment because I was too _____."
(busy)

D. Improve these sentences by replacing the suggested *malapropisms:*

When my daughter is naughty, she is _____ of her toys and
(depraved)
sent to bed.

Someone was taking pictures of the accident scene with a _____
(paranoid)
camera.

Gina's boyfriend is too _____ to be _____
(conceded)   (tolerable)
of criticism.

This week the home team seems to be in _____ for the
(contraction)
championship.

Checking up: To use specific words, think what kind of *hat,* what kind of *vehicle,* what kind of *apparel; how* did the child go into the street? What are the connotations of *cheap, immaterial,* and *contrary,* and why are those words not appropriate to the contexts? What would be the general intention of a writer using such euphemisms as *previously owned, fuel-supply technician,* and *too busy?* If the writer uses such malapropisms as *depraved* (for *deprived), conceded* (for *conceited),* and *contraction* (for *contention),* do we pay much attention to what he says?

Suggestions for Writing

D. Suppose that you have a close friend whose life seems a bit confused. Would you describe his way of life as *chaotic,* or *disorderly,* or *sloppy?* Write a passage of about 300 words, telling why you would choose one of those words rather than either of the others. What are the connotations of those words? How would your choice among those words contribute to the *tone* of your description of your friend?
E. Today's everyday language is much more frank than was the language of 30 years ago; nevertheless, even today people have their euphemisms, ways of avoiding harsh or distasteful words. What are some *euphemisms* you find used often in the world around you? Write a passage of about 300 words, discussing a few of them and commenting on whether to use them is good or bad.
F. Nearly everyone knows some famous sayings that are short and to the point, such as "Seeing is believing." That saying could be put into fancy words, such as "Visual observation creates credibility." What are some famous brief sayings that you know? Have some fun by writing a passage of about 300 words, quoting about three such sayings and showing how they might be put into *fancy words.*

After Writing: Reread your passage, considering its *tone.* Do you believe a reader would find your passage friendly, or showy, or dull, or unconvincing? Why?

Avoiding Confusion of Words: Many words in English have sound-alikes, such as *too-to-two, there-their-they're,* and *principal-principle.* The context usually makes clear which is meant, but if the writer uses the wrong one, he may get attention for his carelessness rather than for his ideas.

There are some words that have easily confusable spellings, sounds, or meanings—yet important differences that the careful writer must take time to know:

    accept, except   *Accept* means to receive, take in, or admit. *Except* means to rule out or exclude.

    adapt, adopt   To *adapt* is to adjust to something new. To *adopt* is to acquire or accept.

    advice, advise   *Advice* is a noun; *advise* is a verb.

    affect, effect   *Affect* is a verb meaning to influence or to change. *Effect* is usually a noun meaning result or consequence; used rarely as a verb, *effect* means to bring about.

    allusion, illusion   An *allusion* is an indirect mention of something well known; an *illusion* is a false idea or image.

between, among Between can be used only when two things are involved: *between* you and me. *Among* must be used when three or more things are involved: *among* the three of us.

capital, capitol *Capitol* refers to the building where a legislature meets; for all other meanings use *capital*.

censor, censure To *censor* is to suppress as objectionable. To *censure* is to reprimand.

choose, chose The double *o* has the long sound as in *boo*.

cite, sight, site To *cite* is to mention or refer to. A *sight* is something seen; *sight* is the sense of seeing. A *site* is a place.

complement, compliment A *complement* is that which fills in or completes. A *compliment* is something favorable said about someone.

conscience, conscious *Conscience* is a noun; *conscious* is an adjective.

coarse, course *Coarse* is an adjective meaning rough or crude. *Course* is a noun meaning progress or route of progress.

desert, dessert The one to eat has two *s*'s.

detract, distract To *detract from* is to diminish. To *distract* is to divert (someone's attention).

due to, because of *Due* is an adjective used to modify a noun: the *illness* is *due* to fatigue. *Because* is an adverb used to modify a verb; he *fell because* of fatigue.

famous, notorious One who is *famous* is widely known for good (or at least acceptable) events or accomplishments. One who is *notorious* is widely known for doing bad things.

formally, formerly *Formally* means in a formal manner. *Formerly* means previously.

human, humane *Human* means characteristic of people. *Humane* means compassionate, kind.

imply, infer To *imply* is to hint or suggest without saying. To *infer* is to draw a conclusion from evidence.

incredible, incredulous *Incredible* means unbelievable. *Incredulous* means reluctant to believe. If someone does *incredible* things, others may be too *incredulous* to believe them.

its, it's The possessive *its* has no apostrophe. The contraction *it's* means *it is*.

lead, led Though both are pronounced to rhyme with *bed, lead* is the metal, but *led* is a past-tense verb.

less, fewer *Less* cannot properly be applied to things that can be counted, but only to things that cannot be counted: *less* water, *less* tension. *Fewer* is properly applied to things that can be counted: *fewer* people, *fewer* flowers.

loose, lose *Loose* (with the *s* sound) means "not fastened." *Lose* (with the *z* sound) means to part with by accident or neglect.

many, much *Many* applies to things that can be counted: *many* days, *many* children. *Much* applies to things that cannot be counted: *much* fun, *much* emotion.

number, amount *Number* applies to things that can be counted: a *number* of spectators, a *number* of hours. *Amount* applies to things that cannot be counted: an *amount* of land, an *amount* of love.

passed, past *Passed* is a verb or participle; the parade *passed* by. *Past* is an adjective or noun: the *past* hour is now in the *past*.

persecute, prosecute To *persecute* is to mistreat cruelly. To *prosecute* is to bring to trial in court.

precede, proceed To *precede* is to go before. To *proceed* is to go forward.

principal, principle *principal* means chief or most important. *Principle* means a guiding law or truth.

quiet, quite The one that means "noiseless" has two syllables.

respectfully, respectively *Respectfully* means with respect or high regard. *Respectively* means severally, not both together.

stationary, stationery *Stationary* means not moving. *Stationery* means materials for writing.

than, then *Than* is used in comparatives: more *than* six. *Then* means at that time or under that condition.

their, there, they're *Their* is the possessive. *There* means at that place. *They're* means *they are*.

to, too, two The one with the double *o* means excessively or also: *too* much for *two* people *to* eat.

weather, whether The one that means atmospheric conditions does not have the *wh*.

who's, whose *Who's* means *who is*. *Whose* is the possessive.

your, you're The possessive *your* does not have an apostrophe. *You're* means *you are*.

Some further problems in choice of words often arise with prepositions. Review "Some Problems With Prepositions," pp. 231–232.

A Choice of Words

Time for Review

A writer must avoid mistaking one word for another that is similar (but not the same) in spelling, sound, or meaning.

Do-It-Yourself Exercise

Write in the blank the most appropriate of the suggested words to complete the sentence:

Violators of campus parking regulations will be _____.
(persecuted/prosecuted)

My favorite Western star is _____ for his award-winning performances.
(famous/notorious)

The way the center _____ that ball behind his back was simply _____.
(passed/past)   (incredible/incredulous)

The defense counsel then _____ with his testimony.
(preceded/proceeded)

My father never _____ his poise when we try to _____ him.
(looses/loses)   (detract/distract)

I certainly didn't mean to _____ that the _____ was _____ sweet to eat.
(imply/infer)   (desert/dessert)   (to/too)

The best _____ we can give you is to keep calm when _____ under pressure.
(advice/advise)   (your/you're)

Melvin could not easily _____ the grade he received in his political science _____.
(accept/except)   (coarse/course)

He must _____ according to his own _____.
(choose/chose)   (conscience/conscious)

354   Chapter Nineteen

The person who lacks self-assurance may not _____ easily
                                              (adapt/adopt)

to new situations.

The interviewer asked _____ _____ the
                      (respectfully/respectively) (weather/whether)

senator had ever been _____ for his activities.
                      (censored/censured)

A large _____ of accidents happen _____
        (amount/number)   (because of/due to)

bad _____.
    (weather/whether)

_____ going to eat _____ calories just to
(Who's/Whose)   (fewer/less)

maintain her _____ ?
             (principals/principles)

Avoiding Faulty Comparisons: Comparisons in English are expressed in two degrees, the comparative (with such words as *less, more, better*) and the superlative (with such words as *least, most, best*). The *comparative* is used when *two* things are involved in the comparison:

>   Mat is *shorter* than John.
>   Which city, Reno or Las Vegas, is *nearer* to California?
>   The truck is *bigger* than the bus.
>   Does your job pay *less* money than mine does?

The *superlative* is used when *three or more* things are involved in the comparison:

>   Mat is the *shortest* man on the team.
>   Which of the airlines flies *nearest* to Spruceville?
>   This is the *biggest* bus in the fleet.
>   Among all of us, I make the *least* money.

With modifiers of more than two syllables the word *more* or *less* (rather than the *-er* ending) is used to form the comparative:

>   Mat is *more inhibited* than John.
>   Reno is *less expensive* than Las Vegas.

With such longer words the word *most* or *least* (rather than the *-est* ending) is used to form the superlative:

>   This is the *most comfortable* bus in the fleet.
>   Which is the *least difficult* of the ten problems?

When a writer states comparison, he must be sure that the items or terms are really capable of being compared. Consider these faulty comparisons:

> The *voice* of a soprano is higher than a *tenor*.
>
> The *rainfall* in Hawaii is much greater than *Arizona*.
>
> *Gas consumption* on the highway is much less than *town*.

It is illogical to compare the *voice* to a *tenor*, the *rainfall* to *Arizona*, or the *gas consumption* to the *town*. The comparisons must be more accurately stated:

> The *voice* of a soprano is higher than *that* of a tenor.
>
> *Hawaii's* rainfall is much greater than *Arizona's*.
>
> *Gas consumption* on the highway is much less than *that* in town.

Incomplete comparisons may result in misunderstanding:

> I love animals more than most people.
>
> We have more money in our cookie jar than the bank.

The comparisons mislead the reader, who may assume that the writer loves animals more than he loves people—or that the bank has some money in the cookie jar. It is necessary to revise such sentences to state the full terms of the comparisons:

> I love animals more than most people *do*.
>
> We have more money in our cookie jar than *we have in* the bank.

Time for Review

Comparisons are expressed in two forms: the *comparative* and the *superlative*.

The *comparative* (with *less, more,* or *-er* ending) is used when *two* things are being compared.

The *superlative* (with *least, most,* or *-est* ending) is used when *three or more things* are being compared.

Terms in a comparison must be capable of being compared.

To avoid misunderstanding by the reader, a writer must state the full terms of a comparison.

Do-It-Yourself Exercise

Write in each blank an appropriate word or phrase to complete a clear and proper comparison:

Of the Kirschner twins, Dave is the _____ runner.
(fast)

Are you still worrying about which is the _____ (intelligent) sex?

Does Karen swim _____ (well) than Mark?

We try to buy groceries at the _____ (inexpensive) of the five markets in town.

Women last year wore the _____ (short) skirts the fashion industry had ever put out.

Who has the _____ (good) appetite, Sid or Charlie?

For solo parts the director always picks the _____ (attractive) girls from the chorus.

The gum on postage stamps doesn't seem so tasty as _____ (last year).

I like this kind of music because it is _____ (contemporary) than the _____ (earlier generations).

Wages in the airline industry are not really _____ (high) than _____ (banking).

Checking up: Remembering that the comparatives *(less, more,* or words with *-er* endings) can be used only with two things being compared, you should have written: *faster* runner, *more intelligent* sex, swim *better*, the *least expensive* market, *shortest* skirts, *better* appetite, *least* (or *most*) attractive. In the last three sentences of the exercise the comparisons must be made complete and clear: tasty as *it was* last year, *more contemporary* than the *music of* earlier generations, *higher* than *those in* banking.

Choosing Concise Words

Readers do not want many words; they want many ideas. They want what they read to be full of details, yet concise and to the point. For just that reason a writer needs to pay attention to brevity.

Word thrift is an attainment. It is much easier to write many words than to write few, and the writer who has some experience knows that filling three sheets of paper with words is easier than filling one sheet with ideas.

When college instructors ask for "an essay of 1,000 words," they are not really talking about words. Rather, they are estimating the degree of development expected in the essay. If the student writes 1,000 words but does not present a well-developed, rounded essay of organized ideas, the paper does not deserve praise.

From the student's point of view the assignment may seem quite different. The instructor may seem to be interested in words, not ideas. Since it is more difficult to develop and organize ideas than it is to write words, the student may set to work with one main goal—to fill space with words. His chief device for that purpose is *padding*.

Writing is padded when it uses more words than are needed to develop its ideas. Some devices of padding are *signposts, redundancies,* and *fat phrasing*.

Avoiding Signposts: The signpost is a statement that tells the reader what is about to be covered, or one that serves as a transition or organizer among ideas. The signpost can be a useful device in a book or in a very long paper. In a short essay, however, the signpost is usually wasted. These are some typical signposts:

> In the paper which I am about to write I shall attempt to fulfill the assignment by . . .
>
> Before we can begin a discussion of the topic that has been assigned, we must first consider . . .
>
> Let me say before I begin that what I am about to write is nothing more than my personal opinion, and . . .
>
> It is difficult to begin writing an essay on the topic of --------, but here goes. . . .
>
> In conclusion let me point out the fact that . . .

Useful as such signposts may be to the public speaker or to the writer of long books, they are generally wasteful in shorter college essays. The student who uses them appears more interested in counting all those words towards his required 1,000 than he is in getting on with his message.

Avoiding Redundancies: A redundancy says something twice without seeming to. Perhaps the writer overlooks the fact that *pre-* means ahead or before; he writes, "It isn't easy to *predict ahead*." Or, if he forgets that *re-* means back or again, he writes, "Let me *repeat again*" or "When I *returned* the book *back* to the library . . . ." But readers do not need to be told that babies are young, that today's times are modern, or that what is sufficient is enough:

> In these *modern times of today,* of course, *young babies* don't usually get *colic pain* unless they have not had *sufficient enough* medical care.

The redundancies, by adding unneeded words, boost the word count without providing new information. The sentence says no more than:

> Today babies don't usually get colic unless they have not had enough medical care.

Some other typical redundancies:

and etc.	*necessary* requirements
combined *together*	now *at this time*
consecutive times *in a row*	*of a* purple *color*
consensus *of opinion*	short *in length*
different varieties	*still* persists
many *in number*	*youthful* child

Avoiding Fat Phrasing: If the *library door* always becomes "the *door of the library*" or if *continue* always becomes "continue *on*," useless words help fill the page. These are some typical devices of fat phrasing:

Prepositional phrases:

the corner of the street (for *street corner*)
men with employment (for *working men*)
circle around the globe (for *circle the globe*)
at the hour of six (for *at six o'clock*)
first of all (for *first*)

Relative clauses:

the car *which was* parked (for *the parked car*)
the girl *who was* seated on the bench (for *the girl on the bench*)
the cake *that was* in the oven (for *the cake in the oven*)

Unnecessary adverbs:

climb *up* the hill
fell *down* to the floor
try again later *on*
rarely *ever* forget
pass *by* the door

Such examples of fat phrasing are not always bad style in themselves, but they may contribute to the wordiness of a style that becomes heavy with other kinds of deadwood:

Wasted Words	Concise Words
We heard him speak a number of times because Miss Roy, the teacher who was teaching our class, invited him to attend and put in a speaking appearance. We have not come into contact with him for a great many years, but have heard tell that he is at the present time acting in the capacity of president of the Toastmasters Club.	We heard him speak often, because our teacher, Miss Roy, invited him to speak to the class. We hadn't seen him for years, but have heard that he is now president of the Toastmasters Club.

Time for Review

Padding fills space with words, not with ideas.

Signposts are statements that tell a reader what is to be or has been covered, or statements that offer hedging or apology.

Redundancies are disguised repetitions, such as a *round circle,* an *old, elderly* man, or *too much overdone.*

Fat phrasing occurs when a writer uses a phrase or clause where fewer words would do.

The careful writer trims signposts, redundancies, and fat phrasing from his work.

Do-It-Yourself Exercise

Reduce the wordage in these passages by rewriting to eliminate *signposts, redundancies,* and *fat phrasing:*

At the beginning let me say that all of my entire family have lived in the state of California for a number of years.

The brakes on my Ford car, which are of the disc variety, never do slip after I happen to drive through a wet puddle of water.

My old grandmother is conserving and saving on power and energy. She currently lives at a home for the aging senior citizens, where the directors who run the place hardly ever only very seldom give their permission to keep the lights on and burn them after 10 P.M. at night.

My employment at the shop where they sell discount furniture goods first began on a Monday in the month of July. Now I will tell something about that first opening day of my job career. It was hard, difficult work lifting heavy tables and mattresses that people sleep on. I was worn out before my noon lunch hour came.

_____

_____

_____

Checking up: Reread each of your trimmed versions. As a reader, do you believe you would want to read the passages with many words—or would you prefer the passages with the same ideas in concise style?

Choosing Fresh Words

Words do not wear out easily. But when a writer puts words into wornout combinations, his work may lack spark. The wornout word combination is a *cliché*.

The greatest shortcoming of a cliché in writing is that it leads the reader's mind into a rut instead of giving him a fresh viewpoint. When that happens, of course, the reader may wonder why he bothered to begin the reading; then the writer has lost his audience. How might a reader react to something like this?—

> Last but not least, it is interesting to note in this connection that the finer things in life seldom come to you if you have your heart set only on filthy lucre. History tells us that in a vast majority of cases the pursuit of happiness does not in any shape or form depend upon mere money. So take it from me, if your eye is only on the almighty dollar, you might just as well forget about true happiness. Money, after all is said and done, can be lost at the drop of a hat.

The writer has strung together about a dozen phrases that everyone has heard before. He might have written the whole thing in one sentence:

Money can't buy happiness.

But it would do little good to put that idea down at all, for the reader might say to himself, "I know that already." The whole message was "just another cliché."

Good writers do not necessarily avoid every cliché. Some ready-made phrases are easily acceptable without their making a whole essay seem stale. To be original is hard work, and the overconscious attempt to avoid a cliché may produce an unnatural tone. Trying to be original is less important than trying to be clear and honest.

Time for Review

A cliché is a wornout combination of words, so often used that nearly everyone recognizes the phrasing.

A Choice of Words

An occasional cliché may be appropriate, but the writer who uses many such ready-made phrases may bore his reader.

Do-It-Yourself Exercise

Underline as many of the *clichés* as you can find in the "Last but not least" passage above. Then, to prove to yourself that such phrases lack originality, complete the sentences below by writing in each blank a word that you think the writer probably intended:

It only stands to _____ that everybody these days has an

_____ to grind.

The shoplifter slipped the bracelet into his pocket, just as slick as a _____

_____. Then, cool as a _____

and looking for all the _____ like an innocent customer, he

sauntered toward the door. When he got outside, quick as a _____

he was off like a _____.

The hero of the story stood by his brother through _____ and

_____, even though the brother was obviously _____

to the core. It's as plain as the _____ on your _____

that _____ is thicker than water.

A rumor is something we should all avoid like the _____,

because a thing like that can spread like _____ before

you can say _____.

Of course, coin collecting is only a common or _____ variety

hobby, but it is by all _____ the most interesting one to me.

To put the story in a _____, I couldn't remember him from

_____. But then all of a _____ his name

came to me like a _____ from the _____

I knew that life was not all a bed of _____, but I never thought

I would get emotionally _____ in the old _____ race.

Checking up: If you were able to fill in most of the words quickly, remember that your own reader would be able to recognize such clichés in your work. Do the sentences in this exercise indicate that their writers had interesting ideas?

Avoiding "Incorrect" Words

Although what is "correct" in language is really whatever is appropriate to a context or to a situation, usage in writing is generally free of certain words and phrases that abound in everyday speech. Effective writers usually avoid using such words and phrases as these:

aggravate Should not be used to mean *annoy* or *irritate*. Aggravate means *to make worse:* "Don't *annoy* me, or you'll *aggravate* our misunderstanding."

ain't, aren't I Never appropriate for use in serious writing, unless in dialogue.

all the farther, all the faster Should not be used for *as far as* or *as fast as*.

alot A misspelling of the two words: *a lot*.

alright A misspelling of the two words: *all right*.

amidst, amongst Should not be used for *amid* and *among*.

anyplace Should not be used for *anywhere*. (Other such forms to be avoided are *every place, some place, no place;* the appropriate forms are *everywhere, somewhere, nowhere*.)

anyways Should not be used for *anyway*.

as Should not be used for *since*.

awful Should not be used for the adverb *awfully*.

being as, being that Should not be used for *since* or *because*.

busted Should not be used for *burst*. (As slang for *arrested* this word would be appropriate only in writing whose purpose makes slang appropriate.)

but what, but that Should not be used for *that:* "I don't know *that* I'll go."

can Should not be used for *may:* "I *can* drive if I *may*."

can't hardly Should not be used for *can hardly:* "She *can hardly* walk."

A Choice of Words

can't help but   Should not be used for *can't help:* "We can't help agreeing" (rather than "We can't help but agree.").

centers around   Should not be used for *centers upon.* (Since a center cannot go around, the phrase is illogical.)

complected   Should not be used for *complexioned:* "He is dark complexioned."

don't   Should not be used for *doesn't.* (See verb agreement, p. 128.)

dove   Should not be used for *dived.*

drug   Should not be used for *dragged.* (See p. 315.)

enthused   Should not be used for *enthusiastic.*

equally as   The *as* is unnecessary: "They are equally good."

ect.   Mistaken form of *etc.*

firstly, secondly   Should not be used for *first, second.*

funny   In most writing *funny* should not be used for *strange* or *odd* (or their *-ly* forms): "He was acting very strangely."

for . . . to   The *for* should be omitted: "I want him *to* go" (not "I want *for* him to go").

hanged, hung   Pictures and other objects are *hung* in place; a person may be *hanged* (as capital punishment).

hisself   Should not be used for *himself.* Other improper forms include *ourself, themself, theirself,* and *theirselves.* The proper forms: *ourselves, themselves.*

his or her   Despite the wish to avoid male chauvinism, the awkwardness of *his or her* and *he or she* makes for bad writing. *His* is the standard reference when the sex is unspecified.

hopefully   Should not be used for *I hope.*

if   Should not be used for *whether.* Use *if* to begin an adverb clause, *whether* to begin a noun clause: "I don't know *whether* she is here."

I'am   Should not be used for *I am* or *I'm.*

in that   Should not be used for *because* or *since:* "Many people worry about inflation, *because* wages are not going up" (not "*in that* wages are not going up").

individual   Should not be used for *person.*

irregardless   Should not be used for *regardless.*

is when   Should not be used in writing a definition: "Hypocrisy is the pretense of having worthy qualities" (not "Hypocrisy *is when* you pretend to have worthy qualities").

kind of   Should not be used for *rather* or *somewhat:* "His speech was *rather* awkward" (not "His speech was *kind of* awkward").

kind of a   The *a* is unnecessary and awkward: "It just seemed to be that *kind of* day" (not "that *kind of a* day").

leave   Should not be used for *let:* "*Let* us try again" (not "*Leave* us try again").

let   Should not be used for *leave:* "*Leave* him alone" (not "*Let* him alone").

off of   The *of* is unnecessary and awkward: "He pushed the books *off* the desk" (not "*off of* the desk").

real   Should not be used for *very* or *really:* "She swims *very* well" or "She swims *really* well" (not "She swims *real* well").

reason is because   Should not be used for *reason is that:* "The reason for the score is *that* our team is unprepared" (not "The reason for the score is *because* . . .").

revelant   Should not be used for *relevant*.

snuck   Should not be used for *sneaked*.

some   Should not be used for *somewhat:* "Conditions are *somewhat* improved" (not "Conditions are *some* improved").

sure   Should not be used for *surely* in standard writing: "General Custer was *surely* surprised" (not "General Custer was *sure* surprised").

suspicion   Should not be used as a verb for *suspect:* "They *suspected* a conspiracy" (not "They *suspicioned* a conspiracy").

them   Should not be used as a demonstrative adjective for *those:* "I bought *those* books" (not "I bought *them* books").

these kind, those kind   Should not be used for *this kind* or *that kind,* since *kind* is singular.

thusly   The *-ly* is unnecessary and awkward: "The candidate *thus* lost the election" (not "*thusly* lost the election").

type   Should not be used for *type of*: "I enjoy that *type of* movie" (not "I enjoy that *type* movie").

undoubtably   Should not be used for *undoubtedly*.

use to   Should not be used for *used to*. (See pp. 314–315.)

ways   Should not be used for *way:* "His goal was still a long *way* off" (not "a long *ways* off").

where . . . at   Should not be used for *where*: "No one knew *where* the bicycle was" (not "where the bicycle was *at*").

which   Should not be used as a pronoun referring to a complete idea. (See p. 255.)

would have   Should not be used for *had:* "If she *had* been able to drive" (not "If she *would have* been able to drive").

QUIZ 19

Choosing Effective Words

On the blank within each sentence write the item that you think completes the sentence most effectively, avoiding inappropriate, inexact, wasteful, or stale words. Then mark the **letter** of that item on your answer blank. After marking your choice, explain briefly why you chose it *(Because:* . . .).

Example A: The newspaper account of the fire was obviously full of ___*errors*___.
(a) erroneousness (b) errors (c) baloney (d) wrong errors
(e) contortions   Ex A __b__
(Because: "*Errors*" *avoids (a) fancy word, (c) slang, (d) redundancy, (e) malapropism.)*

Example B: Proponents of economic controls were unable to analyze why the measures ___*failed*___.
(a) came to naught in the end (b) were counterproductive (c) bombed out
(d) failed (e) enjoyed small success   Ex B __d__
(Because: "*Failed*" *avoids (a) out-of-date word, (b) jargon, (c) slang, and (e) euphemism.)*

1. The truck driver said he was _____ that the brakes had failed.
(a) without a shadow of a doubt (b) incredible (c) more then surprised
(d) doubtful (e) aggravated   1. ____

(Because: _____ .)

(Questions: Which completion avoids both cliché and confusion of words? What does *incredible* mean? See p. 351).

2. The attorney _____ a recess.
(a) respectively requested (b) snuck in a plea for
(c) asked weather the judge would declare (d) asked if he could have
(e) respectfully asked for   2. ____

(Because: _____ .)

(Questions: Is *snuck* a proper verb? Would *respectively, weather,* or *if* be effective? See pp. 352 and 363.)

368   *Chapter Nineteen*

3. The coach said he believed his team would win _____
the opposition's strength.
(a) alot of games despite   (b) regardless of   (c) careless of
(d) less games because of   (e) irregardless of

3._____

(Because: _____

_____.*)*

(Questions: Would *alot, regardless,* or *less* be proper usage? What are some connotations of *careless?* See pp. 350–352 and 362–365.*)*

4. The welterweight challenger has no _____
about winning the match.
(a) allusions   (b) conscious   (c) principals   (d) fear in hisself
(e) illusions

4._____

(Because: _____

_____.*)*

(Questions: What is an *allusion*? Would *conscious, principals,* or *hisself* be proper usage? See pp. 350–352 and 362–365.*)*

5. When she called the hospital, she was told that the patient was feeling

_____.
(a) some better   (b) painlessly   (c) fresh as a daisy
(d) better than the day before   (e) cheerful

5._____

(Because: _____

_____.*)*

(Questions: Should *feeling* be followed by an adverb like *painlessly* or by an adjective like *cheerful?*—See p. 166. Is "fresh as a daisy" a fresh phrase? How does "the day before" feel? Is *some better* a proper phrase?—See p. 364.*)*

6. One driver in the car pool has a six-passenger wagon with _____

_____.
(a) four on the floor   (b) fuel dejection   (c) room for a large amount of tools
(d) everything accept air conditioning   (e) an economy engine

6._____

(Because: _____

_____.*)*

(Questions: Would *four on the floor* be understood by all readers? Would *dejection, amount,* or *accept* be proper usage?—See pp. 350–352 and 362–365.*)*

7. As a newcomer, I did not _____ easily.

(a) enter into meaningful relationships   (b) make friends   (c) turn people on
(d) relate to strangers   (e) scrape up acquaintance   7._____

(Because: _____

_____.)

(Questions: Which of the completions would be psychologists' jargon? Which is slang? Which is a cliché?)

8. _____, free luncheon will be served to all the delegates.

(a) Now at this time   (b) If the session continues on   (c) Later on
(d) After the morning session   (e) Hopefully   8._____

(Because: _____

_____.)

9. Members of the zoology class made a detailed study of _____

_____.

(a) certain marsupials   (b) some animals
(c) animals with pockets in their abdomens
(d) kangaroos, opposums, and wombats   (e) a few Australian mammals   9._____

(Because: _____

_____.)

10. The new police chief has said he will _____

_____ of traffic control.

(a) pursue a follow-up of improvement
(b) try to make an attempt toward improvement
(c) facilitate formation of an association for cooperation in administration   10._____
(d) make a simplification   (e) simplify methods

(Because: _____

_____.)

370   Chapter Nineteen

11. If the public _____ more careful, much of today's pollution might have been avoided.
(a) would have been   (b) would of been   (c) had been   (d) was
(e) conducted themself   11_____

(*Because:* _____

_____.)

12. Our company loses many customers _____

_____.

(a) because of its high prices   (b) due to their policy of cash payment
(c) as it honors no credit cards   (d) who's appliances break down
(e) which means lower profits   12_____

(*Because:* _____

_____.)

13. The chairman _____ that the council would meet again on Tuesday afternoon.
(a) made an announcement   (b) stated the notification   (c) said
(d) volunteered the information   (e) insinuated   13_____

(*Because:* _____

_____.)

14. Which car burns the _____ fuel, yours or mine?
(a) least   (b) fewer   (c) greatest amount of   (d) less   (e) most   14_____

(*Because:* _____

_____.)

15. Spectators at our stadium produce more noise than _____

_____.

(a) you can shake a stick at   (b) Philadelphia   (c) last year
(d) those in Seattle do   (e) us   15_____

(*Because:* _____

_____.)

16. _____
1980's will surely be years of scientific achievement.
(a) In final conclusion, the   (b) We can say without fear of contradiction that
(c) It is possible to forecast ahead of time that the   (d) Undoubtably the
(e) The   16____

(*Because:* _____

_____.)

17. Through years of teaching, Professor Swift had learned to make his lectures

short _____.
(a) and sweet   (b) in length   (c) and enthused   (d) and informative
(e) and kind of humorous   17____

(*Because:* _____

_____.)

18. Radio reports said that the highway patrol was looking for _____

_____.
(a) a stolen vehicle   (b) a stolen motorcycle   (c) a police type motorcycle
(d) a police car, which seemed odd   (e) a police car that a thief had stolen   18____

(*Because:* _____

_____.)

19. Members of my family have always seemed particularly susceptible to those

_____ diseases that cause sneezing.
(a) contiguous   (b) crummy   (c) communicative   (d) contagious
(e) conspiratorial   19____

(*Because:* _____

_____.)

20. The commentator's special report _____
that the councilman had not conducted a fair campaign.
(a) inferred   (b) incinerated   (c) implied   (d) contained an inducement
(e) suggested by hidden innuendo   20____

(*Because:* _____.)

A Train of Thought 20

How to work with . . . expanding ideas
idea-linking devices
consistency of topic
consistency of reference
consistency of person
consistency of tense
parallelism
repetition

How to avoid . . . fragments
shift of topic
faulty pronoun reference
shift of person
shift of tense
awkward repetition

UNTIL NOW THIS BOOK has been discussing the use of words, phrases, and clauses to build clear and effective sentences. Yet, all the while, the writing suggestions have been asking the student to "write a passage" on such and such a topic. And writing a passage means something more than writing a sentence; it means putting several sentences together in some meaningful way.

This chapter concerns some ways and means of putting sentences together to build a train of thought. How does a partial idea expand into a full one? How does one idea link to another? How does a train of thought stay on a clear, straight track? In short, how does a writer develop his ideas and keep them moving smoothly along, getting them not only *on paper* but also *off the paper* and into the mind of the reader?

Expanding Ideas

A full sentence is not always a full idea. Some sentences demand explanation and detail if they are to be understood:

My old dog is really odd.

That sentence says something, all right, but not enough. It leaves us asking, "Why? What do you mean? So what?" The idea needs something more to make it worth saying:

My old dog is really odd. He won't eat anything but cat food.

Now the idea is better; we've been given some evidence that the old dog is odd—a reason for that remark.

From your practice with sentences you already know that these two ideas could be linked as one. They may be *coordinated:*

My old dog is really odd, and *he won't eat anything but cat food.*

But, since the second part of the whole idea gives a reason for the first, it would probably be better to *subordinate:*

My old dog is really odd, because *he won't eat anything but cat food.*

Even when the two parts of the idea are written as separate sentences, they are really linked as one idea. The subject, *my old dog,* is repeated as *he.* They are linked also because the second part *(won't eat anything but cat food)* is a specific way in which the old dog *is really odd.*

By linking such sentences we build a train of thought. We hook one idea onto another, each depending upon the other to form a larger idea, all of them going in one direction.

Of course, the two sentences about *my old dog* still do not make a fully satisfactory idea. We're left wanting still more. *Why* won't the dog eat anything but cat food? The idea would become more complete with added detail and explanation:

My old dog is really odd. He won't eat anything but cat food. When he was a pup, he loved to play with balls of yarn. Once he wore himself out trying to climb a tree, and even now he gets most of his exercise by chasing mice. These habits make me think the mutt was orphaned at birth and raised by a cat.

Now the idea has become much more satisfactory. To build the train of thought has taken five sentences. It certainly wouldn't do to put all those details into one sentence; yet the five sentences all belong together as parts of the *larger* idea.

How have we tied the sentences together? We have used some coordination *(and);* we have used some subordination *(When . . .);* we have also used pronouns and synonyms *(my old dog, he, a pup, his, the mutt)* to keep the main subject constantly in the reader's mind. Still other links between the sentences appear in words that show the passage of time *(When he was a pup, even now, once).* And the summarizing phrase, *These habits,* serves as a reminder of all the details mentioned earlier. We build the train of thought by making words in one sentence repeat, vary, or refer to words in another.

Time for Review

A full sentence is not always a full idea. It usually takes more than one sentence to develop *a train of thought.*

Links in a train of thought are such words and phrases as conjunctions *(and, but, therefore, because, still),* pronouns *(he, they, both),* demonstrative adjectives *(this, that),* adverbs showing how things are related in time *(once, then, later),* in space *(upward, downward, around),* or as cause and result *(as, as a result, because of),* and synonyms that rename.

Do-It-Yourself Exercise

A. Circle the words and phrases that help to link the sentences in this passage:

With the coming of September each year, we are reminded, as the song says, that the days are dwindling down to a precious few. By the calendar, we know that soon the chill winds of winter will begin to blow; and—before we are ready for the end to come—the year will be gone.

As it is with the calendar, so it sometimes seems to be with our country and its system. For there are those among us who would have us believe that America has come to its own September; that our days are dwindling down to a precious few; that before long we will feel the first chill of a long American winter—and that our nation's stand as mankind's "last best hope" will be done.

For those who preach this prophecy—and for those who believe it—this

376 Chapter Twenty

period of our affairs can only be a melancholy season. It is not for me. . . . I live, as I have always worked—by the faith that with each passing day we are always approaching a new springtime.

—Lyndon Baines Johnson
(in a speech at Temple, Texas,
on September 16, 1972)

Checking up: Your markings reveal how many words and phrases are simply repeated as links in the train of thought: *September, year, days, calendar, winter, chill; dwindling down to a precious few; will be gone/will be done; with the calendar/with our country; those who preach/those who believe.*

B. Write in the blanks some appropriate synonyms (either words or phrases) to keep the subject *(automobile)* continually in the reader's mind:

The *automobile* will not easily give way to the bicycle as the average American means of getting around. In most cities the _____ has become a real _____ to the environment. When the _____ moves, it burns gasoline and makes smog. When the _____ doesn't move, _____ takes up valuable parking space. And when the old _____ stops running, _____ owner trades _____ in, and the _____ becomes a _____ in an unsightly junkyard beside the highway. Still, Americans are very slow to give up their precious _____ for something that burns muscle power instead of gasoline.

Checking up: Since the word *it* is the most likely pronoun to rename *automobile*, you've probably used *it* several times—and in one case *its*. Other useful synonyms: *car, vehicle, wheels, bus, pile of junk, clunker, gas burner, smog maker, menace, hazard, speedwagon.*

C. Write in the blanks some appropriate *adverbs* (words, phrases, or clauses) to link the sentences in this passage:

Mankind _____ got around on foot. _____ _____ men learned to harness animals for transportation. It was not until _____ that the wheel was invented, and

_____ that, a means of propelling a wheeled vehicle—

_____ by manpower, _____ by steampower,

_____ by internal-combustion power. _____

mankind has almost forgotten how to walk.

Checking up: Dozens of adverbs would fit the passage. You can get extra practice in using sentence links by writing the passage in several ways. Some useful adverbs; *once, long ago, at one time, in early history, then, later, first, finally, at last, today, now, as time went on, after many centuries.*

More Linking Devices

Sentences may be linked in a train of thought by still other words and phrases that help *parts* of an idea to become elements of a *whole* idea. For example, the word *other* (in the sentence just before this one) obviously shows that what is about to come is related to what came before. What's more, the phrase *for example* (in the sentence just before this one) clearly links that sentence to the one before it. And the clause *What's more* (in the sentence just before this one) continues the process of linking sentence to sentence in the train. *Not only that, but* . . . and the train might go on.

It would be impossible to list all of the words and phrases that can be used as links between ideas, but here are some of those most often used:

also	in fact	so much for
as a result	in short	such
as well	instead	that
at first	later	that is
at last	likewise	then
earlier	more	therefore
finally	moreover	these
first, second	once	this
for example	on the contrary	those
further	on the other hand	to sum up
however	other	what's more
in addition	rather	
indeed	similar	

To show how these linking devices work, let's use a few of them to develop a train of thought:

Who is a winner? Who, *that is,* wins what he goes after in games, in business, in life, or in love? *First,* the consistent winner is usually one who knows the odds. *Second,* knowing the odds, he does not go against them; *for example,* he does not venture when danger or failure is more likely than success. *On the other hand,* the winner does not shrink from a venture and, *in short,* do nothing. When the goal is worthy and the odds not overwhelmingly dark, *then* he moves. *Such* is the winner: one who is careful yet unafraid.

Time for Review

Sentences may be linked in a train of thought by many words and phrases such as those listed on p. 377.

Do-It-Yourself Exercise

Write in the blanks some appropriate words or phrases that link the sentences of this passage in a train of thought.

When I was very small, the _____ thing I wanted to do in life was get rich. All _____ hopes, it seemed to me, depended on _____ one. _____ I came to learn that getting rich was not likely without hard work. _____ thoughts brought me to know what a comedy life is, for I _____ realized that it was only to avoid hard work that I wanted to be rich. _____, I gave up both hard work and riches.

Checking up: Try writing a second entry in each blank to show that several versions are possible. Some useful words and phrases: *first, main, other, less important, that, on the other hand, more recently, such, those, soon, later, further, in short, indeed, to sum up, finally, at last.*

Suggestions for Writing

A. Write a brief account (about 100 words) of an incident in which you had a near accident. In developing the account use words that show time sequence, such as *once, then, later, afterwards, finally.*
B. Write a passage (about 100 words) telling what you think of one widely **played sport.** In developing the passage use (and underline) several adverbs of cause **and result.**
C. Write a passage (about 100 words) telling why you prefer indoors or **prefer outdoors.**

A Train of Thought   379

In developing the passage use words and phrases that show order of importance, such as *first, second, chief, more important, of less importance, further, most of all.*

Keeping Topic Straight

If a train of thought begins with one topic and then shifts to another, the change must be clear and justified. What can happen when the writer doesn't stick to his original topic?

> One of the common methods of advertising is to compare two kinds of toothpaste, saying that one is better than another. My father hates commercials. Probably both the toothpastes are about the same anyway.

The sentence *My father hates commercials* does not continue the train of thought started with *One of the common methods of advertising;* the sentence is not a part of the idea to be developed but is only a side remark. It should be omitted from the sequence and perhaps developed elsewhere as a separate idea.

Time for Review

Any change of topic within a train of thought must be clearly justified.

If a sentence is not clearly a part of the idea to be developed in a passage, that sentence should be omitted.

Do-It-Yourself Exercise

Each blank has under it a sentence that would derail the train of thought by shifting to a different topic. Write in the blank a brief sentence that develops the central thought appropriately.

In some cities the police departments have set up a cop-and-citizen program. Officers who patrol an area in a police car get acquainted with the people in that area. _____
(Crime grows when people are suspicious of their law enforcement

_____. Public meetings are arranged to give
   officers.)
citizens a chance to meet and talk with the officers on their beat.

Student council members suggested that the campus parking problem be

solved by issue of special permits. _____
_____ (Every morning there is a traffic jam when students
_____. Each student would
try to park.)
have an assigned space for so many hours a day.

While talking about health habits, the instructor mentioned the need for
good lighting in study halls. _____
(Many students wear dark glasses even
_____. Inadequate light puts a strain on student
when reading.)
eyes and may cause fatigue and nervousness, which are both health problems.

Checking up: Your sentences to replace the faulty ones should stick clearly to the topics: how the cop-and-citizen program works; how the parking problem might be solved; why good study-hall lighting is essential to health. Perhaps in the first passage the *Crime grows* sentence could be kept in line by making the idea positive, like the rest of the sentences: "The people get over their suspicion of law enforcement, and crime rates go down."

Keeping Reference Straight

Another important way to keep an idea clear as it grows is to be careful with pronoun references. Since a pronoun usually substitutes for a noun, the reader needs to know just what noun is meant by the pronoun. What can happen to a train of thought when the reference isn't clear?

> Downtown that morning a couple of girls were fixing up a new display of shoes in the window of the Supreme department store. *They* were really good lookers. Benny and I decided to just hang around until maybe the girls came out for lunch.

What does the pronoun *they* mean? Were the *shoes* good lookers—or the *girls*? We gather that *they* means the girls, but the train of thought was not easy to follow. When a pronoun could refer to any one of several nouns in the context, the writer needs to make sure that the meaning will be immediately clear to the reader.

> Most of the street was dark, but there was a light burning in the back of Xavier's jewelry store, and the door was wide open. It was midnight, and *that* really made me suspicious.

What does the pronoun *that* mean? Does *that* refer to the *light,* the *store,* the *door*?—to the fact that the light was burning? that the door was open? that it was midnight? The writer needs to avoid using the pronoun unless he is sure the reader will know what it stands for. Just what "made me suspicious"? Maybe it was the whole situation:

> . . . It was midnight, and *the situation* made me suspicious.

Or perhaps it was just the open door:

> . . . It was midnight, and *the open door* made me suspicious.

The writer can, in other words, avoid the pronoun *that* and put in what he really means.

Time for Review

A train of thought can be derailed by a pronoun whose reference is not immediately clear.

Any pronoun whose reference is unclear should be replaced by the noun that the writer intended it to stand for.

Do-It-Yourself Exercise

Each blank has under it a pronoun that could be misunderstood in its context. Write in the blank a noun (or noun phrase) to replace the pronoun and develop a clear train of thought:

Most of the puppies at the pet shop had sad eyes and waggly tails. Teresa just

had to have _____.
(one)

There was a loud roar when the usher tried to make the girls leave. _____

_____ showed how the crowd felt about _____.
(This)   (it)

Willie obviously wanted to be the star. The coach just couldn't keep him from

running with _____.
(it)

Betty spilled hot soup all over the customer's dress. Naturally, _____
                                                                                                (that)

really made _____ mad.
(her)

Next time I'm going to take a course in Italian conversation. Believe me, _____ is where _____ really know how to talk.
           (that)   (they)

Checking up: One, they, this, that, it, and her—all these pronouns would be confusing in their contexts. If you have replaced them with nouns that are fitting and clear, you have developed more consistent trains of thought. Some possible entries: one—*a puppy;* they —*the people* or *the officials;* this—*the roar;* it—*the ball;* that—*Italy* or *the accident;* her—either *Betty* or *the customer.*

Keeping Person Straight

In grammar *person* concerns whether what is named by a noun or pronoun is the *speaker* (*first* person), the *audience* (*second* person), or the *topic* (*third* person) in a sentence or larger idea. To develop a clear train of thought, the writer needs to keep in mind which of these he has started with, then stick to that one. What happens when a writer switches from one *person* to another?

> Someday *I* want to learn to drive a truck. When *you* can drive a truck, *one* can always get a job.

A clearer development might be:

> Someday *I* want to learn to drive a truck. If *I* can drive a truck, *I* can always get a job.

The train of thought comes near jumping the track in these badly linked sentences:

> *A person* should always try to smile. Smiling helps *you* win friends.
> *Riley* has buckled down to studying. After all, *your* education is the most important thing when *one* is young.
> *People* should read with open minds. Don't expect everything to reflect *your* own private ideas.

Time for Review

A train of thought can be derailed by the writer's shifting from first person to third, from third to second, from second to first, and so on.

Any pronoun that switches from the *person* already established in a passage should be replaced by a pronoun that maintains that *person.*

Do-It-Yourself Exercise

Each blank has under it a noun or pronoun. Write in the blank an appropriate word to keep a consistent train of thought throughout each passage:

When _____ can vote, _____ can in-
     (one)   (they)

fluence public affairs. Voting is one of _____ biggest
                                 (your)
responsibilities.

In telling a story _____ must decide what _____
           (the writer)   (you)

will need to make _____ understand.
             (them)

In police work _____ should always be informed of
         (the accused)

_____ rights and have an opportunity to
  (your)

defend _____.
     (oneself)

Of course _____ knew that _____ was likely
        (she)   (a girl)

to talk to _____ when _____ emotions
       (myself)   (your)
got upset.

Checking up: To make the ideas clear, be sure that all the blanks in each context are filled by nouns or pronouns in the same *person*. Some possible appropriate ones are these: *one, he, his; the writer, he, readers; the accused, his, himself; Marcia, a girl, herself, her.*

Suggestions for Writing

D. The popularity of zoos and of the movies of Walt Disney indicates that people are fascinated by animals. Write a passage of about 150 words describing an animal you have known (either wild or domestic). In developing the passage use as many *pronouns* and *synonyms* as you can to refer to that animal.

E Write a passage (about 100 words) telling why you believe something (such as gasoline, water, food) should not be wasted. After you've written the passage, circle words in each sentence to show that the same *topic* has been used throughout the passage.

Chapter Twenty

Keeping Time Straight

Pronouns, synonyms, repetition of key words—all these help keep a developing thought on a clear track. Still another way to keep a thought in line is to be consistent with *past, present,* and *future*. What can happen to a train of thought when the treatment of time gets mixed up?

When summer *came,* I *needed* a job. I *go* out and *look* all over town.

The switch from *came* and *needed* (past tense) to *go* and *look* (present tense) jolts the train. The idea comes through, but not smoothly. The verb tense should be consistent:

When summer *came,* I *needed* a job. I *went* out and *looked* all over town.

Time for Review

A train of thought can be derailed by the writer's shifting from one verb tense to another.

Once a verb tense has been established in a passage, all verbs in that passage should maintain that tense or follow an appropriate *sequence of tenses* (see p. 149).

Do-It-Yourself Exercise

Write in each blank an appropriate verb, being careful to avoid any shift of tense:

One afternoon I *met* Joey on the street outside the shoe factory. He _____ me that he _____ a job in the factory.

He _____ making pretty good money, and he _____ the work. Right away I _____ my chance. I _____ maybe Joey _____ some influence and _____ help me get a job in the factory. Well, he _____. The next day I _____ to work. I _____ that job all summer and _____ enough to buy clothes and books that fall.

Checking up: All the verbs should be in the *past tense*, like *met*. If you had any trouble thinking of appropriate verbs, try some like these: *told, asked, had, was, liked, enjoyed, saw, grabbed, thought, believed, could, might, did, agreed, started, went, reported, kept, earned, made.*

Suggestions for Writing

F. Retelling a story that you have heard is a way of sharing experiences with friends. But retelling a story and making it clear is almost as much of an art as writing an original one. Write a passage of about 150 words, retelling what happened in a movie, book, or television story. In developing the story use the *past tense* consistently.

G. Like starting a cold engine, getting up in the morning can produce a lot of sputtering and coughing and groaning before the day really gets moving. Write a passage of about 200 words, telling what you did from the moment you awoke until the moment you got to class or to work one morning. Tell the story in the *present tense,* as if it were happening *now*.

Avoiding Fragments

Not every sentence, as we have seen, is a full idea. In fact, not every "idea" will make a full sentence. Earlier chapters have shown that a *phrase* is not a sentence, since the phrase contains no subject-verb combination; and a *clause* is not a sentence if it is introduced by a subordinator. These, for example, are not sentences:

> *sitting on his motorbike*
> *because he was careless*
> *to stay awake until the end*

The participial phrase, adverb clause, or infinitive phrase does not serve as a completed sentence. That is why careful writers do not write such phrases and clauses as if they were sentences. These are improperly written:

> There's my cousin Alfie. *Sitting on his motorbike.*
> Sam lost his paycheck. *Because he was careless.*
> I have a problem in history class. *To stay awake until the end.*

The word groups shown in italics are *fragments*. The fragment is a nonsentence written as if it were a full sentence—with a capital at the beginning and a period at the end. The fragment is considered a serious fault in most kinds of writing, since it indicates that the writer may not know what a sentence is. To repair a fragment, the writer needs to make the word group a part of a sentence near it:

> There's my cousin Alfie *sitting on his motorbike.*
> Sam lost his paycheck *because he was careless.*
> I have a problem in history class: *to stay awake until the end.*

Time for Review

A *fragment* is a nonsentence—a sentence fault.

A fragment should be rewritten as part of a sentence near it.

Do-It-Yourself Exercise

Rewrite the *fragments* so that they become parts of the full sentences:

The council used to meet every day. *Right after lunch.*

Revision: _____.

Donna came from Northern Michigan. *Where it's cold. From October to April.*

Revision: _____
_____.

The glass shattered. *All over the street.* Most of the guys ran, but I just stood there. *With the bat.* Old Pickleface came out of his delicatessen. *Obviously mad. Holding the ball in his left hand and a knife in his right.*

Revision: _____
_____
_____
_____
_____
_____.

Checking up: Remember that every full sentence has both *subject and verb*. Prepositional phrases *(all over the street, with the bat)*, unattached modifiers *(obviously mad, holding the ball . . .)* must be written as parts of the full sentences.

Avoiding Run-Together Sentences

Just as the writer must know how to tie sentences together, so must he know how to keep them properly apart. If two ideas crash together without proper linking, the writer risks throwing his reader off the train of thought. What happens when the writer doesn't know that a sentence has ended? He may start another without any warning to the reader:

> Her mother couldn't teach her to drive, the father was too busy to do so.

The comma is not enough to separate two sentences. Standard writing calls for a *semicolon* when two sentences have elements that relate them closely, as the adverb *so* relates to *teach her* to drive:

> Her mother couldn't teach her to drive; her father was too busy to do so.

Some further examples of sentences improperly written with the *comma fault:*

> The hippies seem to be disappearing, they know when they're beaten.
> He caught a glimpse of himself in the mirror, he felt very tired then.
> I told the doctor my ache was nothing, he said he would have to decide that for himself.

All three examples need to be written with the *semicolon* rather than the comma:

> The hippies seem to be disappearing; they know when they're beaten.
> He caught a glimpse of himself in the mirror; he felt very tired then.
> I told the doctor my ache was nothing; he said he would have to decide that for himself.

Now and then two sentences may run together without anything at all to mark the linking. The result is not linking, but crashing:

> Our college is getting funds from the U.S. government probably cutting a class will be a federal offense.
> Ice was all over the road the pickup truck slid into a ditch.
> Racial prejudice in the hearts of men cannot be legislated out of existence laws alone are not enough.
> Billy learned where babies come from now he thinks he is related to his mother by birth and to his father by marriage.

Repairs for comma-faults and run-together sentences can be made in several ways:

1. Use *period* and *capital*:

> Our college is getting funds from the U.S. government. Probably, cutting a class will be a federal offense.

2. Use *semicolon*:

> Ice was all over the road; the pickup truck slid into a ditch.

Chapter Twenty

3. Use *comma* with *coordinator*:

Racial prejudice in the hearts of men cannot be legislated out of existence, *for* laws alone are not enough.

4. Use *subordinator* to begin one of the ideas:

Since Billy learned where babies come from, now he thinks he is related to his mother by birth but to his father by marriage.

Do-It-Yourself Exercise

Repair these comma-fault and run-together sentences by using several of the means listed above:

People really have to wait a long time to see that new _____
(doctor in his

_____ he has whole books instead of magazines.
waiting room)

Women's lib is _____ needs a feminine touch.
(all right it just)

A couple that never get married will never have any _____
(in-laws they)
will only have outlaws.

That old lady really looked _____ spilled the jam on her rug.
(disgusted, I had)

We went to a movie _____ wasn't very
(the other night the popcorn)

_____ certainly was.
(salty the picture)

Dad said we might go on a trip to see the folks _____
(back home he had)
a vacation coming up.

Don't just sit there, _____ the sunset.
(Mom, come and see)

The group leader said we shouldn't _____
(worry, everything)
would come out all right.

There is plenty of time to do things ———————————————————
                                    (in this world, all anybody needs)

——————————————————————————————————— is imagination.

"Why," she asked, "are you looking at me ————————————

———
         (like that," I answered that I thought she was lying.)

Checking up: Some of the entries could be varied, since more than one of the four listed means of repairing comma faults and run-together sentences would make the ideas clear. Probably among the best possibilities are these: *doctor. He; all right; it just; in-laws; they; disgusted. I* or *disgusted, because I had; back home, since; Mom. Come; in this world. All anybody needs; like that?" I answered* . . . . Notice that you need a question mark in that last one.

Using Parallel Structures

Another way of showing that two ideas are related is to put them into *parallel structures*. Repetition of form can be as effective as repetition of words:

> One of the most popular word games today is the definition game. *Someone says,* "Happiness is . . . ," and gives his own definition. *Someone else says,* "Love is . . . ," and gives a definition. *Usually* the *definitions are personal. Always* the *definitions are different.* The game helps to teach us all that most words mean *different things* to *different people.*

In such a passage the coherence is emphasized by repetition of words as well as by repetition of structure.

President Lincoln in his Gettysburg Address used parallelism to emphasize the coherence of his ideas:

> . . . that government *of the people, by the people,* and *for the people* shall not perish from the earth.

And President Kennedy in his inaugural address used parallelism to build a train of thought:

> And so, *my fellow Americans,*   *ask* not
> ║ *what your country can do* for you: *ask*
> ║ *what you can do* for your country.
> *My fellow citizens* of the world,   *ask* not
> ║ *what America will do* for you, but
> ║ *what* together *we can do*
>   for the freedom of man.

Chapter Twenty

Finally, whether ‖ *citizens of America* or
‖ *citizens of the world,* ‖ ask of us
here the same high standards of strength
and sacrifice which we ‖ ask of you.
‖ *With a good conscience* our only sure reward,
‖ *with history* the final judge of our deeds,
let us go forth to lead the land we love,
‖ *asking* His blessing and His help, but
‖ *knowing* that here on earth God's work
must truly be our own.

Do-It-Yourself Exercise

Each blank has under it a group of words that could be revised to make the structure parallel to one of the italicized word-groups in the passage. Write in each blank a revision that achieves *parallelism:*

For the girls the problem was easy; after all, *all of them had learned to* use needle and thread. _____
(The boys had a difficult time with the problem;

_____.
sewing was an entirely new experience.)

Weeds grew along the fence. _____.
(The stone walks had weeds growing along them.)

_____. _____
(In the flower beds there were weeds.)   (There were weeds

_____. It was obvious that gardening was not among Mr.
everywhere.)
Olaski's interests.

I had a happy outlook *when I was a kid. I still have* it now _____

_____.
(as an adult.)

And I hope _____.
(it is still with me)   (in my old age.)

Checking up: Probably your revisions read something like this in the first passage: *For the boys the problem was difficult; after all, none of them had learned to sew.* In the second passage each may begin with *Weeds grew . . . .* In the third: *I had . . . when I was a kid. I still have . . . when I am* an adult. *I'll still have* it *when I am old.*

Time for Review

Sentences may be linked in a train of thought by words, phrases, or clauses that show relationships of time *(once, later, then, at last),* of order *(first, second third . . .),* of division *(one, another, still another, the last),* of comparison *(similarly, like, just as),* of contrast *(however, but, on the contrary, on the other hand),* of summary *(in short, that is),* or of illustration *(for example, for instance).*

Sentences in a train of thought should stick to one *topic.*

Sentences in a train of thought should keep *pronoun reference* clear, (See "Pronoun Reference," p. 252.)

Nouns and pronouns in a train of thought should be consistent in *person.* (See "What Person Means," pp. 240–241).

Verbs in a train of thought should stick to the *past,* to the *present,* or to the *future* (or should develop a clear sequence) rather than shift from one tense to another. (See sequence of tenses, pp. 149–150.)

Sentences in a train of thought should not be *run together* without proper coordination, subordination, or separation.

Sentences in a developing train of thought may gain coherence by *parallelism,* the use of similar structures for similar parts of the idea.

Suggestions for Writing

H. Table manners often differ according to situation—or according to what is being eaten. Consider fried chicken or watermelon. Write a passage of about 150 words, telling how to eat it, either gracefully or otherwise. Use several *infinitive phrases* in *parallel* to show the steps in the process.

I. Big news has a way of being bad news. Write a passage of about 150 words, telling what you believe is the *worst news event* you have heard about recently. In developing the passage use at least three subordinate *clauses* in *parallel.* Try also to use several *prepositional phrases* in *parallel.*

After Writing: Reread your passage to be sure that you have maintained consistency of *person,* of *tense,* and of *topic.* Be sure you have not written any *fragments.* Circle the linking devices that you have used; see the list on p. 377.

A Note on Repetition

From what has been shown in this chapter it should be clear that *repetition* is a commonly used device for tying together the ideas in a train of thought. Indeed, repetition can help a writer to achieve emphasis and clarity as well as coherence. But like most other devices, repetition can be awkwardly used; an overdose of it can spoil a writer's effects.

With all that in mind, use repetition with care. As you reread and revise what you have written, ask yourself whether repetition would help or hinder. In general, do not repeat unless you believe the repetition really improves the intended effect upon your reader.

A Train of Thought 393

QUIZ 20

Building a Train of Thought

On the blank within each passage write the item that you think completes the passage most effectively; then mark the *letter* of that item on your answer blank. After marking your choice, explain briefly why you chose it *(Because: . . .)*.

Example: Students must prepare for the future. After all, the future will bring changes, and _students_ will have to be ready.

(a) we (b) the class (c) they (d) students (e) you   Ex _d_

(Because: "Students" avoids shift of person and faulty reference.*)*

1. It was my first day on the new job. By noon I had a rope-burn on my left hand. By midafternoon I had a charley horse in my right leg. Before quitting time ___

_____.

(a) I had a huge knot on my head (b) a huge knot appeared where a 2×4 hit my head
(c) a falling board had hit my head (d) my head ached
(e) it was an aching head   1.____

(Because: _____.*)*
   (Question: Which completion provides a structure parallel to the *I had a rope-burn* and *I had a charley horse* elements of the preceding sentences?)

2. Most modern highways are designed for safety. They are angled for drainage. Their curves are banked, and _____

_____.

(a) drivers can speed on them (b) nonskid surfaces
(c) they are paid for by public funds (d) their surfaces are of nonskid materials
(e) your car won't skid   2.____

(Because: _____.*)*
   (Question: Which completion provides both clear pronoun reference and parallel structure?)

394   Chapter Twenty

3. Writers of history sometimes leave out important details. _____

_____. Their omissions, however, may cause distortion.

(a) In order to be concise   (b) Because of the need for brevity
(c) They would no doubt find it impossible to include everything
(d) We can't expect one to tell all that happened   (e) It makes the story briefer

3._____

(*Because:* _____.)
  (*Question:* Is a *fragment* permissible? Would *we* or *it* provide clear and consistent pronoun reference?)

4. In the chapter Rome is burning. Meanwhile, there _____ Nero playing his violin.

(a) sits   (b) was   (c) sat   (d) they had   (e) stood

4._____

(*Because:* _____.)
  (*Question:* Which verb is consistent in tense with the *is* of the first sentence?)

5. The two guys sitting right back of us had floppy hats and long beards. After a while the conversation got pretty loud and full of jokes, and _____ really tickled us.

(a) they   (b) when they   (c) both of them   (d) the jokes   (e) one of them

5._____

(*Because:* _____.)
  (*Question:* Would *they* or *them* provide clear pronoun reference?)

6. It is hard to keep smiling when someone is always putting you _____

_____ in public.

(a) down, especially if they do it   (b) down. They shouldn't do it
(c) down. Especially   (d) down, even if he doesn't do it
(e) down. Because they often do it

6._____

(*Because:* _____.)

7. Really good traffic cops cannot be talked out of giving a ticket when it's deserved. _____ can be jollied into giving the ticket in a friendly way.

(a) For example, he   (b) After all, they   (c) What's more, one
(d) In addition, they   (e) On the other hand, they

7._____

(*Because:* _____.)

8. The newspaper story made it appear that only one man had been involved in the robbery. Mrs. Oliva, however, said she had seen two men. _____

_____ may cause a lot of confusion.

(a) This   (b) That   (c) These two   (d) It may
(e) The difference between the two stories   8_____

(Because: _____.)

9. These days there is a lot of discussion of different types of automobile engine. Some say the rotary will replace the piston. _____

_____.

(a) Others hope they don't   (b) Certainly we burn too much gas
(c) Because it burns less fuel   (d) When people come to accept it
(e) Others defend the piston engine   9_____

(Because: _____.)

10. The language of young people seems almost foreign to their elders because of the slang used so much by the young. _____ an older person has to ask for a translation into plain English.

(a) When   (b) However,   (c) Often   (d) Because   (e) Such that   10_____

(Because: _____.)

11. From where Jack Eagle stood his life looked useless. He thought of quitting, giving up. Then the fog lifted. _____ was ridiculous, he thought.

(a) It   (b) This   (c) Quitting   (d) That   (e) Such   11_____

(Because: _____.)

12. Perhaps America today is beginning to listen to the people, of all backgrounds, who may be without financial power but who love their country. For years little attention was paid to such people, but now their voices _____ heard.

(a) were becoming   (b) arose   (c) had to be   (d) are being
(e) having been   12_____

(Because: _____.)

396 Chapter Twenty

13. Together we planned the little business. Together we built it. Together we saw it prosper. _____ watched it go up in smoke.
(a) We   (b) Then   (c) At last   (d) Then one night   (e) Then together we   13_____

(*Because:* _____.)

14. She was a lovely little birdlike creature who filled my days with song. She seemed so happy with me, until one day she fluttered her wings and _____ out of my life.
(a) split   (b) walked   (c) flew   (d) ran   (e) popped   14_____

(*Because:* _____.)

15. The trouble with planned parenthood is that the average couple may be too ambitious. They may plan well enough but _____ carry out the plan.
(a) be unable to   (b) couldn't   (c) not persistent to
(d) careless in trying to   (e) failing to   15_____

(*Because:* _____.)

16. The army has no business forcing a man to get a haircut. _____ is entirely out of line.
(a) Such force   (b) They are   (c) It   (d) That   (e) Because doing so   16_____

(*Because:* _____.)

17. In the battered old wagon sat a hairy youth. The hair fell to his shoulders, down over his eyes, down over a dirty collar. _____ to music on the radio.
(a) Listening   (b) He is listening   (c) Keeping time
(d) Absorbed in listening   (e) He was listening   17_____

(*Because:* _____.)

18. It was very quiet along the street _____.
(a) nothing stirred   (b) , nothing stirred   (c) , not a sound
(d) , hearing nothing   (e) . Nothing stirred   18_____

(*Because:* _____.)

19. His ego was about to take a beating _____ didn't know what was coming, though.

(a) , he   (b) . He   (c) ; He   (d) he   (e) He   19_____

(*Because:* _____.)

20. A secretary usually uses up more energy than a woman who is moving around all day. _____ can't wait to get home and relax.

(a) She   (b) They   (c) I   (d) Such a hard worker
(e) The weary secretary   20_____

(*Because:* _____.)

From Thought to Paragraph   21

How to work with . . . paragraphs
unity of idea
development of idea
coherence of idea
the topic sentence
controlling purpose
transition

How to avoid . . . underdevelopment of idea
incoherence
faulty transition

AS WE HAVE JUST SEEN in the preceding chapter, it usually takes more than one sentence to develop a train of thought. Now we move ahead to consider how a train of thought becomes a *paragraph,* a developed, coherent, and unified element within a longer piece of writing.

One sentence by itself may present an idea without developing that idea enough. Consider this sentence written by Mark Twain:

> When I was a boy, there was but one permanent ambition among my comrades in our village on the west bank of the Mississippi River.

That sentence certainly did present an idea—or part of an idea. But Mark Twain could not have stopped there, for he had aroused the reader's curiosity: "What was that ambition? Why was it permanent? Were there other ambitions that didn't last?" The writer had to go on to satisfy his reader's curiosity by providing answers and details:

> When I was a boy, there was but one permanent ambition among my comrades in our village on the west bank of the Mississippi River. That was to be a steamboatman. We had transient ambitions of other sorts, but they were only transient. When a circus came and went, it left us all burning to become clowns; the first negro minstrel show that ever came to our section left us all suffering to try that kind of life; now and then we had a hope that, if we lived and were good, God would permit us to be pirates. These ambitions faded out, each in its turn; but the ambition to be a steamboatman always remained.

The idea that began with a sentence, teasing but not satisfying, has become a *paragraph,* a group of sentences linked in a train of thought. The paragraph presents the topic of the idea (the "one permanent ambition") and develops that topic by offering specific *detail* ("to be a steamboatman") and *contrast* ("transient ambitions of other sorts," to be clowns, minstrels, pirates).

What Makes a Good Paragraph?

A paragraph presents an idea (usually an aspect of a larger topic) and develops that idea in a coherent group of sentences. The key words here are *idea, development,* and *coherence.* What looks like a paragraph may be a very bad one, or none at all, if it fails in any of these.

1. *Unity of Idea.* The paragraph sets forth its basic idea and sticks to it. Any wandering from that idea violates the *unity* of the paragraph.

2. *Development of Idea.* Mere presentation of idea may be of some interest—but interest cannot be held unless that idea is developed by *illustration,* by *example,* by *comparison,* or by some other means appropriate to that idea.

3. *Coherence of Thought.* All parts of that development must hang together—be consistent and follow a clear line. Any shift from first person to third, from past tense to present, from image to clashing image, or from premise to unreasonable conclusion can weaken or destroy the paragraph.

All these virtues of the good paragraph, of course, are in addition to others that good writing demands: clarity and variety of sentence structure, appropriateness of word choice, helpfulness of punctuation.

The Topic Sentence

Usually the topic of a paragraph is presented in the first sentence. That sentence serves as a point of attention, something to keep the reader's mind focused on as the train of sentences develops to complete the paragraph. The topic sentence helps the reader to grasp the topic in general, and the development keeps the reader's mind on that topic as it presents specific details.

The topic sentence is often a *generalization,* a broad statement that needs to be supported by *specific details.* The generalization stirs the reader to ask, "Why? What makes you think so?" In other words, the topic sentence may be a sort of decision or verdict by the writer—and the rest of the paragraph a presentation of evidence to support that verdict.

> My cousin Marty is a loser.
>
> It is impossible to be friendly with someone who has lent you money.
>
> Science is a means of destroying nature.

Obviously these sentences are not necessarily fact or truth, although the writer presents them as if they were. The alert reader will not accept them without question; he will want to know *why* the writer thinks those things. Each of the topic sentences must be followed by development of the idea, setting forth certain details and evidence to convince the reader of the worth of the statement.

Time for Review

It usually takes more than one sentence to develop a train of thought.

A *paragraph* is a group of sentences linked in a train of thought.

A *paragraph* presents a topic and develops it by offering *specific detail.* The key to a successful paragraph is its combination of topic and development.

Usually the topic of a paragraph is presented in the first sentence: the *topic sentence.*

The topic sentence is often a generalization that makes the reader ask, "Why? What makes you think so?"

Do-It-Yourself Exercise

A. Each blank represents a topic sentence for its paragraph. After reading the development of each paragraph, write on the blank an appropriate topic sentence:

1. _____

_____. When we were kids, he could never win at games. He lost his clothes when we went swimming, and he lost his lunch money on the way to school. As we grew up, he couldn't keep a girlfriend and he couldn't win a bet, though he was always eager to find a girl or take a bet. Now he works for a plumber and is always losing tools. When he gets paid, he usually loses his money in a card game or at the pool hall. And lately he's losing his hair.

2. _____

_____. The modern farmer uses chemical fertilizers that can kill the natural taste of foods. The high-speed saws of the lumber industry turn the forests into wastes, and the scientific machines of industry spoil the waterways and poison the air. Indeed, the more our laboratories learn about nature, the more is nature threatened.

3. _____

_____. Once you owe him a dollar, you may as well owe him the world. Every chance meeting reminds you of the debt. At last you come to believe the lender is a devil, hounding you to pay, so that it becomes necessary to avoid him as he comes along the street.

Checking up: Each topic sentence should be a generalization that is supported by the details in the rest of the paragraph. If you had trouble writing appropriate topic sentences, try possible ones on p. 401.

B. Each of these topics is a suggested basis for a paragraph. Write for each a generalization, a statement of your opinion about the topic, in a brief sentence that could serve as a topic sentence for such a paragraph:

1. *Getting revenge*

_____

_____

2. *Red tape in college life*

_____

_____

3. *People who bore their friends*

_____

_____

4. *Something for nothing*

_____

_____

5. *Believing what you hear*

_____

_____

Checking up: Each topic sentence should be a statement that you believe is generally true, even though other people could have opposite opinions. The sentence should be a generalization, not a specific detail. For example, "Getting revenge takes a lot of planning" is a generalization, an appropriate topic sentence; but "My dictionary says revenge is 'punishment in return for harm done' " is a specific fact and would not make a good topic sentence, though it could be used in the paragraph's development. (It is seldom wise to cite dictionary definitions to make a point.)

C. The next step in developing a paragraph is to list several details (such as specific facts or bits of reasoning) that led you to hold the opinion stated in your topic sentence. For each of the topic sentences that you have written above, list three or four *specific details*:

1. Details to support topic sentence on *getting revenge*.

   a. _____

   _____

   b. _____

   _____

   c. _____

   _____

   d. _____

   _____

2. Details to support topic sentence on *red tape in college life*.

   a. _____

   b. _____

   c. _____

   d. _____

3. Details to support topic sentence on *people who bore friends*.

   a. _____

   b. _____

   c. _____

   d. _____

4. Details to support topic sentence on *something for nothing*.

   a. _____

   b. _____

   c. _____

d. _____

_____

5. Details to support topic sentence on *believing what you hear*.

a. _____

_____

b. _____

_____

c. _____

_____

d. _____

_____

Checking up: Be sure that each supporting detail really does lead to the opinion you have expressed in your topic sentence. If your topic sentence were "My cousin Marty is a loser," it would not be proper to list such a detail as "He was born in Brooklyn" or "He is 18 years old"; such facts would not in any way support the topic sentence. But such evidence as "He will bet on anything, including tomorrow's weather, the color of the next car to pass, or the number of peanuts in a bag"—these are details that might easily lead to the idea that Marty is a loser. Do not try to list any detail that doesn't lead to the conclusion stated in your topic sentence.

Controlling Purpose

The topic sentences that you have written are statements of opinion. They are not necessarily facts; still, by an adequate presentation of details you might lead your reader to agree with your opinions.

Not every paragraph presents an opinion, however. We often write to set forth information: to explain things or give directions about things. Sometimes we write to tell a story, and sometimes we write to describe things for readers to see or feel. These reasons for writing, if we keep them in mind as we write, help us to form appropriate topic sentences and build effective paragraphs.

The controlling purpose of a paragraph is usually one of these four:

1. *To inform:* presenting facts, details, explanations, or directions. Using this controlling purpose we may define things, classify, illustrate, compare, or contrast.
2. *To describe:* presenting details that put images before the reader's mind, giving him a picture to see, sounds to hear, or other sense impressions to experience.

3. *To tell a story:* presenting a sequence of events, either real or imagined, with a beginning, a complication, and an ending.
4. *To persuade:* presenting an opinion and the support of that opinion by evidence and reason, trying to lead the reader to accept or agree with the opinion.

To understand the difference between one controlling purpose and another—and to see the effect of that difference—consider these paragraphs, all on the same basic topic:

Paragraph To Inform.

    Stance and footwork are the basis of good boxing for they make it possible for the boxer to keep his balance while punching and moving. The left foot of the right-handed boxer should be a step ahead of the right, the toes of both feet pointed slightly toward the right. Both knees are bent slightly. The weight of the body rests largely on the right leg. The right heel lifts when a punch is delivered. In advancing the left leg leads, the right follows. In retreating, the reverse takes place. The chin is usually sunk slightly behind the left shoulder. The left hand is advanced, ready to strike or parry, and the right hand is held close to the body, sometimes in front of the chin.
                                –*Encyclopaedia Britannica* (1972)

Paragraph To Describe.

    A groan went up as Spider Hagerty peeled Rivera's sweater over his head. His body seemed leaner because of the swarthiness of the skin. He had muscles, but they made no display like his opponent's. What the audience neglected to see was the deep chest. Nor could it guess the toughness of the fiber of the flesh, the instantaneousness of the cell explosions of the muscles, the fineness of the nerves that wired every part of him into a splendid fighting mechanism. All the audience saw was a brown-skinned boy of eighteen with what seemed the body of a boy. With Danny it was different. Danny was a man of twenty-four, and his body was a man's body. The contrast was still more striking as they stood together in the center of the ring receiving the referee's last instructions.
                                —Jack London, "The Mexican"

Paragraph To Tell a Story.

    There could not have been much time left but Louis fought viciously to punish him anew. He had switched to left hooks and these—at least six in succession—sent Baer down again. Max was bruised, bloodied. It was doubtful if he could have gotten up. He didn't need to—the bell clanged at four, his seconds half-dragged, half-carried him to the corner.
                      —Lester Bromberg, *Boxing's Unforgettable Fights*

Paragraph To Tell a Story.

    Patterson started swiftly again in the second, attacking from a bob and weave, his left hook stinging in fast and often repeating. But, roughly a minute

in the round, he stopped in his tracks, apparently undecided as to which move to go into next. The lull was not lost on Johansson. His straight right came over, zooming into the chin zone, unprotected with Patterson's left hand only chest high. It was true to the mark and a solid smash. Floyd's body seemed to sag slightly forward, yet his head must have remained clear; he immediately took off in ring-circling flight. Ingo followed him, his right at the ready. But he continued guarded pursuit for 25 seconds without throwing a second punch. When he finally tried one, with Patterson backed to the ropes, it was sadly wide.
—Lester Bromberg, *Boxing's Unforgettable Fights*

Paragraph To Persuade.

In America, we give maximum expression to our blood lust in the mass spectator sport of boxing. Some of us are Roman enough to admit our love and need of the sport. Others pretend to look the other way. But when a heavyweight championship fight rolls around, the nation takes a moral holiday and we are all tuned in—some of us peeping out of the corner of our eye at the square jungle and the animal test of brute power unfolding there.
—Eldridge Cleaver, *Soul on Ice*

Time for Review

The controlling purpose of a paragraph is usually one of these four: (1) to inform, (2) to describe, (3) to tell a story, (4) to persuade.

Do-It-Yourself Exercise

A. Return to your plans for developing a paragraph on the subject of *people who bore their friends*. Assume that you are to write a paragraph whose controlling purpose is *to describe*. On the blank below write a topic sentence to introduce the descriptive paragraph:

_____

_____

Checking up: Remember that the topic sentence itself does not have to be descriptive; it must, however, be the sort of generalization that could naturally lead into a description (of, probably, a person who bores his friends).

Continue this exercise by jotting a list of possible *descriptive details* that would support your topic sentence:

_____   _____

_____   _____

_____   _____

B. Return to your plans for developing a paragraph on the subject of *something for nothing*. Assume that you are to write a paragraph whose controlling purpose is *to tell a story*. On the blanks below write a *topic sentence* to introduce a story-telling paragraph (perhaps about a time when you thought you were getting "something for nothing").

_____

_____

Continue this exercise by jotting a list of possible specific *details* (in this case things that happened) in the experience of trying to get "something for nothing":

_____	_____
_____	_____
_____	_____
_____	_____

Checking up: Be sure that each of your topic sentences is a generalization about the topic and that each really leads to a description (as of a boring person) or a story (about getting something for nothing). Are all your listed details really items of description (in the first) and of things that happened (in the second)?

Suggestions for Writing

A. One of Shakespeare's characters (who, by the way, was an old hand at boring his friends) said, "Neither a borrower nor a lender be, for loan oft loses both itself and friend." Can you agree that a person may lose a friend by lending money? Write a paragraph on that topic, using *to tell a story* as your controlling purpose.
B. Returning to your topic sentence on *red tape in college life* (p. 402), write a paragraph using *to inform* as your controlling purpose. Try to give your reader some information on where such red tape is most likely to be found (as in the enrollment process, the required courses, and so on). This paragraph, remember, is to inform, not to persuade, so try to present facts rather than mere opinions.
C. Your topic sentence on *believing what you hear* (p. 403) could be developed in several different ways. Write a paragraph on that topic, using *to persuade* as your controlling purpose. You should try to present details that will persuade your reader that it's good (or that it's bad) to believe what you hear.

After Writing: Underline the topic sentence in your paragraph. Do all the details in the paragraph really stick to that topic? Does the paragraph stick to its controlling purpose?

Maintaining Unity

The topic sentence sets out the territory to be covered in the paragraph, and all other sentences in the paragraph relate to that territory. The paragraph does not attempt to include any facts, details, or impressions that are not directly a part of that topic.

Like all full sentences, a topic sentence has two basic parts—*subject* and *predicate* (see p. 50). The subject presents what the sentence is about; the predicate presents what is said or asked about that subject. Consider this topic sentence:

> Recent awareness of the energy shortage in America has brought the bicycle into renewed popularity.

The subject part of that sentence concerns *awareness of the energy shortage;* the predicate part concerns *the bicycle and its renewed popularity.* If that topic sentence is to be developed into a paragraph, the writer will need to know which part of the sentence he really wants as the topic of his paragraph. If the subject part, awareness of the energy shortage, is to be his topic, he may develop the paragraph like this:

> Recent awareness of the energy shortage in America has brought the bicycle into renewed popularity. Small cars, rather than huge gas-gulpers, are winning sales. More and more people are riding buses and forming car pools to help reduce consumption of fuel, with some of the larger cities putting new push behind efforts to develop rapid-transit systems. Many Americans of all ages, in fact, are learning how to walk again.

Every detail in that paragraph relates to the awareness of the energy shortage. The paragraph presents specific ways in which that awareness is showing itself. But quite a different paragraph would result if the true topic were to be the predicate part of the topic sentence: the bicycle and its renewed popularity.

> Recent awareness of the energy shortage in America has brought the bicycle into renewed popularity. Citizens who own bikes find themselves pedaling to work and school rather than getting the car out of the garage. Owners of bicycle sales-and-repair shops find their business booming. Many cities have set aside "bikeways" for the convenience and safety of cyclists. Police reports show bicycle theft growing, and sellers of padlocks and chains for bike protection are making new profits. More and more Americans are discovering that pedal-pumping is cheaper than gas-pumping and that bicycles don't make smog.

In this second version of the paragraph the topic, the bicycle's new popularity, remains constantly before the reader. Every detail develops that topic. The paragraph makes no mention of any detail unrelated to the bicycle. Any wandering from that topic would violate the unity of the paragraph.

Time for Review

A *topic sentence* limits the territory to be covered by the paragraph.

All sentences in a paragraph should relate to the central idea set forth in the topic sentence.

Do-It-Yourself Exercise

Each of these paragraphs has in it one sentence that derails the train of thought by mentioning details unrelated to the topic. Underline that sentence; then write a new sentence to take its place—one that appropriately completes the paragraph and sticks to the topic:

I remember, even as a small boy, having a lot of pride in my mother. I thought she must have some kind of magic to be able to do all the things she did, to work so hard and never complain and to make us all feel happy. We had our family squabbles and spats, but we were a well-knit unit. My pride in my mother was tempered with a sense of sadness that she had to bear most of our burdens. At a very early age I began to want to relieve her in any small way I could. I was happy whenever I had money to give her.
—Jackie Robinson, *I Never Had It Made*

Rewrite of Faulty Sentence:

_____

_____

_____

Much is being made these days of freedom of speech. Some feel that if speech is really free, then anyone can say anything he wants and say it any time or anywhere. But perhaps they forget that every freedom carries with it some responsibility to use that freedom for the general good. If free speech means the right to say things that create panic or riot and cause destruction, then free speech does not really promote the general good. Modern television plays its part in communication of ideas in our society. Does government have a right to control what is said on television and thus to protect the public good?

Rewrite of Faulty Sentence:

_____

_____

_____

Patterns of Development

Specific Detail: If a topic sentence is a generalization, the other sentences of the paragraph must offer details that support that generalization: evidence that will lead the reader to accept or agree with it. Observe how details support the topic sentence in these paragraphs:

With boys like mine, clothes just don't stand a chance. Whatever I select, they jam the zippers. And pop the buttons. All of a sudden, gaping holes appear. And every remaining accessible surface gets covered with wrinkles and stains for which modern science has yet to find a cure.
—Judith Viorst, "Little-Boy Blues"

What "inflation" really means is that nearly everything that a consumer needs will cost him more than it did before. He will pay more for a quart of milk or a gallon of gasoline. He will pay more for a ticket to the movies. He will pay more for his daily newspaper, more for the light that he reads it by. If he does not pay more for a candy bar, he finds that the bar is smaller than one like it used to be. Prices go up, or values go down.

Illustration: The topic of a paragraph is often developed by a single example expanded to illustrate the topic idea. Perhaps the illustration takes the form of a brief story:

Most Americans eat their food too fast, but they are apparently ashamed of the habit. One midwestern coffee shop recognized the habit by naming itself the Squat & Gobble. But the place soon went out of business. Apparently most people were ashamed to be seen eating in a place that advertised their eat-and-run habits.

And another illustrative paragraph:

Cheaters often give themselves away by getting results that are too good. When a 14-year-old Colorado boy won the Soap Box Derby by getting off to an unlikely fast start, Derby officials investigated and found that he had rigged his car with an electromagnetic device that gave him a thrust when the metallic starting gate was opened.

Comparison: An idea can often be made clearer to a reader by a paragraph that compares something else in the reader's experience:

Once you're out of school, you discover that education really goes on for the rest of your life. A formal education in school or college is something like a Chinese dinner. It leaves you feeling filled when you finish it, but it doesn't last long.

Readers who are familiar with the well-known idea that Chinese food doesn't "stick to the ribs" will understand the comparison more easily than they would understand the topic sentence by itself.

Contrast: Sometimes an idea can be made clearer or more convincing if the writer shows one thing in contrast to another:

Those who claim that baseball is too slow to be interesting are overlooking a basic fact: that baseball was designed to be played in the heat of summer. It is not like basketball, played in winter and usually indoors. And it is not like football, played in the nip of autumn. If baseball were played at the speed of basketball or football, players might suffer heat exhaustion.

Time for Review

A paragraph may be developed by presenting *specific details* that support the generalization made in the topic sentence.

A paragraph may be developed by *illustration*—a single example expanded to show that the topic sentence has basis. An illustration is often a brief story.

A paragraph may be developed by *comparison,* making a new idea seem more familiar by pointing out how it is similar to something probably already known to the reader.

A paragraph may be developed by *contrast,* making a new idea clear by showing how it differs from something else that the reader probably is familiar with.

Do-It-Yourself Exercise

A. Develop this topic sentence into a paragraph by using the pattern of *specific details:*

College education includes a great many things that do not occur in class.

_____
_____
_____
_____
_____
_____

B. Develop this topic sentence into a paragraph by using the pattern of *illustration,* expanding a single detail into a brief imaginary story of something that has happened:

A holiday can turn out to involve harder work than the ordinary working day. _____

C. Develop this topic sentence into a paragraph by using the pattern of *comparison*. The topic (looking forward to a test) may, for instance, be compared to going to the dentist, having to dive off the high board, fighting a bull, facing a judge in court, expecting an earthquake or a hurricane, or being told there is a wild tiger loose in your neighborhood.

Taking a test in college is seldom as bad an experience as the student thinks it is going to be, and the test itself is less frightening than looking forward to it.

D. Develop this topic sentence by *contrast,* showing how the central topic (color television or movies) differs from some other familiar thing (such as black-and-white television or movies):

Color has brought much new excitement to movies and television. _____

414 Chapter Twenty-One

Checking up: Reread each of your paragraph developments to be sure that each does follow the pattern of development indicated. Check for *unity,* making sure that all your sentences clearly relate to the topic.

Suggestions for Writing

D. Write a paragraph (at least six sentences) on the topic of *learning to drive.* Use *to tell a story* as your controlling purpose and *illustration* as your pattern of development.
E. Write a paragraph (at least six sentences) on the topic of *campus elections.* Use *to persuade* as your controlling purpose and *comparison* as your pattern of development.
F. Write a *how-to* paragraph (at least six sentences) on the topic of *avoiding work.* Use *to inform* as your controlling purpose and *specific detail* as your pattern of development.

After Writing: Reread your paragraph to be sure that you have written a clear *topic sentence.* Check each other sentence to be sure that it relates to the topic directly. In the paragraph of illustration, did you tell a brief story? In the paragraph of comparison, is the comparison one that obviously clarifies your point? In the paragraph of specific detail, is each detail really a good example of how to avoid work?

Achieving Coherence

In building a paragraph a writer achieves coherence in several ways. One of those ways is *sticking to the topic.* You have already practiced that technique by completing paragraphs and checking their sentences for unity of topic.

Another way of achieving coherence is *repeating* key words or phrases. For instance, if the topic of a paragraph is *learning to drive,* the reader is kept on a train of thought by any repetition of that phrase or of the words *learn* or *drive.* In a paragraph on *campus elections* any repetition of that phrase or of either of those words will help to keep the reader's mind on that topic. Notice how repetition of word, phrase, and sentence structure helps build the train of thought in this paragraph:

> *Never* in our history has there been such freedom of expression as there is today; *never such concern* with the downtrodden by the so-called Establishment; *never such concern* for youth; *never such concern* for defendants by police and court authority. Many who are young will take that as an astonishing statement. That is because youth can *measure* in only one direction—from *things as they are, forward* to their ideal of what *things ought to be.* They cannot *measure backward* to *things as they used to be, because they have not* lived long enough; and they cannot *measure laterally,* to the condition of other societies on this earth, *because they have not* yet had the opportunity to know them well. Older people must add these two *measure*ments. This is the core reason *why* the generation gap *exists* and *why* it will always *exist.*
>
> —Eric Sevareid

The repetitions of *never such concern; measure* forward, *measure* backward, *measure* laterally; *things as they* are, *things as they* used to be; *because they have not* lived long enough, *because they have not* yet had the opportunity; *why* the generation gap *exists, why* it will always *exist*—all these are repetitions that drive the paragraph forward emphatically.

But mere repetition may annoy the reader if it is overdone or done awkwardly. To avoid using the same words too often, the writer may use synonyms (words of nearly the same meaning) or pronouns (stand-ins for nouns). Notice how *the husband* and *his wife* are referred to by synonym and pronoun in this paragraph:

> Few situations are more frustrating than that of *the husband* teaching *his wife* to drive. *He* is sure to be impatient of her awkward attempts, and *she* of his impetuous demands. *The husband* cannot understand why *the wife* cannot simply do as *he* directs; *she* cannot understand why he wants the impossible. *The learner* grows more and more obtuse as the teacher grows more and more impatient. Unless an end is put to the lesson quickly, *the couple* are sure to become uncoupled, for *the two egos* are on a collision course.

Every use of the synonyms and pronouns for *husband* and *wife* helps to keep before the reader the "characters" in the situation—and helps to hold the paragraph together.

Still another way of achieving coherence is to maintain a single frame of *time*. If a paragraph begins with verbs in the present tense, any change from the present tense must be clearly justified and easy to follow. The writer should not shift to verbs in the past or future tense unless the sequence is clear and purposeful. Notice that the *present tense* is maintained throughout this paragraph, so that the incident seems to be happening *now:*

> Desperation *grabs* at him as he *crouches* behind packing cases. The warehouse *is* surrounded by police. He *knows* they *are* ready with tear gas bombs. He also *knows* that he *is* ready to shoot at any sound, at anything that *moves*. For the first time he *sees* his own capture, or his own death, as real. The thought *tightens* his throat and *dries* his tongue. His muscles *contract,* and the trigger finger *squeezes* off a shot at nothing at all.

If the incident were to be told in the past tense, all the verbs would be in past-tense forms: *grabbed, crouched, was, knew, were, moved, saw, tightened, dried, contracted, squeezed*.

Another means of achieving coherence in a paragraph is to keep pronouns in agreement. If a pronoun or noun is singular, it should be later referred to by singulars; if a pronoun or noun is in the third person, it should later be referred to by third-person pronouns. Unnecessary shifting of person and of number can produce some confusion for the reader, as it does in this paragraph:

> Recently a survey on the eating habits of men in our country was published in a health magazine. *They* said that the bachelor has a shorter life span than the married man, because *they* don't eat a well-balanced diet. *This,* of course, could be changed if *you* would simply cook for *yourself*.

Does *they* (plural) clearly refer to *magazine* (singular)? Does the second *they* (plural) refer to bachelor (singular) or to *married man* (singular)? Does the sudden shift to *you* and *yourself* (second person) distract the reader from the problems of the *bachelor* (third person)? A revision could eliminate the problems by clear reference and proper agreement of pronouns:

> In a recent health magazine a survey of the eating habits of men in our country showed that *bachelors, who* do not eat a well-balanced diet, have a shorter life span than married men. The poor diet, of course, could be changed if the *bachelors* would simply cook for *themselves.*

In this revised version of the paragraph the *bachelors* (plural) are clearly referred to by the pronouns *who* and *themselves* (plural), and the entire paragraph sticks to the third-person approach.

One further way of maintaining coherence in a paragraph is to present consistent pictures, or images, to the reader's mind. If a paragraph about campus elections compares the elections to rat races, the comparison should not later shift to pinball machines, as it does in this paragraph:

> Campus elections often become little more than rat races. Each candidate seeks to get ahead of all others regardless of the worth of his platform. There is little regard for the real needs of the campus or the real issues facing students. And when one candidate wins, all the opponents shout, "Tilt!"

Since "tilt" is an expression connected with the playing of pinball, it is inappropriate to the imagined rat races. The inconsistency of image tends to spoil the coherence of the paragraph.

How Long Is a Paragraph?

No one has ever established that a paragraph should be of any certain length or number of sentences. Just as a sentence may have any number of words (even just one word in the case of a minor sentence), a paragraph may have any number of sentences.

This chapter began by saying that it usually takes more than one sentence to develop a train of thought. That is probably why most paragraphs have more than one sentence: A paragraph is, after all, a *development* of an idea, not merely a *statement* of an idea. What is important is that the paragraph must develop its topic adequately and end when that topic has been covered.

Occasionally what is presented as a paragraph may be not a development of an idea but rather a transition between ideas. A paragraph of *transition* is designed to change the subject of discussion; it appears usually as a brief (possibly one-sentence) paragraph between major parts of an essay. Some examples:

> What I have said so far indicates my prejudice against life in the city, but life in the country isn't all fresh air and roses either.

> Thus I learned to drive; nevertheless, the learning process may be more complicated for others.

> So we see that baseball, as slow a game as it is, may have another kind of movement—a movement of strategy and tactics.

Such *transitional paragraphs* summarize or refer to what has gone before, then point forward to what is to come.

It is usually unwise to use mere "signposts" as transition paragraphs. A signpost is something like "Now I shall turn to another part of my discussion" or "In conclusion . . . ."

Time for Review

A writer achieves coherence in a paragraph by maintaining *unity* of topic, by *repeating* words or phrases, by using *synonyms and pronouns,* by maintaining *one tense* or a consistent movement of time, and by maintaining consistency of *person.*

A writer also achieves coherence by being consistent in presenting pictures, or images, to the reader's mind. He avoids mixing images.

A paragraph may have any number of sentences. What is important is that the paragraph develop its topic adequately and end when that topic has been covered.

A *paragraph of transition* may be very short—even a single sentence. Its purpose is to summarize or refer to what has gone before, then point ahead to what is to come.

A *signpost,* such as "Next I shall discuss . . . " should *not* be used as a transitional paragraph.

QUIZ 21

Building Paragraphs

Each of the paragraphs in this quiz contains some fault in its structure. Considering each in turn, read through the paragraph to understand its topic and its development. Then read the paragraph again, noticing that several words or word groups have been italicized. *One* of the italicized items causes the faulty structure of the paragraph. Write the **letter** of that item on your answer blank. After marking your choice, briefly explain the fault by writing in the "Because" blank one of these:

    Lacks development.   Contains unclear reference.
    Shifts verb tense.   Contains inconsistent image.
    Shifts person.   Violates unity (wanders away
    Has incomplete sentence.   from topic sentence).

Example: Competition has different effects on different people. *Some people* (a) like to have stiff competition because *it* (b) makes them work harder to succeed. *Others* (c) may fall apart at the prospect of having to go up against someone better than they are. To go up against inferior competition often causes *people* (d) to loaf and not put out their best. On the other hand, it might get *you* (e) going because you know that you are sure to win.

Ex _e_

(Because: _Shifts person_.)

1. J. T. is in junior high school now, learning responsibility and noticing girls. He *learns* (a) about sex, the different views *people* (b) have on it. He thinks *it's* (c) beautiful, exciting, and very natural. But when he *expressed* (d) his feeling to his parents, *they* (e) said he was too young to know. They believed sex was something that wasn't to be discussed.

1._____

(Because: _____.)

2. Cooking is a very useful art and *takes* (a) some training and practice. It isn't just something you go and do. If *you are a fry cook* (b) or a chef, you have to think about what goes with what and *how it should be cooked.* (c) And sometimes you have about ten to sixteen orders all at once. *Today the prices of food have gone up* (d) very much, and

meat is very expensive. *I myself was a fry cook* for about four years, and I've worked
(e)
in six or seven places. Most of the cooking jobs are about the same.

2_____

(Because: _____*.)*

3. The word "someday" *has influenced* me quite a bit, because for me it has come
(a)
true. I have made *a discovery* in which countless thousands *have found* the same
(b)   (c)
happiness, love, and *peace of mind.* As for others, I can only wish them the same
(d)
fantastic discovery. Maybe one of those "somedays" will bring it *to them.*
(e)

3_____

(Because: _____*.)*

4. I don't see why *some people* would want to go back to earlier times after seeing
(a)
what *earlier generations* have gone through. Think of the Gold Rush era, when
(b)
people *came* to the West in covered wagons. They suffered many hardships, and
(c)
most of them died at an early age. *You* would have to hunt for your food, and there
(d)   (e)
would be no heaters to warm you up in the freezing mornings.

4_____

(Because: _____*.)*

5. In his essay Dimnet showed in many cases where *the thinking man* was way
(a)
above the average person in his seeing into things. *In his rationalizing of a subject.*
(b)
The example of the mechanic who comes to the car, rationally thinks over the problem, and *goes* to the source of trouble. He can see into the subject deeper than others
(c)
who *are* standing around, *because he can really think.*
(d)   (e)

5_____

(Because: _____*.)*

6. The members of *the penguin* group, the first flightless birds, live mainly in the
(a)
South Temperate and Antarctic areas. *They* are excellent swimmers, with wings
(b)
that are reduced to flippers. Penguins' wings cannot bend like wings of all other birds;
they move *at the shoulder joint* only. In water, penguins are quick and agile; *on land,*
(c)   (d)
they move slowly with a clumsy, amusing walk. *The ostriches have many ancestors,*
(e)

such as rheas, cassowaries, emus, and kiwis. Scientists feel sure that once, long ago, the ancestors of the ostrich could fly.

6._____

(Because:_____.)

7. I believe the only *poetry in my life* today is the poetry of a closed-course circuit,
        (a)
of a high-RPM sports engine *revved up tight* to down shift for the next turn, then
                              (b)
hit the brake just before entering, and rap the engine back up tight *in the turn* and
    (c)   (d)
through it, shift back to high, then the following line, the closing line, as the engine settles down to its own purr, or whine, or roar. That to me is poetry, the *poetry of the road race*.
      (e)

7._____

(Because:_____.)

8. I feel that *a person* should have command over a good vocabulary, *yet* that
                  (a)   (b)
he shouldn't be so worried about being correct that *he* destroys what his thoughts
                                                      (c)
really are. Language and writing are the only medium of communication that people have. Correct or not, if people don't understand what *you* are trying to say, you *may*
                                                          (d)   (e)
as well retire to a dark cave and learn hieroglyphics.

8._____

(Because:_____.)

9. Did you ever notice the way people *sharpen pencils?* First there is the coordi-
                                          (a)
nated *pencil sharpener* with a goal to strive for; *he* uses lots of wrist motion and a
        (b)   (c)
steady, revolving motion. *Then* there is the motion waster; he uses big arm motions
                            (d)
and works up a sweat just sharpening his pencil. Then the guy who hates school work; he jams the pencil in, breaking the lead and sharpening it down to a stub; but this type usually forgets his pencil, so he doesn't have to sharpen one very often. Of the girls there are two types: one is the wriggler, who wriggles just for show; and the other is the one who always sharpens her pencil, whether it needs it or not, just to put on a big show when she *walked* up to the pencil sharpener.
                            (e)

9._____

(Because:_____.)

422   Chapter Twenty-One

10. I remember when we were kids we *used to play* baseball and walk to school
                                         (a)
together. We never *thought* of shooting heroin or getting drunk. I guess when you're
                   (b)
kids, you are more innocent. But *when you grow up* and get older, you meet new
                                        (c)
friends who might be heroin addicts, marijuana smokers, or alcoholics. They get you
started, and *you* start liking it. I'm glad *I decided to become a college student,* be-
             (d)   (e)
cause it gives me something to do, and it gives me a chance to study for what I want to
become in the near future, which is a dentist.   10_____

(Because: _____.)

11. The world today offers us an *environment* which engulfs an individual both
                                       (a)
physically and mentally. *Physically* we are engulfed by fellow man, by traffic and
                              (b)
air pollution and buildings taller than any tree, not to mention horns and sirens and
irate taxi drivers. *Mentally* we are *engulfed* in a constant tug-of-war with ourselves.
                         (c)   (d)
Day in and day out it's the same one-act play. And when the curtain falls, *you* take
                                                                           (e)
your aspirin and go to bed and dream of better days.   11_____

(Because: _____.)

12. I will call her Calamity Jane. *She* is what you might call "accident prone."
                                     (a)
One time she *was driving* home from work when a dump truck decided to run into
                 (b)
her car's back end. *Resulting in a totaled Volkswagen.* She *suffered* broken nose
                            (c)   (d)
number two, broken leg number one, and black eyes two and three. Her face was so
messed up that she *had to have* plastic surgery.
                         (e)   12_____

(Because: _____.)

13. War cannot be eliminated in a *world* in which some countries have greater
                                      (a)
resources. *People* are too greedy and power happy. *From Julius Caesar to Hitler*
              (b)   (c)
it has been a fact that throughout the growth of *this nation* greed has prevailed. There
                                                      (d)
will always be *people* who want and take no matter what the consequences.
                  (e)   13_____

(Because: _____.)

From Thought to Paragraph 423

14. If *all men* are the same, *what's the difference* what color they are? *These*
        (a)   (b)   (c)
burdens have been *brought* upon us by ourselves in *this country*.
   (d)   (e)   14_____

(Because:_____.)

15. I remember the blistering heat and the *different type of people* who really
   (a)
couldn't be classified as hippies, long hairs, or freaks, but you could say *they were*
good people; for although they may have been down and out, they were willing to
   (b)
share whatever they had. With every glance the beaches as well as the entire area
provided a fantastic change in *the landscape*. In the morning oranges from a nearby
   (c)
orchard were breakfast; then it was back to the road. The higher up *I had gone,* the
   (d)
cooler it had gotten. Then the snow came; believe me, *I found out* what cold really
   (e)
meant after a few days. But I found the snow to be very refreshing and enjoyable.   15_____

(Because:_____.)

16. My little niece is shy and delicate *like a tiny flower*. She *seldom has anything*
    (a)   (b)
to say, yet everyone likes to be near her because she is *pretty and appealing* in her
   (c)
manner. We all know that one day she will *break out of her shell* and become *the*
   (d)
girl every boy wants to meet.
   (e)   16_____

(Because:_____.)

17. Society often *reacts violently* to a human being, *rejecting* him because he is
    (a)   (b)
different from the group. Surely society would be wiser to offer help to *such an*
(c)   (d)
individual rather than *to ignore him*. We need to extend a hand rather than a foot.
   (e)   17_____

(Because:_____.)

424 Chapter Twenty-One

18. My way of *getting away* from the civilized world is *to go up to the mountains.*
       (a)   (b)
Some place where very few people travel to. There *in the back country* is freedom.
              (c)   (d)
No more road traffic to contend with, no more crowded beaches, and no more air pollution to breathe. In the mountains *I can relax* and enjoy the sights of nature.
                                                       (e)
18.____

(Because: _____.**)**

19. As we crossed desert after desert, it sometimes *got so hot* that I thought I was
                                                    (a)
going to cook. We often *saw unlucky motorists* whose radiators overheated. At first
                        (b)
we stopped to help people. One man asked us *if we had any water*. We answered,
    (c)   (d)
"No, just lemonade." He said, "Fine!" and poured it down his radiator. I was really surprised that our lemonade cooled that car right down. *To save money,* we
                                                                   (e)
ate boxed cereal. We made the entire trip on two hundred and fifty dollars.
19.____

(Because: _____.**)**

20. Bobby was the first child in the family to show any interest in *earning his own*
                                                                        (a)
money. While the other two boys kept asking their father for allowances, Bobby *planted a vegetable garden* and *sold his produce* to neighborhood housewives. He
         (b)   (c)
learned about farming. Unwilling to squander his profits, he *opened a savings ac-*
        (d)   (e)
count at a bank and was soon quite a financial success.
20.____

(Because: _____.**)**

From Idea to Essay

22

How to work with . . . sources of ideas
attitudes
details
evaluating ideas
organizing
transitions
three kinds of essay

How to avoid . . . truisms
hedging
useless signposts
careless editing

WRITING IS A MEANS OF DISCOVERING. As the writer puts down an idea, he finds that still other ideas grow out of that one. He may even discover ideas he didn't know he had. Hidden attitudes present themselves—and sometimes hidden knowledge.

Writing also puts ideas to a test. As a writer finds *faulty verb agreement* or *indefinite reference of pronouns* or *dangling participles* in his work he discovers that what seems clear in his own mind may be puzzling indeed to anyone else. That is why much of this book has asked the student to avoid those faults and to practice making clear and effective sentences.

Our recent chapters have shown that the attempt to develop and support an opinion may lead to a writer's discovering that his opinion is weak and needs changing; or, by revealing the sources of opinions and attitudes, writing may help the writer discover *why* he believes what he believes.

Since writing leads to discovery and testing of ideas, it can also lead to the writer's discovery of himself. That is one reason why the written essay is among the most useful of college assignments: It gives the student an opportunity to see his own mind at work, to expand his grasp of experience, and to evaluate himself in relation to the world.

This chapter considers how ideas are found, how they are evaluated, and how they are developed into fully rounded discussions, or *essays*.

Sources of Ideas

Where do ideas come from? They come from personal experience. They come from observing, from listening, from reading. They come from reasoning about what has been experienced or read or heard. And they come from imagination, the ability to picture in the mind things that have not been experienced in fact.

The person who has "nothing to write about" is rare. The student who feels lost when he is asked to write can soon get over that feeling if he knows how to go about "discovering" ideas. His first step is to recognize that he does, in fact, have a wide range of experience and knowledge.

Time for Review

Writing is a means of *discovering*. As he works, the writer discovers facts, his own attitudes and opinions, and himself.

Ideas come from *experience,* from *listening,* from *reading,* from *reasoning,* and from *imagination*.

Almost everyone has something to write about once he recognizes his own range of experience and knowledge.

Do-It-Yourself Exercise

What do you know something about? The following is an arbitrary list of items that you may have experience with or knowledge about. Check the items that you do know something about:

___air	___farm	___moonlight	___time
___anger	___fear	___mountain	___traffic
___animal	___fight	___music	___tree
___argument	___fire	___noise	___trick
___automobile	___fish	___original	___trip
___beach	___fly	___pictures	___truth
___bird	___food	___poison	___voice
___book	___friendship	___politics	___water
___camera	___gadget	___praise	___weather
___clothes	___garden	___prejudice	___weight
___color	___glass	___pride	___wood
___competition	___greed	___quiet	___young
___complaint	___hair	___record	___ ___
___cook	___hate	___religion	___ ___
___crime	___height	___safety	___ ___
___danger	___hospital	___sew	___ ___
___date	___insect	___shop	___ ___
___death	___jealousy	___sky	___ ___
___desert	___joke	___sleep	___ ___
___dive	___laugh	___smoke	___ ___
___doctor	___lazy	___sport	___ ___
___draw	___lie	___star	___ ___
___dream	___love	___sunlight	___ ___
___electric	___medicine	___suspicion	___ ___
___envy	___money	___swim	___ ___

Checking up: The extra blanks at the end of the list are for your own additions. Obviously the list is incomplete, for the number of possible items is limitless. How many of them did you check? Do not assume that "knowledge" means specific training or skill, for you have some experience with *sunlight* if you've ever watched a sunrise, with *time* if you ever kept a date, with *medicine* if you've ever taken any. Does the number of items you have checked indicate that you do, in fact, have some range of experience?

Expanding the Sources of Ideas

Since ideas seldom come unmixed, the association of one idea with others may trigger whole new possibilities for topics to write about. The student who has a writing assignment and must select a topic may use the list of "idea" items in an imaginative way. He may, for instance, choose one item, like *water*. Then, scanning the list again, he may pick another, like *fear*. The association gives him a new topic, a topic more specific than either alone: the *fear of water,* indeed something interesting to write about.

Consider some other possibilities from the pairing of items from that list:

medicine—laughter	(Is laughter good medicine?)
glass—friendship	(Is friendship fragile like glass? Can a person see through his friends?)
hair—politics	(Do voters like beards on candidates? Can a "long-hair" get elected?)
bird-camera	(How to take pictures of birds. Birdseye views of things. Aerial photography.)
food—weight	(Do supermarket packages tell honest weight? Does eating really make you fat?)

Naturally many such pairings would produce nonsense without much possibility for development. Perhaps you would be unlikely to write a good essay suggested by *hair-voice* or *fight-praise*—but even those might suggest something. The number of useful pairings is certainly high.

Do-It-Yourself Exercise

By selecting *pairs* of items from the list on p. 427, suggest several possible ideas for writing:

Pair of Items   Idea for Writing

_____ — _____   _____

_____ — _____   _____

_____ — _____   _____

_____ — _____   _____

_____ — _____   _____

Checking up: Did you come up with any pairings that you had to reject as nonsense? Which of your ideas seems most promising or most interesting to you? Did any of your ideas come from items that you added to the original list yourself? Still more ideas may arise from combining items in threes; imagine what might be done with *sport— competition—jealousy, beach—date—laugh,* or *dream—glass—clothes.*

Choosing a Topic

Many writing assignments in college are on topics selected by the instructor. The student is asked to show, in writing, that he has learned something about a given topic. When that sort of assignment is made, the student's chief source of ideas for the essay is the lecture, the class discussion, the lab experiment, the textbook, or library materials. But in the first-year course in English the student is often asked to write on topics of his own choice, using his own experience, observation, opinion, and reasoning. That is the sort of essay that gets the student started in college writing.

Choosing a worthwhile topic involves some steps beyond the selection or pairing of items from an arbitrary list like the one on p. 427. For once the student has decided to write on a general topic, he must make that topic his own by discovering his attitudes toward it and narrowing his approach to it.

Revealing Attitudes

What does the writer really think and feel about his topic? If he immediately knows some of his own thoughts and feelings about that topic, he may begin by jotting those down before he starts to plan the structure of the essay. But he can also expand his discovery of attitudes by referring to a list of possible attitudes.

Right now, pick a possible topic by referring to the list of items that you have checked on p. 427. Then go ahead to the following exercise.

Do-It-Yourself Exercise

On the top blank write the topic that you have selected. With that topic in mind, check any of the following statements that you believe applies to that topic:

Chosen topic: _____

Attitudes

_____ It is useful.	_____ It is dull.
_____ It is a waste of time.	_____ It is puzzling.
_____ It is dangerous.	_____ It helps win friends.
_____ It is easy.	_____ It may help lose friends.
_____ It is difficult.	_____ It is healthful.
_____ It is impossible.	_____ It is unhealthful.

_____	It is expensive.	_____	It is dignified.
_____	It is inexpensive.	_____	It is undignified.
_____	It is dishonest.	_____	It is demoralizing.
_____	It is unethical.	_____	It is attainable.
_____	It is profitable.	_____	It is unattainable.
_____	It is unprofitable.	_____	It is a science.
_____	It may produce happiness.	_____	It is an art.
_____	It may produce unhappiness.	_____	It requires training.
_____	It is inevitable.	_____	It comes naturally.
_____	It is avoidable.	_____	It requires practice.
_____	It is fascinating.	_____	It produces prejudice.
_____	It is up-to-date.	_____	It increases enjoyment.
_____	It is outmoded.	_____	It reduces enjoyment.
_____	It sharpens the senses.	_____	It is painful.
_____	It dulls the senses.	_____	It is ordinary.
_____	It is natural.	_____	It is unusual.
_____	It is unnatural.	_____	It is worthless.
_____	It is romantic.	_____	_____
_____	It is unromantic.	_____	_____
_____	It is realistic.	_____	_____
_____	It is unrealistic.	_____	_____
_____	It is frightening.	_____	_____
_____	It is economical.	_____	_____
_____	It is wasteful.	_____	_____

Checking up: At the end of the list are several extra blanks where you may add further statements about the topic. The statements you have checked have helped you to expand your thinking about the topic and clarify your attitudes toward it. Do any of the checked statements seem to conflict? If so, your attitudes are not yet fully established and will have to become clearer to you as you work on your essay. Keep this list in mind and refer to it when you have later writing assignments; then you may also want to add further attitude statements to the list.

Evaluating Attitudes

How worthy are the attitudes you have checked in the exercise just above? Though a statement may be true, it may still not add much of value to a discussion of the topic. If you have checked "It is up-to-date," you must now ask yourself, "So what?" Will the topic's up-to-dateness really matter to a reader? Will that opinion (or fact) be worth including in the essay? If any of your checked attitude statements brings a "so what" feeling, perhaps that one should be eliminated from your present thinking as you develop the essay.

Which of the attitudes you have checked seems most interesting of all? Could that one be developed as a *central idea* for an essay on the chosen topic?

Discovering Details

The next step in developing plans for an essay might be called "brainstorming." It puts to work a process of thinking that happens almost naturally when an idea is presented to the mind: the process of *free association*. The chosen topic and its central idea call to mind a series of related memories, images, impressions, opinions. Brainstorming is the process of recording those thoughts as they come.

Brainstorming is a kind of game played with the writer's own mind. And like other games, brainstorming has some rules. One rule is: Don't be critical; jot down *every thought*, whether it seems useful or not. If you come up with a thought and immediately say to yourself, "That's no good," you have created a negative response to the natural working of your own mind. When you reject the thought by not jotting it down, your mind tends to be disappointed, as if the mind were saying to itself, "He doesn't like my ideas. All right, then, I won't give him any more." Then, of course, you'll probably sit wondering why your mind has gone blank and you "can't think of anything to write."

So the act of brainstorming must be honest and uncritical. Whatever comes to your mind must go down on your scratch paper. The time for critical selection and rejection of ideas will come later.

Free associations will come almost faster than you can write them down, so it is best to jot down only a word or phrase (or even an abbreviation) to represent each thought as it comes. Even if the thought that comes is entirely unrelated to your topic, jot down a word about that thought.

Do-It-Yourself Exercise

Return to the topic that you chose at the top of the last do-it-yourself exercise (p. 429). You have already checked some of your attitudes toward that topic. Now, in about three or four minutes of *brainstorming,* jot down a word or phrase (or abbreviation) to record every thought that comes to mind about that topic. Remember: Don't be critical; write down everything that comes to mind, and don't worry whether it's useful:

Chosen topic: _____

Brainstorming Notes

_____   _____

_____   _____

_____   _____

_____   _____

_____   _____

_____   _____

_____   _____

_____   _____

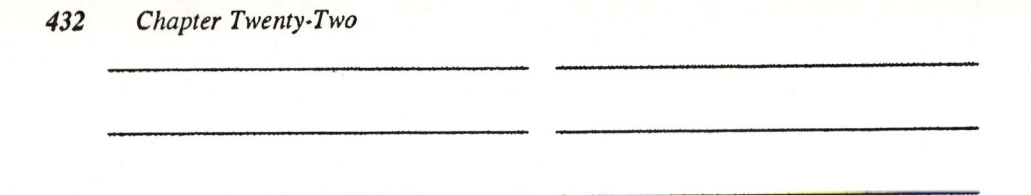

Checking up: When you get some practice with *brainstorming*, it will be easy to come up with 25 to 30 jottings from a four-minute brainstorming session on a given topic. If some thoughts that came up include something like "Have to pick up Tom" or "My hand hurts," you should not have rejected those thoughts; the jottings should include something like "Tom" and "hand." Such wandering thoughts can be eliminated later—but they must not be rejected during the brainstorming.

Evaluating the Ideas

After the brainstorming it is time to look critically at the list of jottings. Anything that seems entirely unrelated to the central idea or topic (such as "Tom" and "hand") should be crossed out. Of the jottings that are left, which is the most interesting? Would that thought make a good *central point* for an essay on the topic? Is that thought consistent with the attitudes checked on p. 429? If so, circle that jotting and assume that it will become the basic thought to be developed in your essay.

Organizing the Material

Once the central point has been determined and the attitude adopted, you may determine the order of details. If any of the jotted ideas now seems not to support or relate to the central one that you have circled, you may rework that thought so that it does relate to the central one—or you may eliminate the unrelated idea by crossing it off the list.

On the list of jottings that remain, which should be dealt with first in an essay on the topic? Which second—and so on. Number the items in the order you think they may best be treated to amplify the central point.

At this step it may be helpful to expand each of the jottings into a full sentence. The sentence will serve as the core of the development of that idea within the whole essay.

Do-It-Yourself Exercise

Return to the do-it-yourself exercise on p. 431. You have already circled one jotting that is to become the basic thought to be developed in your essay. If any of the other items seems unrelated, either adjust it to relate to the basic thought, or cross it out. Then number the remaining jottings in the order of their possible appearance in your essay. Now, following the order you have indicated, write a full sentence that expresses the idea behind each jotting:

Idea Sentences in Order

1. _____.
2. _____.
3. _____.
4. _____.
5. _____.
6. _____.
7. _____.
8. _____.
9. _____.

Checking up: Now written as sentences, your ideas have begun to "jell." They are beginning to take on the character of your essay itself, and they appear in some reasonable order to help you develop your central point.

Giving Body to the Skeleton

Your list of idea-sentences forms a kind of skeleton of the essay. But they must be given substance; each idea must be developed according to its needs.

The central point that you have chosen will serve as a focus for keeping the essay unified. You will not want to wander from that main thought to bring in details that will not help develop it. And that central point should be placed in the reader's mind, at least by tone and implication, very early in your essay.

Your next step in writing is to develop each of your listed sentences, in order, expanding it into a paragraph. Perhaps the sentence will serve as a topic sentence for a paragraph.

Do-It-Yourself Exercise

Taking each of your idea-sentences in turn, develop a full paragraph based on it. Remember that a paragraph must be based upon *one* idea only and must develop that idea by some appropriate means, such as illustration, example, or comparison. You must also decide, as your work develops, whether each paragraph is intended to inform, to describe, to relate a story or happening, or to persuade. A review of Chapter 21 may be helpful as you develop your paragraphs.

Checking up: Reread all of your paragraphs in order. Do they maintain an orderly progression, achieving *coherence* by sticking to the central topic, avoiding unnecessary shifts of pronoun person or verb tense?

Transition—Means of Coherence

Transition is a picking up and moving forward; it is the passing of the thought from one paragraph to another in a kind of relay. Standard devices of transition include these:

1. Conjunctions: *and, but, so, therefore, however, nevertheless, still,* and others—all suggesting that something has gone before and something is to come after.
2. Adverbs of time and place: *then, meanwhile, after, elsewhere, later, also, in addition*—all helping to move the reader from one thought to another.
3. Adverbs of order: *first, second, third, next, last, finally, at last*—all helping to outline points and to indicate an order of things.
4. Comparatives: *similarly, conversely, in other words, on the other hand, on the contrary, for example, also to be considered, still more,* and other such words and phrases—all reminding the reader of what went before and introducing him to what is to come after.

In addition to these standard devices of transition, the picking up and carrying forward of ideas is achieved by repetition in a succeeding paragraph of some word or phrase that appeared in the paragraph before. Consider how transition is handled in this brief essay about paragraphs:

> Anyone who has ever seen a circus parade will remember the elephants. Of all the animals and people in the big parade it was the elephants who showed most order and style. Each elephant was imposing in itself, yet each contributed to the group, to the show. Each linked itself to the elephant before, grasping in its own trunk the tail ahead. In essays, paragraphs are like elephants on parade.
>
> Like those elephants, each paragraph in an essay has its own central self: a controlling idea, a body with legs to stand on. Each has a trunk, or lead sentence; each has a torso, or development of idea by illustration, reason, or explanation; and each has a tail, or finish.
>
> But however finished in itself, the paragraph is only a part of the complete essay. Just as each elephant contributes to the circus parade, each paragraph contributes to the development of the larger idea. Neither the elephant nor the paragraph can wander away on its own path, for if it does, the parade is broken, the movement muddled.
>
> Orderly movement in the circus parade is assured by linking. Each elephant grasps the tail of the one before. Similarly each paragraph in an essay grasps the tail of the one ahead, linking to it by repetition of key words, by transition, or by reflection.

Look again at the paragraphs that have begun this essay. The lead paragraph presents the analogy between elephants on parade and paragraphs in an essay. The second paragraph picks up that idea by repeating the word *elephants* and developing the analogy part by part (trunk—lead sentence; torso—development; tail—end sentence). The second paragraph ends by emphasizing that each paragraph has its own full development, or *finish,* and the third picks up the idea of *finish,* using *but* as a transition word to turn to the idea of the paragraph as contributor to the whole, a part of the *movement.* The fourth paragraph picks up *movement* and shows that it is accomplished by *reflection* upon what has gone before. And the fifth paragraph invites the reader to *look again,* or *reflect* upon what went before it.

Thus the linking process, by reflection and movement forward, continues until the parade comes to an end. The final paragraph, as in a circus itself, brings the reader full circle—returning to the idea with which the essay began.

A circle is a finished form, one of obvious singleness and order. Why does the elephant trainer teach his animals to parade in the linking fashion? He has two reasons. For one, the elephants so linked to one another cannot get out of line; they can't get lost. For another, they make a good show; everyone watching the parade can say to himself (or at least feel) that the elephants have style, that they know what they're doing. And those, of course, are the same reasons why a writer presents his ideas in good paragraphs. The parade of paragraphs makes sense, keeps ideas in order, and produces an effect of form. When the parade comes to an end, the reader feels that the writer knew what he was doing, that the essay has point and style.

A brief outline may emphasize how the essay was developed in its ordering of paragraphs:

Title: "Ideas on Parade"
Thesis: In an essay, paragraphs are like elephants in a circus parade:
   (a) Each *is a unit* in itself.
   (b) Each *contributes to the group.*
   (c) Each *links to the one before.*

Paragraph 1: An introduction presents the idea of the circus parade of elephants, and the thesis statement is presented.

Paragraph 2: The paragraph is like the elephant according to point (a).

Paragraph 3: The paragraph is like the elephant according to point (b).

Paragraph 4: The paragraph is like the elephant according to point (c).

Paragraph 5: The paragraphs in this essay illustrate the linking process, (c).

Paragraph 6: The linking process brings the reader full circle, back to the idea with which the essay began.

Paragraph 7: The thesis is restated and the essay concluded.

This book began with *and* because of the importance of conjunctions as links between ideas. It is the linking of ideas that gives them order, relationship, and emphasis. So it is by linking, the transition from one idea to another, that paragraphs take order, relationship, and emphasis within a complete essay.

Chapter Twenty-Two

Do-It-Yourself Exercise

Return to the developing essay that you have written for the last do-it-yourself exercise (p. 433). What devices of transition have you used to give coherence to the train of thought? Write those devices here:

Conjunctions: _____.

Adverbs of time and place: _____

_____.

Adverbs of order: _____.

Comparatives: _____

_____.

Continue this exercise by examining the opening sentence of each of your paragraphs. Has it used repetition or reflection to pick up the thoughts near the end of the paragraph before? Write here the words that you have used for that purpose:

End of first paragraph: _____

Beginning of second: _____

End of second paragraph: _____

Beginning of third: _____

End of third paragraph: _____

Beginning of fourth: _____

End of fourth paragraph: _____

Beginning of fifth: _____

End of fifth paragraph: _____

Beginning of sixth: _____

End of sixth paragraph: _____

Beginning of seventh: _____

Checking up: If you were unable to find such linkings in any of your paragraphs, go back now and revise your essay with attempt to provide repetitions or reflections.

Bringing the Essay Full Circle

The end of your essay, of course, must leave the reader with two things: (1) clear understanding of your central point, and (2) feeling of completeness and finish in the essay. One way of providing both of those things for the reader is to be sure that your opening paragraph clearly indicates, if only by hint, your central point—and that your final paragraph clearly restates that point. This device of using the end to remind the reader of the beginning will seem to bring the essay to "full circle" and leave an impression of completeness and finish. Reread the sample essay on *paragraphs* (pp. 434–435) and notice how the final paragraph of that essay returns the reader to the opening idea of elephants on circus parade.

Do-It-Yourself Exercise

Return to the developing essay that you have written for the do-it-yourself exercise on p. 433. Does your final paragraph pick up (by repetition or reflection) some words that you used in your opening paragraph? Do those words in both paragraphs relate directly to your central point? If you do not find such repetition or reflection, try now to revise the two paragraphs (at least in part) with attempt to provide it. When you have finished, write here the words or phrases that are picked up at the end to bring the essay full circle:

Words in beginning paragraph: _____

_____

Words in final paragraph: _____

_____

Checking up: Does your essay, either as first written or as revised for this exercise, now have a "finished" effect? Does the essay as you have developed it now leave a reader with a clear idea of the central point?

Considering the Audience

Before you can present the essay as a finished product, you must consider its probable effect upon the reader. Your facts, your opinions, your attitudes, your reasons and arguments must all depend for their success upon how the reader responds to what you have written.

What sort of person or people are likely to read your essay? You are not, after all, writing merely to please yourself; your purpose must include a wish to inform, entertain, or persuade your reader.

In college writing it is often a temptation to assume that the instructor is to be the reader of the essay. But if you write for the instructor, you are likely to find yourself saying only what he wants to hear or what will bring you a good grade. And you may, when writing to the instructor, spoil otherwise good writing by assuming that he knows your material. For instance, you may include such phrases as "in your discussion yesterday" or "as you said in class"; and such references would be meaningless to any reader other than the instructor.

It is usually best to write for a general, public audience. You should assume that your work may be published in a magazine or newspaper and be read by many people you do not know. They are people who may have quite different backgrounds from your own, different attitudes and beliefs, different knowledge. You know things they do not know—but they also know things that you are perhaps unaware of. You need to consider how you can interest such a variety of people and convince them that what you have to say is worth considering.

To win such consideration by readers, of course, requires that you keep their feelings in mind. The reader must not be insulted; he must not be treated like a mere child or a foolish adult; he must not be expected to accept your conclusions or even "facts" without supporting evidence.

Your ideas, worthy as they are, may yet be opposed by other ideas equally worthy. You need to present yours without denouncing people who believe the opposites. To do that, you need not depend upon such hedging and weak expressions as "It is only my opinion, but . . ." or "I may be wrong . . . ." It is best to avoid those approaches and to state your own ideas as firmly as possible without deliberately knocking those of other people. Try to show why your ideas are worth considering; if you attack opposed ideas, do so while acknowledging that they are possibly held by worthy people also.

Some Things To Avoid

Avoid writing *truisms,* statements that are obviously true but are hardly worth writing. ("There are many different kinds of religious belief" is an example of *truism.* To begin an essay with such a sentence can get you off to a dismal start.)

Avoid using your title as part of your essay. As you write the essay, assume that the reader has not read your title; you must make the idea clear in the essay itself.

Avoid assuming that your reader knows what you are discussing. The reader is not a member of your college class and has not been in on your assignments and discussions. He must be told what you want him to understand.

Avoid writing as if the instructor were your reader. Never refer to the instructor as "you," for that word would be meaningless to other readers.

Avoid quoting definitions from the dictionary. You may refer to dictionary definitions of terms, but remember that the reader is concerned with what *you* have to say, not with what the dictionary says.

Avoid *hedging* words and phrases such as "maybe" or "I suppose I could be wrong" or "it is not impossible to assume."

Avoid using many *signposts* such as "I am going to write about . . . " or "In conclusion . . . ." These devices are more useful to the public speaker whose audience is present; they are not much needed by the writer.

Avoid wasting words (or padding). Even if you do have to fill out a thousand-word assignment, don't do it by wasting the reader's time with such things as "Finally I want to say that . . . ." or "In this modern contemporary world of today . . . ."

Avoid turning in your essay to an instructor before you have read it carefully yourself. The work should be carefully checked for the kind of obvious error that nearly every writer makes but that good writers never let anyone else see.

Some Kinds of Essay

Although the term *essay* cannot be defined to exclude any reasonable discussion of a limited topic, most college essays are of types shown here under controlling purposes:

Essays To Inform.

    What is it? (definition)

    What is it like? (description)

    How is it done? (process)

    What happened? (narrative)

Essays To Persuade.

    What does it mean? (interpretation)

    How worthy is it? (criticism)

    What does it lead to? (reason and conclusion)

Essays To Entertain.

    What happened? (personal experience narration)

    What is life? (philosophy and comment)

    What's funny about it? (satire)

These several purposes, of course, are easily blended so that one essay may achieve all three. An essay to persuade may use definition and description and narrative; an essay to inform may use interpretation; and any essay may entertain. But these kinds of essay usually take one of the controlling purposes as a focus for approach and tone.

Supplement 1
A Guide to Punctuation

MARKS OF PUNCTUATION have four distinct uses: (a) to join things, (2) to separate things, (3) to group things by enclosing them, and (4) to mark the ends of things. The marks conventionally used are these:

Joiner—the hyphen.
Separators—the comma, the semicolon, the colon, the dash, the apostrophe.
Enclosures—commas in pairs, parentheses, dashes in pairs, quotation marks.
Terminators—the period, the question mark, the exclamation point.

How To Use the Hyphen

h1—Use the hyphen to join certain prefixes to base words: *self-defense, ex-governor, pro-American*. Unless the base word begins with a capital, do not use the hyphen with *non* or *un: nonprofit, nonagression, unacceptable*.

h2—Use the hyphen to join words that form a compound: *sergeant-at-arms, president-elect, two-thirds, twenty-one, well-trained, a leave-me-alone* attitude. (Refer to pp. 193–194.)

How To Use the Comma

c1—Use the comma between clauses of a compound sentence formed with a coordinator or correlative. (Refer to pp. 54–55.)

c2—Use a comma to separate words, phrases, or clauses in a series. (Refer to pp. 4–5.)

c3—Use a comma to separate consecutive coordinate modifiers. (Refer to pp. 188–189.)

c4—Use a comma to set off an introductory adverb clause. (Refer to p. 87.)

c5—Use a comma to set off an introductory verbal modifier. (Refer to pp. 293, 310, and 330.)

c6—Use a comma to set off a nonrestrictive appositive. (Refer to pp. 104 and 227.)

c7—Use a comma to set off a nonrestrictive adjective (word, phrase, or clause). (Refer to pp. 268, 294, and 310.)

c8—Use a comma to set off a nonrestrictive adverb clause. (Refer to pp. 86–87.)

c9—Use a comma to set off an absolute phrase. (Refer to p. 294.)

c10—Use a comma (or a pair of commas) to set off such transitional adverbs or adverb phrases as *of course, naturally, on the other hand, however, for example.*

c11—Use a comma to set off an interjection like *oh, well, yes.*

c12—Use a comma to set off terms of direct address: "Did you get the assignment, Mike?"

c13—Use a comma to set off items like *he said* in dialogue: *"The preacher urged, 'Don't be discouraged'."*

c14—Use a comma to indicate an omitted verb in certain incomplete yet meaningful structures: "My sister has a cold; *my mother, the flu."*

c15—Use a comma to prevent misreading when the same word is used twice consecutively: "Whatever *goes, goes* well; what *doesn't, doesn't."*

c16—Use a comma before (rather than after) a closing quotation mark: The word *"leaves,"* he wrote, has many meanings.

c17—Use a comma after an especially long introductory prepositional phrase—or one whose last word might be misread with the following word: *"In the long months of those miserable winters that my family lived through during my childhood,* life was enough to bore me." *"In the evening, twilight* settled softly."

How Not To Use the Comma

cf1—Do not use a comma between independent clauses that are *not* joined by a coordinator or correlative. Use a semicolon, or make two separate sentences. (Refer to pp. 68–69 and 387.)

cf2—Do not use a comma between a subject and its verb unless for one of the clear reasons shown under "How to Use the Comma." *Faulty:* "My old friend, greeted me at the corner." *Proper:* "My old friend greeted me at the corner."

cf3—Do not use a comma between a verb and its object or complement. *Faulty:* "Who shot, the bear? It *was, Davy Crockett." Proper:* "Who shot the bear? It was Davy Crockett."

cf4—Do not use a comma to set off a restrictive modifier (word, phrase, or clause). (Refer to pp. 86–87 and 268.)

cf5—Do not use a comma to set off a restrictive appositive. (Refer to p. 104.)

cf6—Do not use a comma to set off a short introductory prepositional phrase—unless misreading could result without the comma. (Refer to *c17* above.)

cf7—Do not use a comma *after* a coordinator (unless for one of the clear reasons shown under "How To Use the Comma").

cf8—Do not use a comma between the two items in a pair.

How To Use the Semicolon

semi 1—Use a semicolon to separate independent clauses that are not joined by a coordinator or correlative. (Refer to pp. 68–69 and 387.)

semi 2—Use a semicolon to separate independent clauses that are joined by a conjunctive adverb. (Refer to pp. 68–69.)

semi 3—Use a semicolon to separate independent clauses that are joined by a coordinator—if the first clause contains several commas: "She's tired, hungry, and ill-tempered; *but* she'll cook our dinner."

semi 4—Use a semicolon to separate items in a series—if those items themselves include commas: "The governor has speaking engagements in South Bend, Indiana; Columbus, Ohio; Iowa City, Iowa; and Lexington, Kentucky."

How To Use the Colon

col 1—Use a colon to direct attention to what comes next: "Just one thing kept me from volunteering: *devout cowardice.*"

col 2—Use a colon in writing precise times of day: *7:42 P.M.*

How To Use the Dash

dash 1—Use a dash to mark or set off an element that repeats, emphasizes, or summarizes what went before: "Old Finley is selfish—*incredibly selfish.* Thin, crumbling, shaky—*these* were the best descriptions of the walls and floors."

dash 2—Use a pair of dashes to set off a remark that is not part of the main sentence: "Papa knew—*he always knew!*—what we were up to."

How To Use the Apostrophe

ap 1—Use an apostrophe to indicate the omission of letters in contractions: "It's late, and we're tired; let's go home."

ap 2—Use an apostrophe to indicate the possessive of nouns and of certain indefinite pronouns: *"Henry's* friend is for *women's* rights, but he is *everybody's* candidate." (Refer to pp. 100–101.)

ap 3—Use an apostrophe with *s* to form the plural of words and numbers that are used as examples of themselves: "Let George count the *yes's* and *no's.*" "How many *4's* and *5's* did you see?"

How To Use Parentheses

paren 1—Use parentheses to enclose elements that interrupt a main thought and have only minor connection with that thought: "Danielle had stopped to buy fresh cherries *(so delicious!)* and a pound of cheese."

paren 2—Use parentheses to enclose numbers, dates, and references that help organize an essay or offer sideline information: "He would tell nothing to reporters except *(1)* his name, *(2)* his address, and *(3)* his birthdate *(1957).*"

How To Use the Period

pd 1—Use a period to mark the end of a declarative sentence or a polite and unemphatic command: "Tomorrow is expected to be cold. Don't forget your coat."

pd 2—Use a period after an initial in a name: *J. T. Salvieri.*

pd 3—Use a period after certain standard abbreviations: *Mr., Dr., Ave., St., A.M., U.S., B.A.*

pd 4—Use a period to mark the decimal place in figures: *8.6* gallons, *$5.68.*

pd 5—Use a period before (rather than after) a closing quotation mark: "This usage is conventional."

How Not To Use the Period

pf1—Do not use a period to make a fragment look like a sentence. (Refer to pp. 385– and 386.)

pf 2—Do not use *two* periods if an abbreviation falls at the end of a sentence; use one period only: *Faulty:* "The class meets to 9 A.M.." *Proper:* "The class meets at 9 A.M."

pf 3—Do not use periods in all-initial abbreviations of three or more letters: *Faulty:* Y.M.C.A., N.A.T.O., U.C.L.A. *Proper:* YMCA, NATO, UCLA.

pf 4—Do not use a period at the end of a question; use a question mark.

How To Use the Question Mark

qm 1—Use a question mark at the end of a question.

qm 2—Use a question mark *before* a quotation mark if what is quoted is a question; otherwise, use a question mark *after* the closing quotation mark:

> Have you seen the movie "Where's Charlie?" Is there any real value in "blue movies"?

qm 3—Use only one question mark at a time. *Faulty:* "Can you imagine my embarrassment????" Proper: "Can you imagine my embarrassment?"

How To Use the Exclamation Point

ex 1—Use the exclamation point after an exclamatory interjection or sentence: "Wow! I thought you'd never get here!"

ex 2—Use the exclamation point after an emphatic command: "Get down from there!"

ex 3—Use the exclamation point after an emphatic declarative sentence: "This is the sort of friendship you show me!"

ex 4—Use an exclamation point *before* a quotation mark if what is quoted is an exclamation; otherwise, use an exclamation point *after* the closing quotation mark:

"You've certainly got nerve!" he said.
Don't call me a "snow bunny"!

ex 5—Use only one exclamation point at a time. *Faulty:* "Gee!! This game is really fun!!!" *Proper:* "Gee, this game is really fun!"

How To Use Quotation Marks

qt 1—Use quotation marks to enclose directly quoted matter, from a single word up to many paragraphs. If the quoted matter consists of more than one paragraph, quotation marks should be used at the beginning of each paragraph—but at the end of *only the last* paragraph.

qt 2—Use quotation marks to enclose words or phrases that deserve special notice:

He's very "intelligent," she said bitterly.

qt 3—Use quotation marks to enclose titles of chapters, articles, short stories, and poems—as well as movies, songs, and other works of art. (The titles of complete books, plays, newspapers, magazines, and pamphlets are underlined usually rather than quoted.)

qt 4—Use quotation marks *after* a comma or period at the end of quoted matter; use quotation marks before a colon or semicolon that follows quoted matter. (For the use of quotation marks in connection with a final question mark or exclamation point see *qm 2* and *ex 4* above.)

Supplement 2
Spelling: A Study List of Three Hundred Useful Words

accept	article	committee	description	exceed
accidentally	assignment	comparatively	desert	except
achievement	association	comparison	desirable	excess
acquaintance	athlete	competitive	despair	excitement
acquire	attendance	complement	desperate	exercise
across	basically	completely	dessert	exhaust
address	becoming	compliment	destroy	exhibited
adequate	beginning	concede	destruction	existence
advice	believable	conceivable	difference	experience
advisable	believe	conference	disappeared	experiment
advise	benefited	conscience	disastrous	explanation
affect	bicycle	conscientious	discipline	extremely
all right	buried	conscious	discouragement	familiar
a lot	business	consistent	dissatisfied	fascinating
altogether	calendar	conspicuous	does	foreign
amateur	candidate	continually	duty	forty
among	capital	controlled	effect	fourth
analysis	capitol	convenience	efficiency	freight
analyze	category	counselor	eighth	government
angle	certain	courageous	either	guarantee
anniversary	changeable	course	eligible	height
answered	character	courteous	embarrassed	hindrance
anxious	chief	courtesy	emphasize	hoping
apologize	choose	criticism	encouragement	humorous
apparent	chose	curiosity	enthusiastic	hypocrisy
appearance	citation	deceive	entrance	illegal
approach	cite	decision	environment	imagination
appropriate	clothes	definitely	equipped	immediately
argument	coarse	dependent	especially	incredible
arrangement	committed	describe	exaggerate	independent

ingredients	neighbor	personnel	resistance	than
interesting	neither	physically	restaurant	their
interpretation	nevertheless	politics	rhythm	then
irrelevant	ninety	possession	ridiculous	there
irresistible	ninth	possibility	sacrifice	they're
it's	noticeable	precede	safety	thorough
its	nowadays	preferred	said	thought
judgment	obstacle	prejudiced	satisfied	through
knowledge	occasion	principal	schedule	to
laid	occasionally	principle	science	too
lead	occurred	privilege	scientific	tragedy
led	occurrence	probably	secretary	traveling
leisure	omission	procedure	seize	tried
let's	operate	proceed	self-conscious	truly
library	opinion	professional	sense	uncontrollable
license	opportunity	pronunciation	sensible	undoubtedly
loneliness	optimistic	psychology	separate	unforgettable
loose	original	quiet	sight	unnecessary
lose	outrageous	quite	similar	unusually
machinery	paid	quitting	sincerely	weather
maintenance	parallel	receipt	site	weight
management	particularly	receive	source	whether
marriage	passed	recipes	speech	who's
marvelous	past	recognize	stopping	whose
meant	perceive	reference	strength	woman
merely	performance	referred	studying	writer
mischievous	permanent	regardless	supersede	writing
mortgage	permissible	regrettable	surely	written
mysterious	permitted	religious	surprise	you're
necessary	personal	repetition	temperamental	your

Supplement 3
A Guide to Revision

Your instructor may use some of these abbreviations and symbols to indicate points that need revision or correction in your papers. To be sure that you understand what the instructor advises, you may use this guide to refer to pages of this book for study or review before you begin revising a paper.

abr — The *abbreviation* is undesirable. Spell the word out.
act — The *active* voice would be more effective than the passive in this passage. (Refer to pp. 172–173.)
amb — This wording is *ambiguous*.
ap — An *apostrophe* is needed (or is used improperly). (Refer to pp. 100–101 and p. 252.)
bw — The unnecessarily *big word* tends to produce stuffy writing. (Refer to pp. 341–342.)
c — A *comma* is needed here. (Refer to the indicated number on pp. 441–442.)
cf — The comma here produces a *comma fault*. (Refer to the indicated number on p. 442.)
cs — The comma here produces a *comma splice*. (Refer to cf1, p. 442.)
cap — The marked letter should be a *capital*. (Refer to pp. 110–111.)
coh — The passage is not *coherent*. (Refer to pp. 391–392.)
col — A *colon* would be proper here. (Refer to p. 443.)
d — The *diction* here is not appropriate to the established tone of your paper. (Refer to pp. 340–365.)
dash — A *dash* would be appropriate here. (Refer to p. 443.)
dead — The marked words are *deadwood;* they may be omitted to produce a more economical effect.
dang — The marked word is a *dangler* and needs revision. (Refer to pp. 84–85 and 295–297.)
emph — This point deserves a greater *emphasis*. It may be expanded by example or illustration.
ex — An *exclamation point* would be appropriate (or is wrongly used) here. (Refer to pp. 444–445.)
fc — This is a *faulty comparison*. (Refer to pp. 190–191, 354–355.)
frag — This *fragment* needs to be made part of a full sentence. (Refer to pp. 385–386.)
h — A *hyphen* is needed (or is misused) here. (Refer to p. 441.)

jarg	—	The marked words are examples of *jargon*. (Refer to p. 344.)
lc	—	The marked letters should be *lower-case*, not capital letters. (Refer to pp. 110–111.)
mal	—	This word is apparently a *malapropism*. (Refer to pp. 347–348.)
mm	—	This *misplaced modifier* makes a revision necessary. (Refer to pp. 204–205, 220–222, 272–273, 311–312.)
pagr	—	The *pronoun agreement* is faulty. (Refer to pp. 253–254.)
para	—	The *paragraphing* is faulty, lacking unity, or coherence, or development. (Refer to pp. 400–417.)
paral	—	The *faulty parallelism* makes a revision necessary. (Refer to pp. 22–23, 190–191, and 326–327.)
paren	—	It would be appropriate to use *parentheses* here. (Refer to p. 443.)
pd	—	A *period* is needed (or is wrongly used) here. (Refer to p. 444.)
pers	—	The marked word is in the wrong *person;* it needs to be consistent with the approach established in your essay.
pf	—	This is a *period fault*. (Refer to p. 444.)
qm	—	A *question mark* is needed. (Refer to p. 444.)
qt	—	the *quotation marks* are missing (or misused) here. (Refer to p. 445.)
red	—	The marked words produce a *redundancy*. (Refer to pp. 357–358.)
ref	—	The marked pronoun has *faulty reference*. (Refer to pp. 254–255.)
ro	—	As written, this is a *run-on* sentence; the punctuation needs revision. (Refer to pp. 386–389.)
sc	—	The *standard of comparison* has not been expressed. What are the *two* things being compared?
semi	—	A *semicolon* would be appropriate here. (Refer to pp. 442–443.)
sp	—	The *spelling* of the marked word is wrong. (Refer to pp. 447–448 or to your dictionary.)
spec	—	Be sure to *specify* or give example here.
st	—	The *shift of tense* distracts the thought. (Refer to pp. 384–385.)
sub	—	This idea should be subordinated; for best result place it less emphatically or revise it as a subordinate clause. (Refer to pp. 78–79, 374, and 391.)
syl	—	The word is wrongly divided in *syllables*. (Refer to the use of the hyphen, pp. 193–194 and 441.)
t	—	The marked verb is in the wrong *tense*. (Refer to pp. 149–152.)
vagr	—	The marked *verb* does not *agree* with its subject. (Refer to pp. 128–129 and *Verb agreement* in index.)
w	—	Is this the right word?
whc	—	The word *which* is needed (or wrongly used) here. (Refer to p. 268.)
whm	—	The case of *who* or *whom* is wrong here. (Refer to pp. 252–253.)
x	—	The marked item is an error of oversight or carelessness. Always be sure to read and correct your work before submitting it.

Supplement 4
Review Quiz A

This quiz reviews the materials in Chapters 1 through 7. Before beginning this quiz, you should review those chapters and their exercises as well as all class notes covering the study of conjunctions, verb agreement, adverbs, subordinate clauses, parallelism, danglers, nouns, possessives, capitalization, sentence structure, and fragments.

On the blank within each sentence write the item that you think most appropriately completes the sentence; then mark the *letter* of that item on your answer blank. Do not overlook the punctuation included in some of the offered completions.

Example: Councilman Spaggiera is not expected to run for re-election, *be-cause he has not recovered from illness*.

(a) due to illness.   (b) . Because of his illness.   (c) because of his illness.
(d) , because he has not recovered from illness.   (e) for he has a continuing illness.   Ex *d*

(*Note:* Completion (d) properly provides a comma before a nonrestrictive adverb clause; the completion avoids (a) a misplaced modifier, (b) a fragment, (c) a misplaced modifier, and (e) the lack of a comma between independent clauses joined by a coordinator.)

1. The company's new product is inexpensive, effective, and _____ _____.

(a) available   (b) benefits everyone   (c) has plenty of power
(d) never breaks down   (e) what everybody wants   1._____

2. When either snow or rain _____, the work stops.

(a) come   (b) have fallen   (c) begins   (d) are on the ground
(e) make driving dangerous   2._____

3. Next year we'll have time for rest, recreation ———————— amusement.

(a) and (b) , and (c) and, (d) , and, (e) or   3._____

4. The case was clear cut ———————————————— the jury could not reach a verdict.

(a) however (b) yet (c) ; still, (d) for (e) nevertheless   4._____

5. My friend Oscar is a man of intelligence, honor, and ————————

(a) respected widely. (b) he is brave. (c) has courage. (d) integrity.
(e) with complete honesty.   5._____

6. ———————————————— doing my homework, the phone rang.

(a) While (b) After (c) Although (d) Disturbing me while
(e) Interrupting when I was   6._____

7. Some species of birds fly ————————————————.

(a) South every Winter (b) North in the Spring (c) south in the Winter
(d) north in the Spring (e) south in the winter   7._____

8. The new stadium, though modern, holds ———————————— than the old one.

(a) as much people (b) less spectators (c) fewer fans (d) as much seats
(e) fewer comfort   8._____

9. Sometimes we avoid a person because he has bad breath, ———————— talks too much, or is too nosy.

(a) dandruff (b) has dandruff, (c) dandruff, (d) or dandruff
(e) or dandruff,   9._____

10. Jack and his wife sometimes ———————————————— their baby along when they visit us.

(a) have brought (b) brings (c) did bring (d) has brought (e) bring   10._____

11. Last night it sounded as if the ———————————————— were fighting again.

(a) Farber's (b) Martinezes (c) Kelly's (d) Thomas (e) Levines'   11._____

12. Lana designs _____ clothing fashions.

(a) womens' (b) childrens' (c) ladies' (d) expensive women's
(e) mens   12_____

13. My _____ is the only girl in our family.

(a) sister Susie (b) sister, Susie, (c) sister Susie; (d) sister Susie,
(e) , sister Susie,   13_____

14. The nation awaits appointment of a _____.

(a) assistant secretary (b) ambassador to Spain (c) interior secretary
(d) chief justice (e) attorney general   14_____

15. No jury, if it is fair, ever _____
without sufficient evidence.

(a) make a decision (b) delivers a verdict (c) reach a verdict (d) convict
(e) determine conviction   15_____

16. At the Olympics many nations _____
medals but also for honor.

(a) not only compete for (b) compete not only for (c) either compete for
(d) compete not for only (e) both compete for   16_____

17. Mrs. Sorenson applied for a fine job at the _____.

(a) Public Library (b) Police station (c) City Hall (d) stationery store
(e) Century City Chamber of commerce   17_____

18. Our company has decided to open a _____
department.

(a) childrens' (b) sport's (c) mens (d) women's (e) ladys'   18_____

19. Pete is almost sure to win a scholarship _____
his average tops the class.

(a) although (b) , because (c) for (d) . Because (e) , if   19_____

20. When the time _____ will be ready to
go.

(a) has come we (b) had come, she (c) arrives he (d) is ripe they
(e) comes, you   20_____

21. While looking for parking space, _____ wastes a lot of gasoline.

(a) a truck (b) most cars (c) bus drivers (d) any driver (e) a big car

21.____

22. The team's captain is a man of quick reflexes, great stamina, and _____

(a) with remarkable skill. (b) has talent. (c) very talented.
(d) who has a lot of skill. (e) remarkable talent.

22.____

23. The Browns and the Joneses seldom meet, because the Browns' classes are earlier than the _____

(a) Jone's classes. (b) Jones's class's. (c) Joneses class's
(d) Joneses' classes. (e) Joneses' class's.

23.____

24. There's just no arguing with _____

(a) mother. (b) Dad. (c) the Sergeant. (d) professor Fiero. (e) Me.

24.____

25. When advertising and junk mail _____, we just throw them away.

(a) is delivered (b) arrive (c) begins to pile up (d) annoys us
(e) becomes annoying

25.____

26. All of the players _____ showed up on time.

(a) but Tom (b) yet he (c) , but Eddie (d) but also him (e) , yet they

26.____

27. My letter of application was ready _____ put it into the mail.

(a) and I (b) so I (c) , I (d) , therefore I (e) , so I

27.____

28. The rain let up after a _____ the wind started to blow hard.

(a) hour; then (b) week; then (c) few days then (d) while, then
(e) time and

28.____

29. I learned most of my math during my last year at _____

(a) nigh school. (b) High School (c) Culver high school.
(d) Elementary school. (e) Junior High.

29.____

30. No amount of _____ can keep him from his duty.

(a) people (b) influence (c) complaints (d) obstacles (e) men

30_____

31. Some _____ have noted a decline in attendance.

(a) church'es (b) churchs (c) church's (d) churches' (e) churches

31_____

32. Before my dog was six months old, she could sit up, roll _____ for food.

(a) over and beg   (b) over and could beg   (c) over, and would beg
(d) over, and beg   (e) over, and begged

32_____

33. We saw a flicker of headlights _____ they disappeared.

(a) then   (b) , then   (c) ; but   (d) ; then   (e) , however,

33_____

34. The referee never raised his _____ several players shouted at him.

(a) voice although   (b) voice, when   (c) hand but   (d) eyes, however
(e) head, although

34_____

35. Once replaced by a smile, _____ again.

(a) you'll never want to frown   (b) your face will never wear a frown
(c) no one will see you frown   (d) we may never frown
(e) your frown may never be seen

35_____

36. Usually the tires or the upholstery _____ before anything else.

(a) wear out   (b) are worn   (c) have to be replaced   (d) wears out
(e) go bad

36_____

37. Most people seem to think that April is a really beautiful _____.

(a) girl.   (b) Spring month.   (c) Month.   (d) Time.
(e) time in the south.

37_____

38. Barnes not only qualifies but _____

(a) he is prepared.   (b) also prepared.   (c) prepared.
(d) also has enthusiasm.   (e) the job was made for him.

38_____

39. The crowd went wild _____ the band played louder and louder.

(a) . While   (b) and   (c) , also   (d) as   (e) , when

39_____

40. The team, when it comes back on the field, _____ to use a different strategy.

(a) are going   (b) was sure   (c) have   (d) is likely   (e) had

40_____

41. Either you drive carefully, or _____

(a) dangerously.   (b) risk arrest.   (c) run the risk of death.
(d) lose your license.   (e) you may be arrested.

41_____

42. Panning for gold _____ can be fun.

(a) a popular pastime,   (b) , popular, and profitable,
(c) both popular, and profitable   (d) , a popular pastime,
(e) , a profitable pastime

42_____

43. Ernville is bothered by mosquitoes only during warm weather and _____

(a) when it has been raining.   (b) after a rain has fallen.
(c) if it has been raining.   (d) after a rain.   (e) it has been raining.

43_____

44. Neither having money _____, I had to eat very little.

(a) or a job   (b) , nor a job   (c) nor having a job   (d) and not having a job
(e) nor as yet no job

44_____

45. All the major exams _____ to be taken.

(a) , however are   (b) are, however   (c) nevertheless, are   (d) are yet
(e) , yet are

45_____

46. Our _____ often gives us free doughnuts.

(a) friend the baker   (b) friend, the bakers   (c) friend the baker,
(d) , friend the baker   (e) friends the bakers,

46_____

47. The auditorium tower has been condemned _____ must be demolished.

(a) , and   (b) , therefore,   (c) ; therefore,   (d) ; therefore
(e) ; therefore, it

47_____

48. Certainly rain is welcome on weekdays. ——————————
——————————————

(a) Never on weekends. (b) But not on holidays.
(c) On weekends, however, not. (d) But it shouldn't rain on holidays.
(e) Except on holidays. 48_____

49. A business recovery is expected next ——————————————
a recovery is predicted.

(a) year, (b) spring; at least, (c) month at least (d) summer indeed,
(e) fall; at least 49_____

50. The campaign against pollution cannot succeed in ——————————
the public does not cooperate.

(a) America, (b) our nation if (c) this country, while
(d) this town, as long as (e) fact, 50_____

Review Quiz B

This quiz reviews the materials in Chapters 8 through 12. Before beginning this quiz, you should review those chapters and their exercises as well as all class notes covering the study of action verbs, auxiliary verbs, linking verbs, complements, verb agreement, adjectives, adverbs, restrictive and nonrestrictive modifiers, misplaced modifiers, and danglers.

On the blank within each sentence write the item that you think most appropriately completes the sentence; then mark the *letter* of that item on your answer blank. Do not overlook the punctuation included in some of the offered completions.

Example: Our new chairman is a woman ____*whose*____ political experience we admire.

(a) whose had (b) , who has (c) whom has (d) whose (e) , who's   Ex *d*

(*Note:* Completion (d) properly completes the sentence, avoiding (a) misuse of *whose* for *who has,* (b) faulty use of comma to set off a restrictive clause, (c) faulty use of *whom* as subject, and (e) faulty use of comma and misuse of *who's* for *whose*.)

1. The two boys _____ watching the stars.

(a) lay (b) was lying (c) laid (d) lain (e) had laid   1._____

2. When Hector was a pup, a black spot _____ under his muzzle.

(a) appears (b) develop (c) use to be (d) grew (e) turns up   2._____

3. A voter in one of the big cities _____ much excuse for not voting.

(a) don't have (b) shouldn't of had (c) doesn't have (d) haven't
(e) never have   3._____

4. Everybody who can play two instruments _____ really valuable to the band.

(a) was (b) were (c) is (d) are (e) have been   4._____

5. The soprano has a cold, so the quartet really sounds _____ today.

(a) bad   (b) poorly   (c) badly   (d) sourly   (e) inharmoniously

6. Apparently your cat doesn't like the new canned food; perhaps the food doesn't taste _____.

(a) well   (b) as good as yesterday   (c) very good   (d) spicily
(e) so deliciously

7. _____ kind of stories always frightened me.

(a) Many   (b) These   (c) Those   (d) Them   (e) That

8. Susie folded the sweater she had washed _____.

(a) up in a drawer   (b) carefully into a box   (c) quickly away
(d) and beautifully   (e) in tepid water

9. The battle of the sexes _____ for many centuries.

(a) have been going on   (b) is something, that has gone on   (c) has gone on
(d) has continued going on,   (e) were in conflict

10. My mongrel pup lay _____ faithfully at my feet.

(a) the stick   (b) himself   (c) down   (d) the bird   (e) a paper

11. Many attractive deals but never a profitable one _____ to come my way.

(a) seem   (b) appears   (c) apparently   (d) , it seems, is   (e) was

12. In the early 1920's Babe Ruth _____ for Boston.

(a) play   (b) plays   (c) played   (d) plaid   (e) playing

13. When he has finished college, Alf _____ most of the music courses.

(a) would take   (b) will have taken   (c) has taken   (d) was taking
(e) had taken

14. Members of the group have set _____
almost overnight.

(a) up   (b) a record   (c) there deliberating   (d) around the table
(e) they're arguing   14._____

15. Mr. Dinero brags that his new little car gets better mileage than _____

_____.

(a) his secretary.   (b) last year.   (c) he did before.   (d) his secretary's.
(e) the neighbors.   15._____

16. The _____ president took his oath today.

(a) newly-elected   (b) recent named   (c) popularly-chosen
(d) high school   (e) high-school   16._____

17. Any bird _____ is usually frightened.

(a) in the hand,   (b) , in the hand   (c) held in the hand
(d) , held in the hand,   (e) held in the hand,   17._____

18. What the family likes most _____ that new dessert.

(a) , is   (b) are   (c) was   (d) were   (e) is   18._____

19. If overweight, _____

(a) the team won't accept you.   (b) your eligibility is in question.
(c) the scales will show it.   (d) you may be ineligible.
(e) a diet may be advisable.   19._____

20. A fragile blue vase had been _____ on the table.

(a) sitting   (b) setting   (c) sat   (d) lain   (e) laying   20._____

21. The child and her mother _____ seen sitting on the sand.

(a) was   (b) are   (c) has been   (d) often   (e) is   21._____

22. Victoria has a smile much more attractive than _____

(a) me.   (b) her sister.   (c) anyone else.   (d) her cousin's.   (e) her's.   22._____

462 Supplement Four

23. A person should never carry a lot of cash _____ he cannot afford to lose it.

(a) which   (b) , since,   (c) if   (d) for   (e) who

23._____

24. Pete's father _____ is a counselor for our club.

(a) who drives a bus   (b) , whom is a druggist,   (c) , which designs tools,
(d) whom we admire   (e) , who sells real estate,

24._____

25. When the audience laughed, the contestant just stood there looking _____

(a) real serious.   (b) obviously disturb.   (c) real seriously.
(d) really serious.   (e) really seriously.

25._____

26. The workers, not the employer, _____ to gain from negotiations.

(a) expect   (b) has much   (c) stands   (d) hasn't a chance   (e) is sure

26._____

27. Usually one of the minor characters _____ on the scene first.

(a) appear   (b) , come   (c) , appears   (d) comes   (e) enters,

27._____

28. The two boxers weighed in yesterday, and Joe was the _____ by nearly two pounds.

(a) weightiest   (b) heavier   (c) most heavy   (d) more heavier
(e) least heavy

28._____

29. The fans like Stan because he is a _____ player.

(a) quick, intelligent   (b) modest, basketball   (c) flashy fascinating
(d) extremely experienced   (e) really, dedicated

29._____

30. Some of _____ are too ripe to be eaten.

(a) this grape   (b) those vegetable   (c) these apples   (d) them pears
(e) that food

30._____

Review Quiz B   463

31. Barney, the night watchman, is very conscientious; he never sleeps _____.

(a) , while on duty.   (b) , when he is on duty.   (c) while he is on duty.
(d) , if on duty.   (e) , or shirks his duty.

31. _____

32. Our new secretary types fast, but she doesn't answer the telephone very _____.

(a) skillful   (b) good   (c) cheerfully   (d) friendly   (e) nice

32. _____

33. Frank came late for class because he had _____ down for an hour and had fallen asleep.

(a) set   (b) layed   (c) lied   (d) laid   (e) lain

33. _____

34. When I was younger _____ to have a lot of prejudice.

(a) people seemed   (b) , I used   (c) it was common   (d) my friends seem
(e) , the world appear

34. _____

35. The mailman as well as two neighbor children _____ bitten by our dog.

(a) has been   (b) were once   (c) could of been   (d) were almost
(e) never have been

35. _____

36. Neither misfortunes nor good luck _____ any change in his attitude.

(a) have caused   (b) has cause   (c) has caused   (d) produce   (e) nor

36. _____

37. In the summer Len usually _____ nothing all day.

(a) do   (b) will do,   (c) doesn't do   (d) does   (e) have done

37. _____

38. The critics couldn't agree on which was the _____ of the two films.

(a) least offensive   (b) more amusing   (c) most artistic   (d) best
(e) excitinger

38. _____

39. Professor Marlboro always takes a deep breath _____ he begins a new phrase.

(a) , as   (b) , when   (c) before   (d) , before   (e) then   39_____

40. Do you know what kind of _____ I like?

(a) girl which   (b) person who   (c) show whom   (d) people
(e) characters who   40_____

41. After Ernie _____ risen each morning, they had chores to do.

(a) have   (b) and Fred   (c) had   (d) and Bill had   (e) , and Mike had   41_____

42. Every village and town _____ own council.

(a) have their   (b) have its   (c) has their   (d) has its   (e) and its   42_____

43. Police investigators _____ erased by the rain.

(a) found the fingerprints almost   (b) almost found the fingerprints
(c) found almost the fingerprints   (d) found the almost fingerprints
(e) found the fingerprints most   43_____

44. One of my favorite topics _____ sports.

(a) have always been   (b) are winter   (c) is   (d) were   (e) have to be   44_____

45. There goes the little lady _____ wrote the music for our show.

(a) who   (b) , who   (c) , she   (d) she   (e) which   45_____

46. He always had the idea of becoming a pilot _____.

(a) in the back of his head   (b) when he was a child
(c) and he grew up to be one   (d) for commercial airlines
(e) , when he finished school   46_____

47. The orchestra tuned up, the director arrived _____.

(a) and the symphony began   (b) , and the symphony was begun
(c) and tapped on the rostrum   (d) as the rehearsal began
(e) , and the audience applauded   47_____

48. At some colleges the older students _____ are most serious.

(a) who   (b) if they   (c) where most   (d) apparently   (e) that   48_____

49. If only she _____ the exam, she could have qualified.

(a) would have taken   (b) has taken   (c) had took   (d) hadn't failed
(e) will take   49_____

50. Every man, woman, and child on board _____ to use the safety equipment.

(a) have been shown how   (b) know how   (c) are able
(d) has been told how   (e) learn   50_____

Review Quiz C

This quiz reviews the materials in Chapters 13 through 18. Before beginning this quiz, you should review those chapters and their exercises as well as all class notes covering the study of prepositions, pronoun usage, adjective clauses, gerunds, present participles, past participles, and infinitives.

On the blank within each sentence write the item that you think most appropriately completes the sentence; then mark the *letter* of that item on your answer blank. Do not overlook the punctuation included in some of the offered completions.

Example: A good newscaster must be one of those people *whom* listeners believe they can trust.

(a) who   (b) whom   (c) who's   (d) which   (e) whoever

Ex. *b*

(*Note:* Completion (b) properly provides a relative pronoun in the object case, to begin the adjective clause "whom they can trust"; the completion avoids (a) improper case (*they* is the subject of the clause), (c) a meaningless use of *who's (who is . . . ?)*, (d) improper use of *which* to refer to *people*, and (e) improper case.)

1. Everyone must bring _____ lunch ticket.

(a) they're   (b) there   (c) their   (d) her   (e) your

1._____

2. Any candidate _____ is elected must serve a full term.

(a) who's   (b) who   (c) whom   (d) whose   (e) whomever

2._____

3. Speaking very little Italian _____ were difficult to express.

(a) my thoughts   (b) our needs   (c) , we found ideas   (d) , what we needed
(e) , most things

3._____

4. Both Jackie and _____ were given another opportunity.

(a) her   (b) him   (c) our   (d) me   (e) I

4._____

5. Taking cat-like steps, the speaker crept _____ the room.

(a) within (b) in (c) inside (d) into (e) passed

5._____

6. The dean said that he could never approve of _____

(a) her behavior. (b) him stealing. (c) us defacing property.
(d) them cheating. (e) me taking time off.

6._____

7. Taken from my wallet, _____ credit card was stolen.

(a) my gasoline (b) I think my (c) I discovered a (d) my report said the
(e) my mother told police that my

7._____

8. All the honors went to six teammates and _____.

(a) I (b) we (c) us (d) ourselfs (e) hisself

8._____

9. If the troop wants to win an award _____ will have to work as a unit.

(a) , they (b) it (c) , it (d) members (e) we

9._____

10. _____ new girlfriend?

(a) Who's James's (b) Whose James' (c) Who's Jame's
(d) Who'se James's (e) Whose James's

10._____

11. If you have a spot on your coat, _____ removed.

(a) it has to be (b) they have to be (c) the coat have to be
(d) the spot has to be (e) you must have it

11._____

12. Judging by his clothing, _____ a coal miner.

(a) he must be (b) I'd say he is (c) it appears that he's
(d) our friend looks like (e) it makes him look like

12._____

13. The old mule _____ its stance, the boy couldn't make it move.

(a) took (b) taking (c) having took (d) had taken (e) has taken

13._____

14. To do his duty _____ only thought.

(a) was the officer's (b) , was the captain's (c) , all the watchman
(d) were the lieutenant's (e) are most men's

14._____

15. Although a person can sometimes have a strong opinion, no one can ever be certain that _____ right.

(a) they are (b) you are (c) he is (d) we are (e) he was   15_____

16. After all the work we've done, do you think you are _____ us?

(a) prouder than (b) proud of (c) more excited than (d) as experienced as
(e) tired as   16_____

17. The voters _____ will make the best decision.

(a) theirselves (b) themself (c) ourself (d) themselves (e) itself   17_____

18. I love to go to the mountain forests and breathe freely _____ all those big trees.

(a) amidst (b) among (c) between (d) with (e) besides   18_____

19. Any soldier _____ could not see his sergeant.

(a) behind the rock,   (b) , who took cover,   (c) , in a jeep
(d) who stayed under cover   (e) who's glasses had broken   19_____

20 No engineer _____ worth his fee will do a careless job.

(a) whose (b) that is (c) which is (d) who's (e) , who is   20_____

21. It was discovered that the sergeant had sometimes opened the _____

(a) mail of the captain.   (b) captains mail.   (c) locker of the major.
(d) general's letters.   (e) safe of Lieutenant James.   21_____

22. Mrs. Peale was eating some strawberries that were raised by her neighbor _____.

(a) in a bowl of cream   (b) with sugar on them   (c) sliced over ice cream
(d) across the street   (e) fresh from the refrigerator   22_____

23. She is an artist _____ we have always admired.

(a) whom (b) who's work (c) who (d) , who (e) , whom   23_____

24 Have confidence in yourself and state your ideas in a straightforward manner.

Then you will probably get a better grade and probably _____
a much more interesting paper.
(a) be   (b) writing   (c) , write   (d) you will write   (e) write   24_____

25. There sat Louisa, studying at a table in the library _____
notice of Hank.
(a) , and not taking   (b) . Not taking   (c) not taking   (d) , not taking
(e) . Taking no   25_____

26. Many colleges have grade requirements that are too high _____
isn't fair to many good students.
(a) this   (b) , which   (c) , and that   (d) , it   (e) ; having such standards   26_____

27. By doing what I think and by saying what I think, _____
much more genuine as a person.
(a) makes me   (b) lets me be   (c) I become   (d) allows me to be
(e) life makes me   27_____

28. Having a girlfriend usually gives a fellow new incentive _____

_____ _____.
(a) for which to work for   (b) to work for   (c) for which to work
(d) toward which to work   (e) on which to concentrate on   28_____

29. _____ must do the best they can at every
job.
(a) Everyone   (b) All employees   (c) Each worker   (d) Us new employees
(e) A person   29_____

30. Jerry told his uncle that _____ was to blame.
(a) I   (b) he   (c) they   (d) both   (e) all of us   30_____

31. Neither of the winners _____ made a speech.
(a) having   (b) has   (c) have   (d) after having   (e) were   31_____

32. Psychologists often say we should choose friends whose beliefs we respect

_____ have attitudes like our own.
(a) , and who   (b) and   (c) and they   (d) and who   (e) but   32_____

33. Riley is an experienced employee _____ no beginner could replace.

(a) which   (b) who's   (c) who   (d) whose   (e) whom   33_____

34. There goes the _____ who led us to victory last season.

(a) player,   (b) , halfback,   (c) coach   (d) , fellow   (e) man,   34_____

35. All my _____ had to be hung out to dry.

(a) clothes soaked through   (b) clothes, soaked through
(c) clothes, soaked through and   (d) clothes, soaked through,
(e) clothes soaked, through   35_____

36. Stuffed into the suitcase _____ a voice-recording device.

(a) the traveler carried   (b) , he had concealed   (c) , investigators found
(d) was   (e) the equipment included   36_____

37. The professors have complained about him _____.

(a) never studying   (b) causing trouble   (c) cheating   (d) constantly
(e) not being in class   37_____

38. _____ the rays warm you all over.

(a) Laying in the sun,   (b) Lying in the sun,   (c) The sun beating down,
(d) While you lay there,   (e) Beating down upon you   38_____

39. There should be no one to tell us how to live, unless _____ hurting someone else.

(a) when   (b) you're   (c) we're   (d) their   (e) they are   39_____

40. I have never accused anyone _____ myself.

(a) but those who have hurt   (b) who seemed honest with
(c) who showed interest in   (d) who didn't accuse   (e) but   40_____

41. Usually the crowd listen to whoever _____.

(a) pleases them   (b) it likes   (c) they like   (d) we present
(e) you introduce   41_____

42. Those jurors who have read the facts of the case should disqualify _____ .

(a) themselves   (b) theirselves   (c) themself   (d) theirself
(e) theirselfs

42_____

43. I don't know much yet about politics, but I hope to _____ someday.

(a) become one   (b) go into them   (c) learn more about it   (d) gain some
(e) succeed at them

43_____

44. An accident victim was brought in by an ambulance _____ .

(a) with a crushed leg.   (b) obviously near death.   (c) seriously bruised.
(d) that had a back injury.   (e) and treated immediately.

44_____

45. When _____ , we saw that it was empty.

(a) opened   (b) it is opened   (c) the box was opened   (d) broken open
(e) open

45_____

46. Jack always takes the blame for Charlie and _____

(a) her.   (b) I.   (c) they.   (d) we.   (e) myself.

46_____

47. The year's winning contestants _____ Georgina and me.

(a) were   (b) had to be   (c) were as proud as   (d) were tutored by
(e) appeared to have been

47_____

48. Looking forward to exams, _____ to study daily.

(a) there are assignments   (b) a resolution is needed   (c) the best plan is
(d) my decision was   (e) Arnie decided

48_____

49. Since the streets were covered with _____ kids decided to skate to school.

(a) ice some   (b) ice we   (c) ice, us   (d) ice, the   (e) ice, although

49_____

50. Most applicants said they wanted the job _____

(a) to get rich.   (b) to avoid poverty.   (c) to try something new.
(d) to be challenging.   (e) not to seem lazy.

50_____

Review Quiz D

This quiz reviews the materials in Chapter 19 and 20 as well as the punctuation and spelling in Supplements 1 and 2. Before beginning this quiz, you should review all those materials, including those on diction, idea-linking devices, parallelism, fragments, run-on sentences, and shifts of reference, person, tense, and voice.

On the blank within each sentence write the item that you think most appropriately completes the sentence; then mark the **letter** of that item on your answer blank. Do not overlook the punctuation included in some of the offered completions.

Example: The experience was not so exciting as you *would have expected*.

(a) might of supposed.   (b) could of expected.   (c) might have suppose.
(d) would have expected.   (e) had of imagined.

Ex. *d*

(*Note:* Completion (d) avoids the misspelling of *have* and the faulty omission of *d* on *supposed*.)

1. Suddenly the movie stunt man _____ down on the roof of the saloon.

   (a) dove   (b) lay   (c) set   (d) laid   (e) snuck

   1._____

2. Walking with her head held high, the old lady looked neither left nor right as she _____ Elson's door.

   (a) preceded past   (b) proceeded past   (c) past   (d) lead her dog past
   (e) strutted past

   2._____

3. People do not work so efficiently when _____ uncomfortable.

   (a) there   (b) their   (c) they're   (d) its   (e) the whether is

   3._____

474   Supplement Four

4. They walked along the deserted beach and found it strewn with all kinds of _____.

(a) refuge   (b) drags of humanity   (c) waist products   (d) rabble
(e) refuse

4_____

5. We must recognize that in _____ we still have poverty.

(a) these modern times of today   (b) today's modern times   (c) these times
(d) times that are adequate enough   (e) our wealthy, affluent times

5_____

6. Tell your friends that we don't expect to go _____.

(a) anyplace   (b) nowhere   (c) no how   (d) anyways   (e) anywhere

6_____

7. A person should never carry a lot of cash _____ may be robbed.

(a) , he   (b) ; you   (c) ; they   (d) ; she   (e) , or they

7_____

8. One of the passengers carried a gun aboard the plane _____ had not detected it.

(a) but authorities   (b) the gate-check   (c) ; pre-flight checks
(d) he said they   (e) apparently the machine

8_____

9. Dr. Shane's discovery was _____ remarkable.

(a) real   (b) more then   (c) nothing accept   (d) no less than   (e) sure

9_____

10. _____ an Indian, he had to fight hard.

(a) Due to his being   (b) Because of his being   (c) Since being
(d) Him being   (e) Due to he was

10_____

11. The child had disappeared after he _____ into the water when no one was looking.

(a) jump   (b) crawl   (c) dove   (d) dived   (e) had went

11_____

12. The orchestra tuned up, the director arrived _____.

(a) and the performance began   (b) , and the performance was begun
(c) , and the performance began   (d) , and tapped on the rostrum
(e) as the rehearsal began

12_____

13. Government is seldom successful in trying to control individual enterprise. _____ leads to business recession.

(a) It   (b) That   (c) Such control   (d) Because such control
(e) Especially when it

13._____

14. We were all invited to a party at our friend Perry's _____.

(a) domicile   (b) place of residence   (c) humble abode   (d) house
(e) habitat

14._____

15. People who expect something for nothing are _____ disappointed.

(a) all too often   (b) more often then not   (c) many times and oft
(d) often times   (e) often

15._____

16. Each department has assured us that _____ account will be reported on time.

(a) its   (b) it's   (c) its'   (d) their   (e) they're

16._____

17. Dr. Stern _____ until he found an answer.

(a) left no stone unturned   (b) did not rest   (c) continued on
(d) worked laboriously   (e) worked like a Trojan

17._____

18. Each specimen had been mounted in a portable glass case, so the term project _____ ready to submit.

(a) is now   (b) would soon be   (c) has been made   (d) were almost
(e) takes form

18._____

19. Joe wanted to win, and he prayed constantly—before breakfast, after lunch, and _____.

(a) at bedtime   (b) when retiring   (c) as he went to bed   (d) going to bed
(e) kneeled beside his bed

19._____

20. Feeling exhausted, the players drug themselves _____.

(a) downfield   (b) off the field   (c) to the locker room   (d) with soft drinks
(e) back to the line

20._____

476   Supplement Four

21. If the newcomer won't cooperate on the hike, leave him _____.
(a) go   (b) stay here   (c) behind   (d) go back to camp
(e) shift for himself   21_____

22. After Ernie _____ risen each morning, they had one duty.
(a) have   (b) and Tom   (c) had   (d) and Mike,   (e) and Bill had   22_____

23. Last summer when I nearly _____
I had a vision of my life.
(a) past a tough course,   (b) drownded,   (c) lost my breathe,
(d) run out of money,   (e) drowned,   23_____

24. Reduction of speed limits has resulted in _____
highway deaths.
(a) a smaller amount of   (b) less   (c) not so much   (d) fewer
(e) downward reduction of   24_____

25. This brand of perfume has a very _____ odor.
(a) punctual   (b) flagrant   (c) simulating   (d) stimulating
(e) intoxicated   25_____

26. The director obviously resented the _____ment.
(a) arrang----   (b) discourage----   (c) gover----   (d) argue----
(e) judge----   26_____

27. His usual behavior was hardly _____able.
(a) notic----   (b) chang----   (c) permiss----   (d) manage----
(e) irresist----   27_____

28. The general's dis_____ was widely known.
(a) ---cription   (b) ---cision   (c) ---pair   (d) ---cipline   (e) ---truction   28_____

29. What they have done is certainly _____ious.
(a) conspic----   (b) mischiev----   (c) outrage----   (d) myster----
(e) court----   29_____

30. The teacher did not try to _____ise me.
(a) anal---   (b) recogn---   (c) adv---   (d) not---   (e) supr---   30_____

31. The championship bout had been _____ly exciting.
(a) true--   (b) unusua--   (c) definit--   (d) especial--   (e) sur--   31_____

32. Their _____ance had not been reported in the news.
(a) resist---- (b) confer---- (c) occurr---- (d) independ----
(e) differ----   32_____

33. Some of the workers had not been _____ed by the agency.
(a) benefit-- (b) commit-- (c) try-- (d) refer-- (e) pay--   33_____

34. An inadequate law was _____eeded by a new one.
(a) prec----- (b) succ----- (c) supers----- (d) ex----- (e) perc----- 34_____

35. _____ty rules are observed by our organization.
(a) Four-- (b) Nine-- (c) Eight-- (d) Saf-- (e) Due--   35_____

Punctuation Quiz

Write in each numbered blank the most appropriate punctuation (selected from the alternatives offered below each sentence or passage). If no punctuation should be used, make no mark in the blank. Then mark the *letter* of your choice on your answer blank at the right.

Example: Facing a shortage of space___ the authorities___ decided to con-
                                        1   2
struct a three___level parking building on the campus.
              3   Ex 1_____
                                                                            Ex 2_____
(a) ,   (b) ;   (c) -   (d) :   (e) none   Ex 3_____

A. Skeptics may disbelieve it___ but the movie industry does have its wise
                              1
men___
    2   1_____
(a) ,   (b) ;   (c) :   (d) -   (e) .   2_____

B. Doctors___ who specialize in arthritis___ know that the treatment must
          3   4
do more than relieve pain___ it must also reduce inflammation.   3_____
                         5   4_____
(a) ,   (b) ;   (c) :   (d) '   (e) none   5_____

C. One panelist said___ that he wanted his future wife to be self___sufficient
                    6   7
but not "independent___
                    8   6_____
                                                                            7_____
(a) ,   (b) " .   (c) -   (d) ."   (e) none   8_____

D. Assignments being rather dull___ I fell into the habit___ of ignoring them in
                                9   10
favor of television.   9_____
(a) ,   (b) ;   (c) —   (d) .   (e) none   10_____

478   Supplement Four

E. Yes___ the friend in need___ is a friend indeed___ especially when he is
     11   12   13
very much in need___
                  14

(a) ,   (b) ;   (c) :   (d) !   (e) none

11_____
12_____
13_____
14_____

F. Not all the voters___ who are Democrats___ can be expected to support the
                           15   16
party___s candidate.
     17

(a) ,   (b) —   (c) :   (d) '   (e) none

15_____
16_____
17_____

G. Swimming in a riptide___ is not a procedure___ that can be recom-
                         18   19
mended by any lifeguard___ who is really responsible.
                    20

(a) ,   (b) —   (c) '   (d) ;   (e) none

18_____
19_____
20_____

H. Warned about her habit___ of arriving late___ Miss Allen assumed an attitude
                            21   22

of tardier___ than___ thou superiority.
       23   24

(a) ,   (b) ;   (c) -   (d) "   (e) none

21_____
22_____
23_____
24_____

I. Most of us___ of course___ are less disciplined than any self___respecting
            25   26   27
jellyfish.

(a) ,   (b) ?   (c) -   (d) ;   (e) none

25_____
26_____
27_____

J. Ms. Peerless___ who is a tall___ winsome___ blonde___ is otherwise rather
              28   29   30   31
non___descript.
     32

(a) ,   (b) -   (c) ;   (d) :   (e) none

28_____
29_____
30_____
31_____
32_____

K. The aircraft carrier___ Ticonderoga___ sailed today from San Diego___
                        33   34   35
California___ bound for duty___ in Southeast Asia.
      36   37

(a) ,   (b) ;   (c) :   (d) !   (e) none

33_____
34_____
35_____
36_____
37_____

L. Wildlife is important to us___ we all know that fact___ But how much do we
                                38   39
know about that importance___ Can we back our concern___ with knowledge___
                                  40   41   42

(a) ,   (b) ;   (c) .   (d) ?   (e) none

38_____
39_____
40_____
41_____
42_____

M. "A women⎯⎯s lib enthusiast whom I know introduced some guests⎯⎯
              43   44
saying, 'We are happy to have with us Mr. and Mrs. Brown—not necessarily in that
order⎯⎯ of course!⎯⎯
      45   46

(a) ,   (b) "   (c) '   (d) ' "   (e) none

43⎯⎯
44⎯⎯
45⎯⎯
46⎯⎯

N. I asked Grandpa⎯⎯ what I could do to save money on a daily basis. His
                  47
answer⎯⎯ was interesting⎯⎯ "You must know exactly where your money is⎯⎯
      48   49   50
all of it."

(a) ,   (b) —   (c) :   (d) ,"   (e) none

47⎯⎯
48⎯⎯
49⎯⎯
50⎯⎯

Index

A, an
  as determiner, 185, 187
  before vowel, 112
  in title, 110
Abbreviation, 444
Absolute phrase, 294–295, 297
  comma with, 294–295
  use of, 294–295
Abstract noun, 96–97, 103, 291
Action verb, 120–138, 162
Active voice, 173–175, 312–314
Address, term of, 442
Adjective, 182–195
  as clipped-form adverb, 206–208
  comparative, 189–191, 354–356
  compound, 193–195, 441
  coordinate, 187–189, 441
  defined, 37
  demonstrative, 186–187, 375
  descriptive, 37–38, 182–184, 187–189
  determiner as, 185–187
  distinguished from adverb, 166–167, 206–207
  infinitive as, 323–326, 331–332
  -ing word as, 62, 107, 291–297
  in pairs and series, 187–189
  limiting, 186–187
  misplaced, 191
  modified by adverb, 202–204
  past participle as, 304–306, 312–313, 315, 322
  prepositional phrase as, 193–194, 216–220
  present participle as, 291–297, 304, 322
  subordinate clause as, *see* Adjective clause
  superlative, 190, 354–356
  to modify gerund, 288
  to modify noun, 37–38, 182–183
Adjective clause, 182–183, 193–195, 265–273, 441
  incomplete, 277
  nonrestrictive, 268–270, 441
  placement of, 272–273
  restrictive, 268–270
  subordinator in, 265–267
  use of, 269–270
  who in, 270–272
Adjective complement, 163, 165–169, 207
  comma fault with, 442
  defined, 165
  distinguished from noun complement, 165
  past participle as, 172–173, 308–309, 312–313
Adjective phrase, 182–183, 193–194
  defined, 41

Adverb, 202–210
  as idea link, 375–377, 434
  as transitional device, 434, 436, 442
  clipped form of, 206–208, 310
  comma with, 72, 441–442
  comparative, 434
  conjunctive adverb as, 68
  defined, 38, 202
  descriptive, 38
  distinguished from adjective, 166–167, 207
  distinguished from conjunctive adverb, 71
  distinguished from preposition, 228–229
  in compound-adjective, 193
  infinitive as, 324, 330–332
  in series and pairs, 208
  -ly ending of, 206–208, 210
  modified by adverb, 204
  negative, 210
  placement of, 204–206, 210
  prepositional phrase as, 216–217, 221
  restrictive, 86–88
  subordinate clause as, *see* Adverb clause
  subordinator in, 88, 209–210
  to modify adjective, 40, 202–203
  to modify adverb, 40
  to modify infinitive, 108, 328
  to modify gerund, 288
  to modify verb, 40, 202–208
  to modify verbal, 286–288, 292, 310, 324, 328–329
  unnecessary, 358
Adverb clause, 209–210
  as idea link, 376–377
  comma with, 82, 87–88, 297, 441–442
  defined, 81–82, 202, 209–210
  distinguished from sentence, 385
  incomplete, 83–85
  nonrestrictive, 86–88, 442
  placement of, 82–83, 88
  restrictive, 86–88
  to begin sentence, 81–84, 87, 441
  use of, 83–89
Adverb phrase, 202–204
  as idea link, 376–377, 442
  comma with, 442
  defined, 41
Advertising, euphemisms in, 347
Affirmative subject, 132–133
Agreement, *see* Pronoun, Verb agreement
Amount, 98–99
Apostrophe
  as separator, 443

  to indicate contraction, 252, 443
  to indicate possessive, 100–103, 184, 225, 227, 443
Appositive
  commas with, 103–104, 277, 441–442
  defined, 103–104
  infinitive as, 331
  nonrestrictive, 103–104, 277, 331, 441
  noun clause as, 274, 277
  restrictive, 104–105, 331, 442
Appropriate words, 340–365, 401
Articles, 186–187
Association, 430–431
Attitude, 340–341, 437
  discovery of, 426, 429–430
  evaluation of, 430
Audience, 437–438
Auxiliary verb
  be as, 162–163
  defined, 144
  endings of, 126–128
  lacking past participle, 308
  list of, 146
  person of, 126–127, 146
  tenses of, 149
  to form future tense, 146–147
  to form perfect tense, 146–148
  to form progressive tense, 145–146, 162–163
  to form verb phrase, 145–148, 162–163, 304
  use of, 149, 154–155

Be
  as auxiliary verb, 162–163
  as linking verb, 163–176
  forms of, 162
  synonyms for, 168–169, 171
Brainstorming, 431–432
Brevity, 356

Capitalization
  in abbreviations, 110, 444
  in hyphenated compound, 441
  in titles, 110
  of *I*, 110
  of proper nouns, 96, 110–111, 113
  summary of, 110–111
  to begin sentence, 80, 96, 110–111, 113, 385
  to revise comma fault, 387–388
Case, *see* Pronoun
Cause, clause to indicate, 81–82
Choice of words, 340–365, 401
Classifying, in paragraph development, 405
Clause
  as subject, 41, 170–172

as word group, 41–42, 57, 109
defined, 41, 109
distinguished from phrase, 41, 223, 228–385
distinguished from sentence, 41, 78–79, 89, 385–386
in series, 441
subject in, 41, 270–272
see also Adjective clause, Adverb clause, Conditional clause, Incomplete clause, Independent clause, Subordinate clause
Cliché, 360–362
Clipped form of adverb, 206–208, 210
Coherence
among ideas, 389, 391–392
in essay, 434–437
in paragraph, 400–401, 414–416
parallelism for, 391
transition for, 434, 436
Collective noun
as subject, 131–132
defined, 105
number of, 105–106, 131–135
use of, 135
verb agreement with, 131–132
Colon, 443
Comma
after adverb clause, 82, 87, 297, 441
after prepositional phrase, 442
after verbal modifier, 293–294, 310–311, 313, 330–332, 441–442
before coordinator, 4–5, 7–9, 21–22, 388, 441
in compound sentence, 54–55, 388, 441
in dialogue, 442
in series, 4–5, 8–9, 12, 21–22, 441
paired, 86–87, 104–105, 442
summary of uses of, 441–442
to prevent misreading, 442
to replace omitted verb, 442
to separate coordinate adjectives, 188–189, 441
to set off absolute phrase, 294, 442
to set off adverb, 72, 441–442
to set off conjunctive adverb, 68–69, 72, 442
to set off interjection, 442
to set off nonrestrictive appositive, 104–105, 277, 331, 441
clause, 86–87, 268–270, 277, 442
modifier, 294, 310–311, 313–315, 330–332, 441–442
to set off transitional words, 442
with quotation mark, 445
Comma fault
after coordinator, 442
after prepositional phrase, 442
between items in pair, 12, 442
between simple sentences, 387, 442
between subject and verb, 330–331, 442
between verb and complement, 330–331, 442
between verb and modifier, 300–331, 442
between verb and object, 330–331, 442

revision of, 387–389
summary of, 442
with infinitive phrase, 330–331
with restrictive appositive, 277, 442
with restrictive modifier, 86–88, 268, 277, 331, 442
Command, 50, 444
Comment, as controlling purpose, 438
Common noun, 96–97, 103
Comparative
adjective, 189–190, 354–355
adverb, 434
Comparison
as description, 189–190
as idea link, 391
consistency in, 416
faulty, 190–191, 354–355
incomplete, 355
in paragraph development, 401, 405, 411–414, 416, 433
Complement, *see* Adjective complement, Noun complement
Complex sentence
defined, 56
independent clause in, 56, 78
subordinate clause in, 56–57, 72, 78
subordinator in, 60–61
use of, 57, 62, 72
Compound adjective, 193–194, 441
Compound-complex sentence
coordinator in, 57–60
defined, 58
independent clause in, 58
subordinate clause in, 58
subordinator in, 58–59
use of, 61
Compound noun, 41
Compound predicate, 52
Compound sentence
comma in, 54–55, 388, 441
conjunctive adverb in, 68–69
coordinator in, 53–55, 60–61, 68–69, 78
defined, 53
independent clauses in, 53–54, 68–69
semicolon in, 68–70, 387, 442–443
use of, 55, 61, 68, 78
Compound subject, 52
Concise words, 356–361
Conclusion, 401, 405, 438
Concrete noun, 96–97
Conditional clause, 80–81, 86
Confusion of words, 350–354
Conjunction
as device of transition, 434, 436
as idea link, 58–62, 375
as key to sentence structure, 59–63
defined, 37
distinguished from preposition, 223–224
in title, 110
see also Conjunctive adverb, Coordinator, Correlative, Relative conjunction, Subordinator
Conjunctive adverb, 68–72
as adverb, 68
as conjunction, 68
comma with, 69, 72
defined, 68
distinguished from adverb, 71

distinguished from coordinator, 58
in compound sentence, 68–69
list of, 70
phrases as, 70
placement of, 68–69
semicolon with, 68–69, 72, 443
to replace coordinator, 442
use of, 69, 71–72
Connotation, 346 347, 350
Consistency
of comparison, 416
of image, 401, 416–417
of number, 105
of person, 391, 415–416
of pronoun usage, 249, 380–382, 391, 415–416
of tense, 151–155, 384–385, 391, 401, 415, 417
of topic, 379, 383, 391
of voice, 173
Context, 254
Contraction, 252, 443
Contrast
as idea link, 391
coordinators to indicate, 18–19
correlatives to indicate, 22
in paragraph development, 400, 405, 411–413
Controlling purpose
of essay, 437–439
of paragraph, 405–408, 413–414, 433, 437
Coordinate adjectives, 187–189, 441
Coordination, as idea link, 374–375, 391
Coordinator
as idea link, 374
between coordinate adjectives, 188
between items in pair or series, 2–12, 18–22, 66, 128–129, 327–328
comma fault with, 442
comma with, 4–9, 21–22, 441
distinguished from conjunctive adverb, 68
in compound-complex sentence, 57–58
in compound predicate, 54
in compound sentence, 53–54, 59–61, 68–69, 78–79
list of, 58
omitted, 187–188
replaced by conjunctive adverb, 69
to indicate contrast, 18
to revise comma fault, 388
use of, 6–9, 12, 20–21
Correctness in writing, 431
Correlative
comma with, 441
to indicate contrast, 22
to link pair, 9–12, 22–27, 29, 129–130, 327–328
use of, 23–26, 29, 131
Count noun, 98–99, 352
Criticism, as controlling purpose, 438

-d
as past-participial ending, 307–309
faulty omission of, 123
Dangler
incomplete clause as, 84–85, 88–89
infinitive as, 329–332
modifier as, 191
participle as, 295–297, 311–313, 426

revising of, 84–85, 295–297
Dash, 443
Deadwood, 358
Decimal, 444
Definition
　as controlling purpose, 438
　from dictionary, 403, 438
Degree
　comparative, 190, 354–355
　superlative, 190, 354–355
Demonstrative adjective, 186–187, 374
Demonstrative pronoun, 247–248, 256
Definite article, 186–187
Description
　adjective for, 37, 182–184, 187–188
　adverb for, 38
　as controlling purpose, 438
　comparison as, 189–190
　in paragraph development, 404, 406–408, 433
Details
　discovery of, 431
　in description, 407
　in paragraph development, 400–405, 407–408, 410, 412, 414
　order of, 432–433
　organization of, 432–433
　sensory, 404
　to persuade, 408
　use of, 182, 188–189, 356, 400–401, 403–405, 407–408, 410, 412–414
Determiner, 185–187
Development
　of essay, 357, 426–438
　of idea, 356–357, 374, 379, 400–405, 416, 426–438
　of paragraph, 400–417, 433, 435
　of passage, 374–392
Dialogue, comma in, 442
Dictionary, 346, 348, 403, 438
Discovering
　of attitudes, 426, 429–430
　of details, 431–432
　of ideas, 426–429
　of opinions, 426–429
　of rules of grammar, 36, 39
　writing as, 426

-*e*, silent, 121
-*ed*
　as past-participial ending, 304–308, 314–315
　as verb ending, 120–123, 305–307, 314–315
　faulty omission of, 123
Emphasis
　dash to indicate, 443
　exclamation point for, 444–445
　fragment as device of, 89
　in paragraph development, 415
　quotation marks to indicate, 445
　transition as device of, 435
Encloser, 441
Entertaining, as controlling purpose, 437–438
-*er* as comparative ending, 354–356
-*es*
　as noun ending, 98–99, 127
　as verb ending, 126–129, 243–244

Essay
　as self-discovery, 426
　coherence in, 434–437
　controlling purpose of, 438–439
　development of, 357, 426–439
　title of, 438
-*est* as superlative ending, 354–355
Euphemism, 347–350
Everyday words, 342–343, 346
Exact words, 346–356
Example, in paragraph development, 401, 411, 414, 433
Exclamation point
　after command, 444
　as terminator, 444–445
　for emphasis, 444–445
　with quotation mark, 445
Experience
　as controlling purpose, 439
　as source of ideas, 426–428

Fact
　distinguished from opinion, 405–406
　presentation of, 405, 409, 430, 437–438
Fancy words, 341–343, 346
Fat phrasing, 357–359
Faulty agreement
　of pronoun with noun, 247, 253–256
　of verb with subject, 243–244, 426
Faulty comparison, 190–191, 354–356
Faulty parallelism
　in comparison, 190–191
　in pairs and series, 22–23, 208, 326–327
Faulty pronoun reference, 248, 254–257, 380–382, 426
Feminine gender, 254
First person
　defined, 126, 240, 382
　shall as, 146
Five W's, 264
Formal writing, 342
Fragment
　avoiding, 385–386, 391, 444
　distinguished from sentence, 385–386, 444
　for emphasis, 89
　prepositional phrase as, 386
　revising of, 385–386
　subordinate clause as, 79, 89, 385
Fresh words, 360–362
Future-perfect tense, 146–148
Future tense, 146, 384, 391, 415

Gender, 254
Generalization, 401–403
General words, 347–350
Gerund
　as modifier, 288
　as noun, 106–109, 286–291, 322
　defined, 106, 286–287
　distinguished from present participle, 292
　distinguished from verb, 322
　-*ing* word as, 106–107, 109, 287
　modified by adjective, 288
　modified by adverb, 288, 328
　object of, 286, 288, 290
　plural noun before, 291
　possessive before, 290–291

to modify noun, 288
transitive, 286, 288, 290
Gerund phrase
　as subject, 108
　defined, 108, 288
　use of, 289–290
Grammar, 36 38

Happening, 120
Hedging, 438
Hyphen
　in compound adjective, 193–194, 441
　in compound noun, 441
　summary of uses of, 441

I, 110, 240
Ideas
　coherence among, 389, 391–392
　development of, 356–357, 374, 379, 400–405, 416, 426–438
　discovering of, 426–429
　distinguished from sentence, 374–375, 385
　evaluating of, 432, 438
　expanding of, 374–375, 428–429
　in paragraph, 400–401
　linking of, 374–378, 383–384, 387, 389–392, 414–417, 434–437, 441–442
　noun clauses as names of, 109
　nouns as names of, 37, 96–97
　order of, 432–433, 435
　sources of, 426–429, 431
　statement of, 416
　unity of, 400
Illustration
　as idea link, 391
　in paragraph development, 400, 405, 411–414, 433
Image
　consistency of, 401, 416–417
　shift of, 301, 416–417
Imagination, as source of ideas, 426
Inanimate object, 291
Incomplete clause
　as dangler, 84–85, 88–89
　defined, 84–85, 276–277
　use of, 87–89, 278
Incorrect words, 362–365
Indefinite article, 186–187
Indefinite pronoun
　as subject, 132–133, 248–249
　defined, 132, 248–249
　list of, 132–133
　person of, 132
　plural of, 132–133, 248–249
　possessive of, 443
　singular of, 132–133
　use of, 135, 249–250
　verb agreement with, 132–133, 254
Independent clause
　comma with, 54, 388, 441
　defined, 53
　distinguished from subordinate clause, 78
　in complex sentence, 56, 78
　in compound-complex sentence, 56, 78
　in compound sentence, 53–54, 68–69
　interrogative pronoun in, 263–264
　semicolon with, 68–69, 387, 442–443

verb tense in, 149
Indirect object, 225–226, 243
Infinitive, 322–334
　as adjective, 323–326, 331–332
　as adverb, 324, 330–332
　as appositive, 331
　as dangler, 329–332
　as noun, 105–109, 113, 322–323, 332
　as noun complement, 331
　as object, 323, 331
　as subject, 323, 331
　defined, 322
　distinguished from prepositional phrase, 229, 325–326
　distinguished from verb, 105–106, 110, 276
　in pairs or series, 326–328
　intransitive, 328
　modified by adverb, 108, 328
　placement of, 329–330
　split, 333–334
　to as marker of, 105–107, 320, 322–323, 325–326
　transitive, 328
　verb as element in, 230, 323, 325–326
Infinitive phrase
　comma fault with, 330–332
　comma with, 330–332
　defined, 108
　distinguished from sentence, 385
　in parallel, 391
　placement of, 329–330
　restrictive, 331–332
　structure of, 108–109
Informal writing, 89, 343
Informing, as controlling purpose, 405–407, 433, 437, 439
-ing words
　as adjectives, 62, 107, 291–397
　as nouns, 106–107, 109, 286–291
　distinguished from verbs, 286–287, 304
　in verb phrases, 162
Initials, 110, 444
Intensive pronoun, 246–247, 256
Interjection, 43, 442, 444
Interpretation, as controlling purpose, 439
Interrogative pronoun, 250–251, 256, 263–265
Intransitive
　defined, 123–124
　infinitive as, 328
　verb as, 123–124, 135–137
Irregular verb
　defined, 121–122, 149
　distinguished from regular verb, 122
　past participle of, 306–309
　past tense of, 121–123
　use of, 122–123, 149

Jargon, 344–346
Joiner, 441

Leave-out test, 245
Like
　as preposition, 82
　as subordinator, 82
Limiting adjective, 186–187

Linking devices
　in developing ideas, 374–378, 383–384, 389–392, 414–417, 434–437
　in paragraph development, 414–415, 417, 433
Linking verb
　agreement with subject, 169–172
　be as, 163–176
　defined, 163–164
　in passive voice, 312–313
　list of, 167–169, 171
　sense verb as, 169, 171
　use of, 169, 172
　with noun complement, 164, 170–172
　with past participle, 308
Listening, as source of ideas, 426
Long possessive, 100, 225
-ly
　as adverb ending, 206–208, 210
　unnecessary, 207

Malapropism, 347–348, 350
Manner, clause to indicate, 81–82
Masculine gender, 254
Mass noun, 98–99
Misplaced modifier, 88, 191, 193, 204–206, 220–222, 272–273, 311–313, 330
Modifier
　as dangler, 191
　as fragment, 386
　defined, 40
　linked by preposition, 216
　misplaced, 88, 191, 193, 204–206, 221–222, 272–273, 311–313, 330
　noun as, 288
　of infinitive, 108, 328
　of past participle, 310–311, 328
　of present participle, 292–293
　restrictive, 86–88, 268–269, 310, 331–332, 442
　see also Adjective, Adverb, Dangler, Gerund, Infinitive, Past participle, Prepositional phrase, Present participle

-n as past participial ending, 306, 308
Name
　noun as, 37, 96
　of idea, 37, 96–97
　of person, 37, 62, 96–97, 100–103, 225–226, 240, 250
　of place, 37, 110
　of thing, 96–97
Narrative, as controlling purpose, 438–439
Negative adverb, 210
Negative subject, 133
Neuter pronoun, 254
Nonrestrictive
　adjective clause, 268–270, 441
　adverb clause, 86–88, 442
　appositive, 103–104, 277, 331, 441
　participial phrase, 293–295, 310–311, 314–315
Nonsentence, *see* Fragment
Noun, 96–113
　abstract, 96–97, 103, 291
　as indirect object, 225–226, 243

as modifier, 288
as name, 37, 96–97
as object of verb, 123–125, 135, 144
as object of verbal, 288, 290, 292, 328–329
as subject of verbal, 294, 322
between subject and verb, 129–130, 132
collective, 105–106, 131–135
common, 96–98, 103
compound, 441
concrete, 96–97
count, 98–99, 352
defined, 37, 96
distinguished from verb, 127, 326
-es ending of, 98–99, 127
gerund as, 106–109, 286–291, 322
infinitive as, 105–109, 113, 322–323, 332
-ing words as, 106–107, 109, 286–291
in prepositional phrase, 129–130, 193, 217–218, 226, 230, 325–326
linked by preposition, 216
mass, 98–99, 352
modified by adjective, 40, 182–183
modified by gerund, 288
modified by infinitive, 325
modified by past participle, 304, 312, 315
modified by present participle, 291–292, 295–297
number of, 98
person of, 240–241
plural of, 98–99, 101–103, 105, 128–129, 241, 291
possessive of, 100–103, 184–187, 225–227
proper, 96–97, 110–111, 113, 269
replaced by pronoun, 42–43, 240, 251, 253–254, 267, 271–272, 380–381, 415
-s ending of, 98–99, 127
singular of, 98–101, 105
sorts of, 96–97
subordinate clause as, *see* Noun clause as
verbal, 106–109, 286–291, 322–323
Noun clause, 273–279
　as appositive, 274, 277
　as name of idea, 109
　as noun complement, 274
　as object of preposition, 218–220, 274
　as object of verb, 109, 274
　as object of verbal, 274
　as subject, 170, 274–275
　defined, 109, 274
　incomplete, 276–277
　structure of, 109–110, 274
　use of, 109–110, 113, 219–220, 275–276
　with *who* as subject, 273–274
Noun complement
　comma fault with, 442
　defined, 163–164
　distinguished from adjective complement, 165
　infinitive as, 331

linking verb with, 164, 170–172
noun clause as, 274
noun phrase as, 165
use of, 164–165, 172
with subordinate clause as subject, 170–172
Noun markers, 185–186
Noun phrase
as noun complement, 165
as object of preposition, 218–219, 325–326
as object of verbal, 329
defined, 41, 107–108
gerund phrase as, 108, 288
introduced by *a* or *an*, 112
to revise faulty pronoun reference, 381–382
with gerund as modifier, 288–289
Number
consistency of, 105, 133
of academic course, 111–112
of collective noun, 105–106, 131–135
of noun, 98
of pronoun, 132–133, 241–242, 248–249, 253–254, 415
of verb, 126–130
ordinal, 207
parentheses with, 443
shift of, 105, 132–133, 415
Number, a
plural of, 443
with count noun, 98–99, 352

Object
comma fault with, 330–331, 442
defined, 123, 225
indirect, 225–226, 243
infinitive as, 323, 331
of gerund, 286, 288, 290
of preposition, 218, 219, 220, 225–226, 232–233, 274, 325–326
of verb, 109, 123–125, 135, 144, 225, 274
of verbal, 274, 288, 290, 292, 328–329
pronoun as, 219, 230, 241, 243, 252–253, 325–326
whom as, 252–253
Observing, as source of ideas, 426
Opinion
discovering of, 426
distinguished from fact, 405
presentation of, 402, 405, 426, 430, 437–438
Order
of details, 432
of ideas, 432–433, 435
Ordinal number, 207
Organizing
numbers to indicate, 443
of details, 432
Out-of-date words, 344–345
Ownership, possessive for, 100

Padding, 357, 359, 439
Pair
adjectives in, 187–189
adverbs in, 208
as object of preposition, 232–233
as plural, 10–11, 129, 245

as predicate, 51–52
as singular, 10–11, 21–22, 128–130
as subject, 9–12, 20–25, 51, 128–131, 133–134
comma fault in, 12
of commas, 86–87, 104–105, 442
of infinitives, 326–328
of pronouns, 244–245
parallelism in, 6–8, 12, 18–19, 22–25, 244, 326–327
verb agreement with, 128–129
with coordinator, 2–12, 18–22, 66, 128–129, 327–328
with correlative, 9–12, 22–27, 29, 129–130, 327–328
Paragraph, 400–417
coherence in, 400–401, 414–416
controlling purpose of, 405–408, 413–414, 433, 437
development of, 400–417, 433, 435
ideas in, 400–401
length of, 416–417
linking devices in, 435
of transition, 416–417
quoted, 445
topic of, 400–405, 409–411, 414, 416–417, 433
unity in, 400, 409–410, 414, 417
Parallelism
as idea link, 389–391
faulty, 22–23, 190–191, 208, 326–327
in comparisons, 190–191
in pairs, 6–8, 12, 208, 210, 219, 326–327
in series, 6–8, 12, 208, 210, 219, 326–327
Parentheses, 443
Participial phrase
distinguished from sentence, 385
nonrestrictive, 293–295, 310–311, 314–315, 441
restrictive, 293–294, 310, 442
see also Past participial phrase, Present participial phrase
Participle, *see* Dangler, Past participle, Present participle
Parts of speech, 37–40, 42–44
defined, 37–38, 42–44
summarized, 38, 43
Passage
development of, 374–392
distinguished from sentence, 374–375
Passive voice, 145–146, 162, 172–176, 312–314
Past participial phrase
comma with, 310–311, 313
dangling, 311–313
defined, 310
nonrestrictive, 310–311, 314–315, 441
placement of, 310–313, 315
restrictive, 310–311, 442
use of, 311, 313–314
Past participle, 304–315
as adjective, 304, 312, 315, 322
as adjective complement, 172–173, 308–309, 312–313
-d ending of, 307–309
defined, 304

distinguished from verb, 122, 304–305, 307–308, 322
-ed ending of, 304–308, 314–315
in passive voice, 173, 312–314
in verb phrase, 304
irregular, 306–309
linking verb with, 308
modified by adverb, 310–311, 328
-n ending of, 306, 308
of *drag,* 315
of *sneak,* 315
recognizing of, 308
regular, 305–306
sound change in, 307–309
-t ending of, 307
Past-perfect tense, 146–147, 162
Past tense
consistency of, 384–385, 391, 401, 415
defined, 120
distinguished from past participle, 122
-ed ending of, 120–123, 305–307, 314–315
in paragraph development, 415
of *be,* 162
of irregular verb, 121–123
of regular verb, 121–123
use of, 152–153, 384–385
Pattern, of paragraph development, 410–414
Perfect tense
agreement in, 128
auxiliary verb in, 146–147
defined, 146
in sequence of tenses, 154–155
of *be,* 162
past, 146–147, 162
present, 136, 146–147, 154–155
use of, 155
Period
after abbreviation, 444
after initial, 110, 444
after polite command, 444
as decimal, 444
as terminator, 441, 444
to end sentence, 9, 385, 444
to revise comma fault, 387
with quotation mark, 445
Period fault, 444
Person
agreement in, 128, 169, 253–254
consistency of, 391, 415–416
defined, 126, 240–241, 382
of auxiliary verb, 126–127, 146
of noun, 240–241
of pronoun, 132, 241–243, 433
of present-tense verb, 125–126
shift of, 382–383, 401, 415–416, 433
use of, 243–244
who or *whom,* 267
see also First person, Second person, Third person
Personal pronoun, 241–246, 256
Persons, names of
capitalization of, 96, 111
possessive of, 100–101, 225–226
proper noun as, 96
titles as, 225
Persuading
as controlling purpose, 437, 439

in paragraph development, 406–408, 433
Philosophy, as controlling purpose, 439
Phrase
　as conjunctive adverb, 70
　as word group, 41–42, 107–108
　defined, 41, 107–108
　distinguished from clause, 41, 223, 228, 385
　distinguished from sentence, 385
　in series, 441
　see also Adjective phrase, Adverb phrase, Gerund phrase, Infinitive phrase, Noun phrase, Past participial phrase, Present participial phrase, Verb phrase
Place, clause to indicate, 81–83
Place names, 37, 110
Plural
　before gerund, 291
　collective noun as, 105–106, 131–135
　defined, 241
　formed by pair, 10–11, 129, 245
　of *a number,* 443
　of indefinite pronoun, 132–133, 248–249
　of noun, 98–99, 101–103, 105, 128–129, 241, 291
　of possessive, 101–103
　of pronoun, 132–133, 241–242, 253–254
　of subject, 169–170
　of verb, 128–129, 169–170
　pair or series as, 10–11, 129, 245
　sound change to indicate, 98–99
　verb agreement with, 98–99
Poetry, diction in, 344
Possessive
　apostrophe to indicate, 100–103, 184, 225, 227, 443
　before gerund, 290–291
　long form of, 100, 225
　of names, 100–103, 225–226
　of nouns, 100–103, 184–187, 225–227
　of personal title, 22
　of pronoun, 443
　placement of, 227
　plural of, 101–103
　pronouns, 184, 241–242, 252–253, 256
　singular of, 100–103
　s sound in, 100
　to indicate ownership, 100
　with gerund, 290–291
Predicate
　as element in clause, 41–42
　compound, 52
　defined, 50
　in simple sentence, 51
　in topic sentence, 409
　pair as, 51–52
　placement of, 401
　series as, 51
Prefix, 441
Preposition, 216–233
　at end of sentence, 228–229
　confused with other words, 223–224, 229
　defined, 216–217
　distinguished from adverb, 228–229
　distinguished from conjunction, 223–224
　in title, 110
　like as, 82
　list of, 217
　object of, 218–220, 232–233, 274, 325–326
　omitted before indirect object, 226
　omitted before paired object, 232–233
　restrictions on use of, 231–232
　to as, 229–230, 325–326
　to link modifiers, 216
　to link noun and verb, 216
　to link nouns, 216
　with noun clause as object, 218–220, 274
　with noun phrase as object, 218–220
　see also Prepositional phrase
Prepositional phrase
　as fragment, 386
　as long possessive, 100, 225
　as modifier, 43, 216–222
　comma fault with, 442
　comma with, 442
　defined, 43
　distinguished from infinitive, 230, 325–326
　distinguished from subordinate clause, 223–224, 226–228
　in parallel, 391
　noun in, 129–130, 193, 217–218, 226, 230, 325–326
　overuse of, 358
　placement of, 220–222
　use of, 194–195, 220, 222–228, 230
Present participial phrase
　comma with, 293–294
　defined, 292–293
　distinguished from sentence, 385
　nonrestrictive, 294, 441
　restrictive, 293, 442
Present participle
　as adjective, 291–297, 322
　as dangler, 295–297
　defined, 292, 304
　distinguished from gerund, 292
　distinguished from verb, 322
　in absolute phrase, 294–295
　modified by adverb, 292–293
　placement of, 292
　transitive, 292–293
　with subject, 294
Present-perfect tense
　agreement in, 128
　defined, 136, 146
　in sequence of tenses, 154–155
　of *be,* 162
Present tense
　agreement in, 9–11, 128–131, 134–135
　consistency of, 153–154, 384, 401
　defined, 120–121
　in paragraph development, 415
　of *be,* 162
　person in, 125–126
Process, as controlling purpose, 439
Process verb, 166
Progressive tense, 145–146, 162–163
Pronoun, 240–257
　agreement with noun, 247, 253–256, 415–416
　as idea link, 375–376, 383, 387, 417
　as name, 62, 240
　as object, 219, 230, 241, 243, 252–253, 325–326
　as subject, 132–133, 241–245, 249–250, 252–254
　before gerund, 290–291
　capitalization of, 110
　case of, 241–242
　consistency of, 249, 380–382, 391
　defined, 42–43, 240, 242
　demonstrative, 247–248, 256
　gender of, 254
　indefinite, 132–133, 248–250, 254, 256
　in pair, 244–245
　in parallel, 244–245
　intensive, 246–247, 256
　interrogative, 250–251, 256, 263–265
　number of, 132–133, 241–242, 248–249, 253–254, 415
　objective, 241–243, 252–253
　personal, 241–246, 256
　person of, 132, 241–243, 433
　possessive, 184, 241–242, 252–253, 256
　plural of, 241–242, 253–254
　reference of, 248, 254–257, 380–382, 391, 415, 426
　reflexive, 246–247, 256
　relative, 251–253, 256–257, 265–268, 270–272
　singular of, 241–244, 253–254
　subjective, 241–243
　to avoid repetition, 415
　verb agreement with, 243–245
Proper noun
　capitalization of, 96, 110–111, 113
　defined, 96–97
　with nonrestrictive modifier, 269
Punctuation, 4–6, 441–445
Purpose, controlling, 405–408, 413–414, 433, 437–439

Question
　as sentence purpose, 50
　punctuation of, 444
Question mark
　as terminator, 389, 441, 444
　with quotation mark, 445
Quotation mark
　at end of paragraph, 445
　colon with, 445
　comma with, 445
　exclamation point with, 445
　for emphasis, 444–445
　period with, 445
　question mark with, 445
　semicolon with, 445
　to enclose title, 445

Reading, as source of ideas, 426
Reasoning
　as controlling purpose, 439
　as source of ideas, 426
Redundancy, 357, 359–360
Reference of pronoun, 248, 254–257, 380–382, 391, 415, 426
Reflection, as device of coherence, 434–437
Reflexive pronoun, 246–247, 256

Regular verb
  defined, 120–122
  distinguished from irregular verb, 122
  -ed ending of, 120–122, 305
Relative clause, 251–253, 265–268, 270–272, 358
Relative conjunction, 251
Relative pronoun, 251–253, 256–257, 265–268, 270–272
Repetition
  as idea link, 384, 389–392, 414–415, 417, 434, 436–437
  awkward, 392, 415
  dash to set off, 443
  pronoun to avoid, 240, 415
  synonyms to avoid, 415
Restrictive
  adjective clause, 268–269
  adverb clause, 268–269
  appositive, 104–105, 277, 331, 442
  modifier, 86–88, 268–269, 293–294, 310, 331–332, 442
Revising
  of comma fault, 387–389
  of dangler, 84–85, 295–297
  of faulty pronoun reference, 255–256, 380–382
  of fragment, 385–386
  of misplaced modifier, 191–192, 205–206, 221–222
  of run-together sentences, 387–389
  of sentence structures, 60–63
Rules of grammar, 36, 38
Run-together sentences, 386–389, 391

'*s*
  in contractions, 252, 443
  in possessives, 100–103, 184, 225, 227, 443
-*s*
  as noun ending, 98–99, 127
  as verb ending, 10–11, 20, 126–129, 132, 243–244
Satire, as controlling purpose, 439
Second person, 126, 241, 246
-*self*, 126, 246–247
Semicolon
  after quotation mark, 445
  as separator, 442–443
  between independent clauses, 68–69, 387, 442–443
  between items in series, 443
  to revise comma fault, 388–389
  with conjunctive adverb, 68, 72, 443
Sense verbs, 168–169, 171
Sensory details, 404
Sentence
  adverb clause to begin, 81–84, 87, 441
  as word group, 41
  basic elements of, 37
  capital to begin, 80, 96, 110–111, 113, 385
  comma fault with, 387, 442
  defined, 41, 50
  distinguished from clause, 40, 78–79, 89, 385
  distinguished from fragment, 385–386
  distinguished from idea, 374–375, 385

distinguished from passage, 374–375
distinguished from phrase, 385
kinds of, 50–62
period to end, 9, 385, 444
predicate in, 40
preposition at end of, 228–229
purpose of, 50
revising structure of, 60–63
subject in, 41, 50–51, 62
subordinator to begin, 79
topic, 401–403, 407–414, 433
  see also Complex sentence, Compound-complex sentence, Compound sentence, Simple sentence
Separator, 441
Sequence of tenses, 149–155, 384, 391
Series
  adjectives in, 187–189
  adverbs in, 208
  as predicate, 51
  as subject, 51
  clauses in, 441
  comma with, 4–5, 8–9, 12, 21–22, 441
  coordinator to link, 4–7, 18–22, 68
  infinitives in, 326–328
  parallelism in, 6–8, 12, 208, 210, 219, 326–327
  phrases in, 441
  semicolon with, 443
  verb agreement with, 128
  verbs in, 50
Shift
  of image, 401, 416–417
  of number, 105, 132–133, 415
  of person, 382–383, 401, 415–416, 433
  of tense, 384–385, 391, 401, 415, 433
  of topic, 379–380
  of voice, 173
Signpost, 357, 359, 416–417, 438
Silent -*e*, 121
Simple sentence
  defined, 51
  use of, 55, 62
Singular
  collective noun as, 105–106, 131–135
  defined, 241–242
  of indefinite pronoun, 132–133, 248–249
  of intensive pronoun, 246
  of noun, 98–101, 105
  of paired items, 10–11 21–22, 128–130
  of possessive, 100–103
  of pronoun, 241–244, 253–254
  of reflexive pronoun, 246
  of verb, 10–11, 125–131
  verb agreement with, 169–171
  who as, 270–272
Slang, 343–346
Sound
  an before vowel, 112
  change of, 89, 307–309
  of *s* in possessive, 100
  similarity of, 347–348, 350–354
  "swallowing" of, 123, 314–315
Specific words, 347–350

Spelling
  confused, 350–354
  of final -*y* words, 121
  of silent -*e* words, 121
  list for study, 447–448
Split infinitive, 333–334
s sound in possessive, 100
Statement
  as sentence purpose, 50
  of idea, 416
Status verb, 120
Story telling
  as controlling purpose, 439
  in paragraph development, 406–408, 411–412, 414, 433
Style, 358, 435
Subject
  affirmative, 132–133
  as element in clause, 41, 270–272
  as element in sentence, 41, 50–51, 62
  change of, to revise dangler, 296
  collective noun as, 131–132
  comma fault with, 330–331, 442
  compound, 52
  defined, 9–10, 37–38, 50
  described by adjective complement, 165
  gerund phrase as, 108
  indefinite pronoun as, 132–133, 248–249
  infinitive as, 323, 331
  in noun-complement pattern, 170
  in passive voice, 312–313
  in relative clause, 270–272
  in topic sentence, 409
  negative, 133
  noun clause as, 170, 274–275
  of verbal, 294, 322
  omission of, 84–85
  pair or series as, 9–12, 20–25, 51, 128–131, 133–134
  placement of, 50–51
  pronoun as, 132–133, 241–245, 249–250, 252–254
  renamed by noun complement, 164
  subordinate clause as, 170–172
  there before, 170–172
  verb agreement with, 10–11, 20, 128–135, 169–172, 243–245, 249–250, 254, 270–272, 426
  who as, 252–253, 270–272
Subjective case, 241–243
Subordinate clause, 78–79
  as adjective, 182–183, 193–195, 265–273, 277, 441–442
  as adverb, 82–89, 202, 209–210, 297, 385–386, 441–442
  as fragment, 79, 89, 385
  as noun, 109–110, 170, 218–220, 273, 279
  as subject, 170
  conditional, 80–81, 86
  defined, 56
  distinguished from independent clause, 78
  distinguished from prepositional phrase, 223–224, 226–228
  distinguished from sentence, 78–79, 89, 385
  incomplete, 84–85, 88–89, 276–277
  in complex sentence, 56–57, 79–80

in compound-complex sentence,
  56–57, 79–80
in parallel, 391
placement of, 57, 80–83
relative, 251–253, 265–268,
  270–272, 358
replaced by absolute phrase, 294
subordinator in, 56–60, 78–83,
  88–89, 109, 358
to indicate cause, manner, place,
  time, 81–82
use of, 79–81, 83, 85, 87–88,
  269–270, 275–276, 278–279
verb tense in, 149–150
Subordination
as idea link, 374, 391
pattern of, 78–79
subordinator for, 78
Subordinator, 78–79
defined, 79
in adjective clause, 265–267
in adverb clause, 88, 209–210
in complex sentence, 60–61
in compound-complex sentence,
  58–59
in incomplete clause, 88
like as, 82
list of, 59
omission of, 276–278
placement of, 79
to begin sentence, 79
to begin subordinate clause, 56–60,
  78–83, 88–89, 109, 385
to revise comma fault, 388
who as, 265–268, 270–272
Summary
as idea link, 391, 417
dash to indicate, 443
Superlative, 190, 354–356
Synonym
as idea link, 375–376, 383, 417
for *be*, 168–169, 171
to avoid repetition, 415

-*t* as past-participial ending, 307
Tense
consistency of, 151–155, 348–385,
  391, 401, 415, 417
defined, 120–121
in independent clause, 149
in subordinate clause, 149–150
of auxiliary verbs, 149
of *be*, 162
sequence of, 149–155, 384, 391
shift of, 384–385, 391, 401, 415,
  433
verb change to indicate, 120–121
see also Future tense, Past tense,
  Perfect tense, Present tense,
  Progressive tense
Terminators, 441
The
as determiner, 185–187
in titles, 110
use of, 186–187
There before subject, 170–171
Thesis, 435
Third person
as point of view, 401
defined, 126–127, 129, 241, 382
indefinite pronoun as, 132
of auxiliary verb, 126–127
of personal pronoun, 241–244

of reflexive pronoun, 246
of verb, 126–127
pronoun agreement with, 243–244
shift from, 401, 415
use of, 127–128
Time, 81–82, 120–121, 443
Title
capitalization in, 110
of essay, 438
of literary work, 445
possessive of, 225
quotation marks with, 445
To
as preposition, 229–230, 325–326
in infinitive, 105–107, 230,
  322–323, 325–326
omission of, 327
Tone, 340–341, 433, 439
Topic
attitude toward, 340–341
choosing of, 428–429
consistency of, 379, 383, 391
of paragraph, 400–405, 409–411,
  414, 416–417, 433
of writing, 343, 379–380, 428–433
shift of, 379–380
Topic sentence, 401–403, 407–414,
  433
Transition
as device of coherence, 434–437
devices of, 434–437
paragraph of, 416–417
signpost as, 357
Transitive
defined, 123–124
gerund, 286, 288, 290
infinitive, 328
participle, 292–293
verb, 123–125, 136–137, 144
Troublesome verbs, 136–137
Truism, 438

Underlining, 445
Unity in paragraph, 400, 409–410,
  414, 417

Vagueness, 104
Verb, 120–137, 144–155, 162–176
agreement with subject, *see* Verb
  agreement
auxiliary, 126–127, 144–155,
  162–163, 304, 308
changed to adjective, 62
comma fault with, 330–331, 442
defined, 37, 120
distinguished from infinitive,
  105–106, 110, 276
distinguished from noun, 127, 326
distinguished from verbal,
  105–106, 110, 122, 276,
  286–287, 304–305, 307–308,
  322
-*ed* ending of, 120–123, 305–307,
  314–315
forming infinitive, 230, 323,
  325–326
in passive voice, 312–314
in series, 50
intransitive, 123–124, 135–137
irregular, 121–123, 149, 306–309
linked by preposition, 216
linking, *see* Linking verb
modified by adverb, 40, 202–208

number of, 126–130
object of, 109, 123–125, 135, 144,
  225, 274
omission of, 84–85, 442
person of, 125–128
regular, 120–122, 305
-*s* ending of, 10–11, 20, 126–129,
  132, 243–244
sense, 168–169, 171
singular of, 10–11, 125–131
tense of, *see* Tense
to indicate action, 120–137, 162
to indicate happening, 120
to indicate process, 166
to indicate status, 120
transitive, 123–125, 136–137, 144
troublesome, 136–137
Verb agreement
defined, 128–129
faulty, 243–244, 426
in noun-complement pattern,
  170–172
in perfect tenses, 128
in relative clause, 270–272
of linking verbs, 169–172
use of, 131, 135
with affirmative subject, 133–134
with collective noun, 131–132
with pair or series as subject,
  10–11, 19–20, 128–129
with pronoun as subject, 132–133,
  243, 245, 249–250, 254
with singular, 169–171
with *who* as subject, 270–272
Verbal, 286–297, 304–315, 322–334
comma with, 441
distinguished from verb, 105–106,
  110, 122, 276, 286–287,
  304–305, 307–308, 322
object of, 274, 286–288, 290, 292,
  328–329
subject of, 294, 322
see also Gerund, Infinitive, Past
  participle, Present participle
Verb phrase, 145–146, 162
defined, 41
-*ing* words in, 162
with auxiliary, 144–145, 162, 304
with past participle, 304
Voice
active, 173–175, 312–314
consistency of, 173
passive, 145–146, 162, 172–176,
  312–314
shift of, 173
Vowel
an before, 112
in past participle, 307–309

Who, whom
as interrogative pronoun, 250–252,
  264–265
as object, 252–253
as relative pronoun, 250
as singular, 270–272
as subject, 252–253, 270–272
as subordinator, 265–268, 270–272
distinguished, 252–253
in adjective clause, 270–272
in noun clause, 273–274
to refer to persons, 267, 270
verb agreement with, 270–272

Word choice, 340–365, 401
Word group, *see* Clause, Phrase,
　　Sentence
Wordiness, 358–359
Writing
　as discovering, 426
　correctness in, 431
　formal, 342
　informal, 89, 343
　topic of, 343, 379–380, 428–433

-y spelling rule, 121